"Thomas Aiello's book is an exciting and detailed account of Muhammad Ali's return to the ring after three and a half years in exile, with a special focus on how Atlanta, with its sophisticated Black politicians like State Senator Leroy Johnson, was able to overcome racist opposition to present the bout against white hope Jerry Quarry in the heart of the Deep South."

—LEWIS A. ERENBERG, author of *The Rumble in the Jungle: Muhammad Ali and George Foreman on the Global Stage*

"Contrary to the beloved figure he would become years later, the Muhammad Ali of 1970 was a man under siege. Stripped of the heavyweight championship and exiled from the ring for 3½ years for evading the draft during the Vietnam War, he was hated by a large segment of white America for his perceived uppity attitude and his affiliation with the Black separatist Nation of Islam. Improbably, Atlanta stepped forward to provide him with a venue to launch his comeback in an event that would prove pivotal both for Ali and the city itself. In his thoroughly researched book, *Return of the King*, Thomas Aiello offers up an erudite study of that long ago encounter that is a welcome addition to the Ali canon."

—MARK KRAM JR., author of *Smokin' Joe: The Life of Joe Frazier*

"Thomas Aiello rivetingly chronicles the powerful convergence of culture and politics, time and place, for cultural icon Muhammad Ali and Black powerbroker Leroy Johnson during a decisive moment in Atlanta. Anyone interested in exploring the possibilities and limitations of Black Power politics will admire *Return of the King*."

—WINSTON A. GRADY-WILLIS, author of *Challenging U.S. Apartheid: Atlanta and Black Struggles for Human Rights, 1960–1977*

"*Return of the King* is essential reading for anyone interested in Muhammad Ali and boxing as transcendent figure and institution respectively. Aiello frames his treatment of the 1970 fight between Jerry Quarry and Ali, in the racial politics of Atlanta, the state of Georgia, and the nation. After reading this book no one can ever see Atlanta as 'the city too busy to hate.' This study is sports history at its best and reveals that when properly contextualized and theorized the discipline is invaluable to a clearer and more accurate understanding of the past."

—JEFFREY T. SAMMONS, author of *Beyond the Ring: The Role of Boxing in American Society*

"Both local and national in scope, *Return of the King* is a fascinating account of the Ali-Quarry fight. It offers a fresh look at the political culture of Atlanta through the prism of Leroy Johnson's story and a closer focus on one of the most underappreciated periods of Ali's career. This is an early contender for the best sports history books of 2025."

—CLAYTON TRUTOR, author of *Loserville: How Professional Sports Remade Atlanta—and How Atlanta Remade Professional Sports*

"In *Return of the King* Thomas Aiello deftly reconstructs Muhammad Ali's boxing comeback after being exiled for refusing to serve in the United States military at the height of the Vietnam War. Aiello offers a compelling narrative that reveals why Ali's return could only have occurred in Atlanta, the Black mecca of the American South. This is the origin story of Ali's second act: when the self-proclaimed King of the World found redemption in the ring, emerging as a triumphant symbol of Black Power."

—JOHNNY SMITH, coauthor of *Blood Brothers: The Fatal Friendship Between Muhammad Ali and Malcolm X*

RETURN OF THE KING

RETURN

OF THE KING

THE REBIRTH OF MUHAMMAD ALI AND THE RISE OF ATLANTA

THOMAS AIELLO

University of Nebraska Press | Lincoln

Manufactured in the United States of America

The University of Nebraska Press is part of a land-grant institution with campuses and programs on the past, present, and future homelands of the Pawnee, Ponca, Otoe-Missouria, Omaha, Dakota, Lakota, Kaw, Cheyenne, and Arapaho Peoples, as well as those of the relocated Ho-Chunk, Sac and Fox, and Iowa Peoples.

For customers in the EU with safety/GPSR
concerns, contact:
gpsr@mare-nostrum.co.uk
Mare Nostrum Group BV
Mauritskade 21D
1091 GC Amsterdam
The Netherlands

Library of Congress Control Number: 2025031573

Set in Minion Pro by A. Shahan.

For C. G.

CONTENTS

ILLUSTRATIONS

FOLLOWING PAGE 98

TABLES

RETURN OF THE KING

PROLOGUE

On September 7, 1892, the Olympic Club of New Orleans hosted what it called a "fistic carnival," the most important night of boxing in the United States to date. The bare-knuckle days were over, boxing was legal in Louisiana, and the heavyweight champion, John L. Sullivan, who had fought illicitly in the area several times prior, headlined the card, defending his title against James Corbett. The two could not have been more different. Sullivan had won his title ten years earlier, the last of the bare-knuckle champions. "Gentleman Jim," by contrast, had trained with a coach and had only fought under the Marquis of Queensbury rules that now governed the sport. When the gentleman defeated the brawler, the world took notice. Boxing had changed forever.[1]

But if it was the beginning of one era, it was the end of another. On the undercard of the heavyweight title fight between Sullivan and Corbett was another championship bout, this one for the bantamweight title. The champion was George "Little Chocolate" Dixon, a Canadian boxer, defending against a newcomer, Jack Skelly, making his first professional fight. Skelly came from Brooklyn and had a strong amateur background, but he wasn't ready for a championship match. Dixon knocked him out in the eighth round. That a recognized champion defeated a debutante on the undercard of a major fight was not particularly newsworthy. But in this fight, the Canadian, Little Chocolate, was Black, and his Brooklyn opponent was white. By 1892, New Orleans was two years into its experiment with formal segregation, but though the Olympic Club was a white venue, the draw of Dixon did convince the club to allow Black fans to watch its "fistic carnival." Those fans entered through a separate entrance and sat in a segregated section. But they were there.[2]

When the night was over, white newspapers throughout the country blared headlines that Jim Corbett had defeated John L. Sullivan and won the heavyweight crown. Black newspapers, meanwhile, blared headlines that George Dixon had successfully defended his title by defeating a white opponent. The culture makers in New Orleans, while generally polite to the bantamweight champion, were horrified by what they had seen. White fans "winced every time Dixon landed on Skelly. The sight was repugnant to some of the men from the South," the *Chicago Tribune* explained. "The idea of sitting quietly by and seeing a colored boy pommel a white lad grates on Southerners." The *New Orleans Times-Democrat* lamented that it was "a mistake to match a negro and a white man, a mistake to bring the races together on any terms of equality, even in the prize ring."[3] There would be no more interracial boxing contests in New Orleans, not in an era of social Darwinism, when boxing was an easy shorthand for evolutionary might, particularly for those who didn't trouble themselves with science books. When another interracial bout was scheduled in Mississippi in 1897, a white man stepped in and stopped it. "The idea of n——s fighting white men," he said, "Why, if that darned scoundrel would beat that white boy the n——s would never stop gloating over it, and, as it is, we have enough trouble with them."[4]

The Dixon-Skelly fight would be the first time a Black man pummeled a white man in front of a large crowd of onlookers in the Deep South without facing retributive incarceration or the hangman's noose.

And it would be the last—for the next seventy-eight years.

—

Seventy-one years after the fistic carnival, the March 1963 edition of *Ebony* magazine arrived at the homes of hundreds of thousands of subscribers across the country with two feature articles, one profiling a new phenomenon in politics, the other a new phenomenon in sports. The first told the story of Leroy Reginald Johnson, the first Black state senator in Georgia since 1870 and the only Black state senator in the South, whose political success in another Deep South state would have been difficult to fathom as Skelly hit the mat in the eighth round back in 1892. The article closed with a quote from a member of Johnson's team, describing the new senator's electoral win. "This is a victory for the whole community, and not just for Negroes," he said. "It was a good day for the race—the human race."[5]

Johnson was an Atlanta native, a Morehouse graduate who had gone to law school, established a private practice, then became a politician. He was aided by a powerful Black voting bloc in the city that provided the Black middle and upper class a measure of influence unavailable to many others in the Deep South. That bloc, buoyed by the elimination of Georgia's county unit system, which judged representation by majority vote in a county rather than by individual districts, sent Johnson to the state senate in 1962. While he faced bigotry early in his new job, he was able to overcome it largely through a willingness to negotiate and compromise with his colleagues. He took that same attitude into the world of business, as well, expanding his reach and growing his profile not only in the city but throughout the state and nation as a new exemplar of modern Southern politics, even though most Black residents of Atlanta would have argued, despite Johnson's success, that no modern Southern politics actually existed. Still, Johnson's election was a watershed, opening the door for further Black representation in the state legislature in the next several election cycles. He had "no illusions about what one Negro can accomplish in an otherwise all-white legislature," *Ebony* claimed, but "he thinks he can 'alter the image of the Negro as conceived by so many Southern legislators.'"[6]

On the edition's next page was a profile of the next big sensation in boxing, made notorious partly for his skill in the ring and partly for his boastful rhetoric. A picture of the fighter screaming was at the top of the page next to the article's title, "A Look at Cassius Clay: Biggest Mouth in Boxing." Clay told the magazine about his greatness, about the surety that he could defeat heavyweight champion Sonny Liston. "There're a lot of things I want to be in this fight game," he told the magazine, "but I sure don't want to be a Joe Louis. That is, I don't want to have the income tax trouble he had. Man, you can't fight or do nothing without peace of mind. I don't want anything to take my mind off going straight up—up—up."[7]

That is exactly what he would do. A young Clay had begun boxing at age twelve and would rise through the amateur ranks to win the national Golden Gloves and ultimately the gold medal at the 1960 Rome Olympics. After that he would become professional, rising through those ranks, as well, until he defeated Sonny Liston in 1964 to become world's heavyweight champion. In the ring after his victory Ali screamed into a microphone, "I'm the king of the world!"[8] After defending that championship for three years, Clay would face scrutiny from the federal government; he would lose much of that peace of mind. And when he was no longer going straight up—up—up, he would eventually turn to Georgia's Black state senator, who would restore much of that peace of mind and put his career back on its upward trajectory. The connection between the two was only cosmetic in 1963, but it would move from the pages of *Ebony* in 1970, and in the process would fundamentally change sports in the remainder of the twentieth century.

—

In the months following the *Ebony* profiles of Johnson and Clay, John F. Kennedy would be assassinated, as would Ngo Dinh Diem, American puppet governor of South Vietnam. The deaths would pave the way for the presidency of Lyndon Johnson, who would escalate in Vietnam, including an expansion of the military draft. Cassius Clay had originally been disqualified from the draft after failing a military intelligence test. But Muhammad Ali's eligibility would prove a very different story.[9]

Clay first became acquainted with the Nation of Islam in, of all places, Johnson's Atlanta during his amateur boxing days in 1958. His introduction continued the following year during a boxing tournament in Chicago in 1959. After the fighter turned professional and moved to Miami to train with Angelo Dundee, he began attending Nation of Islam meetings at the local mosque there. When he met Malcolm X the two became close, the NOI minister even conspicuously attending Clay's training camp for his first fight with Sonny Liston. After that fight, after Clay won the heavyweight title, he announced that he was a member of the Nation of Islam, a follower of Elijah Muhammad who had changed his name to Cassius X. Weeks later Muhammad gave Cassius a new name: Muhammad Ali.[10]

Much of white America experienced his conversion as a trauma. The fighter was already brash and braggadocious, an avatar of professional wrestling's Gorgeous George mapped onto the boxing world. He played the heel, but he did it in an entertaining way that had always divided sports fans. Now, however, they were divided more than ever; the heavyweight champion in a sport that came to define American masculinity, itself an avatar of the leftover remnants of social Darwinian assumptions about survival of the fittest, was part of an organization considered by many to be a hate group. Many fans interpreted the conversion as a threat.

So too did the US government. It wasn't long after Ali's public conversion that his draft status was changed. A complicated call and response with the military followed, leading ultimately to Ali refusing his draft induction and facing indictment as a consequence. His choice was motivated in part by a sincere belief in the immorality of the conflict and a need for more of those resources to be used at home in service to racial equality. But even more pressing for Ali was a directive by Elijah Muhammad, who had refused induction during the World War II draft and served several years in prison as a result, that the Nation's most famous acolyte not step forward when his name was called. In the end, however, the result was the same. Even before he was convicted and sentenced to five years in prison, Ali was stripped of his championship and his boxing license in every state with a licensing body. For the next three years the former champion engaged in a series of legal appeals, surviving on revenue from public speaking engagements, guest television appearances, and even a role in a Broadway musical.[11]

It was a difficult time for Ali, the boxer publicly claiming that he was done with the sport but privately hoping that popular opinion would find its way back to him. After one television appearance wherein he admitted that he needed money and could get it if allowed to fight again, Elijah Muhammad suspended him from the faith, in part because Ali was, in Muhammad's thinking, playing into the hands of white capitalists, but also in part because the former champion was no longer the financial and recruiting boon to the Nation of Islam that he had been as champion. For a true believer like Ali, the suspension was a devastating blow, but it allowed more secular management to come back into his camp, a management that began securing him more lucrative deals and searching for possible venues open to permitting the fighter back into the ring.[12] Surely, publicists thought, there was a liberal city, one with a substantial majority of its population opposed to the Vietnam War and dedicated to racial equality, a city willing to resist the pressures of patriotic orthodoxy to provide a fighter treated unfairly a chance at redemption.

—

Atlanta was none of those things.

The city began the twentieth century accepting a variety of Black migrants coming from rural areas of the state, those seeking to escape tenant farming and the financial ravages of the crop lien system. That group added to an agglomeration of Black wealth in Atlanta that only grew with a broadening customer base in the segregated sections of the city. White business and civic leaders, meanwhile, realized that if they wanted to draw national financial interests and private venture capital to the region, they needed to create an image of Atlanta that included sedate if not amicable race relations that would differentiate the city from its Southern contemporaries. In 1925 a "Forward Atlanta" campaign by the Chamber of Commerce invested in publicizing opportunities in the city and helped expand its population further. Part of that program, and part of the reality of municipal politics in a segregated city with significant Black wealth, was white leaders working with Black leaders to limit the dangers of more overt acts of racial violence and mollify those Black residents still stagnating under the status quo.[13]

And there were plenty of them stagnating. Atlanta's Auburn Avenue was hailed as the wealthiest Black street in the country, but the vast majority of Black Atlanta still struggled in low-wage jobs with no real chance of advancement. Their neighborhoods were kept artificially poor by zoning restrictions and highway construction. Segregated facilities that were separate and decidedly unequal were the norm. A wealthy and powerful Black leadership group advocated for those in the working class and negotiated regularly with powerful white interests to ensure a kind of tolerable stasis, but actual progress among poor residents, despite the growth in per capita income bred by the success of affluent Black businesspeople, was rare.[14]

When the civil rights movement began in earnest in 1955, Atlanta watched as white officials in other Southern cities cracked down on protesters and made sweeping racial pronouncements that trumpeted a white supremacy that played to a white working-class base but only damaged the prospects of those cities to make themselves appear cosmopolitan to potential investors. White leadership in Georgia's capital city chose instead a path of mollification through negotiation, maintaining the reputation of Atlanta as a reasonable alternative to Montgomery or New Orleans, where more overt acts of retributive violence had met civil rights activism. In 1955, mayor William Hartsfield declared Atlanta a "city too busy to hate," emphasizing the spread of civic capitalism that would later become known as the Sunbelt. And it worked. While the rest of the white South found itself in the newspapers for all the wrong reasons, corporate capital came to Atlanta in droves. Coca-Cola, Delta, and other companies expanded. The city added tens of thousands of jobs per year.[15]

When the sit-in movement arrived in 1960, Atlanta's politicians responded with a token desegregation that made white leaders appear conciliatory. The following year those leaders authorized the desegregation of four city high schools. The year after that Johnson joined the state senate as a representative from Atlanta. It was a strategy that earned the city a reputation for racial moderation, a Southern oasis in a sea of massive resistance, a reputation only bolstered by comparisons with neighbors like Birmingham, which, in the summer after Johnson took office, violently repressed civil rights protesters and stunted the growth of a city that originally had similar economic aspirations.[16]

But the reputation of Atlanta belied a racial reality incongruent with its public profile. Segregation remained. The schools would battle in court for years. Residential segregation limited the scope of Black prospects for all but the wealthiest on Auburn Avenue. Underneath pictures of upper-class negotiation, modern integrated facilities, and corporate boosterism lay the reality of a Black mass seething with discontent in neighborhoods kept artificially small and artificially indigent, cut off from vital services by city planning designed to keep white residents from ever having to see them. Black students were also seething on the campuses of the Atlanta University Center, the large conglomeration of Black colleges and universities in the heart of the city. The students had been the authors of the sit-ins in 1960 and had become disillusioned by the accommodationist negotiating aid they received from influential Black leaders seeking to maintain amicable relations with the white business and civic elite. "It is a sad but true fact that for most black people, Atlanta has been more dream than reality," admitted Julian Bond.[17]

—

The governor of Georgia at the time of the 1963 *Ebony* profile, while Birmingham was seemingly on fire next door, was Carl Sanders, a racial moderate, a liberal by Southern standards. Sanders guided the state through the tumultuous middle years of the 1960s, and while Georgia's race relations were in many ways just as problematic as those of its neighbors, the presence of Sanders and the reputation of Atlanta made the state look far more stable than others in the region. When Sanders left office, however, he was replaced by a very different kind of politician. Lester Maddox had long been a symbol of racial intransigence, a restaurateur who made himself infamous for chasing off Black customers with guns and pickax handles rather than serve them. His run for governor had seemed quixotic at first, and he lost the vote of his home city of Atlanta by a substantial margin, but rural white voters in the rest of the state saw in the paragon of massive resistance someone still willing to push back against the tide of racial equality laws they saw as crashing down upon them.[18]

Though Maddox did not give the state the kind of George Wallace–esque administration that many feared, his reputation preceded him, and his antics only reminded people that while Atlanta had so carefully curated a reputation as a city too busy to hate, the most powerful man in the city was very much a hater.

Sanders, however, hadn't disappeared from the scene. During his time as governor, he oversaw perhaps the most important element of Atlanta's project of national and international legitimacy: the arrival of major league professional sports. The South had missed out on the boom in professional sports, as all of the major sports leagues, save the NHL, had desegregated prior to the birth of the classical civil rights movement, and even the NHL had done so by the 1960s. But the gains of the civil rights movement, combined with the size, wealth, and reputation of Atlanta, made the arrival of pro sports a real possibility for the first time. In 1965, Major League Baseball's Milwaukee Braves agreed to move south; in 1966 Atlanta secured an expansion franchise in the National Football League, the Atlanta Falcons. The following year the city would debut the Atlanta Chiefs, competing in the newly formed North American Soccer League.[19]

Sports teams were important to Atlanta powerbrokers because for so many they served as the front-facing image of the cities where they played. The Braves and Falcons, and to a lesser extent the Chiefs, gave residents a sense of legitimacy, a feeling that the public relations work they had done since the Forward Atlanta campaign early in the century had finally paid dividends. But even as the city's new teams began play, the specter of race loomed. Both the Braves and the Falcons would play in Atlanta Stadium on land made available to the local stadium authority through a slum clearance program that displaced Black residents and further diminished the territory open to Black residents. The year that play began, 1966, opened with the Georgia state legislature refusing to seat Julian Bond, who had been elected from an Atlanta district, claiming that the refusal was a direct result of his vocal opposition to the war in Vietnam. The year ended with the reactionary Maddox's gubernatorial victory and a decision by the US Supreme Court forcing Georgia legislators to seat Bond.[20]

After Sanders left office to make way for Maddox, the former governor became involved in a variety of other ventures. Among them was an effort with local real estate developer Tom Cousins to bring the National Basketball Association to Atlanta. They found success in 1968 when they purchased the St. Louis Hawks and brought them to the city, using the effort as an excuse to develop a new downtown arena, the Omni Coliseum, which they hoped would revitalize downtown and bring white suburban residents, and their money, back to the city. Those white suburban dollars never really materialized, so they tried again several years later, debuting the Atlanta Flames in the National Hockey League in 1972, hoping that a sport with all white players would draw customers, even though the game itself was foreign to most Southern sports fans.[21]

—

Between the arrival of the Hawks and the arrival of the Flames, Atlanta managed to bring another major league professional sport to the city. The spectacle of championship boxing wasn't entirely new to Atlanta, but the arrival of a fight with the publicity and magnitude of Muhammad Ali certainly was.

Ali's return to the ring was a convergence of time and place. While advocates for the former champion had searched far and wide for a venue that would host a bout, Atlanta was something of a last resort. It was a majority Black city with professional sports and a reputation for racial moderation, but it was also the home of Lester Maddox; Atlanta, however, had two benefits that other potential suitors for an Ali fight didn't have. First, Atlanta was in a state with no athletic commission, meaning that Ali would not have to justify his presence to a state board as he would in other states. Second, Atlanta had an influential Black leadership that marshaled a large voting bloc responsible for putting many of the city's politicians in power. And chief among those leaders was Leroy Johnson.[22]

Johnson was able to convince the city's mayor, Sam Massell, that the fight would be a value added to the city's reputation. Johnson had endorsed Massell's candidacy, even though there was a Black competitor for the job, and helped deliver him the votes he needed to win, so Massell, in turn, reluctantly agreed to hosting a potential match. After securing Ali a license to fight in the city, the search was on for an opponent. Johnson wanted a championship bout between the undefeated Ali and the current champion, Joe Frazier. When that effort fell through, however, the group decided on the next best thing: a Great White Hope.[23]

Jerry Quarry was a California fighter, the number-one-ranked contender, the closest approximation of a star white heavyweight since the retirement of Rocky Marciano. He had also previously been critical of Ali's unwillingness to abide by his draft notice. Failing the availability of Frazier, Quarry was the best of second-best options.[24]

The choice of Quarry as Ali's Atlanta opponent was an intentional effort to infuse race into the narrative of the fight. But in Atlanta race was going to be part of it even if no one made the attempt. Lester Maddox railed against the presence of a Black draft dodger getting his opportunity to return in Georgia, and even declared the day of the fight a day of mourning throughout the state. Patriotic groups like the American Legion protested. Atlanta's Municipal Auditorium, where the fight would take place, received bomb threats, and Ali's camp received any number of threatening phone calls and notes. Gunshots even rang out near the home where Ali stayed while training in the city. All of it laid bare the myths behind the stories Atlanta told about its progressive identity.[25]

Despite efforts to stop the fight, however, on October 26, 1970, Muhammad Ali returned to the ring after three years of forced exile, defeating Jerry Quarry after a cut over the white fighter's eye left him unable to answer the bell for the fourth round. He did so in front of five thousand fans—most of them Black, most of them rooting for Ali and celebrating his return—in downtown Atlanta. It was the largest collection of Black wealth and power in the city since the funeral of Martin Luther King, Jr., more than two years prior. The festivities at Municipal Auditorium that night became a celebration of Black protest and independence, a demonstration that though white Atlanta's self-deceptions about its racial progressivism had real consequences for real people in the city, Black power in the state capital was also real, and that Black power could come together to rehabilitate an athlete whose infamy had kept him from boxing everywhere else in the country, including in cities that had actual progressive bona fides to celebrate. It was a watershed moment, a defining cultural victory for Black Atlanta that helped make the city the Black mecca that it became. At the same time, it did for Atlanta what boosters had always wanted. The fight was shown on closed-circuit television at more than two hundred venues across the country and scores of others around the world. It was the first American sporting event shown live in the Soviet Union. Atlanta had officially become an international city.[26]

—

The emergence of Atlanta, the new visibility of its Black population, the reemergence of Muhammad Ali, and the sea change in boxing that it generated all came from the convergence of three distinct entities: Leroy Johnson, Ali, and Atlanta itself. And even as they came together, each of them presented images that obscured the reality of who they really were.

Johnson presented himself as acting in the interests of Black Atlanta, and, to be sure, he was. But he was also acting in his own best interest. His effort in making and promoting the fight netted him roughly $175,000. He was a state senator, but he was also a businessman, a member of the Black elite that so many working-class residents saw as disconnected from the real problems faced by the majority of Atlanta's Black citizens. Johnson worked tirelessly, in his own way, to amplify Black issues and push the race forward, but he also wore diamonds, drove luxury cars, and smoked expensive cigars. Johnson was, in many ways, an enigma, and while he was celebrated for his effort in bringing Ali back to boxing and giving Atlanta a publicity coup in the process, many younger civil rights activists would go back to mistrusting him when the national and international sports reporters left town.[27]

That mistrust was built on the reality that although Atlanta presented itself as a paragon of Southern racial moderation, it had long used that reputation as a cudgel to promote white civic and business interests over and against the quality of life of its poorer Black residents. Atlanta was beset by racial strife in the years before Muhammad Ali's return, and it would be beset by racial strife in the years after. But the demonstration of legitimate Black power embodied by one October fight night in 1970 would demonstrate that Black power would have to be accounted for in any future political negotiations. When, for example, the election to replace mayor Sam Massell took place in 1973, the victor in that contest would be Maynard Jackson, the city's first Black mayor, fundamentally altering the political reality in Atlanta. No white mayoral candidate has ever won an election since then.[28]

Ali's return wasn't the only reason for that change, of course, but it certainly played a role. And just as the politician and the venue were presenting images of themselves different, to varying degrees, from reality, so too was the boxer. Ali was a complicated figure. He was not an advocate of integrationist civil rights. He was decidedly against women's rights. His opposition to the Vietnam War was rooted principally in fear of the NOI rather than any sustained or considered convictions. And yet he became one of the most beloved figures among those who preached the gospel of civil and women's rights and vehemently opposed the war in Vietnam. He also represented such movements to those who did not love him, white Southerners in particular, who saw in him a symbol of Black radicalism and anti-American sentiment, a threat by his very popularity to patriotic white identity. Ali came to represent so many things that he wasn't really part of—for better and worse—largely because he was so entertaining and because he could fight. Still, as historian Othello Harris has explained, "More than anyone else, Ali made sports into contested political ground for blacks, and athletes who followed would find it easier to challenge the sports establishment."[29]

"For some reason, people don't want fighters just to be fighters," wrote Gary Wills in 1975. "They have to stand for an era, for the color of hope, for a metaphysics of the spirit." It was that attitude that created caricatures of good and evil that dominated the sport, that made Jerry Quarry, at least temporarily, "the voice of the new ethnics." Sonny Liston was a criminal, Joe Louis a patriot. Ali was a draft dodger to many, a hero to others. "It is as if the *art* were not enough to redeem boxing's violence, all that cruelty inflicted on the face—so we prefer to think the loser is being destroyed for some deeply ideological reason."[30]

Much of the art got lost in 1970 in the politics of ethnicity, ideology, and cruelty. But that was largely because the art, at least this time, was really beside the point. It was the politics of race, the wielding of Black political power, and the courage of Ali to return to the ring in the heart of the Deep South that governed the meaning of his fight with Jerry Quarry.

—

Thus it was that on October 26, 1970, for the second time in history, for the first time in the twentieth century, a Black man pummeled a white man in front of a large crowd of onlookers in the Deep South and was celebrated as a result. There was no threat of jail or lynching. Those screaming at the fighters weren't attempting to impose a white supremacist order on a Black man who knew that no matter the result of the combat, the real consequence was still to come.

At the same time, however, there was still—for so many in the Deep South, for so many among those screaming at the fighters—a remaining white supremacist order that decidedly limited their opportunities and governed the scope of their lives. The fight between Muhammad Ali and Jerry Quarry that October night would forever change boxing. Ali's presence in the ring enlivened a moribund sport that had suffered in his absence. His victory in Atlanta created the opportunity for his better-known bouts with Joe Frazier, George Foreman, and Ken Norton. It would provide him a larger platform to use his fame for racial equality and religious freedom.

And it would, in its way, forever change Atlanta. It was a night that encapsulated the intersection of race and urban economics in the Deep South, demonstrating—even against the history of Atlanta race relations—that metropolitan development, civic pride, and, ultimately, money, could on occasion temporarily abrogate the uglier vicissitudes of formalized racism without the necessity of Black concessions and compromise. That it did so at the hands of Leroy Johnson, a member of the city's Black elite that had been responsible for so many of those concessions, made the moment all the more stark. In the wake of the fight Johnson didn't abandon his legislative strategy of quid pro quo or take a more hard-line Black Power position. Racism, and even segregation, didn't magically disappear. But on October 26, 1970, the Black population owned Atlanta, and the city, the state, the country, and the world reaped a legitimate benefit from its ownership, however temporary it may have been.

The King of the World had returned.

1. CLASS, RACE, AND THE RISE OF LEROY JOHNSON IN ATLANTA

1895–1968

Atlanta's Black middle class had made itself a dominant part of the city's community since the last decades of the nineteenth century, an entrepreneurial group that had cast down its bucket since the days of Booker Washington's Atlanta Compromise speech in the city during the 1895 Cotton States Exposition. The political relationship that they developed with influential whites continued until 1908, when the state instituted its white primary.[1] Political influence, however, wasn't the only kind of influence. By 1911 the city had roughly two thousand Black businesses. At the close of the nineteenth century the Black elite was largely composed of entrepreneurs who sold products and services to white customers, but change was afoot. Just as in northern markets responding to the early birth pangs of the Great Migration, an influx of rural Black migrants into Atlanta turned many whites away from Black service industries, leading to an erosion of the old hierarchical order and its replacement with a new entrepreneurial class that built a business infrastructure reliant instead on Black customers. Among Black business owners in the 1890s, for example, only pharmacists, grocers, and undertakers served a predominantly Black clientele. Those early members of the Black elite lived in a city, unlike nearby Augusta and Savannah, that never really had a substantial antebellum free population, and so came principally, as August Meier explains, "from the mostly mulatto house-servant group."[2] The core institutions of that original aristocracy were the First Congregational Church, Atlanta University, and a variety of exclusive social clubs.

The shift that created the new leadership class largely came from entrepreneurs in the finance, insurance, and real estate industries. Alonzo Herndon famously arrived in Atlanta in poverty but founded the Atlanta Life Insurance Company in 1905. Hemon Perry arrived from Texas in a similar state in 1908, but in 1911 he was able to create Standard Life Insurance, which in turn developed a variety of subsidiaries, including Citizens Trust Bank in 1921. Though Standard Life folded in the late 1920s, Citizens Trust would grow to become one of the most influential and profitable Black banks in the country, just as Atlanta Life grew in the insurance industry, becoming the largest Black life insurance company in America. The new economic order had arrived. While much of Atlanta's Black business and cultural life still centered on Auburn Avenue, many of those new power brokers moved to Atlanta's West Side residential areas.[3]

The business elite was joined by the presidents of the city's Black colleges, a group of doctors and lawyers, and some college professors to create a dominant core of influence peddlers, almost none of them coming from the original nineteenth-century Black upper class. The older families, then, were left to either marry into the new money or migrate to other cities, which most of them ultimately did, creating what Meier has called "a considerable elite circulation in Atlanta."[4] Still, while the new money made for a larger Black upper class and a spread of wealth to more entrepreneurs, the expansion of Black wealth also came with a growing income disparity, as the bulk of poor rural migrants coming to Atlanta did not have the good fortune of Herndon and Perry and never made it to the nicer neighborhoods of the West Side. As Virginia Hein explains, "There were two Atlantas within the city and two black Atlantas within the black community itself." One of those Black Atlantas enjoyed wealth and the power to negotiate with white leaders; the other, in the words of Anne Rivers Siddons, suffered "inadequate housing, poor municipal services, idleness, dirt, decay, overcrowding, poor playground facilities or none at all, and poverty—always, endlessly, too little money."[5]

That Black elite's first real electoral success came in the 1920s, when the Black voting bloc helped defeat a series of bond referenda. Leaders then leveraged that power to get the city's board of education to build its first Black high school. When postwar legal victories, like the elimination of the state's white primary in *Chapman v. King* (1946), helped expand Black political power more broadly, Black influence in Atlanta only increased. Throughout the 1950s Black voters in Atlanta appeared at the polls in greater percentages than whites and continued to grow in number, until in 1962, the year of Leroy Johnson's state senate election, 34 percent of the total electorate was Black, with roughly 52,000 registered Black voters. The percentage of Black registrants remained lower through the early 1960s than the percentage of the total Black population in the city, but the Black voting bloc stood in lockstep behind candidates whereas whites remained split between racial conservatives and racial moderates. Two distinct voting blocs, then, ultimately emerged: one that included middle- and upper-class whites and the vast majority of Black voters, and another that included working-class whites and parts of the middle class. In the 1961 mayoral election, for example, Ivan Allen defeated opponent Lester Maddox by a relatively wide margin, even though Maddox narrowly edged Allen among white voters. Black votes swung that election and had the power to swing any city contest, making Black political power a vital part of white political thinking.[6] It was something that white politicians in other Deep South cities didn't have to contend with, at least not to the same degree; but in return, whites in the city got the ability to contrast Atlanta with more violent civil rights sites like Montgomery, Little Rock, and New Orleans. Georgia's capital city was "the city too busy to hate"—a term coined by mayor William Hartsfield in the year after the Supreme Court's *Brown* decision and popularized by the local Chamber of Commerce—courting northern business development and venture capital to promote itself as a thriving representative of the Sunbelt.[7]

The slogan was part of a long-standing attempt to improve the city's image. In 1925 Atlanta's Chamber of Commerce began a "Forward Atlanta" campaign to increase new business infrastructure in the city. The group invested three-quarters of a million dollars in the effort, and it bore significant fruit, as the population of the city grew 35 percent in the decade and hundreds of businesses and thousands of jobs came to Atlanta as a result. While those jobs largely went to whites, Black enterprises also thrived. By 1956 *Fortune* magazine had named Auburn Avenue the "richest Negro street in the world," and Atlanta Life Insurance and Citizens Trust Bank were two of the most prosperous Black companies in the country.[8]

There were, however, limitations on Black economic and physical mobility. Atlanta's first segregation ordinance appeared in 1913 and was followed by a variety of zoning ordinances that created separate spaces for Black residency, even after the Supreme Court declared racial zoning unconstitutional in 1924. More common, beginning in 1917, was the city's use of highway construction to remove Black residents from downtown areas and bind them into certain sections, a practice that continued well into the 1960s. After a new influx of Black migrants after World War II, residential segregation practices in the city, and even the bombing of Black homes, led the Urban League to create the Atlanta Housing Council in an attempt to leverage Black political power to create more physical space for Black residents, but those efforts met with further highway construction projects and even physical barriers. In 1962, as Johnson was winning his first term in the state senate, the notorious Peyton Road "Wall" was erected after a Black doctor attempted to purchase a house in Atlanta's Peyton Forest subdivision. In response, the all-white board of aldermen approved the barricading of two roads, which stopped north-south travel into a cluster of white neighborhoods. The Atlanta Negro Voters League and other Black leadership organizations protested the move, and the barricades were ultimately removed on the order of the Fulton County Superior Court, but the incident gave lie to the assumption that white racial moderation was somehow akin to racial advocacy—that Atlanta was indeed "too busy to hate." The reality, from any moderate white perspective, was that racial moderation required segregation and necessitated placating racist whites just as much as placating middle- and upper-class Black residents, leaving the bulk of the city's Black population out of the equation entirely.[9]

That equation, however, yielded results for everyone else. After the Lockheed Corporation, an aerospace company, built a factory in suburban Marietta after World War II, other companies followed, expanding the regional economy in the 1950s. In the 1960s Atlanta's population grew by thirty thousand residents every year; its economy added an average of twenty-three thousand jobs annually. From 1945 to 1960 almost three thousand new corporations or branch offices of existing corporations came to Atlanta. Skyscrapers rose; Six Flags and Atlanta Stadium were built; the airport expanded. Atlanta became the financial hub of the South. It was the home of Delta, Southern Bell, and Coca-

Cola. That growth, in turn, prompted the development of the tourism, convention, and entertainment industries, creating a diverse economy that white business and civic leaders didn't want interrupted by civil rights struggles and racial agitation.[10]

In the late 1950s, as Georgia's government was plotting a strategy to avoid school desegregation, even floating a plan to shut down the state's schools, Mayor Hartsfield and Atlanta pushed back. His defense of education, and his suggestion that Atlanta voters should have their say on whether schools in the city should be desegregated, was supported by a glut of white ministers, professionals, and parent-teacher associations. Though that plan was not an endorsement of integrated schools, and the only reason such discussions were taking place was because of the work of Black activists pushing for such changes, white leaders again worked with their Black counterparts to ensure that investment in Atlanta would not stop because of overt statewide racism. A "Save Our Schools" movement was created in 1959, largely by white parents. Both Black and white leaders pushed for a biracial commission to help determine the best route for desegregation. White Atlantans hadn't become egalitarians, of course, but they wanted schools, outside investment, and the reputation that came with them. The state legislature responded in 1960 by holding hearings on school desegregation—a glorified way to delay any actual decision on the prospect.[11]

The legislature was representative of more than just Atlanta and was far less worried about its national reputation than city leaders. White residents who had absconded to the suburbs and no longer had the same vested interest in the city's growth were similarly skeptical of the merits of integration. "We'll see, as time goes on, how wrong they are," wrote one suburban editor of white Atlanta leadership's insistence that desegregation would encourage business relocation and private venture capital to move into the city. "It will have nothing whatever to do with location of plants or growth of business. You can mark these words well." It was a sentiment that would prove to be wrong, but it also demonstrated the broader opinion of white Georgia beyond Atlanta's power brokers.[12]

Still, in August 1961 Black students desegregated four formerly white high schools in Atlanta, and John Kennedy responded by citing the city as exemplary of how Southern communities should respond to court rulings. "Look closely," he suggested, "at what Atlanta has done." For the

New York Times Atlanta was the "new and shining example" of interracial cooperation. Predominantly white magazines across the country echoed the sentiment.[13] Predominantly Black magazines declared Atlanta as a new Black mecca. *Ebony* admitted that much of the "highly publicized racial harmony" was "a fabrication encouraged by the Chamber of Commerce," but the magazine hyped the "Black mecca" nonetheless. "Some say it's the place where black dreams are most likely to come true, that in Atlanta black folks have more, live better, accomplish more and deal with whites more effectively than they do anywhere else in the South—or North." As was its common strategy, *Ebony* focused on the city's talented tenth, noting Black political, civic, and economic influence, the trappings of success that could be seen in Atlanta's shiny new skyline and on the playing fields of its new pro sports teams. Leroy Johnson was part of the hype, publicly claiming that there was "no other city in the nation where a Negro has more opportunity to achieve his ambitions."[14]

All, however, was not as it seemed. Citing school desegregation efforts and the sit-ins that followed, and the outwardly peaceful dispatch with which they were dealt, Julian Bond said that "this city's fathers are not losing their expertise in explaining away Atlanta's racial divisions." The bulk of the Black population in Atlanta was poor, and "it is poorly educated," Bond argued. He noted that a portion of the statistics that bore out that poverty arose from the rural migrant population flooding into the city. But the other part came from segregated schools run by a school board "whose loyalties lay in financial Atlanta, and not in improving the minds of young black men and women." Keeping the peace, in other words, was doing functional harm to the ability of Black Atlantans to get ahead educationally and financially.[15] "Something strange and appalling has happened in Atlanta," Martin Luther King, Jr., explained. "While boasting of its civic virtue, Atlanta has allowed itself to fall behind almost every major southern city in progress toward desegregation." Despite the high-profile high-school integration, the bulk of Atlanta's schools remained decidedly segregated a decade after the Supreme Court's *Brown* decision.[16]

The city's actual desegregation didn't take place until the second half of the sixties, following the Supreme Court's *Heart of Atlanta Motel, Inc. v. United States* (1964) decision, which ruled that the federal government could enjoin a motel from discriminating on the basis of race, fully enabling Title 2 of the Civil Rights Act of 1964. If the government could enjoin the Heart of Atlanta Motel from discriminating, it could enjoin all of the other whites-only businesses in the city. Only when the writing was on the wall and a real threat of government intervention existed did the city too busy to hate follow through with city-wide desegregation. The Supreme Court also issued a ruling on Atlanta's segregated schools that year, but though *Calhoun v. Latimer* (1964) had been initiated by the NAACP's Legal Defense Fund, local Black leaders failed to follow through on the ruling's dictates for fear of alienating white leaders and stymieing progress on other fronts.[17]

Nothing approximating comprehensive school desegregation in Atlanta happened until 1973, years after Ali and the crowds he drew had left the city. At that point the local NAACP, led by onetime Leroy Johnson ally Lonnie King, negotiated with white elites to appoint a Black school superintendent and install other Black administrators while the integration of actual students was de-emphasized, leaving the vast majority of the city's schools at least 90 percent single-race. In response, a group of Black parents filed suit, claiming that the supposed settlement had been negotiated without the consent of the Black working class.[18]

It was a suit at the heart of the class disconnect existing within Black Atlanta. As Julian Bond, another occasional working ally of Johnson, explained of the Black community, Atlanta was "the best place in the United States if you're middle-class and have a college degree, but if you're poor, it's just like Birmingham, Jackson or any other place." Though popular perception cited the educated middle-class status of Black leaders in the city and their negotiation with white leaders about the nature and outcomes of civil rights for its seeming racial equality, Tomiko Brown-Nagin has explained that "the reliance on biracial negotiation further excluded working class and poor black families from discourses about the future." That negotiation actually benefited white leaders, as it neutered civil rights protest efforts by creating a semblance of racial harmony. Atlanta was, in the words of Adolph Reed, "the archetype of the hegemony of development elites in local politics."[19]

But it also benefited Black leaders, as they were able to pursue goals that benefited middle and upper-class Black interests. That they did so while failing to "pursue reforms that might have ensured the well-being of African-Americans as a whole" was a reality that was either willful or the result of willful self-deception. "The would-be black middle-class reformers, like the system of segregation that they opposed, were racially essentialist. They conflated the legal manifestation of white supremacy," Brown-Nagin explains, "with the actual socio-economic conditions in which those constructed as 'colored,' or 'raced,' lived." Even when some Black leaders supported more radical strategies, compromise always won out.[20]

Those leaders boasted that almost 30 percent of Atlanta's municipal workforce in the 1960s was Black and the middle class of the race was constantly expanding. But Black residents in socioeconomically depressed neighborhoods like Dixie Hills and Vine City saw none of that supposed success. Race relations in Atlanta, James Baldwin noted, were "manipulated by the mayor and a fairly strong Negro middle class," which "works mainly in areas of compromise and concession and has very little effect on the bulk of the Negro population." More than half of Atlanta's African-American population had stopped attending school before the ninth grade. In 1965 Black residents constituted 45 percent of the city population, though Black neighborhoods only made up 22 percent of residential land. The Black unemployment rate was double that of whites. The majority of Black Atlantans were caged by economic and geographic limitations that kept them in a state of stasis, even as the broader city economy continued to boom.[21] When Martin Luther King, Jr., toured Vine City in early 1966, he found the conditions there "appalling. I had no idea people were living in Atlanta, Georgia, in such conditions." He described the neighborhood as worse than the Chicago slums. "This is a shame on the community." King suggested a rent strike to the residents, but, with nowhere else to go, they felt that kind of action to be unsafe.[22]

Meanwhile, neighborhoods like Summerhill and Peoplestown had been stymied by freeway construction directed through the areas. Urban renewal programs through the first half of the 1960s led to the demolition of twenty-one thousand housing units in low-income areas, displacing roughly sixty-seven thousand people, most of them Black. Things only devolved when the city built Atlanta Stadium in 1965, forcing out more than twelve thousand Summerhill residents. Those displaced were promised new homes through the Model Cities program, but the closest approximation that the government provided were temporary mobile homes.[23]

Charles Rutheiser has argued that the construction of Atlanta Stadium was "the high-water mark of the old regime; subsequent projects would no longer be decided by a select group of white oligarchs sitting around a table at the Commerce Club." That did not mean, however, that consequences of earlier projects did not cast a long shadow. Frustration in neighborhoods like Summerhill and Peoplestown finally boiled over in September 1966, with the people of Vine City inflamed after police shot and wounded an unarmed man. Residents of the neighborhood, along with those of Summerhill and Peoplestown, took to the streets, and the police responded with officers in riot gear. When the residents threw bricks and bottles, police responded with tear gas. Local ministers attempted to calm the frustrated residents. Ralph Abernathy and other members of the Black ruling elite struggled to convince Ivan Allen to call off the police to get them out of the area. At a meeting of protesters at a local church, younger advocates of Black Power clashed with SCLC officials. The SCLC's Hosea Williams urged nonviolence, telling the group to "go home and cool off." He was followed on stage by a SNCC worker, however, who turned the group back to a Black Power message. "We're not going home to cool off," he responded to Williams. "We're going home to heat up."[24]

They did heat up. Moderate Black leaders blamed the violence of the uprising on the younger activists of SNCC. To counter the radicals, leaders created the Good Neighbor Association, giving membership to residents who made a pledge to disavow violence. The Atlanta Summit Leadership Conference, a local rights group of influential Black leaders like Leroy Johnson, scapegoated SNCC chair Stokely Carmichael, who was, according to physician O. W. Davis, "an albatross around our necks—a parasite on the community." Carmichael was a symbol of the radical rejection of Black accommodationist leadership. "We've got to stop him," said William Holmes Borders, pastor of Wheat Street Baptist Church, "or he's going to stop us." But there was dissent from that position. The SCLC's Hosea Williams, who straddled the divide between traditional leadership and the radical revolt, reminded those at the summit meeting that the uprising was, in fact, a response to white violence. Black leaders denouncing the protests "sort of sound like white men," he said.[25]

One of the principal Black leaders part of the compromise apparatus was Austin T. Walden, Leroy Johnson's mentor. A year after students in

Atlanta began a widespread sit-in campaign to desegregate businesses in the city in 1960, Walden led a group of Black representatives who negotiated with white business and civic leaders to integrate local lunch counters and gradually desegregate other establishments, even though the protesters themselves had not approved the deal. The March 1961 agreement only exacerbated an existing breach. Students were upset that Walden had kneecapped the sit-ins and ignored their demands for immediate integration and improved employment opportunities. Though the kind of private representative dealmaking that Black decision-makers had commonly engaged in had largely gone uncontested by the working poor through the 1950s, the following decade led many, beginning with the students, to question a strategy that primarily benefited the Black middle and upper classes over and against the masses of Black Atlantans. It was a strategy that "delayed the advent of formal equality and thwarted efforts to transform the city's social relations in any fundamental way."[26]

During the sit-ins, members of the Atlanta Committee for Cooperative Action, founded in 1958 by younger Black professionals frustrated by the city's established Black decision-makers, supported the students and provided advice. Leroy Johnson was part of that group, along with Jesse Hill, Whitney Young, Carl Holman, and others. The advice of the committee directed students to target businesses with a large African American customer base, leveraging Black economic power in service to civil rights ends. Johnson, Hill, and others also served as conduits between student protesters and the old guard of Black leadership. Their participation was, in the moment, seen by the students as a value added, but when a compromise was reached without them they targeted their criticism at Atlanta's Black elite writ large, not making any distinctions between the old guard and new.[27]

Hill, who would become one of Johnson's closest allies, was an insurance executive with Atlanta Life who had started in the company as an actuary in 1949 after attending Missouri's Lincoln University for his undergraduate work and graduating from the University of Michigan with a masters in actuarial science and business administration. Hill was a native of St. Louis, but he took to his new city at the same time as the burgeoning civil rights movement. He was, according to Benjamin Mays, a "total community character." He chaired the city's All-Citizens Registration Committee, helping to register more than fifty thousand

Black voters. He helped with school desegregation efforts, as well as other social movements for racial equality. After rising to become vice president of Atlanta Life, he also took over as president of the *Atlanta Inquirer* newspaper and vice president of Enterprise Investments. He was treasurer of the Atlanta Urban League, a member of the executive committee of the Atlanta branch of the NAACP, and sat on the board of the national SCLC. Hill was a titan both of business and of civil rights, an exemplar of the possibilities available to the Black upper class to be involved in both civic negotiations and civil protest. He was, in that sense, a bridge between both sides of the two dominant forces in Black Atlanta and thus a valuable ally to Johnson, who occupied a place on only one side of that divide.[28]

Even before the 1961 Walden agreement, Black leadership was largely opposed to the sit-ins after they began in March 1960. Walden, Donald Hollowell, Rufus Clement, and others believed that student arrests following the first demonstrations gave them standing to sue, making further sit-ins unnecessary. C. A. Scott, editor of the *Atlanta Daily World*, opposed the protests in his paper, arguing that voting rights issues were far more important; desegregating public facilities should be de-emphasized and the sit-in protests should cease. When the student protesters approached Scott with their public appeal, he reluctantly printed it but charged them the regular advertising price. And he followed with editorials criticizing the protests. When the students wanted another advertisement to run in the *World*, Scott refused.[29] That said, local realtor Q. V. Williamson and Martin Luther King, Sr., posted bonds to get the protesting students released from jail. Walden and Hollowell called a special meeting of the NAACP's Legal Defense Fund to discuss the state's anti-trespass law and to chart a legal strategy to counter it. Leroy Johnson and Jesse Hill counseled the students and gave advice to SNCC leaders. There were generational and class divides, to be sure, but Black leaders in the city, even if they disapproved, did not abandon the student protesters.[30]

The sit-ins threatened white support for racial moderation as business owners who originally saw the veneer of progressivism as economically beneficial now saw themselves as targets whose commercial success could be stymied by civil rights activism. The protests also divided the old guard of Black leaders from the more radical students, as power brokers saw activism as, at best, eroding their ability to cut deals with white business elites or, at worst, pushing those elites toward the more virulent forces of segregationist politics. It left leaders like Johnson attempting to provide some kind of generic support for the students while trying to salvage relationships with the white civic and business class.[31]

Three years later, as student protests continued to use sit-ins to desegregate public accommodations, Johnson declared in January 1964 that he was "convinced that the demonstrations will be supported by the total Negro leadership in Atlanta."[32] At the same time, however, Walden, Clement, Hill, and other Black leaders tried to convince Mayor Allen not to testify before Congress on behalf of the bill that became the Civil Rights Act of 1964. They worried that white opposition to the bill and Allen's public support for it would ultimately hurt his ability to make successful race policy in the city. They wanted the Civil Rights Act, of course, but they felt Allen's testimony would play no role in its passage, thus offering the Black elite bad options in Atlanta politics. Allen testified anyway, but the episode demonstrated the willingness of those leaders to make moral compromises for strategic goals that would clearly have come under opposition had the bulk of the city's Black population known about them.[33]

The tide of Black leadership in the city, however, would begin to change the following year, as in 1965 Q. V. Williamson was elected the first Black alderman in Atlanta since Reconstruction. That same year attorney Horace Ward won a seat in the state senate to join Johnson. Even though Lester Maddox won the governorship the following year, eight Black candidates, all from the Atlanta area, won seats in the state legislature in the same election cycle. It was a demonstration of the critical mass of Black voters created by white flight to suburban centers.[34] As Kevin Kruse has explained, white Atlanta was decidedly resistant to racial change, but though whites were "generally less violent in their resistance" than similar groups in Northern cities, they were also less successful in defending against a rising tide of equalitarian politics. That was largely because "the black population they challenged was both larger and stronger than those in the North," which created an earlier and more powerful impetus for white flight out of the city center and into developing suburbs around Atlanta. It was a process that largely developed in the 1960s and 1970s in the North, but happened much earlier in Southern urban hubs like Atlanta.[35]

But there was still confrontation, largely governed by class. In the immediate postwar period, Black residency in Atlanta began to encroach on white working-class neighborhoods. In the mid-1950s, however, issues over racial segregation came to middle-class white areas and to nonresidential public spaces like buses, schools, and parks. Then in the early 1960s, really beginning with the Atlanta sit-in campaign, the white upper class felt the effects as the protests targeted white businesses and challenged the fragile coalition between Black and white power brokers.[36]

White flight in Atlanta led to what Kruse has called the "politics of suburban secession," wherein people in new outlying communities broke ties with Atlanta, cultivated their own smaller city politics, and sought growth that would make them functionally independent of the bigger city. In 1960 Atlanta had more than three hundred thousand white residents, but sixty thousand of them left for suburban communities over the course of the decade, not only growing the percentage of Black residency by the time of the Ali fight but also making the number of white residents demonstrably smaller. The result was a city at the end of the 1960s whose residential segregation was actually greater than it had been in the early 1940s.[37]

Leroy Johnson was one of the beneficiaries of that demographic change. Stephen Lesher wrote a long profile in the *New York Times* of Johnson, arguing that the socially literate all knew names like Ralph Abernathy, Julian Bond, and Coretta Scott King, but "among those who earn their bread in and around politics, one Southern black leader stands a head taller than the rest—a relatively obscure 42-year-old Georgia State Senator named Leroy R. Johnson." Lesher cited the "brazen pragmatism" that allowed Johnson to work with a variety of different representatives to get legislation that benefited Black Georgians; in return he could marshal large voting blocs to support candidates who helped him. "His white enemies believe he is a thief; his black enemies characterize him as a sellout Tom," wrote Lesher. "Neither is correct. He is nothing more or less than a fascinating black Machiavelli."[38]

Born on the west side of Atlanta on July 28, 1928, the son of a mortician, Johnson had to walk carefully to school to avoid the violence coming from the Beaver Slide neighborhood of the city. "I learned two things as a boy," he said. "First, that it's no fun to be poor. Second, that you've gotta outrun the opposition if you want to stay whole." Johnson grew up in the shadow of the capitol he would later occupy, riding on segregated buses and eating at Jim Crow restaurants. But he also knew that the Black middle class in the city was, in the words of Lerone Bennett, "an oasis in a desert: there were Negro bankers on this oasis, and Negro professors, doctors and insurance executives. Leroy Johnson caught a glimpse of their dream." After school at Booker T. Washington High, he attended Morehouse College along with contemporaries like Martin Luther King, Jr. He met a student at Spelman, Cleopatra Whittington, who would, in the late 1940s, become his wife. Their only son, Michael V. Johnson, was born on October 14, 1950. Even though he inclined toward the ministry in his youth, at Morehouse he studied history and political science, falling for the latter after reading about Tammany Hall's George T. Plunkitt. After earning a master's degree in political science from Atlanta University, he began teaching history and geography in Black high schools in the early 1950s. After *Brown v. Board of Education* in 1954, he was recruited by the local NAACP's Austin T. Walden and the Negro Voters League's Warren R. Cochrane to conduct a clinic for Black residents on the use of new voting machines. Johnson had caught the political bug. He gave up his teaching job and attended law school at North Carolina College at Durham (now North Carolina Central University), his wife working part-time as a librarian and Johnson working nights and weekends as a butcher to help keep the family afloat. In the summers he would leave his family and go north to take temporary jobs that would pay Black workers better than they would in the South.[39]

After completing his law degree in 1957, now twenty-nine years old, Johnson returned to Atlanta, still segregated but with a reputation under the leadership of Mayor Hartsfield of being comparatively progressive compared with other Southern cities. With the aid of Walden and Cochrane, he accepted a job on the staff of the Fulton County prosecutor's office, becoming the first Black assistant prosecutor in the southeast. He stayed in the office for five years, but clearly wanted more. He would do favors for those who needed anything, particularly judges, knowing that having legal friends in high places could only be a benefit. He also began joining organizations, becoming part of the connected world of

Black politics in the city. He joined the Masons, rising to the thirty-third degree. Then there were the All Citizens Registration Committee, the Fulton County Citizens Democratic Club, the Georgia Association of Citizens Democratic Clubs, the Georgia Voters League, the Atlanta Junior Voters League. He held officer roles in all of them. Perhaps most important was his role as secretary of the Atlanta Negro Voters League, in which he moved throughout the state at the behest of Walden to advise Black groups about protecting their voting rights.[40]

The Atlanta Negro Voters League had been formed by Walden and John Wesley Dobbs in July 1949 to take advantage of the Fifth Circuit Court of Appeals ruling in *Chapman v. King* that eliminated the state's white primary. In practice the ANVL became one of the chief negotiating organizations of the Black upper class. It used its influence over Black voting blocs to convince white leaders to make concessions, interviewing and endorsing candidates based on their own perception of who might be best for Black interests.[41]

Johnson's opportunity to run for his own political office came in 1962, when the Supreme Court ruled Georgia's county unit system unconstitutional.[42] A response to the urban migration of Black citizens and a bulwark of white supremacy, the county unit structure had been used informally since the late nineteenth century and had been formalized in 1917. It allotted six representatives to the eight most populous Georgia counties, four representatives to the thirty next-most-populous counties, and two representatives to the remainder. Under that system Fulton County, though the state's largest, received only one seat in the state senate, giving disproportionate power to white rural voters. The same system held for city elections in Atlanta. To serve on the aldermanic board, for example, a representative had to live in the ward he would represent, but he had to be elected by a majority of the total city population, which intentionally and overtly favored white candidates. The system had been upheld in federal court in 1946, but sixteen years later, the Supreme Court overturned the original precedent.[43] After the subsequent distribution of senate seats based on population, Fulton County received seven seats, and Walden and Cochrane convinced Johnson to run for one of them, in the Thirty-Eighth District, where roughly seventy thousand of the ninety thousand residents were Black. Johnson took to the role with a flourish, calling Black and white leaders, leaning on Walden and younger power brokers like Horace Ward. Walden and Cochrane convinced him to stop smoking cigars in public, even though he loved them, because they "reminded white people of Negro politicians of the Reconstruction era." He switched to cigarettes. But he also spoke at every available meeting of every conceivable group. He gladhanded whoever was willing to shake. He visited nightclubs on Saturday nights and church pulpits on Sunday mornings. Realizing that a Black official might win a state senate seat, something that hadn't happened since Reconstruction, white leaders in the Democratic Party decided that all seven seats in the primary would be decided by an at-large vote, wherein districts didn't matter, thus giving the majority white population the ability to place white representatives in all seven seats. The subsequent election, wherein Johnson overwhelmingly won his district but was still defeated county-wide by white competitors, was contested, and the courts ruled that voting had to be done by district. That meant that Johnson won his primary against four white candidates. He then handily defeated Republican T. M. Alexander, another Black candidate, in the general election, becoming the first Black man in ninety-two years to serve in the Georgia legislature. He celebrated his victory by declaring that he did not "want to be a Negro senator. I want to be a representative of all the people."[44]

Johnson's victory, when he was only thirty-four years old, was hailed as a portentous moment for the South. Voice of America reported the win across the world. Johnson was given a citizenship award in Louisiana, where Black citizens treated him like a celebrity, like Cassius Clay. They reached out, hoping to just touch the Black man who managed to win an election in the Jim Crow South. All of the leading white politicians in Georgia, seeing at least a vague blur of writing on the wall, sent letters of congratulation to the new state senator. Among them was one of Georgia's US senators, arch–white supremacist Herman Talmadge. He even invited Johnson to the Talmadge estate, where the two discussed Georgia politics with seemingly unrestrained conviviality. Whether Talmadge had an eye on the right side of history or on the pragmatic change in political winds, it was clear that Johnson's election was more meaningful than most state senatorial votes.[45]

But it wasn't particularly meaningful to his colleagues. The Commerce Club, for example, was an exclusive gathering place for the city's white political elite. Newly inaugurated, Johnson arrived for a special luncheon at the club in honor of the new legislative session, then watched angrily as the manager removed the place setting in front of him. Johnson was also initially treated like a pariah by most of his fellow senators, but slowly earned their respect, preferring to gain concessions in back rooms rather than grandstand on the senate floor. His willingness to negotiate and his ability to rally Black voters made him an influential force in the body over the course of the 1960s. "Here was a voice of the New South not sitting in but *getting* in," explained Budd Schulberg. "Adopting the old approaches of the string-tie Southern politicians, sweet-talkin' and favor-swappin' in back rooms, he had put them to work for black power, Atlanta style."[46] Julian Bond remembered that Johnson "became a full-time politician. I mean 24 hours a day, seven days a week." He glad-handed, made connections. "He let it be known that if you did a favor for him, he'd do one for you." He had working alliances with the city's white judges because he always supported pay raises for the judiciary and always opposed shortening their terms in office.[47]

As the first Black Georgia state senator since 1870 and the first Black representative in the statehouse since 1907, Johnson's election gave him a larger profile, but it also gave him a sense of responsibility. He responded by opening a law practice and then going on a national lecture tour. He regularly spoke across the country, like his counterpart, Ali, earning high speaking fees averaging roughly a thousand dollars per speech and making his name. The Georgia Association of Citizens Democratic Clubs, a statewide Black political federation, appointed him vice president, and he would become president of the group in 1966. In 1963 he won the NAACP's Freedom Award; he was also named Scottish Rite Mason of the Year and one of the Atlanta Chamber of Commerce's outstanding young men. He and Walden were both appointed to the Democratic Party's State Executive Committee. He visited Lyndon Johnson in the White House several times; he even traveled to Zanzibar as a special ambassador, sent by the president, to the country's independence ceremony. "There's something special about being the first of anything," he told Lesher. "Everybody wanted to see and hear this black fella who got himself elected to the Georgia General Assembly. But I knew I wouldn't be the last." And he wanted to ensure it. Lerone Bennett told a story of Johnson taking a group of young boys into the senate chamber, sitting them in his chair, and telling them to be regular visitors to the capitol, to plan to sit there one day after school. He saw his election as giving "Negro boys and girls something tangible in terms of what they can accomplish. When I was a boy I never dreamed of being a senator from Georgia," he said. "Now, a Negro boy or girl can aspire to be not only a senator but a governor of this state."[48]

Johnson "wasn't a civil rights guy; he wasn't a Julian Bond or Marion Barry," remembered local Black attorney Stan Sanders. "He was a wheeler-dealer. He was slick. He could talk to the black guys as well as to the white guys."[49] But he was, in his way, a civil rights guy. When he took office at the state capitol and was refused service in the building's cafeteria, he stayed and ate nonetheless, desegregating the cafeteria as one of his first acts in the legislature.[50] In the second half of the 1960s Johnson worked with the Southern Regional Council's Voter Education Project, led by Vernon Jordan. The group registered voters, provided training to Black political leadership, including newly elected officials, and funded hundreds of grassroots enfranchisement projects. Johnson's work with the VEP demonstrated that while he believed in a political pragmatism that sacrificed doctrinal purity for a more results-based horse trading model of success, he was still willing to do that horse trading in aid of Black equality and political power.[51]

Among the new Black leaders he mentored was Julian Bond. Bond had attended Morehouse as the sit-in movement began in 1960, helping to coordinate the protests in Atlanta. He would become one of the founding members of the Student Nonviolent Coordinating Committee. Over the next several years, he expanded his activism to include both Southern civil rights and vigorous opposition to the Vietnam War. In 1965 he won a seat in the Georgia House of Representatives, but white legislators used that opposition as a pretense to refuse to seat him. So his district elected him again—and again, repeating their electoral decision to make their choice of representative clear. Still he was denied, so Bond turned to Johnson. "You'd be surprised at the people who were known as being much more militant than Leroy who urged me to really Tom—to get up and apologize for what I said. But not Leroy." Over in the state senate, Johnson denounced the actions of his colleagues on the other side of the capitol. Johnson hosted strategy sessions at his house involving Bond, James Forman, Donald Hollowell, and others to plot the best way to respond to the controversy. By 1966 there were more Black legislators than just Johnson. Black representatives J. C. Daugherty, William H. Alexander, and Benjamin Brown, and Black senators Johnson and Horace Ward all spoke at a special committee hearing on Bond's place in the legislature. At the end of that year, in December 1966, the Supreme Court finally ruled the actions of the Georgia House unconstitutional. Bond was finally sworn in as a member of the legislature in January 1967, and he was in a stronger position for not having sold out his ideals.[52]

In that election cycle Lester Maddox's gubernatorial campaign actually received fewer votes than Howard "Bo" Callaway, a Republican who also had a history of racism. Calloway, however, did not get 50 percent of the votes because of a write-in campaign for former governor Ellis Arnall, which meant that the election fell to the general assembly. Arnall was a Democrat in the Franklin Roosevelt style who had previously served as governor in the 1940s. He had been among Maddox's principal rivals in the Democratic primary and had taken Maddox to a primary runoff. While the majority of Atlanta bemoaned a Maddox candidacy as an embarrassment, a racist throwback to what they hoped was an earlier era, much of the state's rural white population gravitated to a traditional racist Southern Democrat whose politics looked far more like those of Herman Talmadge than Franklin Roosevelt.[53]

Johnson knew that the predominantly Democratic body would choose Maddox, but he didn't want to vote for either of the racist candidates. The body's parliamentarian told him that he was unable to abstain from the vote, so he rose in the chamber, declared that "conscience must prevail over party expediency." He told his colleagues, "I cannot today in good conscience vote for Lester Maddox nor for Howard Callaway." When asked by the clerk how he voted, Johnson smiled and voted "present." It was Johnson's pragmatism at work. He was able to preserve his integrity while not putting himself in conflict with Maddox, to whom the Democratic majority gave the governorship despite his having fewer votes than his Republican opponent. It was a controversial decision that ultimately ended in the Supreme Court, where a split court ruled five to four that the state assembly did have the authority to decide the outcome of the race, even if it chose the candidate who received fewer votes. The Maddox election in 1966 was interpreted as a white conservative backlash against the increasing pace of desegregation efforts, and it caused controversy among more liberal Democrats. Still, less than a year later,

Johnson managed to pass his first bill, providing aid to families forcibly evicted by landlords, and Maddox signed the bill into law, despite the fact that his more moderate predecessor, Carl Sanders, had previously vetoed a similar Johnson effort.[54]

Maddox came to be seen as something of an enigma in the governor's mansion. For more than a decade his Pickrick restaurant had run advertisements combining promotions for fried chicken with denunciations of liberal politicians, civil rights workers, and the push for Black rights more broadly. After the Civil Rights Act of 1964 Maddox had chased Black customers away at gunpoint. His well-publicized intransigence made him a pariah among the city's Black population and among advocates of civil rights more broadly, but it made him a celebrity to many white Georgians who saw him as manning the barricades of both white supremacy and free enterprise. When a federal court enjoined him from refusing service to Black customers—at the same time it enjoined the Heart of Atlanta Motel from doing the same thing—Maddox attempted an appeal to the Supreme Court. When that failed, he closed his restaurant rather than operate an integrated establishment. The lasting image of his fight against potential Black patrons was a red pickax handle that he used to chase away activists, and in the weeks after the restaurant shuttered its doors, Maddox sold souvenirs in front of the building that included bumper stickers, political pamphlets, and red pickax handles with "Pickrick drumsticks" emblazoned on them.[55]

When running for governor he made a typical litany of campaign promises, but after his victory, controversial as it may have been, he did not reject federal money for public schools. He did not get into a high-profile showdown with the Johnson administration. He appointed more Black government administrators than any previous administration. He appointed the first Black Georgia State Patrol officer, created food assistance and expanded Medicaid programs, and integrated the Governor's Summer Intern Program. He appointed more than forty Black officials to county draft boards across the state, providing many draftees a fairness that would not be evident in Kentucky when Muhammad Ali first appeared before a similar body. He raised teacher pay, began an early release program for state prisoners, and attacked chain gangs and county prison camps as ineffective. In his inaugural address he discussed equal justice for everyone in Georgia. Just ten days into his term he met with a delegation of Black leaders, including Leroy Johnson and Martin Luther King, Sr. He told them he wanted to be "the best governor this state has ever had and I can't possibly do that by working against any group of citizens or creating any special conditions for any group." He told Johnson, King, and others, "I'll do more for you than my predecessor did."[56]

But he was still Lester Maddox. He had, as Norman Mailer described him, "the face of a three-month-old infant who is mean and bald and wears eyeglasses." Maddox had always hated Martin Luther King, Jr., and after the rights leader's April 1968 assassination, he showed no grief at the loss. Maddox railed against the state flag flying at half-staff in response to King's death. On the day of the Atlanta funeral the governor refused to close the Capitol and filled it with armed officers, directing them to shoot any mourner if they came onto the grounds.[57]

In 1968 Leroy Johnson was one of seven Black members of Georgia's delegation, appointed by Lester Maddox, to the Democratic National Convention. Bond, meanwhile, led an all-Black challenge group to Maddox's delegation and attempted to recruit Johnson. But the political pragmatist had not seen any value in the challenge. Johnson had served as a delegate in 1964, when he had been the only Black delegate. Now there were eight. In this case his willingness to compromise with white authority failed him.[58] After contentious hearings at the Democratic National Convention, the party's Credentials Committee decided to split Georgia's votes between the two slates of delegates, with each getting twenty-one representatives. Maddox was incensed, comparing the compromise proposal to the Soviet invasion of Czechoslovakia. William P. Trotter, a white member of the Maddox delegation, described the decision as creating "the 51st state of our union" and claimed that the move would lead to a "mass exodus of Georgians to the Republican party."[59]

Bond's delegation was celebrated at the convention, but its counterpart group from Georgia was less enthusiastic. Many of the Maddox delegates left the convention, refusing to be seated next to a group of civil rights leaders and antiwar activists. Johnson, of course, wasn't among those who walked out. He was no friend of Maddox and had a good relationship with Bond. All seven of the original Black delegates stayed to be part of the newly constituted Georgia delegation. But even though he remained in Chicago, being part of the Maddox faction was not a good look. It was clear that political pragmatism had its uses, but it was a millstone around the neck of the pragmatist in public ideological fights. When an opposition plank on Vietnam was called to a floor vote at the convention, one that called for immediate American withdrawal from Vietnam, Johnson the pragmatist voted with his fellow Maddox delegates against it, while almost all of the Bond delegates voted in favor. The referendum was like a glowing sign standing between Johnson and the civil rights activists with whom he now caucused: We are similar, but we are not the same.[60]

But while Johnson lay low, Julian Bond's profile was raised significantly for his efforts. Charles Negaro, a Connecticut lawyer in the camp of candidate Eugene McCarthy, marveled that Bond was able to "capture the hearts of America. Bond was Fannie Lou Hamer! A much different type, but Bond was the Fannie Lou Hamer of 1968! He became a television idol overnight." One Wisconsin delegate even nominated the twenty-eight-year-old Bond for vice president. It was symbolic, as Bond's age disqualified him, but the roar of the crowd demonstrated that Bond was a star. Even when the vote to seat all of the challenge delegates failed on the floor of the convention, chants of "We want Bond, we want Bond!" echoed through the chamber.[61]

"Imagine how Leroy could have looked if *he* had been the one to be nominated," said Lonnie King, president of Atlanta's chapter of the NAACP. Johnson would have been seen as the leader of the challenge group, had he joined, and thus surely would have been the one nominated. Instead he appeared to be allied with Maddox against Black protesters. But "he was too myopic to see it," King said. "His pragmatism clouds his national vision." But Johnson met with Bond after the protest delegation was seated and reminded him that he had done several favors for Bond over the years. By the time Bond announced victory for the delegation on the floor of the convention, "Who was standing there holding the microphone for him?" asked King. "Nobody but Leroy Johnson. And I said to myself, 'Man, he's good. He's *really* good.'"[62]

And he stayed good by facilitating deals whenever he could. As Jack Walker explained in 1964, "In order to build a majority, a Negro politician in Atlanta must develop a political style which combines enough of the themes of protest to capture the loyalty of the Negro voters with enough of the themes of accommodation and 'responsibility' to win the confidence and acceptance of the more liberal whites."[63] No one mastered that Black Atlanta political style better than Johnson. "Johnson's influence—and his willingness to use it for friends," Lesher explained, "has kept his enemies, if not at a minimum, at least at a safe distance."[64]

But there were further problems with that 1968 election cycle, problems that laid bare the divide between the Black middle- and upper-class decisionmakers and the mass of Atlanta's Black citizenry. Among those running for the state legislature was Louise Watley, a public housing advocate who herself lived in Atlanta public housing. She received less than two hundred votes. *The Great Speckled Bird*'s Eliza Paschall speculated that perhaps her lack of support stemmed from her advocacy against the city's slums. Or perhaps it was because she was a woman. "Where were the black Atlanta office holders who go around the U.S. discussing the need for whites as well as blacks to vote for blacks?" she asked. Was the reason for their silence that Watley "does not come from the Negro elite background?" Or that "she 'makes trouble' for the Housing Authority?" Could it have been that "if you have people who actually live in public housing who are that articulate, pretty soon there'll be no need for the 'professional?'" Johnson, Ward, Bond, and others were all, she assumed, "so busy making speeches to middle class audiences about the importance of more black officials" that "they didn't have time to help."[65] Watley's campaign was, from the beginning, a decided long shot, but Paschall's screed highlighted a disconnect between Black leaders and the bulk of Black Atlanta citizens that was not only real; it was really frustrating to many among the working poor trying to create a path for representation for those who lived as they did.

It was a frustration made all the more intense by the reality that it took place behind a curtain of a public-facing progressivism that Atlanta showed to the nation, one that provided supposed benefits like professional sports. Allen and civic leaders in the city constructed a new stadium and courted the Milwaukee Braves to come to Atlanta to play in it.[66] Then came the NFL's Falcons, then the North American Soccer League's Chiefs.[67] Mayor Ivan Allen once bragged that the city built Atlanta Stadium "on ground we didn't own with money we didn't have for clubs we had not yet signed."[68] It was a demonstration of the business imperative of the city, of Atlanta's sense of self and possibility.

Neither the Braves nor the Falcons played well or drew well in their new home, but that did not stop city leaders from coveting more professional sports to bolster its major-league image. Building a basketball arena downtown, for example, offered the possibility of an NBA franchise and another round of slum clearance. Downtown gentrification would price out poor Black residents from the construction area while keeping suburban white Atlantans engaged with the city center, keeping those white economies tied to downtown and perpetuating the pleasing myth of racial accord. Postwar stadium construction erased much of the urban diversity of downtown neighborhoods, as Benjamin Lisle explains. Working-class Black residents, then, suffered further as Black athletes began to arrive. And arrive they did, Atlanta bringing in the NBA's St. Louis Hawks in 1968.[69]

Sports were important for gilding the veneer of racial moderation the city had cultivated for itself, but they were not a racial cure-all. In June 1967, the year after the debut seasons of the Braves and Falcons, an uprising began in the west Atlanta neighborhood of Dixie Hills. Two weeks earlier the Ku Klux Klan had marched through Dixie Hills with a police escort. On June 17 a Black youth quarreled with a security guard at the Flamingo Grill after trying to enter the restaurant with a can of beer. His sister and another teenager arrived and accosted the security guard, leading to the arrest of all three. The following evening a group of residents held a meeting at the shopping center where the restaurant was located. They were frustrated with the Klan and the Flamingo, but also with inadequate sanitation and a lack of local playgrounds. Then on Monday, June 19, police shot a Black youth as he disabled a burglar alarm. The boy wasn't killed, but the incident was the principal subject of a protest meeting at Saint Joseph Baptist Church. Leroy Johnson and alderman Q. V. Williamson spoke at the meeting, encouraging the crowd to draft a petition enumerating the problems that faced them. "Some of us may differ about procedure, but all of us are serious about obtaining first class citizens rights for Negroes in Atlanta," Johnson told the crowd. "If we have to march, then march we must, but within the confines of the law." But his effort was shouted down by Stokely Carmichael and other younger members of SNCC, who saw the strategies of the older generation as inadequate to the task of creating viable change. The group cheered for Carmichael. One member told Johnson he was "wearing a white man's shirt." Carmichael encouraged those at the meeting to march in the streets, to "force the police department to work until they fall in their tracks." They did, ultimately throwing bottles and rocks as police officers fired warning shots into the air. Law enforcement restored order, but several police cars were damaged and ten protesters were arrested, including Carmichael. It was a demonstration of the growing influence of a younger, more radical strategy and the growing disapproval of working-class Black citizens for the more pragmatic governmental approach embodied by politicians like Johnson.[70]

The city responded by building new neighborhood playgrounds, on one hand, and by expanding the police presence in Dixie Hills, on the other. Ivan Allen announced the creation of the Negro Youth Patrol, a group of Black men in their early twenties who would serve as volunteer monitors of behavior in the neighborhood to ensure everyone's safety. Johnson introduced the volunteers at a Dixie Hills meeting, but SNCC interrupted with criticism of Johnson, the patrol, and similar "Uncle Tom groups."[71]

The rejection by young radicals of the efforts of leaders like Johnson ensured that protests would continue. In one demonstration fewer than two hundred protesters attempted to confront more than three hundred police officers arrayed against them. The officers responded violently, killing one man sitting on his porch nearby and wounding a nine-year-old child. Ultimately, the overwhelming police presence limited further large-scale demonstrations, but it only exacerbated neighborhood discontent. Johnson and other Black moderate leaders drafted a petition and gathered more than a thousand signatures to demand that Stokely Carmichael and other SNCC organizers leave Atlanta.[72]

The signatures demonstrated that frustration with more radical groups was growing in impoverished neighborhoods, residents alienated by the retributive police violence brought to their doorsteps for protests rooted in rhetoric rather than pragmatic solutions, something that Johnson, in however imperfect a fashion, was better able to provide. Still, the city had responded with playgrounds, which was more than political leaders had managed previously. The Atlanta Committee for Cooperative Action met following the Dixie Hills violence at Leroy Johnson's house, attempting to figure out the best ways for moderation to be coupled with tangible results. If Black power brokers couldn't actually make the lives of working-class Black residents in Atlanta better, they reasoned, the influence of more radical groups would always remain a threat. "We must have some victories," Johnson said at the meeting. "Then we'll have the ammunition to fight the forces which come and tear up our communities." It was clear that the system of biracial agreements, so celebrated among white business and civic leaders, wasn't working for the majority of Black residents, who understood all too clearly that, in the words of Matthew Lassiter, "the dialectic of white moderation and black pragmatism produced a politics of civility that permitted modest reforms but reinforced systemic inequality." SNCC's Atlanta office, for example, published its "We Want Black Power" tract soon after the Dixie Hills protests. Its argument stressed that "the man in the ghetto" had to lead the movement. Trusting traditional Black power brokers was tantamount to trusting white people to lead civil rights efforts.[73]

More than half of the city's Black workers were unskilled labor. The average Black family earned less than half of what the average white family earned. Average white workers were high-school graduates, while the average Black Atlantan had less than an eighth-grade education. Pushed by overcrowded and deteriorating housing and real economic disparities, family life for many was markedly unstable. In roughly 40 percent of Black Atlanta homes, a single mother was the head of household, a number that rose to more than 60 percent in public housing. The uprisings in the city were not simply the result of individual incidents. They were part of a protest against a systematic bigotry that was eroding Black lives, economies, and families.[74]

By 1968 Atlanta's population was 45 percent Black, and by 1973 it would be 54 percent Black. Roughly three-quarters of that population was squarely in the working class. In 1969 the city had ninety-three thousand registered Black voters, up from forty-one thousand in 1961. And much of that new population was northern born, as many students coming to Atlanta for collegiate education stayed in the city and contributed to a reverse migration. So too did industrial expansion in the city that created jobs for those both with and without college degrees. That demographic shift over the course of the decade forced white politicians to respond to Black concerns and campaign for the Black vote.[75]

Table 1. African Americans as Percentage of Atlanta's Population[1]

Date	Total Population	African-American Population	Percentage
1940	302, 288	104, 533	34.6
1950	331,314	121,416	36.6
1960	487,455	186, 820	38.3
1970	496,973	255,051	51.3

1. Brown-Nagin, "Class Actions," 55.

The shift to a Black majority in Atlanta, with white residents responding to increasing African American population growth and civil rights activism by moving to the suburbs, "created new needs and new roles for the local government."[76] While white leaders were reluctant to take those roles, politicians like Johnson stepped into the resulting breach to create pragmatic solutions to difficult problems. It was, in many ways, a thankless job, earning him the begrudging respect of fellow Black leaders, the begrudging toleration of white politicians, and the overt skepticism of many in the working-class population who wondered whose interests he really had at heart. But whatever the slings and arrows he may have accrued in relation to his power, it was clear that he had accrued power, as well. And when opportunities arose he would be ready to use it.

2. BLACK POWER, BLACK SPORT, AND THE FALL OF MUHAMMAD ALI

1942–1968

Cassius Marcellus Clay, Jr., was born in Louisville on January 17, 1942, the first son of a sign painter and a domestic worker. Clay, Sr., had dreamed of being an artist and entertainer before settling into his commercial craft. That sense of ambition, of dreaming beyond the bounds of cloistered expectations, was as much an inheritance for his son as the name itself. The elder Clay remembered looking at his son as a baby and thinking, "That's gonna be nothing but another Joe Louis." The name, both the father's and the son's, came from a nineteenth-century Kentucky plantation owner, a distant relative of Henry Clay who freed his slaves and became an abolitionist. That legacy, along with the name, was itself part of the inheritance.[1]

A young Clay had first been moved to racial consciousness after learning of the murder of Emmett Till in 1955. "I stood on the corner with a gang of boys, looking at pictures of him in the black newspapers and magazines," he remembered. Ali felt "a deep kinship to him." The murder was a glaring demonstration of white hatred, of the inability of dominant white systems to defend Black lives.[2]

Clay began boxing in the basement of the Grace Community Center, which doubled as the gym of trainer Fred Stoner, but he was kicked out, ostensibly for doing things his own way, displaying an individualism anathema to Stoner. After Clay's bicycle was stolen in October 1954, less than a year before Till's murder, Clay began taking boxing lessons at the local Columbia Gym from Louisville policeman Joe Martin. His first knockout came the following year, when he beat up a classmate at

DuValle Junior High who had threatened him. Clay's early trainer didn't see much special in the twelve-year-old, but "he was a kid willing to make the sacrifices necessary to achieve something worthwhile in sports." Those sacrifices made him one of the best amateurs in the country. He won 100 of his 108 amateur fights and six Kentucky Golden Gloves championships. Then he won the national Golden Gloves. He won the National AAU championship in 1959 and 1960, then won the Olympic gold medal in Rome in the light heavyweight division at only eighteen years old.[3]

After his Olympic triumph Clay turned professional, managed by a syndicate of businessmen based in Louisville who gave him light heavyweight champion Archie Moore as a trainer. The two did not get along, and Clay soon moved to Angelo Dundee, with whom he would stay through the 1970s. The Louisville Sporting Group, however, would remain as his financial backer until the Nation of Islam eventually took over. Many believed that Clay was fortunate to have rich white businessmen as backers, rather than members of organized crime, who often dominated the finances of boxing. But as Robert Lipsyte notes, "In many ways they looked at him and treated him as if he was a prize racehorse," controlling his movement and keeping him within a boundary of their own making by using their investment as a sword of Damocles over his head.[4]

Clay had actually met Dundee in 1957 while the trainer was in Louisville. The young fighter went to Dundee's hotel, asked to see him, then spent three hours asking questions of both the trainer and the boxer he was accompanying, Willie Pastrano. Dundee "had worked with six world champions," notes Dave Kindred, "and he had never had that animated a conversation about the craft with any of them." The two would not join forces for several years, but that meeting would lay the groundwork for their later relationship.[5] Dundee came into the business following his brother, Chris. Their family name was Mirena, but after Chris changed his to Dundee, younger Angelo did the same, apprenticing as a boxing trainer after World War II while Chris promoted fights in New York. The brothers moved to Miami in 1951, where the younger Dundee slowly earned a reputation as a leading trainer in the business. "I remember that he always wanted to work," said Dundee of a young Clay. "Even then you could tell that he had exceptional ability."[6]

Clay began his professional career in October 1960 with a six-round decision victory against Tunney Hunsaker. After that, however, he began to knock out his opponents. After five professional fights, he started to get noticed. Dick Schaap profiled him in the *Saturday Evening Post*. "I'm better than Floyd Patterson was at the same age," he told the journalist. "I bet Sugar Ray Robinson wasn't as good as me when he was eighteen." At the same time Clay admitted to revering Robinson, both for his boxing skill and for his money and style. Schaap interpreted Clay as "a warm, natural young man, totally lacking in sophistication, whose personality could be a refreshing breeze in a becalmed sport." The experts he consulted described the fighter's amazingly fast hands and quick feet. "How good a pro prospect is Cassius Clay?" Schaap asked. "He is almost as good as he says he is."[7] And even though the boxer would later renounce his birth name after his Muslim conversion, that birth name was an integral part of his early identity. "Don't you think it's a beautiful name?" he asked the *New York Times Magazine*'s Howard Tuckner. "Cassius Marcellus Clay. Say it to yourself. Cassius Marcellus Clay. Feel the way it rolls out of your mouth. Say it loud. Cassius Marcellus Clay. It's beautiful. It's a beautiful name."[8]

Clay had first come into contact with the Nation of Islam in Atlanta on a trip with his brother Rudy in 1958. The sixteen-year-old spoke with representatives of the faith outside the group's mosque on Piedmont Avenue. The following year he again met with members of the NOI while at the Golden Gloves in Chicago, where they gave him a record of "A White Man's Heaven Is a Black Man's Hell," performed by the man who would later become Louis Farrakhan. It was a record that he played constantly when back in Louisville. He wrote a paper on the group in his senior year high-school English class. He and his brother regularly listened to Elijah Muhammad's national radio addresses.[9]

After the newly professional Clay moved to Miami to train with Dundee, he met Sam Saxon while the minister was selling copies of *Muhammad Speaks* in front of the NOI mosque in the city. The two became fast friends, bonded by Saxon's interest in boxing and Clay's interest in the Nation. Clay began attending Muslim meetings with relative regularity, but in June 1962 Saxon invited him to a rally in Detroit to hear Elijah Muhammad speak in person. Before the rally Saxon took Clay and his brother to a diner, where he introduced them to Malcolm X. Malcolm's work, beginning in 1952, had grown the number of NOI mosques from ten to thirty by 1959, including the one on Atlanta's

Piedmont Avenue, but Malcolm had not followed boxing and didn't know who Clay was. Still, the two clearly had a connection from the beginning.[10]

That month a plane that had flown from Atlanta crashed in Paris, killing more than a hundred passengers. Malcolm publicly described the crash as "a very beautiful thing." Allah had "dropped an airplane out of the sky with over a hundred and twenty white people on it," and he hoped "that every day another plane falls out of the sky." It was a statement that shocked the nation, but shocked in particular those in Atlanta. Martin Luther King, Jr., had canceled segregation protests in the city in deference to the mourning taking place. "That's my hometown," he said. "I knew many of the people who were killed. Many of them believed in progress."[11]

Clay, not yet publicly associated with the faith that would so enrage Atlanta, continued boxing. And he continued winning. He would finally get his shot at the heavyweight championship in early 1964, against Sonny Liston, but even before the fight rumors circulated that the challenger had joined Elijah Muhammad's group. Muhammad was born Elijah Robert Poole in Sandersville, Georgia, roughly 120 miles outside of Atlanta, in 1897. The son of a sharecropper, Poole left school after fourth grade to help support his family. It was a hardscrabble life of poverty, compounded by experiencing the racism of rural Georgia in the early Jim Crow period. Muhammad claimed to have witnessed three lynchings in his early life; whether or not that was true, his was a life in Georgia defined by race and desperation. And it was ultimately untenable. In 1923 he and his family left, part of the first major wave of the Great Migration, and settled in Hamtramck, Michigan. Eight years later, in August 1931, he attended a meeting led by Wallace Fard Muhammad. After joining the leader's movement he went to work for the organization, moving to Chicago to take over the group's Mosque Number 2 and ultimately changing his name to Elijah Muhammad. When Fard Muhammad disappeared in 1934 there was a fight for power among several different contenders, but Elijah Muhammad eventually won it, taking over the faith and growing it in the years to come by positing that Fard Muhammad had been a savior figure: Allah come to earth. The faith declined in the early 1940s as Elijah Muhammad went to prison for four years after refusing to register for the military draft and absconding to Washington to avoid prosecution. He was indicted both for draft evasion and for sedition, a charge resulting from his instruction to followers not to fight in the war. He was acquitted of sedition but jailed on the draft evasion charge from 1942 to 1946.[12]

After his release the faith began to grow more readily, including the prison conversion of Malcolm Little, who upon his own release from incarceration in 1952 would go to work for the Nation of Islam as Malcolm X. The first reports that Clay had been seen at a Nation of Islam meeting appeared in September 1963. The rumors became even more pronounced when Malcolm X began appearing regularly in Clay's training camp. Malcolm was both a mentor and genuine friend of the boxer. "Not many people know the quality of the mind he's got in there. He fools them," Malcolm told George Plimpton. "One forgets that though a clown never imitates a wise man, the wise man can imitate the clown."[13]

But Malcolm, by that time, had run afoul of Elijah Muhammad and was suspended from the Nation. Malcolm's proximity to Clay prior to his title fight with Liston was largely in aid of attempting to woo the fighter away from Muhammad and the NOI and to use him as a kind of protection against any potential retaliatory violence by the sect. The Nation's leader, frustrated by Malcolm's presence around Clay, called the fighter and explained that "all good Muslims should stay away from Malcolm" while he was suspended from the faith. Clay had already converted and believed wholeheartedly in the word of Muhammad, but that was one instruction he chose not to take.[14]

Eventually the fight took place. Clay won the heavyweight championship in Miami on February 25, 1964, against Sonny Liston, a rural Arkansas native, one of twenty-four siblings, who had previously served time for armed robbery. Liston was a seven-to-one favorite, considered at the time the most intimidating boxer in the game. But Clay took the offensive in the runup to the bout, calling Liston a "big, ugly bear," harassing and baiting the champion and promising that he would win in eight rounds. He caused a near-riotous scene at the weigh-in on the morning of the fight. All of that rhetoric was designed to alter Liston's focus, and it worked. Liston lunged at Clay uncontrollably, while Clay fought a more scientific fight. The damage he was able to inflict over seven rounds left Liston unable to answer the bell prior to the eighth. Clay was the new heavyweight champion.[15]

The victory catapulted him to global celebrity. "Europeans may never have heard of America's Koufax," wrote Jack Olsen, "and North Americans may know little about Brazil's Pelè, and neither Americans nor Europeans know about Red China's Chuang Tse-tung, but who doesn't know who the heavyweight champion is?"[16]

Clay was a phenomenon. "He invented himself out of the cultural and political currents of the early 1960s—black pride, rock and roll, popular entertainment, anti-authority rebellion, generational self-expression and wrestling," Jack Newfield explained. Clay hadn't announced his affiliation with the NOI until after his championship win. He was worried that Florida officials might try to cancel the fight if they knew of his conversion, and the promoter, William B. McDonald, actually threatened to cancel it unless Clay denounced the organization. That was a bridge too far for the fighter, but McDonald acquiesced on the condition that Malcolm stayed away until the fight. Meanwhile, NOI leadership was reticent about an announcement lest Clay lose to Liston and embarrass the organization. Elijah Muhammad was no fan of boxing, but he supported the group's new member because of his fame and his relationship with Malcolm—and the money. Muhammad's son Herbert, owner of a small photography studio and the editor of *Muhammad Speaks*, served as Ali's manager, taking a third of all his earnings. Accounts have portrayed Muhammad as having little interest in Clay prior to the Liston fight, but Randy Roberts and Johnny Smith have argued that Muhammad was actually very interested in the boxer well before his attempt at the heavyweight title. Clay, meanwhile, was seemingly devoted to the faith, at least verbally, but never obeyed its strictures. Though Clay denied being a member of the NOI in the weeks prior to the Liston fight, he had not only become part of the group but had taken the name Cassius X.[17]

The Liston-Clay championship bout took place at the Miami Beach Convention Hall. Its promoter, MacDonald, was enamored of the Cold War possibilities that could come from showing "the world that two colored boys like Liston and Clay could fight in a Southern city and be treated like kings." Ali's brother had made his professional debut on the undercard. In between Rudy's victory and the championship bout against Liston, Malcolm came into Ali's dressing room and gave him a pep talk. "The fight is the truth. It's the Cross and the Crescent fighting in the prize ring—for the first time. It's a modern Crusades—a Christian and a Muslim facing each other with television to beam it off Telstar for the whole world to see what happens!" Allah, Malcolm assured his friend, would not allow him to lose.[18] It was, to be sure, a decidedly different pep talk than Ali would receive from protestant minister Jesse Jackson six years later in his return fight in Atlanta, but it was precisely what the nascent Black Muslim needed in the biggest moment of his professional life to date.

After the fight, and after Clay's famous post-fight interview claiming that he was "the greatest," he returned to Miami's Hampton House Hotel, where he, Malcolm, and running back Jim Brown plotted strategy until four in the morning. The championship was an opportunity to use his new prominence to support racial causes that needed the megaphone of the heavyweight title. At the press conference the next morning, Clay spoke in a subdued tone far different from his rhetoric the night before. He was inevitably asked about the Black Muslims, a reporter asking Clay if he was a "card-carrying" member of the NOI. "I believe in Allah and in peace," he said. "I go to a Black Muslim meeting and what do I see? I see that there's no smoking and no drinking and their women wear dresses down to the floor. And then I come out on the street and you tell me I shouldn't go there. Well, there must be something in there if you don't want me to go there."[19]

The something in there had become a vital part of Clay's identity, and the new champion would defend his new faith. "You call it Black Muslim, I don't. The real name is Islam," he said. "That means peace. Yet people brand us a hate group. They say we want to take over the country. They say we're Communists. That is not true. Followers of Allah are the sweetest people in the world." He was now part of the group, and he gave intelligent descriptions of the faith and of Black separatism. "I don't impose myself on people who don't want me. If I go in somebody's house where I'm not welcome, I am uncomfortable. So I stay away. I like white people. I like my own people. They can live together without infringing on each other. You can't condemn a man for wanting peace."[20]

In the wake of the news of Clay's relationship with the NOI, Marion Jackson, sports editor of the *Atlanta Daily World*, the city's oldest surviving Black newspaper, took a hard line. "Clay, through his association with Malcolm X, Muhammad, and other Black Muslims, has revealed himself as a white-hating racist at the time when intergroup progress is being made throughout the South."[21] But the fighter wasn't in the South, and showed no concern over such criticism. Days after his championship victory, Clay traveled to New York, where on March 2 he visited the offices of the *New York Amsterdam News*. He denied knowing about any rift between Malcolm and Muhammad, but did announce that he had renounced the name of "a Kentucky slave master" in favor of being called Cassius X.[22] Two weeks later Elijah Muhammad proclaimed that Cassius Clay was a name without "divine meaning." The boxer's name from that point forward would be Muhammad Ali, "as long as he believes in Allah and follows me." The typical convert to the Nation of Islam had to wait several years before receiving an Arabic name, but Ali's swift name change was, in Malcolm's interpretation, a strategy for ensuring the fighter would stay loyal to the group.[23]

Clay had originally failed an intelligence test and was disqualified from military service in Vietnam, but three days after his trip to the *Amsterdam News*, Cassius was asked a question about a government announcement that the fighter's intelligence test would be readministered. Would he ever consider conscientious objector status? "I don't like that name," he told the reporter. "It sounds ugly." He said that he would need several hours to explain his position on the war and military service; it couldn't be explained away with a simplistic label.[24]

He then took a month-long trip to Africa, touring Ghana, Nigeria, and Egypt. In every place he visited, he was celebrated as a hero. Ali's trip to Africa would broaden his profile throughout the world, tying him to decolonization efforts on the continent and making him an avatar of liberation and democracy for so many in the Global South.[25] But he was not so celebrated back home. Ali's announcement prompted concern from the federal government, J. Edgar Hoover inquiring at his FBI about Ali's draft status in response.[26] Before Ali's Africa trip, many speculated that the government might attempt to withhold his visa due to a military status that was uncertain after taking that second military intelligence test. Reporters questioned him about the possibility of passing the test and being drafted. The champion was reluctant to make any definitive statements. He didn't want to go to jail or get into trouble. "I just want to do what's right," he told them.[27] It was ultimately reported that he failed the second test attempt in March 1964, an embarrassing outcome for Ali, but one that kept him from any showdown over a potential draft notice.[28]

Ali's rematch with Liston was originally scheduled for November 1964, but an Ali hernia postponed the bout until May 1965 in Boston. In the interregnum Malcolm X was assassinated at Harlem's Audubon Ballroom. By that point Ali and Malcolm were no longer close, Malcolm having left the Nation of Islam the previous year and Ali choosing to stay. But as the three accused assassins were shown to be affiliated with the Nation, promoters began to claim that rumors and even threats of violence had begun to surface surrounding the Liston rematch. They decided to move the fight from Boston to a more remote venue in Lewiston, Maine.[29] Meanwhile, through 1965, Ali became more devout and more public about his devotion.[30] It was almost as if his dedication to his faith increased in direct proportion to the public hostility it engendered.

As a Black man from the South, however, Ali understood that hostility in Boston was decidedly different than hostility in places like Georgia. In April he rode from his base in Miami to Chicopee Falls, Massachusetts, to train for the Liston rematch. Ali had purchased a bus, known colloquially as Big Red, that took him and his team north because of his fear of flying. Before the trip he warned everyone to make sure they were full and satisfied, "cause we ain't stoppin' in Georgia. We flyin' over Georgia." When the bus moved north from Florida, he turned to Edwin Pope, a sportswriter from Georgia who was riding with the team. "I ain't letting you Georgia Baptists get me," Ali told Pope, who denied that he was a Baptist. "Sure you're Baptist," said Ali. "Everybody from Georgia is a Baptist."[31]

The Georgia Baptists, it turned out, didn't get Ali. The group had experienced trouble in Yulee, Florida, when they tried to eat in a restaurant that was still segregated a year after the Civil Rights Act had become law, but when the bus stopped in Brunswick, Georgia, they entered a roadside restaurant where they received some menacing looks but all had a chance to eat.[32]

In his second fight with Liston, Ali won in a controversial first-round knockout with what he described as a "snap punch," which he claimed to have learned from his friend Stepin Fetchit. "You can't see it, but if you hit by it, you all be knocked out." Others were sure it was a phantom punch, their suspicions aided by Liston's known relationship with organized crime. For those who defended the legitimacy of the champion's victory, they suggested that conspiracy theories about the knockout were largely the result of built-in hostility to Ali himself and the faith he espoused.[33]

Ali collected no new supporters later that year when he fought former champion Floyd Patterson, creating a rhetorical battle between a former Black champion that represented an integrationist position and a current champion that advocated for separatist nationalism. As Grant Farred has explained, "Patterson's idea of radical opposition was to drink at a whites-only water fountain in the South and to pronounce the water egalitarian." Ali's defeat of Patterson was, for Farred, a symbolic changing of the guard that mirrored the movement from classical civil rights strategies to those of the Black Power movement.[34]

The rhetoric of Ali and Patterson in the lead-up to the fight really centered on a contest about what it meant to be Black in America. "The Black Muslim influence must be removed from boxing," said Patterson. "Cassius Clay is disgracing himself and the Negro race. No decent person can look up to a champion whose credo is 'hate whites.' I have nothing but contempt for the Black Muslims and that for which they stand. The image of a Black Muslim as the world heavyweight champion disgraces the sport and the nation."[35]

In reality, of course, Ali's image did neither of those things. His presence created a new interest in boxing that raised the profile of an often maligned sport and, in the process, fattened the purses of all the fighters on his cards, including that of Patterson. The following year, in January 1966, Ali formed Main Bout, Inc., a new promotional company that would allow him and the NOI to upend the predominantly white boxing establishment. He wanted his new endeavor to "be one in which Negroes are not used as fronts, but as stockholders, officers, and production and promotion agents," he said when announcing the venture. The company was heavily influenced by Nation of Islam leadership, and it would regulate Ali's public appearances on television and radio, but it was also a legitimate effort to give Black fighters power outside of the ring. Both of those facts kept many in the United States from wanting to work with Main Bout, so the company turned to fights in Canada and Europe. Herbert Muhammad would serve as the organization's president and, by default, Ali's manager, with much of the profit of the promotional group and from Ali himself going directly to the NOI. It was a successful venture but ultimately collapsed after Ali's coming suspension.[36]

Even before his suspension, however, it was clear that Ali was at least somewhat frustrated about Herbert Muhammad and the amount of money that was flowing to members of the Nation.[37] But monetary concerns did not create doubt in his faith. Ali divorced his first wife, Sonji, in early 1966, claiming that she had not been adequately devoted to the teachings of the NOI. While the divorce was a demonstration of his full indoctrination into the sect, Sonji would remain a substantive part of the controversy surrounding the boxer, as he did not pay the alimony required of him and just months after the divorce was back in court after a check he sent to his ex-wife bounced.[38] While Ali was able to make restitution in lieu of spending time in jail, the incident did not speak well of his responsibility. It also seemed to highlight the amount of money leaving his coffers and moving into the hands of the Nation of Islam. If alimony checks were bouncing during his profitable fight career, it was clear that if that career were taken away, he would have little cash left to sustain him.

Despite his devotion, such monetary concerns created tensions. At the annual convention of the NOI in February 1966, Black Muslim officials tried to force Ali to begin attending meetings of the Fruit of Islam, the group's police agency. They were, in the words of an FBI report, "extremely dissatisfied with his attitude and the way he speaks so spontaneously. They feel he needs much more discipline than he presently has to be a satisfactory Muslim."[39]

The following month, March 1966, the champion was scheduled for a title defense against George Chuvalo in Toronto. Before the bout the Miami post of the American Legion denounced Ali and threatened to picket any local theater planning to broadcast the fight. It was among the first instances of long-running hostility by the Legion against Ali. Though he had yet to be drafted and was yet to refuse induction into the military, his status had been changed to eligible and Ali had publicly questioned the change and his potential participation in the conflict. That, along with his membership in the NOI and his unapologetic Blackness, was enough for the Legion.[40] And that kind of patriotic denunciation had real consequences, as a barrage of racist letters began to flood the champion's mailbox. Meanwhile the *Chicago Tribune*, in the words of Jack Olsen, "waged a choleric campaign against holding the next Clay fight in Chicago," which led to a broader national critique of Ali. One of the observers with whom Olsen discussed the furor saw race at the heart of those criticisms. "Americans have become so guilty about Negroes that they bend over further than they want to in their attitude toward them," he said. "Then along comes somebody like Cassius, and they feel free to unload their resentment and pour it on."[41]

As if to counter the rhetoric of outlets like the *Tribune*, the NOI's *Muhammad Speaks* published articles and cartoons bemoaning the military draft as a conspiracy to kill Black men, continuing a long history of NOI opposition to the Vietnam conflict.[42] That kind of retributive propaganda generated by the group's principal media outlet wasn't intended to create public exhibits that Ali's faith guided him against the war, but any dispassionate review would see that such articles and cartoons did so. The problem, of course, was that no one was dispassionate about Vietnam, particularly the government, and with loud denunciations of the conflict from Ali, Muhammad, and *Muhammad Speaks*, the military turned its attention to the heavyweight champion.

Ali learned that the government had changed his draft status to eligible while sitting at his Miami home with journalist Robert Lipsyte. "Why me?" he asked after receiving the phone call. "I can't understand it. How did they do this to me—the heavyweight champion of the world?"[43] In the wake of the resulting public controversy, Ali gave an interview to CBS's Bob Halloran, one that won him few supporters. "Why me?" he asked of having his draft status changed. "A man who pays the salary of at least 50,000 men in Vietnam, a man who the government gets $6 million from a year from two fights, a man who can pay in two fights for three bomber planes . . ."[44]

One of Ali's relatives, speaking anonymously, blamed the Nation of Islam for the fighter's intransigence. "Cassius was searching for a father," the relative said, "and Elijah Muhammad is it. If Elijah tell him don't go to war, go to jail, he'll go to jail. That man have Cassius by the nose."[45] Historians Randy Roberts and Johnny Smith agree. They have portrayed Ali as "searching for a father figure" in the absence of any stability from his own. Angelo Dundee had served in that role, in a sense, but Elijah Muhammad would truly embody it for Ali.[46]

Others, however, were more sympathetic to the fighter's sincerity. "How the hell are you gonna send a kid like that to fight against people of color, *his* people?" one of Ali's friends asked. "How the hell are you gonna send him into battle alongside white Americans that he regards as the real enemy? That kid has a sincere, true, deep hatred of whites that goes all the way back to his childhood and the way his father brought him up. You meet the old man, and you'll know exactly what I'm talking about."[47] It was true that Cassius Sr. had emphasized the pitfalls of racial cooperation during his son's childhood, and that segregated Louisville would give any Black resident plenty of reasons to resent whites. It was also true that Ali devoted himself to a faith that taught that white people were devils—not metaphorical devils, but actual devils. Still, Ali's behavior toward the many white people in his life seemed to give lie to any "deep hatred of whites." Even if it was true, however, Ali's stance toward the military draft was conditioned less by that possible hatred and more by the instruction of Muhammad.

Selective Service originally classified Ali as 1Y, unfit for military service because of his low intelligence test score. While he was abroad boxing in Europe, however, Ali was reclassified to 1A after the military lowered the mental aptitude standard for draft eligibility, which qualified him for induction and prompted him to seek legal aid to again be reclassified, this time as a conscientious objector. "I conscientiously object to any combat military service that involves the participation in any war in which the lives of human beings are being taken," said his statement. Many at the time interpreted the reclassification as a kind of punishment for the champion's publicly stated political views, and Ali didn't shy away from such claims. But one of his more effective arguments was that there was no Black representation on his local draft board at the time of his reclassification, making it unrepresentative of the local community it served. For his part, Elijah Muhammad had refused service in World War II. By the leader's own estimate nearly a hundred members of the NOI went to prison for obeying his command and refusing induction in the 1940s. Herbert Muhammad constantly reminded Ali of Elijah's sacrifice—leaving out FBI claims that when agents arrived to arrest him, he was hiding under his mother's bed, wrapped in a carpet in an attempt to evade the law.[48]

After his all-white Louisville draft board rejected his exemption, Ali took his claim to the Kentucky Selective Service Appeal Board, but it agreed with the local board and ruled in May 1966 that he was not entitled to conscientious objector status.[49] The decision came even though the FBI knew that "Clay is a dedicated member of the Muslim religion." He was "of good character and reputation," and "sincere in [his] claim of conscientious objection." The Justice Department that would ultimately prosecute him—and that recommended that the Louisville draft board deny his appeal—knew from his first conscientious objector declaration that the fighter qualified.[50]

Meanwhile Ali fought George Chuvalo in Toronto in March 1966, then Henry Cooper and Brian London in London, England, in May and August. In September he knocked out Karl Mildenberger in Frankfurt, Germany. In November he returned to the United States and defeated Cleveland "Big Cat" Williams in Houston. In early 1967, even as the trauma over his draft status continued, he fought Ernie Terrell, again in Houston's Astrodome. Terrell had been a sparring partner for Ali before his conversion to the Nation of Islam and refused to refer to his opponent as anything but Cassius Clay. Clay responded by referring to Terrell as a racial sellout and an Uncle Tom, and went even farther during the fight. Instead of working for a knockout, Ali toyed with Terrell, screaming, "White man's n——!" and "Uncle Tom Negro!" as he pummeled him. "What's my name?" he shouted during combinations. "What's my name?"[51]

Upon Ali's return to the United States from Germany, the FBI plotted a potential arrest of the champion after he purchased several thousand dollars' worth of jewelry overseas and did not declare the purchases when he arrived home. Internal memos discussed the possibility of charging Ali with smuggling as a way to get rid of him without airing public debates about conscientious objector status. The smuggling charge never materialized, but the Bureau's intent was clear, which made Ali's draft case all the more problematic when it moved from Louisville to Washington. The Justice Department requested an FBI investigation of the sincerity of Ali's claims—the same FBI that had already noted the champion's sincerity in conscientiously objecting, then attempted to manufacture smuggling charges against him.[52]

Meanwhile Ali went back to Kentucky Selective Service and, on August 23, petitioned for an exemption based on his status as a minister in the Nation of Islam. Later that day Ali had a hearing in Louisville before Lawrence Grauman, a former federal circuit judge. To represent him he hired Hayden Covington, a New York attorney who had represented multiple cases of conscientious objection among Jehovah's Witnesses during World War II. Covington made a convincing case, and in response Grauman concluded that Ali was "sincere in his objection on religious grounds to participation in war in any form," noting that a willingness to fight in self-defense or to "participate in a theocratic war" did not disqualify a potential conscientious objector. Ali "has always been of good character," as demonstrated by witnesses at the hearing and the FBI report that was submitted to Grauman. Ali was "not a hypocrite or a faker." Grauman recommended to the Justice Department that his conscientious objector status be upheld.[53]

The Justice Department, unsurprisingly, disagreed. T. Oscar Smith, chief of the Justice Department's Conscientious Objector Section, wrote a recommendation to the Kentucky Selective Service Appeal Board that acknowledged Grauman's sincerity claim, but reasoned that the NOI did not object to participation in war as a function of religion, but rather as a function of the political and racial policies of Elijah Muhammad. The teachings of the Nation of Islam "rest on grounds which are primarily political and racial" rather than religious, the department reasoned. The group opposed war in certain circumstances, but not all circumstances, and "only a general scruple against participation in war in any form" created eligibility for conscientious objector status. It was a claim that Grauman had dispensed with, using a variety of case law to make his point, but Smith ignored that part of his report. Ali himself, Smith reminded Kentucky, said that if he "thought going to war would bring freedom and equality to twenty-two million of my people, they wouldn't have to draft me." Smith's conclusions were not as well-reasoned as those of Grauman, but his opinion carried more weight in Louisville. With that reasoning in hand, the Kentucky Selective Service Appeal Board denied Ali's claim on January 10, 1967.[54]

An appeal to the National Selective Service Appeal Board also failed the following month. In March Ali fought Zora Folley in Madison Square Garden, knocking him out in the seventh round. During his training for the fight, after doing road work at the Central Park reservoir, he turned to reporter Leonard Shecter and asked, "They let you read the papers in jail?" That was the moment Shecter knew that Ali had already made up his mind to refuse induction. After receiving his induction notice in March 1967, he spoke to Sugar Ray Robinson, who tried to convince him to accept it. He told Ali that his service would be nothing but fighting exhibitions for the troops. He would never see combat. And refusing would only ruin his boxing career. A frustrated Ali told him that Elijah Muhammad had told him he had to refuse induction, and that he was scared. "If you ask me," remembered Robinson after the fact, "he wasn't afraid of jail. He was scared of being killed by the Muslims."[55]

Two days after the Folley fight, on March 24, 1967, Ali successfully requested a transfer of induction location to Houston, then challenged his induction on the basis of unrepresentative white draft boards. Before he traveled there he announced at a Chicago restaurant that, if imprisoned, he would certainly return to boxing. "My ghost will haunt all arenas. The people will watch the fights and they will whisper, 'Hey, Ali could whip that guy.'" He assured everyone that he was only "twenty-five years old now. Make my comeback at twenty-eight. That's not old. Whip 'em all—if I get good food in jail." While Ali wouldn't actually go to jail, his statement was more prescient than he could know.[56]

The U.S. District Court for the Western District of Kentucky took up the boxer's case but concluded that there was no "substantial constitutional question" until Ali actually went through the induction process and refused to submit. The U.S. District Court for the Southern District of Texas said much the same. So on April 28 Ali reported for induction at the U.S. Customs office in Houston, a large crowd protesting outside the building, and declined to submit. The protesters were there, for the most part, to cheer on the champion and encourage him in his stand, seeing in his action a representation of their own beliefs; he was making a stand for all of them. "I have searched my conscience, and I find I cannot be true to my belief in my religion by accepting such a call," he told the crowd.[57]

Inside the building Ali was told to take a symbolic step forward when his name was called. But the name that was first called was Cassius Clay. When the fighter did not step forward, the representative called Muhammad Ali. Still he remained stationary. He was then warned of the consequences and asked a final time. Ali stayed where he was. Lieutenant Colonel J. Edwin McKee left the room and met with reporters. "Ladies and gentlemen, Mr. Muhammad Ali has just refused to be inducted into the United States armed forces." He was followed shortly by Ali himself, who passed out a formal statement to reporters in lieu of answering questions. It acknowledged the possible consequences of his action but argued that a choice between military service and jail was no choice at all. "There is another alternative and that alternative is justice." Though there had been rumors that he would be stripped of his title as a result of his stand, "I insist upon my right to pursue my livelihood in accordance with the same rights granted to other men and women who have disagreed with the policies of whatever Administration was in power at the time." He had earned his title, and those attempting to take it from him "actually disgrace themselves."[58]

Seven days later Ali was indicted for draft evasion. His appeal to the Fifth Circuit Court of Appeals was denied on May 15, and on June 20, a jury in the U.S. District Court for the Southern District of Texas convicted him. The judge, Joe Ingraham, sentenced Ali to five years in prison and a $10,000 fine.[59] Even before the charge and conviction, however, the New York State Athletic Commission suspended his boxing license—just an hour after he refused induction on April 28—in a unanimous vote, arguing that Ali's actions were "detrimental to the best interests of boxing." The fighter got the call while in his Houston hotel room. "I expected that," he said. "I am not surprised."[60]

As went New York, so went everyone else. The World Boxing Association stripped him of his championship, then the British Boxing Board and the European Boxing Union did the same. When told about the decision, Ali told reporters that it was a "continuation of the same artificially induced prejudice and discrimination" that had historically been a part of the sport and the country. And he was right. If anyone else had been stripped of their right to work without due process, their Fourteenth Amendment claim would have been ironclad.[61] While Black fans rallied behind the champ, however, white conservatives celebrated the decision. Ali was a "helpless dupe" of a dissident political sect, claimed the *National Review*, and while dissent was a vital part of the American system, the right to dissent "is not a right to break the law." Edwin Dooley, head of the New York State Athletic Commission, said that it was "a pity that 'Clay' has loused up his image and the image of boxing."[62]

For many, this seemed a long time coming for Ali. "Long before he actually refused induction into the Army and thereby gave the officials of boxing the opportunity to bar him, in the name of patriotism, from the ring and to send their sport back into the sleazy tedium from which he had for a time redeemed it," wrote Jack Richardson, "long before this concrete act, there had been howls of rage over his behavior, over his rodomontade, over his Muslim pieties, over, finally, the glory he seemed to find in himself." There had, in other words, always been an undercurrent of white resentment similar to that undergirding the white hostility toward Jack Johnson two generations earlier.[63] The WBA had made public threats against Ali's title before, claiming that his second bout with Liston was fixed. Ed Lassman, president of the WBA, also argued that Ali's behavior at the Liston press conference was "detrimental to the boxing world" and "a very poor example for the youth of the world." None of the state commissions agreed with Lassman, and the WBA soon had to back down, or at least bide its time.[64] When they finally had an opportunity, they struck.

Opinions on Ali's stand and his punishment fell along a clear dividing line. After someone expressed support for or denigration of Ali, "we would know how you stood on a dozen front-page issues," explained Budd Schulberg, "on the ABM and the SST, on the CIA, the FBI and Kent State, on the Nixon Doctrine and the law-and-order bills. Never before had there been a heavyweight champion who provided this kind of touchstone." Among those critical of Ali was the Californian white heavyweight Jerry Quarry. "Boxing needs a white champion to replace Cassius Clay," he said, advocating for himself as the best option for the role. "I'm the only one who can really help boxing."[65]

At the same time, however, Ali received support from Black voices who normally opposed his stances. Jackie Robinson credited the boxer for "backing up his words with deeds." Floyd Patterson, Ali's former opponent, argued that he was "being made to pay too stiff a penalty for saying and doing what he thinks is right." Ali's act was also celebrated abroad. There were protest demonstrations at American embassies and consulates in Guyana, Pakistan, and Egypt. The press in Ghana editorialized for Ali. The first substantive protest against the Vietnam War in England included leaflets that read, "LBJ Don't Send Muhammad Ali to War."[66]

But Black voices also took the other side. Robinson, for example, later changed his mind, asking how Ali could "expect to make millions of dollars in this country and then refuse to fight for it." Robinson claimed that Cassius Clay was "hurting the morale of a lot of young Negro soldiers over in Vietnam." He "has made millions of dollars off of the American public, and now he's not willing to show his appreciation to a country that's giving him, in my view, a fantastic opportunity." While Robinson's concern about Black soldiers who chose to accept military induction was certainly genuine, his deadnaming of Ali and his equation of participation in war with appreciation for material success rang hollow to many who supported the boxer's stand. Still, the *New York Amsterdam News* surveyed the opinions of Harlem residents and found a mixed reaction, with support outweighing criticism, but criticism still decidedly present.[67]

Martin Luther King, Jr., however, was no critic. Atlanta's most famous resident preached a sermon two days after the boxer's induction refusal in the city's Ebenezer Baptist Church that singled out Ali's courage. "He is giving up even fame. He is giving up millions of dollars in order to stand up for what his conscience tells him is right," said King. "No matter what you think of Muhammad Ali's religion, you certainly have to admire his courage." King was also asked about his thoughts on Ali's conviction while giving a press conference at Ebenezer. "If Cassius Clay or Muhammad Ali is jailed, it will stimulate more activity against the draft." He noted that "many Negroes" were "going to have to face this issue," and they would certainly resent any further government action against Ali.[68]

Public opinion was one thing; the opinion of boxing's sanctioning bodies was another. After the New York State Athletic Commission and the World Boxing Association stripped Ali's championship, all of boxing's sanctioning bodies declared the heavyweight title vacant. Every state with a commission suspended his boxing license. To fill the power vacuum at the top of the heavyweight division, the WBA held a series of elimination matches to name a new champion, but the number one contender, Joe Frazier, a Philadelphia fighter originally from South Carolina, opted out of the tournament to fight Buster Mathis for the championship of the New York State Athletic Commission.[69]

The WBA's tournament began with an eight-man field, promoted by Sports Action, Inc., led by Mike Malitz and Robert Kassel. The group had outmaneuvered Madison Square Garden, the more stalwart contender to promote the contests, because they were able to offer the fighters more money, facilitated by a television contract with ABC, which would broadcast the tournament on its *Wide World of Sports*. It was, in the words of

Tex Maule, both a blessing and a curse, as the tournament "represents the final takeover by TV of a major sports field," a phenomenon that would give access to boxing to more spectators but would likely reduce gates in arenas that held boxing contests. "Among all the pretenders to Ali's throne," Maule claimed in *Sports Illustrated*, "no one stands head and shoulders above the rest." That might not have been a good portent for heavyweight boxing writ large, but it would make for an exciting series of matches. "The lowliest is capable of giving the best an argument." On August 5, 1967, Thad Spencer defeated Ernie Terrell and Jimmy Ellis beat Leotis Martin at Houston's Astrodome. The following month Karl Mildenberger lost to Oscar Bonavena, then the month after that Jerry Quarry defeated Floyd Patterson. Then Ellis defeated Bonavena and Quarry took down Spencer. On April 27, 1968, Jerry Quarry fought for the title, falling to Jimmy Ellis, one of Ali's childhood friends and former sparring partners, in Oakland; when Frazier defeated Ellis in February 1970, he unified the titles.[70]

Ali was devastated by the loss of his championship and livelihood, and by seeing others compete for something he had never really lost. At the same time he also had to worry about the real possibility of incarceration. His trial on draft evasion charges began in Houston in June, five weeks after his indictment, in front of an all-white jury. The district attorney blamed Ali's actions on the Nation of Islam. "That's where his troubles began," said Morton Susman, "I think that's the reason he's here, his being in the Muslims." After two days of testimony and only twenty minutes of jury deliberation, Ali was convicted. Because the decision would be appealed, he was released on $5,000 bail on the condition that he not leave the continental United States.[71]

In the process of Ali's appeal to the Supreme Court, it was discovered that the FBI had recorded five different telephone calls that included Ali. The wiretaps had not originally targeted Ali, but the collection of that data convinced the Supreme Court on March 24, 1969, to vacate the boxer's original conviction and remand the case back to the District Court to determine whether the conviction had been tainted by illegal electronic surveillance. Judge Ingraham ruled that while one of the calls did not merit disclosure, the other four did. Still, he ruled that they did not present evidence that would demonstrate that the Justice Department's case had been tainted, so in July he reimposed the prison sentence and fine.

Again Ali appealed to the Fifth Circuit, but the court ruled that gathering foreign intelligence was a necessary part of the executive function and that since judicial review had determined that Ali's rights had not been violated, the conviction could stand. Once again the former champ was left with his only recourse being an appeal to the Supreme Court.[72]

Meanwhile, in September, Ali attempted to get his New York license reinstated, but in October the athletic commission unanimously denied his request, citing his refusal to be drafted, his felony conviction, and "the best interests of boxing." Ali responded with a lawsuit in the Southern District of New York, arguing that the commission was denying his First, Eighth, and Fourteenth Amendment rights. Judge Marvin Frankel dismissed the complaint in December, however, arguing that the state athletic commission had the right to make those decisions and that there was no proof in Ali's suit that demonstrated that the commission's ruling was arbitrary. If Ali could provide some kind of proof of that charge, Frankel noted that he would be willing to review any evidence that came before him. Ali responded in January by amending his complaint to describe the New York State Athletic Commission's actions as violations of the equal protection clause of the Fourteenth Amendment. This new suit came before Judge Walter Mansfield, who agreed with Frankel that the commission had the authority to deny a boxing license for a felony conviction or military offense, but was less sure about whether this particular denial was a violation of Ali's right to equal protection of the law.[73]

Though Ali's stance was controversial and angered much of the country, Julian Bond noted that it helped crystallize for many the meaning of what was happening in Vietnam. "You could hear people talking about it on street corners. It was on everyone's lips. People who had never thought about the war—black and white—began to think it through because of Ali." Essayist Gerald Early remembered his reaction as a child. "When he refused," he said of Ali's stance, "I felt something greater than pride: I felt as though my honor as a black boy had been defended, my honor as a human being." Historian Jim Jacobs has argued that in many ways, the stripping of Ali's title and his exile from boxing turned many people in his favor. "It showed people that Ali was sincere. It made him an underdog," said Jacobs. "He became a symbol to people who had never been interested in boxing before." There was, he argues, an inherent understanding among many that Ali's success was itself the reason for his exile. "If Ali had been the tenth-ranked heavyweight instead of champion, he never would have been denied a license to fight." Even some mainstream periodicals like *Esquire* defended the fighter, calling the public attacks against his stand on the war in Vietnam "self-righteously patriotic."[74]

After he lost his title, Ali's voice began to change, at least in some circles, criticizing wealthy, influential Black leaders as part of the broader race problem. "All the so-called Negroes worry about is money. He's like the white man now. He'll blow up his mama for some money. Sell out his people for some money," Ali said. "That's why we're nowhere today because all the big Negroes with money are up on the hill with the white folks, riding with the white folks, going to church with the white folks, marrying the white folks, shufflin' and tommin' and lovin' white folks. And they forget all about the brother down there in Harlem. His rent's due, living in a bad home, standin' on a corner, nobody know him, nobody want him, and he rides by in his limousine." It was a decidedly different message than Ali's public persona normally allowed, but it also seemed to be a criticism of the very people in Atlanta who would eventually bring him back to boxing.[75]

Ali told a story in 1968 of a delegation of Black athletes coming to him, trying to convince him to accept induction into military service, arguing that it would be a better look for the race. "I love my people. The little Negroes, they catching hell. They hungry. They raggedy. They getting beat up, shot, killed, just for asking for justice," he told them. "Now I'm the one's catching hell, too. I could make millions if I led my people the wrong way, to something I know is wrong. So now I have to make a decision. Step into a billion dollars or step into poverty. Step into a billion dollars and denounce my people or step into poverty and teach them the truth." Ali claimed not to be interested in the money. "I will die before I sell out my people for the white man's money." He claimed that the athletes left the meeting completely on his side, saying they were with him and wondering what they would do if they were forced to stand up for their beliefs. Whether apocryphal or not, the story spoke to Ali's conception of both his purpose and his influence.[76]

His stand catalyzed a broader athletic activism in the second half of the decade, giving a kind of permission to Black athletes who wanted to use their platforms for social justice. In December 1967 Harry Edwards led the Olympic Project for Human Rights to boycott the 1968 Summer Olympics, inspired in part by Ali's stand.[77] His group had "witnessed the intermingling of politics, religious philosophy, and sports in the tumultuous sojourn of Muhammad Ali to the apex of athletic glory and into the doldrums of disfavor in the athletic world," Edwards remembered. The first of the group's demands was "Restoration of Muhammad Ali's title and right to box in this country." The group also wanted the removal of Avery Brundage as chairman of the International Olympic Committee and a ban on the participation of the apartheid states of South Africa and Rhodesia. They wanted Black coaches added to the American Olympic team and Black administrators added to the U.S. Olympic Committee. They wanted the desegregation of the New York Athletic Club. First and foremost, however, was the restoration of Ali's title.[78]

Edwards saw Ali as a paragon of athletic radical action. He had fundamentally altered the path available to Black athletes seeking both sports achievement and national fame. His stand against the draft had angered a wide swath of his fan base and virtually all of the federal government, but it "enabled him to further transcend the sports arena." Historian Amy Bass has identified a clear affinity between the action and consequence of Ali's stand in 1967 and that of Julian Bond the year before, when he was refused his seat in the Georgia state legislature for his own anti-Vietnam position. Ali's stand "characterized a strategy of cultural resistance effective in a modern media age." Perhaps the single most influential effort in the strategy of using sports media as a site of resistance was the podium protest of Tommie Smith and John Carlos after the 200 meter dash at the same Olympics that Edwards had attempted to boycott. The stand of those runners, heads bowed, one black-gloved fist raised during the playing of the American national anthem, was built, Bass argues, from a strategy "politically illustrated" by Ali.[79]

Ali was, for Harry Edwards, "the warrior saint in the revolt of the black athlete in America." Black athletes had previously avoided overt demonstrations of political activism, fearing a backlash that could hurt their ability to earn a living. Even when Black athletes did become more vocal, particularly following the violence in Birmingham in the summer of 1963, they did so in aid of the integrationist politics of the classical civil rights movement. When Clay, and then Ali, spoke politically but against the traditional goals of the Southern movement, he changed the meaning of Black athletic political activity. "To us," said Edwards, referring to Ali, "he was—is—a god."[80]

But then there was Vietnam. Though the war was unpopular with a wide swath of the country, it had been "a virtual nonissue for athletes, amateur and professional" up to the point of Ali's induction refusal. The boxer's vocal opposition to the war in Vietnam made the conflict "a central issue for athletes," even as they continued to engage in a variety of protests, also inspired by Ali, concerning domestic racial inequalities.[81] "If Ali hadn't done what he did, Harry Edwards wouldn't have gotten a fraction of the support he got in 1968 to boycott the Mexico City Olympics," concluded Arthur Ashe. "Tommie Smith and John Carlos wouldn't have raised their fists. Ali had to be on their minds. He was largely responsible for it becoming an expected part of the black athlete's responsibility to get involved." In 1967 Ashe refused to participate in a Davis Cup match when the United States was scheduled to play South Africa. "There's no question that Ali's sacrifice was in the forefront of my mind."[82]

His sacrifice was also on the minds of collegiate athletes, who began their own activism on campuses across the country. "From the end-zone dance of Elmo Wright to the adoption of Islamic names by black athletic heroes such as basketball great Lew Alcindor (Kareem Abdul-Jabbar) and football star Bobby Moore (Ahmad Rashaad)," explains Jeffrey T. Sammons, "Ali's oppositional style interlaced itself into the social fabric."[83] When thirteen Black athletes at the University of Washington presented a list of demands to their school administrators, they included on the list a call for Jim Owens, head coach of the Huskies football team, to publicly endorse Muhammad Ali. When Bob Pressley, a basketball player at the University of California, Berkeley, clashed with his coach over his desire to wear a natural hairstyle, there was in that effort, too, the influence of Ali, whose near constant rhetoric about his image and his appearance helped elevate the "Black is Beautiful" movement that urged African Americans to eschew traditionally understood white beauty standards.[84]

Newsweek's Pete Axthelm attempted to make sense of the new revolution in Black sports in July 1968. He traced the double lives of Black athletes prior to desegregation, wherein Jesse Owens could be the toast of the world but not get fair treatment back home in the United States, wherein Cassius Clay could win a gold medal in Rome but could not eat at the majority of restaurants in his Louisville hometown. But after Ali's stand, after the Olympic Project for Human Rights, athletes had a louder voice; they had the ability to use sports as "a means toward an ideological end." And because of that ability, sports would never be the same again.[85]

In 1967 Ali served as the grand marshal in a commemorative Watts Riots parade, demonstrating the continued support he received from the frustrated Black masses. And he understood the importance of those masses. "I just don't represent boxing. I'm taking a stand for what I believe in and being one thousand percent for the freedom of the black people," he said. "Naturally those who have the same fight, but on a smaller scale, they come to me." They supported him. They saw his fight as a larger version of their own.[86] So Ali's radicalism was not simply important because it prodded other athletes to use their platforms for meaningful causes. Ali's radicalism was doing work of its own.

But he was still a showman. While Ali was serving what would become a three-and-a-half-year sentence, Joe Frazier lent the former champion money to help him through. Gerald Early has argued that the move was not necessarily altruistic, as "Frazier needed Ali as much as Ali needed Frazier." Mark Kram has gone the other way, claiming that Frazier virtually worshipped Ali, even agreeing to forgo his champion's purse and have a fifty-fifty split were they ever to actually fight. "In those days," wrote Frazier, "we were on a friendly basis—rivals who could talk to each other in a reasonable way." Early in 1969, however, Ali appeared on a Philadelphia radio show and called Frazier an "Uncle Tom" who fought for white men. He was a "coward." He challenged Frazier to a fight at the gym in North Philadelphia that served as Frazier's training home. When the two met at the gym, crowds surrounding them in anticipation, Ali then modified the challenge, telling Frazier to go across the street and fight him in Fairmount Park. Ali led the crowd out of the gym, and when Frazier didn't follow, he was humiliated. The rift between the two was set.[87]

If that rift was ever to become a rivalry, however, the activist icon would have to find his way from the parades, protests, and Black Muslim pulpits back to the boxing ring. And if he were ever going to manage that, Leroy Johnson and Black Atlanta would have to find their way there as well.

3. GROWING PAINS

1969

In October 1968 a new play appeared on Broadway from playwright Howard Sackler. *The Great White Hope* was a fictionalized biography of Jack Johnson. The story's protagonist "possesses three fatal liabilities," explained a review in the *Atlanta Voice*. "He is black, he refuses to conform to the shuffling, obsequious stereotype required of him, and he openly consorts with a white girlfriend." He wins the heavyweight boxing championship but refuses to be cowed by white leaders who despise him. "In a final shattering scene, the black man battles until his body is a blood-smeared wreckage; then, battered and beaten, he watches the new champ—the great white hope parade past in triumph." The play premiered in New York, but there was a reason that it was of interest to Black readers as far away as Atlanta. In the wake of the controversy surrounding Ali, many saw the depiction of Johnson as a statement on the trials of the more modern fighter who had seen his career limited by government interference.[1]

Johnson began fighting professionally in 1897 and won the world heavyweight championship eleven years later, in 1908. In an age of social Darwinism, many Black fans celebrated his victories as a proof against pseudoscientific race claims. There was, however, an ambivalence in Black support for Johnson. He was brash and braggadocious; he caroused with white women and married several of them. Booker T. Washington, for example, believed that Johnson's success hurt the possibility of racial unity and prompted more racial violence. The boxer "has harmed rather than helped the race," he argued.[2]

Sociologists and folklorists have interpreted Johnson as embodying the role of the "bad n——," one who "refuses to accept the place given to blacks in American society, and who frequently challenges the outer perimeters of expected behavior." It was a point of pride to be considered such, to disregard danger in living a life on the social margins. Johnson even criticized white people for actions that much of the Black population praised. It made Johnson an aspirational figure to many working-class Black fans but left him open to criticism by those of the middle class who benefited more directly from the racial status quo. The white population was virtually unanimous in its opposition to Johnson, while Black responses varied, largely based on class. Some saw him as challenging white supremacy and flouting racist laws and customs. Others saw him as exacerbating racial hostilities and stifling any possibility of progress in challenging discriminatory law and policy.[3]

While Ali's controversy never included marriages to white women or social Darwinian scientific claims, his was a similarly polarizing career. There were far more white fans who supported Ali than Johnson, but Black ambivalence was very real in the period following his first defeat of Sonny Liston and the public announcement of his membership in the Nation of Islam. Ali saw the comparison clearly, "except I'm a clean Jack Johnson." Unlike the former champ, Ali didn't drink or "mess with white women." He was a model citizen, "and that makes 'em angry. They know I'm not gonna lose my title in the ring. Now that drives 'em out of their mind. So they take my license away." But, bothered as he was by the theft, Ali put on a brave face, as Johnson had done before him. "I'm fightin' for 22 million black people. I'm fightin' for their freedom, and that's really big. I ain't losin' nothin', but gainin' the world."[4]

As the new year began, Black Atlantans were also fighting for their freedom. They were not, however, gaining the world. "The early part of 1969 was not a time to hold out much hope for black people in America," Julian Bond explained, "in Atlanta or anywhere else."[5] Leroy Johnson, however, was trying. He began an uphill battle for more equitable housing, advocating for changes in the board of the Atlanta Housing Authority. Related to such advocacy was Johnson's fight to keep Atlanta from annexing predominantly white suburbs like Sandy Springs, interpreting the move as an effort by white Republicans to increase their voting power in the city over the dominant position of Atlanta's Black Democrats, which is exactly what it was.[6] He would be forced to fight a similar action later in the year.

Back in January, before the annexation drama escalated, Johnson brought Martin Luther King's father and Rosa Parks to the state legislature to celebrate the fallen civil rights champion on what would have been his birthday less than a year after his death. He then presented a resolution to the legislature to make January 15, King's birth date, a state holiday. In response he began receiving a series of threatening phone calls from racists who saw a King holiday as a bridge too far. Johnson's legislative colleagues agreed. The state senate never even brought the bill to the floor for a vote.[7]

It was a frustrating loss for Johnson, but many in the city saw the effort as largely performative, as they saw much of Johnson's official work. In late 1968, for example, mayor Ivan Allen created an Urban Life Observatory Advisory Council and included Johnson as part of it. The problem, critics said, was that Johnson was the only Black representative on a council that would necessarily be dealing with a substantial number of Black issues. There were also no women on the council. And who exactly, asked Eliza Paschall, would the council advise? She was certain, as were others, that "lots of money" would "go for middle-class professional salaries for studies which will show that the solutions to the problems being studied start with more money."[8] While Johnson's presence on such councils was important, and Black representation, limited as it may have been, was necessary in governmental analyses of urban problems, the makeup of the council and its vague aims made many outside the core of mainstream Black power brokers see Johnson as part of a problem rather than a component of any tangible solutions.

Johnson's work, however, was more than just performative; it was decidedly devoted to tangible solutions, both in Atlanta and throughout Georgia. He represented Black state leadership in civil rights fights in rural parts of the state and was a tireless advocate for issues like tenure reform for teachers.[9] Johnson's activism, and the influence that ultimately stemmed from it, even had him rumored to be a candidate for Atlanta's 1969 mayoral election. He didn't deny the rumors, claiming in March 1969 that he was considering the opportunity but wanted to ensure that there was only one Black candidate so as not to split the votes of city residents.[10] When Ivan Allen announced that he would neither seek a third term as mayor nor endorse a successor, Black leaders met with him about the forthcoming race. Johnson was joined by Jesse Hill,

Martin Luther King, Sr., and others, expressing their interest in playing a role, along with white civic and business leaders, in choosing the next Democratic nominee. White leaders, however, were coalescing around the candidacy of alderman Rodney Cook, whom, Johnson and others explained to Allen, the Black community would not support.[11]

So Johnson was considering a run. Some scholars have interpreted him as "feeling entitled to a black candidacy as mayor," that he "had earned the right to be that man or would broker the person who would be."[12] Though the claims have been made without direct evidence, it is no stretch to assume that Johnson's record did give him some sense of entitlement. He was moderate enough to draw potential support from a segment of the white population, which would be crucial in such an election—but because of that moderation, younger Black organizers distrusted him as someone who would compromise away any bargaining power the African American community might have. In late April, after another Black candidate, Dr. Horace Tate, entered the race, the state senator suggested that the NAACP or another organization administer a kind of Black primary between Tate and himself to see which candidate should represent the community in Atlanta's mayoral race. Tate, a former schoolteacher who served on the Atlanta school board, rejected the suggestion, but it was telling as to Johnson's political calculation and his willingness to try unconventional things.[13] Though speculation would continue into the summer months and Johnson would flirt with entering the race, he ultimately decided not to run for mayor, calling it an "extremely difficult and painful" decision.[14]

That left Tate as the only Black candidate, but his chances were slim, so Johnson gave his endorsement to the eventual winner, Sam Massell, a former vice mayor and realtor. "I knew that Leroy was carrying Sam's water," remembered attorney David Franklin. "And I knew right then that Massell would get 80 percent of the black vote." Johnson decided not to run for mayor because, as a veteran vote counter, his math told him that any Black candidate would need more Black support than the current registration percentage would allow. "To me," Johnson remembered, "the most important thing was to elect a man—white or black—who would feel beholden to the Negro community." A Johnson victory would also require at least 15 or 20 percent of the white vote and the capital investment of the white business community, neither of which, Johnson argued, were yet available to a Black candidate. And if he deemed that he couldn't win, he was sure that Tate couldn't win either. At the same time, Johnson believed that a Massell victory could provide the coattails needed to elevate Maynard Jackson, a Black candidate running for vice mayor, to victory.[15]

Johnson wasn't alone. "Atlanta is not yet ready to elect a Negro Mayor and a Vice Mayor," said Reverend J. D. Grier, chairman of Operation Breadbasket. "There is a good chance that we will be able to elect a Vice Mayor." There were many qualified Black candidates, he reasoned. "However, I would hope and pray that they would put the interest of the community before their personal right." He praised Tate's work on the school board. "I hope that he would stay there where his chances for re-election are good, and where his unique background in education is needed." The editorial board of the *Atlanta Inquirer* agreed, applauding Tate's campaign as "very important, for it focuses on the disappointment of black citizens in many white elected officials," but arguing that Massell was a choice who could actually win. Polls showed Tate receiving only 1 percent of the white vote, making victory impossible.[16] While there were plenty of Black Atlantans who believed that a Black mayor was possible in 1969, the opinion of Johnson, Grier, and the *Inquirer* was shared by many more.

Still, the elevation of Jackson that would result from supporting a white mayoral candidate was a position that Johnson and other Black leaders were reluctant to come around on. "There was a feeling among blacks that Maynard was a maverick," said Johnson, "that he was concerned about his own political interest, that he made no consultation with anybody." He had, in other words, been willing to buck the traditional Black power structure that saw itself as kingmaker in the city. Johnson, meanwhile, had spent his career working within that power structure to garner consensus on development projects that he saw as beneficial to the broader Black community as well as to himself.[17]

Historian Maurice Hobson has portrayed Tate's candidacy as offensive to the city's Black political elite, who were chagrined by the fact that he hadn't consulted them before running. There were late-arriving endorsements for Tate by Ralph Abernathy, Coretta Scott King, Julian Bond, and Jesse Jackson, but those last-minute announcements were unable to put Tate into the runoff, although he did receive a narrow majority of the Black vote. Bond, in particular, was frustrated with the Black leadership coalition, which, he believed, could have pushed Tate's candidacy over the top but decided against it in the name of an unnecessary territorial pragmatism. Meanwhile Johnson and Martin Luther King, Sr., endorsed Massell, a Jewish candidate whose lack of favor among the city's white business leaders was largely assumed to be the result of antisemitism.[18]

Still, it was significant that Black power brokers in the city were choosing a candidate, though not the Black candidate, who was not a member of the white elite who were part of the traditional negotiating structure of Atlanta politics. Massell won in a runoff that didn't include Horace Tate, despite losing the white vote. As Fred Powledge explained in 1973, "Ever since Massell's election, the [white] power structure has seemed willing to accept the fact that the days when it ran City Hall are over and new ways of cooperation must be tried." Black Atlanta voted for Massell in massive numbers, 92.7 percent of its vote going to the candidate in the runoff, allowing him to win the mayoral race in an election that took place under the shadow of controversies over race and police brutality. It was, according to the *Atlanta Inquirer*, the "most productive and effective city election" for Black voters in the city's history; they exercised "great power" and "literally overhauled the city governing bodies, the board of aldermen and the board of education." In the same election cycle Maynard Jackson won election as vice mayor, just as Johnson had predicted, and four new Black aldermen joined the city's board. Black political power had reached a new zenith.[19]

In May, during a meeting of the Hungry Club at the Butler Street YMCA, Jackson was scheduled to give a campaign speech, but before he could take the podium, a frustrated man, George Williams, commandeered the stage and demanded the audience listen to him. The Butler Street YMCA served the traditional functions of a YMCA, but it was also one of the centers of political and social activity of Atlanta's Black elite, known colloquially during the 1950s, 60s, and 70s as "Atlanta's Black City Hall." The Hungry Club was established in 1945 by Black leaders in the city seeking a forum for an exchange of ideas among themselves and between them and white business and civic leaders. The club held luncheons at the Butler Street YMCA, inviting religious and political leaders to address concerns that directly affected the Black population. Those attending were "hungry for food and ideas," and even though the luncheons did not represent a formal organization or a specific political interest, they became important arbiters of power among the Black elite in Atlanta.[20]

At the May 1969 Hungry Club meeting, after Williams commandeered the microphone, he complained that Leroy Johnson had lied to him, that Johnson had failed as legal counsel for Williams's son. His screed against Johnson ultimately ended when a policeman arrested him and dragged him out of the building as the middle- and upper-class crowd buzzed about the crazy man who had interrupted their meeting. It was another example of the very real rift between the Black political class and those they claimed to represent. Johnson was, for so many of those frustrated working-class people, the symbol of that rift.[21]

It didn't help that Johnson wore tailor-made suits and a large diamond ring. He drove a Mercedes most days, a Jaguar or Cadillac on others. In his law practice he represented celebrities like Otis Redding, Hank Aaron, and James Brown. He made himself, in many ways, an easy target for such criticism, even for those who didn't fully understand the history of the city's Black middle and upper classes' strategy of negotiation.[22]

Johnson's career as an attorney and a businessman provided the source of most of his revenue. Not only had he served as an attorney for James Brown, but at the end of March 1969 he was elected to the board of directors of Brown's fast-food organization, Gold Platter, Incorporated, of Macon. When Gold Platter issued its initial public offering in the summer, the two hundred thousand shares sold out at six dollars per share—a surprising outcome, because the company had yet to prove itself viable. There was one Gold Platter restaurant in Macon. The company had sold eleven franchises, but none of them had opened at the time of the IPO.[23] In August, however, two additional Gold Platter restaurants opened in Macon, with Johnson, Brown and the city's mayor, Ronnie Thompson, there for a ribbon-cutting ceremony in the presence of thousands of people. Johnson, touting the restaurants, said that he and Brown "are sincere in our belief that we have 'opened a new door' through which black people can 'get a piece of the action.'"[24]

In addition to having a presence on the board, Johnson owned, along with Atlanta alderman and fellow Gold Platter board member Q. V. Williamson, 14 percent of the stock in Hunter-Peachtree, a holding company that owned twelve thousand shares of Gold Platter stock and had the Atlanta-area Gold Platter franchise. The soul food restaurants were just the first part of what Brown saw as a potential empire, one that also included convenience stores and motor hotels. The effort, however, did not get off the ground; the following year, after a "substantial" financial loss, Gold Platter shuttered. But the venture demonstrated Johnson's desire to create revenue for himself and to stay as close as possible to the orbit of celebrity.[25]

Meanwhile Black frustration moved in April to the Atlanta University Center, the cluster of HBCUs that included Atlanta University, Clark College, Morris Brown, Morehouse, Spelman, and the Interdenominational Theological Center. The leadership of historically Black colleges was historically conservative, and many of the leaders of Atlanta's institutions were part of the city's moderate Black leadership class. The frustration of the working class with middle- and upper-class Black leaders was mirrored in 1969 by student frustration with their administrators, whom they saw as similarly unresponsive to their needs. Morehouse students wanted the AUC colleges consolidated, more Black trustees, and a modified curriculum. They had tried and failed to get a meeting with the Atlanta University Board of Trustees. A day later a group of students representing several schools went to a meeting of the Morehouse Board of Trustees and chained the doors. Morehouse president Hugh Morris Gloster attempted to address the students, but he refused to make concessions under threat and instead submitted his resignation. His letter admitted to being in favor of more Black trustees and closer relations between the schools of the AUC, "but I cannot participate in a meeting in which members of the Board of Trustees are confined in this conference room by force and are subjected to insult and intimidation." He could not "be a party to concessions made under duress"; he was, therefore, "submitting my resignation as President of Morehouse College."[26]

The trustees stayed chained in a room for twenty-nine hours, until a temporary agreement mollified the students.[27] During the crisis the Student Government Association met. The body condemned the protest and voted to refuse Gloster's resignation letter. "Their motives are dubious," said student government president Nelson Taylor of the protesters. "These are the people who are still trying to fan the embers of strife and confusion. These are the people who are making the bomb threats." The crisis seemed to have passed, but days later Taylor proved prescient when the Morehouse campus reading center was firebombed.[28]

George Coleman, associate editor of the *Atlanta Voice*, was sympathetic to the students. "The present dilemma at Morehouse College was looming on the horizon for quite some time," he wrote. "Student interests and demands must be taken seriously, for as an institution of learning cannot exist without a sound faculty, it cannot function without students."[29] In late June Morehouse administrators announced that five students would be suspended for a year for the April protest; five more would be suspended for a semester. In all, twenty-eight students would face some form of discipline. A frustrated Coleman called the administrative crackdown "disgusting." It was a situation, he argued, that called for leniency. "Who knows, but that a future M. L. King or Ralph Bunche may have been thrown out into the streets like a criminal."[30] It was an act of lording power over the powerless, demonstrating the disconnect the students were attempting to highlight in the first place.

The conflicts, however, were not relegated to campus. In August, Robert 8X Birdsong, a twenty-two-year-old member of the NOI, shot two government workers in downtown Atlanta. He had been selling *Muhammad Speaks* newspapers at the post office and attempted to sell one to mail handler Herbert Westbrook. When Westbrook told the salesman, "I don't buy trash like that," the Black Muslims there allegedly attacked him. When Benjamin Smith, a post office traffic guard, came to Westbrook's defense, Robert 8X took Smith's gun and shot both of the postal workers. That was, at least, the way Georgia's white media presented the crime, reminding those in white Georgia that the Nation of Islam and its members were a threat.[31]

The most prominent of those members, Ali, was still far from Atlanta and its racial controversies that summer. In early April he appeared with Howard Cosell on ABC's *Wide World of Sports*. When Cosell asked him about the possibility of returning to the ring, Ali told him, "I'd go back if the money was right. I have a lot of bills to pay." Watching at his home in Chicago was Elijah Muhammad, who responded to Ali's appearance with a signed editorial in *Muhammad Speaks*. The fighter's desire for money from boxing had disqualified him from membership in the faith. "Muhammad Ali is out of the circle of the brotherhood of the followers of Islam under the leadership and teaching of Elijah Muhammad for one year," he wrote. "Mr. Muhammad Ali plainly acted the fool." He demonstrated in his interview with Cosell that he was putting "his hopes and trust in the enemy of Allah for survival," which demonstrated that he didn't trust Allah to meet his worldly needs. "Mr. Muhammad Ali wants a place in this sports world. He loves it." And that, in itself, was a crime. In the next edition of *Muhammad Speaks*, the leader stripped him of his Muslim name, noting that he would revert back to being known as Cassius Clay. Elijah's son Herbert Muhammad would no longer serve as the boxer's manager.[32]

It seemed a strange about-face for the organization, which had, most people assumed, willingly taken so much of Ali's fighting fortune in the past. His stated willingness to fight for money now appeared to many an excuse for the Nation to drop him now that he had no fortune to bleed. Understanding the popular framing, the NOI's national secretary, John Ali, claimed that the former champion's debts were the result of "ignorance and extravagance," of not spending with abstemiousness as taught by the faith. The Nation had never "taken any money from Muhammad Ali."[33] Of course, the Nation had taken plenty of money from Muhammad Ali, but even Ali tamped down the more vicious rumors of the financial advantages the group may have taken. "They say he stole my money and they say he told me not to go to the Army. But they got to let one of them go. I could make ten million dollars if I went to the Army. If he's out to rob me he wants me to go. But he never said a word, either way."[34]

The Nation's reasons seemed a protest too much. "In the era of Black Power," explains historian Claude Clegg, "the boxer was no longer an essential factor in the appeal of the Nation to young African-Americans." The organization could feel relatively confident that it could jettison Ali without prompting an exodus from the faith. Clegg notes that the ouster seemed reminiscent of the group's split with Malcolm X in 1964; "it seemed to raise many of the same issues of authority, generational tensions, and jealousies." It could be interpreted, then, as punishment intended as "a reassertion of Muhammad's dominion over the Nation—a reminder to followers who had become a bit too enamored of Ali."[35]

For Ali, the suspension was devastating. He had devoted so much of himself to the group and had taken such a public risk to be a part of it. He had in many ways replaced his relationship with his birth father with a fatherly relationship with Muhammad. Now those who were supposed to be defending him against the onslaught of white reactionary politics were tossing him aside. He was left, in a sense, a man without a country. In speeches following the suspension, Ali continued unfailingly to praise Muhammad, but after the curtain fell on his appearances, the fighter used the opportunity to rekindle his relationship with Cassius Clay, Sr.[36]

He also reunited with his pre-Nation publicist, Harold Conrad, who had promoted Ali's first fight with Sonny Liston. Conrad had also promoted Liston's fights with Floyd Patterson and many other contests. He was a former scriptwriter and novelist and often moved in literary circles, spending time with Norman Mailer, James Baldwin, Ben Hecht, and others. "Neither an advocate of black power nor a civil rights worker nor a peace marcher," he simply understood that drawing fans to closed-circuit broadcasts required an actual draw. And he knew Ali was it. Conrad was "out of the Damon Runyon canon, a cheery cynic, tall, lean, and dapper, silk scarf bunched at this throat."[37] Immediately upon his return the publicist got the former champ booked on the *Tonight Show*, *What's My Line?*, and *Merv Griffin*. While such appearances were intentionally lighthearted, Ali also appeared on William F. Buckley's show to debate more substantive issues, demonstrating that he wasn't shying away from political stances. When Buckley argued that Ali had "been poisoned" by Elijah Muhammad to see "white people as an enemy," Ali was game for the fight. "It's *you* who taught us that you're our enemy," he responded. "It was white people who bumped off Martin Luther King, it was white people who bumped off Medgar Evers, it was white people who bumped off Adam Clayton Powell. We didn't imagine this."[38]

Conrad also attempted to get Ali back in the ring. One of his efforts occurred in Macon, Georgia, which had been the state's major urban center before being overtaken by Atlanta and which, like Atlanta, was trying to grow its economic base. In August 1969 Conrad contacted Bill Lavery, manager of the nine-thousand-seat Macon Coliseum, about the potential of an Ali fight. Lavery was interested in boxing and had even brought Chris Dundee, Angelo's brother, to the city to sell him on an opportunity for boxing cards at his venue. He brought the national AAU basketball tournament to the coliseum, as well as professional tennis. Macon's mayor, Ronnie Thompson, believed sports was a way to grow the city's economy. He had already contacted both the University of Georgia and Georgia Tech about playing non-conference basketball games at the coliseum. He very publicly argued that championship boxing was something else the city wanted. But it didn't want Muhammad Ali. When Lavery brought the proposal to Macon's board of aldermen and its mayor, both rejected it outright. The aldermen voted unanimously against it. Thompson was more vocal. "This man has refused to fight for his country but he is very willing to fight for the dollar under a free enterprise system that other Americans, both black and white, are fighting and dying to preserve," he said. Lavery wasn't necessarily disappointed in the rejection. He claimed to the *Macon Telegraph*'s Harley Bowers that "there was no fight in the first place," and thus "nothing to vote down." He portrayed the story as one that had grown larger than it really was. Still, that didn't mean that Lavery wasn't interested in bringing boxing back to Macon. "You can't get a bigger name in boxing than Clay," he said, but the banned fighter was only one option. "This was a boxing town once and could be again."[39] Of course, the one thing that Macon lacked was a Black political base with the kind of electoral power that could sway aldermanic and mayoral decisions. As it had in the nineteenth century, then, a recalcitrant Macon was again destined to see Atlanta, which did have that Black political power, pass it by.

Ali attempted to regain his license in New York by appealing to Jackie Robinson, who was friends with Republican New York governor Nelson Rockefeller. Robinson, however, had told Ali that Rockefeller was close to Richard Nixon, and Nixon was as anti-Ali as one could be. Restarting his fight career in New York, as of 1969, seemed impossible. Still, prompted by Ali's attorney Chauncey Eskridge—former lawyer for Martin Luther King, Jr., and the SCLC—the NAACP's Legal Defense Fund brought a case that year against the New York State Athletic Commission, claiming that denying Ali a boxing license violated his rights, arguing that the commission had often given licenses to convicted criminals and that granting a license to Ali would be consistent with past behavior. Though a district court judge did not rule for the former champion, he was clearly willing to see evidence of past instances of licensing criminals by the commission.[40]

It seemed at least a plausible reason for hope. So too did the work of Ali's team. Conrad, Eskridge, Clay Sr., and business agent Gene Dibble combined to help push Ali back into the limelight and to help him profit off the effort. He already owned, with the help of the Nation of Islam, 60 percent of a San Antonio oil well, which provided monthly royalties.

But with his team in place, Ali sold the rights to what would become his first autobiography to Random House for a $200,000 advance. He also signed two lucrative movie deals. The first was for a documentary titled *a.k.a. Casius Clay*, which would tell the story of the boxer's life and activism. The second was for a computerized superfight between Ali and Rocky Marciano, who had retired thirteen years prior. The team also replaced his speaker's agent, Richard Fulton, signing Ali to the American Program Bureau. Under his previous deal, brokered by the NOI and led by Gene Kilroy, Ali was receiving between $1,500 and $2,000 per lecture. But with his new management, he was flying on a private jet to campuses across the country, earning between $15,000 and $25,000 per speech.[41] It was a good deal, but Ali had still "lost three of the best years of his life," argued Pete Hamill, "as he scuffled around the country, making speeches at college campuses and Muslim mosques, followed by a retinue of lawyers, hangers-on, and acolytes."[42]

One of Ali's confidants during his difficult days was Joe Frazier. "You'll be back. Better than ever," Frazier told him. "Joe," Ali responded, "you the big man now. You gotta keep my name out there. Don't let 'em forget." To allay some of his worry, Ali threw himself into his speaking engagements, putting together six different stump speeches. He studied them regularly and practiced in front of a mirror with his wife listening. In public performance the speeches were, as noted by Thomas Hauser, "part sermon and part rap." They started quietly but would usually crescendo into grievance over the loss of his title and profession. "Can my title be taken away without my being whupped?" he would shout at the crowd. "No!" they would respond. "Who's the champion of the world?" "You are!" It was a call-and-response strategy that would turn sedate audiences into cheering fans.[43]

Ali also mirrored Leroy Johnson in joining the restaurant industry. Eskridge negotiated a deal that allowed Ali's name and image to be used for a new fast-food chain called Champburger in return for a 6 percent ownership stake in the company and 1 percent of gross sales. With the company's IPO in 1969, Ali made $900,000.[44] His exile from the NOI had been painful and demoralizing, but without the religious sect and with a new team in place, he had quickly returned to wealth.

In early April Ali traveled to Atlanta amidst a whirl of controversy. He had been convicted and sentenced to five years in prison, and a week prior to his venture south, the Supreme Court had remanded his case back to a lower court over concerns about undisclosed wiretapping information. It was a victory, if only temporary, for Ali, but with it came more antiwar publicity.[45] In Atlanta he spoke to a crowd at Georgia Tech, and after the speech he acknowledged Muhammad's suspension, telling reporters, "I'm retired. I'll never climb into the ring or go into an arena again."[46] It was an auspicious statement to make in Atlanta, as the following year he would climb into the ring and go into an arena only two short miles from the Georgia Tech campus.

Ali's journey across that two-mile, two-year stretch from Georgia Tech to Atlanta Municipal Auditorium, from Black Muslim outcast to Black Muslim hero, from convicted draft dodger to heavyweight contender, has been interpreted by many and in many different ways.[47] Less discussed has been the intersection of time and place, Atlanta after integration, in creating the possibility of that two-mile journey. Ali was fighting in court to stay out of jail; he was fighting on stages like that at Tech for a Black nationalist counter to integrationist and pro-Vietnam messages; and he was, despite his denials, fighting to fight again in rings and arenas. He was aided in those efforts by his own tenacity, but also by a broader turn in public opinion away from support for the Vietnam War. It didn't require a long ethical leap to believe that if Ali could come to Atlanta to speak—particularly with the Black Muslim message he was presenting to his college audience—he could come to Atlanta to box.

Soon after his brief trip to Atlanta, Ali's case resumed in federal district court in Houston, his defense led by Atlanta ACLU lawyer Charles Morgan. Morgan had, in fact, created the southern regional office of the ACLU. A native of Birmingham, he was a white lawyer involved in civil rights who had also defended Julian Bond when he was denied his seat in the Georgia legislature. Morgan's brief in the Ali case requested all of the wiretaps and a list of government officials with access to them. The government countered with a national security argument, claiming that the "surveillance was being conducted to gather foreign intelligence information."[48] The conversations with Ali came from taps of Elijah Muhammad's phone, the FBI admitting that it had monitored the leader's conversations from 1962 to 1966, even though Lyndon Johnson's authorization of those wiretaps had concluded in June 1965.[49]

As the trial continued, the current heavyweight champion, Joe Frazier, was training in New York for a June 23 bout in Madison Square Garden against a California fighter named Jerry Quarry. Quarry's road to such opportunities had been inordinately difficult. A native of Bakersfield, Quarry was the son of amateur boxer Jack Quarry, who had come to California from Texas during the Great Depression. Quarry was from the Dust Bowl, lighting out from home during the Great Depression like so many others, seeking the promised land. He hopped boxcars, often surviving by fighting his way through the clamor of desperation on his way out West. When he arrived he took a job as a seasonal farm worker. He married his wife, Arwanda, and they began having children, eight in total, of whom Jerry was the second. The family was constantly on the move, following the work, Jerry and his siblings growing up in migrant farm labor camps. The "Hard Luck" tattoo on Jack's knuckles spoke to his hardscrabble background, but also the expectations he would have for his children. "My heritage was *The Grapes of Wrath*," Jerry Quarry remembered. Jerry estimated attending at least twenty different schools and, at times, no school at all, forced to pick cotton to help his parents instead. Finally the Quarrys settled in Bellflower, California, where Jack found a job working for Goodyear. It was there that he raised his sons to fight.[50]

Jerry first donned boxing gloves at only three years old and first entered the ring when he was five. He won the junior Golden Gloves at eight. He had to stop at thirteen, however, when he contracted nephritis, an often fatal kidney inflammation that left a majority of survivors semi-invalids. Quarry was in the hospital for nine months, then had a further eighteen-month convalescence after returning home. During that recovery he developed acute appendicitis and had to have an appendectomy. It was yet another strain to his system, but it also became his salvation. "It was miraculous, really," said his father. "It must have been that the poison from his appendix was offsetting the medication for his kidneys. When that was removed, the medication started taking effect." His chance of survival had been low, but he made a full recovery by the time that he was sixteen years old. But his ordeal wasn't over. While swimming with his friends, Jerry attempted a backward dive into a swimming pool. He hit the side of the pool and broke his back and one of his hands. When he finally recovered from yet another devastating injury, his father got him a job changing Greyhound bus tires. The foreman of the crew almost let him go because he was so weak, but Quarry's father convinced the foreman to give him another month. "By the time he quit that job, they wanted to make him the foreman," Jack remembered. Jerry's work ethic carried him through, and soon the younger Quarry wanted to begin boxing again. His father was unsure, worried that his injury-prone son would fall victim to another calamity. But Jack was domineering at best, abusive at worst. "Jerry never really bonded with our father, and he was always insecure about that," remembered his brother Mike. "When Jerry was sick with nephritis, he went to school half days, and my father called him a mama's boy. He became a boxer to try to prove himself."[51]

And box he did. By the time Quarry turned eighteen, he had fought more than two hundred amateur bouts, amassing a record of 170-13-54. In 1965 he won the California Golden Gloves, then went onto the national competition, where he won the championship, knocking out all five of his opponents. Jerry had just graduated from high school; further developing his amateur credentials could have secured him a spot on the 1968 Olympic team. But his father wanted him to turn pro, seeing money in his son's left hook and white skin. Rocky Marciano had retired in 1955; Ingemar Johansson had won the heavyweight title in 1959 and lost it in 1960. But throughout the 1960s the champions had been Black, and Jack Quarry saw in his son the next Great White Hope, supremely marketable despite his youth and comparative inexperience. The young fighter signed a contract with a local trainer and began his professional career, winning his first bout in May 1965 in front of fifteen thousand fans at the Los Angeles Coliseum. He fought professionally nineteen times in his first year, with seventeen wins, two draws, and ten knockouts. Soon afterward, however, he lost his first professional bout to Eddie Machen.[52]

Still, the losses were rare. Quarry was a man's man, in the words of Norman Mailer, with a face "which would give a Marine sergeant pause in a bar fight."[53] And soon, in 1968, he found himself fighting Jimmy Ellis for the heavyweight title at the conclusion of the Ali replacement tournament. Though he went the distance against Ellis, he lost the decision. When he complained of back pain, an X-ray revealed that he had fought Ellis with a broken back. He had been roughhousing with his brother Jimmy; after being pushed into a jukebox Jerry fractured his back for the second time. Prior to the fight, his father had him shot up with cortisone to alleviate the pain and ensure the $12,000 payday.[54]

Ellis was trained by Angelo Dundee. In the weeks prior to the Ellis-Quarry fight, a still-suspended Ali came to Dundee's gym while in Miami for a commercial shoot. He wanted to work out, and Dundee convinced him to spar with Ellis as part of his training for Quarry, known as "The Bellflower Bomber" or "Irish" Jerry Quarry. Ali stayed in Miami through the commercial shoot to keep working with Dundee's man, a Louisville fighter and boyhood friend of Ali who had sparred with the champ while he was still eligible. The fight was held in Los Angeles, and reporters inevitably asked about race, as Ellis, a Black fighter, was taking on the white Quarry, but both downplayed any race questions. Race was always part of the media's presentation of Quarry, less because he emphasized it himself and more because he was a white fighter in a division dominated by Black athletes, in a sport with a history of hunger for a Great White Hope.[55]

From there Quarry had an opportunity to fight Joe Frazier. Frazier, however, seemed less concerned about his opponent and more concerned with Ali. "What kind of a man is this who don't want to fight for his country?" he asked. "If he was in Russia, or some place else, they'd put him up against the wall. He walks around like he's one kind of a big hero but he's just a phony, a disgrace." Frazier understood Ali's religious objections, of course, but he wasn't impressed. "What's this Muhammad Ali and that X stuff he talks about? I don't know what he's talking about and I don't think he does either," he said. Frazier wouldn't fight Ali with that name. "If he walks into the ring with me, you can be sure the announcer will call him Cassius Clay, the name he was born with."[56] As Gerald Early described the strained relationship between Ali and Frazier, "the difference between the two men was rather like the difference between the Town Negro and the Country Negro, and the public drama that played out between them as professional athletes was something like a variation of this."[57]

Atlanta was decidedly interested in the Frazier-Quarry fight. WQXI showed a documentary, "Heavyweight, Inc.," about the champion, and Municipal Auditorium held a closed-circuit broadcast of the event on a large screen.[58] A feature on the bout in the *Atlanta Voice* suggested that Frazier could have been "the best heavyweight to come along since

Rocky Marciano. He is the closest thing to perpetual motion in the ring since Henry Armstrong." At the same time, "Frazier has never fought a man with the dynamite Quarry packs. It all depends on who gets there first with the most."[59]

Frazier, as it turned out, got there first with the most. Quarry fought Frazier in June 1969 at Madison Square Garden, remaining game and competitive for the first six rounds. In the seventh the referee stopped the bout because of a deep cut above Quarry's eye. It was a problem the fighter would have throughout his career—an easiness to bleed that would cost him in larger moments.[60]

Three days after Atlanta boxing fans watched Frazier defeat Quarry on closed circuit, they had the opportunity to watch their own live championship fights. Atlanta promoter Murray Silver staged a light heavyweight championship bout between undefeated champion Bob Foster and challenger Levan Roundtree, a Savannah native with a 21–6 record. The undercard featured Bobby Alford, Georgia's Golden Gloves middleweight champion, taking on undefeated challenger Harry White from Warner Robbins. The card was stocked with Georgians; at least seven of the fighters were from Atlanta.[61] The presence of Bob Foster and a legitimate title fight drew many to the arena, but fights at Municipal Auditorium or the local Sports Arena were a semiregular occurrence, Silver creating cards with local boxers to draw customers to his promotions. Atlanta was a boxing town, even though championship bouts like that of Foster and Roundtree were more rare. Foster knocked out Roundtree in the fourth round.[62]

Eddie Murphy, one of the competitors that night, was the director of the Vine City Recreation Center. The center had served Vine City for years but had fallen on hard times until, in 1967, Murphy took over the operation at the request of the Vine City Youth Council. His salary was paid by the Atlanta Recreation Department, the city seeing the center as a value added to an often tumultuous Black area mired in urban poverty. Funding it obviously did not placate a region beset by a variety of other problems, many of them created by white city leadership, but the center's boxing program did give some an opportunity to fight in venues like Municipal Auditorium, a convenient place for promoters in the area to draw undercard talent for boxing shows.[63]

Nationally, meanwhile, many wanted Ali back at the top of the card. The November 1969 issue of *Esquire* featured a defense of Ali and a plea for him to be able to defend his championship. The cover featured a variety of influential people standing in a boxing ring, pointing at the camera. Among them were Truman Capote, Howard Cosell, Michael Harrington, James Earl Jones, Roy Lichtenstein, Sidney Lumet, George Plimpton, Budd Schulberg, and José Torres. Inside the issue, there were even more names: Isaac Asimov, John Barth, Harry Belafonte, Richard Burton, Dick Cavett, Allen Ginsberg, John Houston, Gloria Vanderbilt, Kurt Vonnegut, Jim Morrison, Ali MacGraw, and so many others. In the article that accompanied the petition, Irwin Shaw described the plight of the former champion, arguing that "justice in America, it turns out, is considerably more selective than Selective Service." He pointed out that Ali was barred from fighting even before he was convicted—a clear violation of his right to work. Then there was the denial of his conscientious objection more broadly. Shaw explained the long ordeal from Ali's original classification all the way through his conviction and his continued battles in court. "It is interesting to speculate what the ruling of the draft board would have been if Muhammad Ali had been astute enough to take up residence in Harlem prior to his original classification and had gone before a draft board there rather than in Kentucky."[64] The names were prominent, of course, but white Georgians voting in elections for Lester Maddox were unlikely to be moved by the opinion of Marshall McLuhan and Kurt Vonnegut. Still, to sell the issue in Atlanta, the magazine placed an advertisement in the *Atlanta Constitution*, boldly headlined "Muhammad Ali Deserves the Right to Defend His Title."[65] It was, if not a demonstration of the city's support of Ali, a demonstration of *Esquire*'s belief that there was enough support in a Deep South city for someone presumed by many conservatives to be a draft dodger to profitably run such an advertisement.

That month, more than 250,000 demonstrators gathered in Washington for the largest antiwar demonstration in American history. In December, for the first time, polls showed that a majority of the population disapproved of the conflict in Vietnam. For many, it seemed, Ali had been an early adopter of a position the country was finally coming around to.[66]

Still, the majority of white Georgians continued to support the conflict, and the confidence of *Esquire* to advertise in Atlanta was all the more interesting because of the reaction to Ali just south, in Florida. When promoter Ron Gorton attempted to rent the forty-eight-thousand-seat Tampa Stadium to host a potential February fight between Frazier and Ali, the Tampa City Council, sports authority, and mayor received thousands of telephone calls opposing the bout. Veterans groups announced that they would picket the contract signing. Florida's governor, Claude Kirk—the first Republican governor of the state since Reconstruction and a staunch supporter of Richard Nixon—said that he saw "no reason why an alleged draft-dodger should be in a position to lay claim to any title." The pressure was such that the city's sports authority voted unanimously to deny the request.[67]

Kirk wasn't the only governor opposed to a potential Ali fight. When the Tampa controversy erupted, reporters inevitably questioned Lester Maddox about the possibility of the former champ boxing in nearby Georgia. There had been rumors that Atlanta attorney John Kirby and advertising executive Ed Hughes had been working to bring an Ali-Frazier bout to the city. "I don't think we have any place here for such an engagement," said Maddox, "or person." Maddox claimed that were the former champion to serve both his military obligation and his prison sentence, then after those combined years of service he would be welcome to fight in Georgia. Until then, "I say phooey!" Ali "has become a damaging reflection on boxing. And I feel his fighting here would be harmful to the community and all its people."[68]

It was a common refrain for many white conservative Georgians. Syndicated boxing columnist Jimmy Cannon argued in early 1970 that "the athlete of the decade has to be Cassius Clay, who is now Muhammad Ali." He embodied the 1960s. "It is as though he were created to represent them. In him is the trouble and the wildness and the hysterical gladness and the nonsense and the rebellion and the conflicts of race and the yearning for bizarre religions and the cult of the put-on and the changed values that altered the world and the feeling about Vietnam in the generation that ridicules what their parents cherish." It was easy to imagine white citizens across Georgia turning to the sports page of their local newspaper and nodding along to Cannon's screed.[69]

During the controversy surrounding potential locations for a would-be Ali fight, and while the boxer was obviously not boxing, he still managed to be knocked out. Needing an infusion of funds to continue his various legal battles, Ali agreed to film sparring sessions with forty-five-year-old Rocky Marciano and allow a computer program to determine a winner in a mythical fight between the champions of two different generations. Advertising executive Murray Woroner paid $10,000 to each fighter, along with a percentage of the movie's profits, to film seventy-five one-minute rounds, the heavy workload required to get all the angles the simulation would need. Both the twenty-seven-year-old Ali and the older undefeated champion acted out various scenarios, neither knowing the outcome that the computer would determine. The computer was supposedly fed more than 120 variables and more than four million facts about the fighters.[70]

While an Ali-Frazier fight was a kind of unattained dream for boxing fans, so too were such generational contests like Ali-Marciano, and computer simulations were a way to bring those fights to life. Only adding to the drama was the fact that Marciano had been a vocal critic of Ali's conduct. "It's a bad situation now because there's a lack of respect for the present champion, and that creates a lack of respect for all past champions," he said early in 1969. "Nobody questions my fights, they were all tough ones, but people just don't treat you the same way since he came along." Marciano would not live to see the result of his fight with Ali. He died in a plane crash in August, but he would get one more victory. Against a blue backdrop and among the cheers of an unseen, artificial audience, the fighters traded blows for twelve rounds until Marciano knocked out Ali in the thirteenth. The simulated bout debuted at Broadway's Cinerama Theater before moving around the country, giving fans a chance to see the two former champions fight at least one more time.[71]

Ali naturally hated the outcome and slammed the film as ridiculous, which prompted its backers to file a slander suit against him. But it was Ali, the *Los Angeles Sentinel* claimed, who "should sue the promoter and the computer for even dreaming that Marciano could have beaten him!"[72] What many didn't realize is that political considerations far more than data mining proved determinative of the fight's outcome. As the white *Philadelphia Inquirer* intoned, "The Computer knows who's who in the equation. Take you, a loud-mouth black racist who brags

'I'm the Greatest! I'm the King!' You won't submit to White America's old image of black fighters, you won't even submit to white America's Army." The American people, the paper said, referring to the white American people, "want your ass whipped in public, knocked down, ripped, stomped, clubbed, pulverized and not just by anybody, but by a real great white hope, and none's around. That's where the computer comes in." And so Marciano knocked out Ali in the version shown to American audiences, largely because Ali had spent the past three years being vilified in the United States. But Ali was still popular in Europe and the rest of the world, and the version of the superfight those audiences saw featured Ali winning the bout.[73]

Woroner was undaunted by Ali's criticism of the fictional fight's outcome and developed several plans to get Ali back in an actual ring. One was for a fight in a small five-hundred-seat arena in Miami; another involved an empty arena match wherein only the fighters, corners, doctors, and officials would know where the fight was to take place. Then the film of the fight would be distributed throughout the country. There was also a plan in place to host an Ali fight in the small, all-Black town of Boley, Oklahoma, a community originally founded by freed slaves, but the only venue available was an outdoor rodeo arena without professional-grade facilities.[74]

In June, as the location search continued, ABC News aired a documentary titled "It Can Be Done," a feature on Atlanta's racial progress and the distance it still had to go to make full equality a reality. Johnson was interviewed for the broadcast as part of a roundtable with other Black city leaders like Lonnie King, Julian Bond, and William Holmes Borders. Mayor Ivan Allen was featured, as was police chief Herbert Jenkins. Calvin Craig, former Grand Dragon of the Ku Klux Klan, explained why he quit the racist group to join the Model Cities program. The documentary only bolstered Atlanta's reputation as a racially moderate version of Southern metropolitanism.[75]

But those who lived in the city knew better. The film showed no homes that represented Black wealth, emphasizing instead Black residents of Atlanta who lived in poverty. At the other end of that spectrum, the documentary showed no examples of white poverty. There was no representation of police brutality—Jenkins and his force were only shown helping the poor. The *Atlanta Voice*'s George M. Coleman countered the documentary by arguing that "the disgrace of 'Inner City U.S.A.' has invaded downtown Atlanta." He argued that white-owned businesses had begun to let their facilities go to seed now that the majority of customers in downtown Atlanta were Black. The restrooms in department stores were no longer clean. Neither were grocery stores. "Garbage pickups are less than when an overflow of whites were walking the streets." Coleman interpreted the declension as a result of the fact that "the general thinking is that now that blacks are shopping it is not necessary to keep things as pleasant as when it was part of the old pattern." That lack of concern by white owners who now served a largely Black clientele was then blamed on the customers themselves. "To those who say the black man is not clean, we say: Look to your traditional hill billers, the poor class of whites in town, if you want to see filth."[76]

The disconnect between the city's reputation and its reality gave so many in the Black population a greater stake in the outcome of constitutional revisions that year. When the legislature began debating a new state constitution, Johnson advocated for an equal housing provision in the document's bill of rights. He admitted that federal law protected equal opportunity in housing after the passage of the 1968 Civil Rights Act, but cited "the problems of interpreting federal laws, especially in smaller counties and cities." It only made sense, then, that such protections be present in Georgia law. "The chances are the committee may defeat it, or the people reject it, but it's my duty to try." The committee did defeat it, but the provision demonstrated Johnson's efforts—even quixotic ones—to use his position to advocate for the Black working class, despite the charges often leveled against him as being an accommodationist member of the elite only out for his own best interest.[77]

In September 1969 Johnson turned his attention to police brutality, prompted by the brutal beating of two Black suspects by five white officers. Johnson and onetime rival Horace Tate called for, at least, suspensions of the officers. The case became a scandal in Atlanta largely because the witness to the beating was a Black officer, DeWitt Smith. His allegations ultimately led to civil rights groups meeting with Ivan Allen to demand the firing of Atlanta chief of police Herbert Jenkins and, when Allen demurred, filing a federal lawsuit seeking Jenkins's ouster. While Jenkins survived the scandal, Smith was expelled from the Fraternal Order of Police for exposing the abuse of his fellow officers. In response

Black police officers in the city created the Afro-American Patrol League as a counter to the white-dominated traditional police union. Johnson responded by introducing legislation that proposed a Citizens Police Review Board to investigate the practice in Atlanta. "The basis of police brutality is racism," he told reporters, "and it cannot be stamped out by investigations conducted by the police department itself."[78]

It wasn't the first time Johnson had tried to establish civilian review of the police department. In 1965 Johnson met with Jenkins and asked for some measure of civilian review. Jenkins responded with an informal process that he called civilian review, but in which no civilians actually heard complaints. Even that nascent attempt only lasted two months. At the beginning of 1969 the Metropolitan Atlanta Summit Leadership Conference (MASLC), a local civil rights group, held a press conference naming the glut of brutality incidents that had occurred in 1968. "Repressiveness and improper procedures appear to be on the rise in Metropolitan Atlanta," the conference argued, warning of an escalation that ultimately came to a head in September. Johnson's Citizens Police Review Board legislation wouldn't pass, and police brutality continued to be a problem, with calls for civilian review remaining loud through the early 1970s after controversial killings in that decade by several Atlanta officers.[79]

That said, Johnson could also stir controversy within the Black community. In October aldermanic candidate Lynn Westergaard turned down the endorsement of MASLC after its leader, Reverend Joseph E. Boone, asked for $500 in return for the endorsement, supposedly to defray the cost of printing flyers. Johnson was among the leadership of the Atlanta Summit Leadership Conference (ASLC), a rival city organization, and criticized Boone for what seemed like a pay-for-play endorsement scheme. "Rev. Boone and his group put themselves in this position," he said. "They have made their own bed, now let them lie in it." Johnson was not alone. Alderman Q. V. Williamson, Reverend Samuel Williams, and insurance executive Jesse Hill of Atlanta Life Insurance Company all presented Black critiques of the MASLC, and Boone pushed back against them all. Johnson and his allies were "pseudo-black leaders" propagating a "vicious lie." They were tools of "the white establishment" and "were selected by the whites" to tear down their own, probably, he surmised, by friends of mayoral candidate Sam Massell.[80] Johnson's record gave lie to such charges, but the internecine fighting, particularly in relation to the city's board of aldermen, which would be crucial in allowing Johnson to pursue the Ali fight, demonstrated that metropolitan politics was not a simple matter of white and Black. And Johnson's willingness to advocate for a level playing field in aldermanic elections and his clear association with Sam Massell, even though Boone's charges were unsubstantiated, would pay dividends with the board and with Massell the following year.

The battle also underscored the complicated role that race played in the city. Nationally syndicated columnist Joseph Kraft noted that Atlanta's Black population had risen from 38 to 47 percent of the total in the previous decade, a population with a solid middle-class core, wherein "a large and disciplined Negro population has tended to cooperate with upper-income whites to elect racial moderates over the extremists supported by the low-income whites, or rednecks." Such coalitions allowed for the rise of Johnson in the state senate and Julian Bond in the state house. Kraft speculated that the sustained growth of the city's Black population could continue pushing the Democratic party to the left, leaving it "to become the black party while the Republicans move right to become the white party." It was a prescient prediction, but his belief that the example of Atlanta "shows that urban growth does not necessarily have to yield racial tension" was far more naive. Racial tension was undeniably present in the city, despite its seemingly moderate politics. "The race thing bores people here," said one political operative, surely only referring to the white population. "They're interested in money."[81] It might have been more accurate to say that white willful boredom with "the race thing" was calculated to facilitate its interest in money. If there was a possibility of demonstrating low-stakes racial progressivism in aid of profit, the white population voting for white liberal mayoral candidates was sure to be open to it.

At the same time, there were real divisions in Atlanta's Black population. Maynard Jackson's upstart candidacy for the city's vice mayoralty was popular among many. The *Atlanta Voice*'s George Coleman saw Jackson as "way ahead of his time" and even questioned why he wasn't running for the city's top office. Jackson was "one of the finest young men active in politics today."[82] But his candidacy simultaneously left Black power brokers angry that once again they had not been consulted. Jackson's resulting campaign portrayed him as an outsider attempting to buck the influence of those who claimed to make candidate decisions for Black voters. In particular he challenged the Atlanta Negro Voters League, which had once been run by Jackson's grandfather, John Wesley Dobbs. By 1969 the ANVL was composed of a new group of Black leaders, Leroy Johnson among them. Joining him was the Butler Street YMCA's Warren Cochrane, the NAACP's Lonnie King, construction mogul Herman Russell, Reverend William Holmes Borders, and Johnson allies Q. V. Williamson and Jesse Hill. The group, which met regularly at Paschal's restaurant and nicknamed itself the "Black Young Men on the Go," had decided that if anyone was going to make a mayoral or vice mayoral run, it should be the Southern Regional Commission's Vernon Jordan or Leroy Johnson. And certainly not Maynard Jackson.[83]

But Jackson would win anyway. The group had more success with the mayor's race, endorsing eventual winner Sam Massell. Massell, though, was not simply a white liberal candidate: he was a white liberal Jewish candidate. As the election drew near, he charged that a group of white business leaders and current mayor Ivan Allen had attacked his integrity and that their motives were antisemitic at base. In response Johnson joined a group of the city's Black leaders, including Martin Luther King, Sr., Andrew Young, and Benjamin Mays, at a press conference at City Hall to reaffirm the "honor and integrity" of Massell and their unshakable endorsement of his candidacy.[84]

Massell would win that election, but just as important were four victories by Black candidates in aldermanic races, bringing the total Black representation on the board to five of the nineteen members. One of them, Marvin Arrington, was a former aide to Johnson.[85] It was a strong Black voting bloc in an important body, which along with the mayor-elect had a close association with Johnson. At a meeting of Black elected officials throughout the state after the election, former candidates expressed the racial realities they faced that gave lie to Kraft's colorblind optimism. It was indeed a large, disciplined voting bloc with a strong middle-class base, but it was also a population beset by artificially imposed poverty, largely segregated from whites through restrictive neighborhood segregation, and still struggling for higher wages in mostly menial jobs. Johnson spoke at the forum and stressed that it was time to take advantage of legislative victories, to leverage representation for actual policy change. "Black people can no longer be planned for," he told the crowd. "They must be planned with."[86]

With the elections out of the way, Johnson's planning turned to Atlanta's housing crisis, an issue he had worked on for much of the year. The new fight centered around Bolton Gardens, an apartment complex in a working-class Black neighborhood. The Atlanta Housing Code Enforcement office had found thirty-eight code violations at the complex in October. Though the building was only six years old, ceiling plaster was falling; there were broken windows, water leaks, and malfunctioning heaters. There was a rat infestation.[87] Despite the violations and management's hesitation to make the necessary repairs, the owner planned to raise rents. After reporting their concerns to Legal Aid, many of the residents planned to pool their rent money and pay it not to the property manager but instead to the Bolton Gardens Tenant Association to begin making the repairs themselves. The property owners threatened to evict them. For all the talk of Black legislative representation and middle-class wealth in Atlanta, the "rent strike" became a symbol of the real problems that existed in the city when race intersected with class. The local NAACP voiced its full support for the rent strikers, as did Johnson and incoming vice mayor Jackson. In November Johnson joined residents at a downtown picket in front of the office of the building's owner. He hand delivered a letter to the owner, claiming to have a "vested interest" in the tenants' "aspirations, their hopes and their desire to live as other human beings live, in the absence of rats and roaches, water flooding their apartments, unsanitary garbage conditions, and no place for their children to play." Acting on behalf of his Atlanta Summit Leadership Conference, he requested negotiations to bring the dispute to a conclusion.[88]

The rent strike was by no means a novel concept, used often by the working poor to gain some measure of leverage in the relationship between landlord and lessee. It wasn't even the first such event in Atlanta. In February 1966 SNCC initiated a rent strike in the Markham Street area, picketing against the city's seeming unwillingness to enforce housing codes. In response Johnson introduced a slum clearance bill in the state senate, but the effort died in committee and there was little functional change in tenants' housing conditions. Among the reasons for that lack of success was Black power brokers' disapproval of the strike tactics; the dominant Black colleges in the city, like Morehouse and Atlanta University, emphasized a respectability politics that endorsed the professional values of those power brokers. And by late 1969, when the Bolton Gardens effort was underway, SNCC had largely lost its influence in Atlanta.[89]

Ultimately, and perhaps inevitably, the dispute ended in the courts. In late November a judge issued an injunction against the proposed rent increase. While that was something of a victory, fifty-eight tenants were sent eviction notices. Legal Aid returned to court to defend them, but a judge ruled in January 1970 that the evictions were permissible. Appeals in federal district court protected most of the residents from actual eviction, but the crisis highlighted the racial inequities hiding under the surface of Atlanta's progressive image. Johnson responded with rent control legislation for impoverished areas, but it would see little legislative progress.[90]

The white supremacy at the heart of such individual housing inequities was, in the minds of many, writ large in the simultaneous Abolish Atlanta movement, a plan to consolidate Atlanta and Fulton County. It wasn't white leaders' first attempt to create a whiter Atlanta. Earlier in the decade a proposed plan to annex predominantly white Sandy Springs, north of Atlanta, would have given white voters a significant majority in the blackening city. Johnson fought the proposal by adding an amendment that would include the annexation of predominantly Black Boulder Park. As both areas had to approve the plan, Sandy Springs residents decided overwhelmingly to reject the proposal now that the plan wouldn't generate the intended white majority.[91]

With the new plan in 1969, Johnson again took the lead in condemning the action as a method of limiting Black political power by folding in suburban whites to the Atlanta voter base. The Abolish Atlanta bill would be more comprehensive than previous schemes and would not require a local referendum to pass. It was, for Johnson, "a shoddy and vicious attempt to suffocate minorities and poor citizens in Atlanta and must be denounced and rejected by every decent public official and private citizen for what it really is." He explained that the plan demonstrated no real financial advantage to the city and could only be a racial move. Though Atlanta had five Black aldermen and a Black vice mayor, who chaired the board of aldermen, the new plan would leave only four of ten proposed districts with Black majorities, and only two with meaningful majorities, potentially limiting Black voting power on the board. Johnson was not alone in denouncing the plan, as the bulk of Black city leaders opposed it. Charles Black, spokesman for Young Men on the Go, described consolidation as "racially and class-inspired," and it certainly was.[92] But Johnson's voice would be far louder than that of Black and others, as for many he was "the most politically powerful Negro figure in the state."[93] His leadership against the prospect helped defeat it in the state senate. He was, according to *Constitution* political editor Bill Shipp, "the man to thank—or blame—for the measure's apparent downfall," as Johnson brokered a backroom deal with some of his white opponents in exchange for Highway Department funding.[94]

Stephen Lesher, in his *New York Times* profile of Johnson, interpreted the politician's effort to defeat the Abolish Atlanta bill as "perhaps his most important achievement for the maintenance of black political power in Atlanta." When the original senate effort appeared as if it had four votes more than it needed to pass, Johnson began the process of whipping votes against it, calling in favors and trading favors of his own to swing the vote against Abolish Atlanta. He called Black officials to find out which legislators needed Black support in their home districts to win reelection, then set those officials to work bombarding their senators with telephone calls and telegrams, sent from individuals and groups throughout the state. When the senate held its vote, Johnson had managed to swing five senators and stop Abolish Atlanta. That kind of power, that kind of effort, defined the political life of one of Georgia's most influential voices: one who would use his influence to help the Black population whenever he could, to help himself when it was convenient, and ultimately to help Muhammad Ali and Atlanta.[95]

That kind of political calculation could also be seen in Johnson's effort to overhaul the city's personnel board by increasing the three-member body to five members. He first submitted a bill to the legislature, but after significant blowback charging him and the mayor of a political patronage scheme, he submitted a measure directly to the board of aldermen in the hopes of creating a powerful endorsement to provide momentum for the legislative bill. Much of Black Atlanta saw the "patronage scheme" charges as "racist propaganda among members of the Fulton County delegation" in the state senate. They supported Johnson's effort, as it would provide more Black representation on the board. The *Atlanta Daily World* called out white senator Armstrong Smith in particular, urging him to "check the population shift in his senatorial district since 1968," as "Black citizens resent his unwarranted attack on Senator Johnson." It was the new normal for many white Atlanta politicians caught in the swell of white flight. Members of the board of aldermen understood the new demographic reality in front of them, and they supported the law and endorsed it in front of the general assembly. Though the plan failed, the effort only bolstered the connection between Johnson and the aldermen.[96]

Meanwhile Ali was also branching out, seemingly moving farther away from the boxing ring that had originally made his name. In late 1969 he agreed to appear in the theatrical production *Buck White*, a musical adaptation by Oscar Brown, Jr., of Joseph Dolan Tuotti's play *Big Time Buck White*. The comedy told the story of a Black Power organization in the throes of radical organizing. The musical, like the play, begins comically, as five members of the group argue with one another, but then their leader arrives and moves the musical to a more serious register. Brown cast Ali as Dick Williams, the chief organizer of the group, understanding that Ali had the credentials to give the more serious advocacy section of the performance a legitimacy not available to traditional actors. The musical opened at New York's George Abbott Theater in December and enjoyed moderate success in its run off and on Broadway. Most surprising to audiences and critics was Ali's ability to sing. "We came in chains, we didn't volunteer," went one of his solos.

> And yet, today, the fact remains
> We're still held captive here
> Now we say, cut us loose
> Though that may go against your grain
> Still, there is no excuse
> We came in chains, and now your choice must be
> To either blow out all our brains
> Or else just set us free.[97]

The musical showcased Ali's wide-ranging talent, but it also allowed him to present a message he had been giving for years in a new format and to a new audience. It was a message to which many Black residents of Atlanta could relate.

FIG. 1. The location of Ali's September 1970 exhibition bout on the campus of Morehouse University. The building is now known as Samuel H. Archer Hall. Photo taken by the author.

FIG. 2. Atlanta's Municipal Auditorium, location of the Ali-Quarry bout. The venue was later purchased by Georgia State University and is now known as Dahlberg Hall. Photo taken by the author.

VOTE

The Straight Democratic Ticket

Return Lyndon Johnson TO The White House

Return Leroy Johnson TO The Senate

Johnson & Johnson

Responsible Leadership

The Johnson Record

Senator Leroy Johnson has represented with distinction the people of the 38th District, Fulton County and the State of Georgia during the last two years in the Georgia Senate. He has:

SERVED: The people of the 38th District and his state as a member of the following standing Legislative Committees:

1. Appropriation Committee
2. Health and Welfare Committee
3. Judiciary Committee
4. Educational Matters Committee

SERVED: The people of the 38th District and his state as a member of the following Temporary Legislative Committees:

1. Rapid Transit Committee
2. Small Loan Study Committee
3. State-wide Teacher Tenure Committee

INTRODUCED: The following legislation for the benefit of the people in the 38th District, Fulton County and the State of Georgia:

1. A Public Accommodations Bill (Before the National Civil Rights Bill passed)
2. A minimum wage law of $1.00 per hour for all workers in the State of Georgia.
3. A State-wide Teacher Tenure Law to protect the jobs of all teachers in Georgia.
4. A slum clearing bill, requiring property to be brought up to standards.

PASSED: The following legislation for the benefit of the people of the 38th District, Fulton County and the State of Georgia:

1. An Anti-Poll Tax Resolution through the State Senate.
2. A bill requiring an election to be held to fill vacancies on the Board of Aldermen for the city of Atlanta.
3. A revenue measure which would provide some $40,000 to the County Treasurer to increase services with no increase of taxes.
4. An Anti-Dispossessory Bill to prevent furniture from being placed on streets and sidewalks (passed the Senate 43-0; passed the House of Representatives 166-2, opposed by the Attorney General and not signed by the Governor).
5. A bill making it easier for persons without schooling to register and vote.

LED: Senator Johnson led the struggle for improvement for all citizens.

1. The fight to desegregate the State Capitol.
2. The fight to desegregate the Drivers License Bureau.
3. The fight for the passage of the mixed drinks referendum.
4. The fight for greater pension benefits for firemen, policemen, and teachers in Fulton County.

APPOINTED: Senator Johnson appointed for the first time in Georgia's history 80 Negro boys and girls to serve as pages in the State Capitol.

VOTED: Senator Johnson voted for progressive legislation in Housing, Education, Health and Welfare for the benefit of all citizens.

DEFEATED: The following legislation for the benefit of the people of the 38th District, Fulton County and the State of Georgia:

1. Four attempts to make Public Accommodation Laws illegal in the new State Constitution.
2. Attempts to pass an anti-picketing bill designed to prevent demonstrations in Georgia.
3. Prevented three attempts to write into the new proposed Constitution a provision requiring segregation in education.

SERVED: As a member of the State Democratic Executive Committee and on the National Community Service Committee to implement the Civil Rights Bill. Appointed by President Lyndon Johnson to serve as special Ambassador to represent the United States at the Independence Celebration in Zanzibar, Africa.

VOTE NOV. 3rd

PULL the Democratic Lever

FIG. 3. A campaign flier for Leroy Johnson's first reelection campaign for Georgia State Senate in 1964. Photo courtesy of the Atlanta University Center Robert W. Woodruff Library.

FIG. 4. Promotional poster used by Atlanta's Voter Education Project, taking advantage of Muhammad Ali's presence in the city. Photo courtesy of the Atlanta University Center Robert W. Woodruff Library.

only LEROY JOHNSON

. . . AFTER TEN YEARS OF GETTING THINGS DONE IN THE GEORGIA SENATE . . .

. . . AND WITH HIS TRACK RECORD OF STATESMANSHIP AND EXPERIENCE . . .

OFFERS THE KIND OF MATURE LEADERSHIP NEEDED FOR A UNITED AND PROGRESSIVE ATLANTA.

REGISTER NOW AND VOTE ON OCTOBER 2ND FOR LEROY JOHNSON FOR MAYOR

"Those issues which dominated the mayoral campaign four years ago are unfortunately the *same* issues that are still with us today. No unified, strong direction or tangible progress has yet been made in the areas of Atlanta's human needs, crime and drugs, or social services. I don't believe in making a lot of campaign promises, but one thing I *do* pledge: to unite the tremendous talents from Atlanta's many and diverse communities into a collective force which can and *will* direct Atlanta to its potential of greatness . . ."

Leroy Johnson
THE ONE FOR ALL

FIG. 5. (ABOVE) Ali being presented with a plaque by Hugh Gloster, president of Morehouse University. Photo courtesy of the Atlanta University Center Robert W. Woodruff Library.

FIG. 6. Campaign flier for Leroy Johnson's mayoral campaign in 1972—an election he would lose, marking the downfall of his political career. Photo courtesy of the Atlanta University Center Robert W. Woodruff Library.

FIG. 7. A cartoon in the *Atlanta Voice* portraying Leroy Johnson as a "political oreo pimp" and a stooge for white politicians. Cartoon courtesy of the *Atlanta Voice*.

FIG. 8. An *Atlanta Journal-Constitution* cartoon by Baldy depicting Johnson's original state senate victory in 1962, using the imagery of the boxing ring to celebrate the politician's ascendency. Photo courtesy of the Richard B. Russell Library for Political Research and Studies, University of Georgia Libraries.

FIG. 9. An *Atlanta Journal-Constitution* cartoon by Baldy depicting Johnson's first year in the legislature, charting a course between the political antics of his white colleagues. Photo courtesy of the Richard B. Russell Library for Political Research and Studies, University of Georgia Libraries.

FIG. 10. An *Atlanta Journal-Constitution* cartoon by Baldy depicting Johnson and Hugh M. Gillis dancing "the old soft shoe" through state senatorial politics. Photo courtesy of the Richard B. Russell Library for Political Research and Studies, University of Georgia Libraries.

FIG. 11. An *Atlanta Journal-Constitution* cartoon by Baldy depicting Johnson and Roy Wilkins in 1964 being walked over by civil rights protesters doing damage to Black politicians attempting more permanent strategies at racial uplift. Photo courtesy of the Richard B. Russell Library for Political Research and Studies, University of Georgia Libraries.

FIG. 12. An *Atlanta Journal-Constitution* cartoon by Baldy depicting Johnson reading a newspaper while his mayoral opponent, Maynard Jackson, lies unconscious. Photo courtesy of the Richard B. Russell Library for Political Research and Studies, University of Georgia Libraries.

FIG. 13. The interior of the Hyatt Regency at its opening in 1967. Photo courtesy of the Kenan Research Center at the Atlanta History Center.

FIG. 14. (ABOVE) Leroy Johnson announcing Ali's return bout in Atlanta with the fighter and Hank Aaron. Photo courtesy of Special Collections and Archives, Georgia State University Library.

FIG. 15. Johnson and Ali at the fighter's introductory Atlanta press conference. Photo courtesy of Special Collections and Archives, Georgia State University Library.

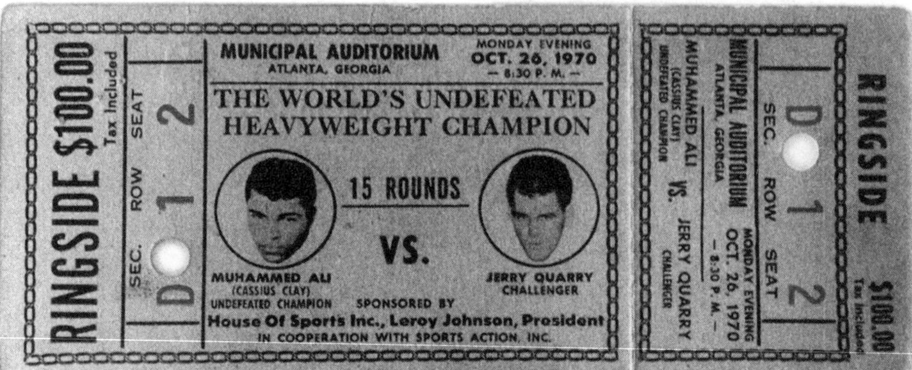

FIG. 16. (ABOVE) Ticket stub for the Ali-Quarry fight. Photo courtesy of Special Collections and Archives, Georgia State University Library.

FIG. 17. Leroy Johnson smoking one of his famous cigars. Photo courtesy of Special Collections and Archives, Georgia State University Library.

FIG. 18. Jerry Quarry training in Atlanta for his bout with Ali. Photo courtesy of Special Collections and Archives, Georgia State University Library.

FIG. 19. Jerry Quarry sparring with a partner at Atlanta's Sports Arena. Photo courtesy of Special Collections and Archives, Georgia State University Library.

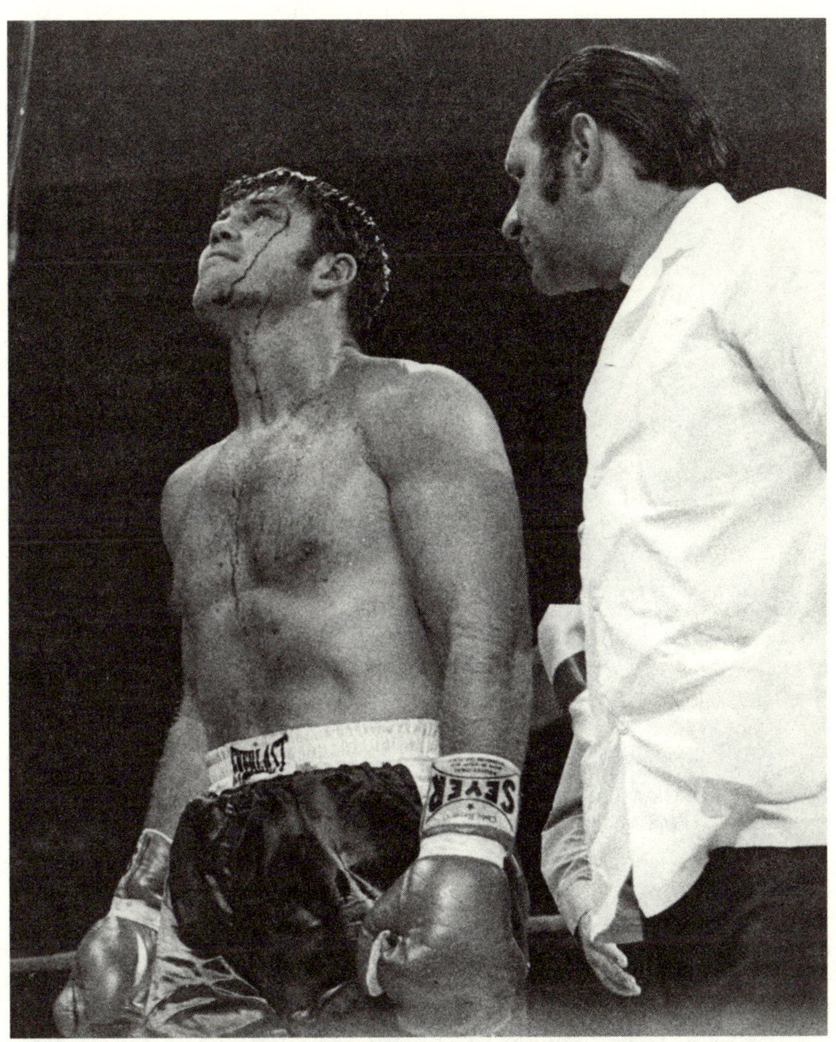

FIG. 20. A bloody and defeated Jerry Quarry standing in the ring after his loss to Ali. Photo courtesy of Special Collections and Archives, Georgia State University Library.

FIG. 21. Lester Maddox fielding questions from reporters outside of the Georgia State Capitol. Photo courtesy of the Kenan Research Center at the Atlanta History Center.

FIG. 22. Activist Hosea Williams, a regular combatant of Leroy Johnson, speaking to a crowd in front of Atlanta's public school administration building. Photo courtesy of the Kenan Research Center at the Atlanta History Center.

FIG. 23. Supporters of the sanitation workers strike marching on Martin Luther King Jr. Drive in downtown Atlanta in March 1970. Photo courtesy of Special Collections and Archives, Georgia State University Library.

FIG. 24. Jesse Hill, civil rights activist, insurance executive, and collaborator of Leroy Johnson in bringing Ali's return fight to Atlanta. Photo courtesy of Special Collections and Archives, Georgia State University Library.

FIG. 25. Mayor Sam Massell, pointing, second from right, looking at a model of an improved downtown Atlanta. Photo courtesy of Special Collections and Archives, Georgia State University Library.

FIG. 26. Lester Maddox and his wife, Hattie Virginia Cox, standing outside of his restaurant, The Pickrick, defying a court desegregation order in 1964. Photo courtesy of Special Collections and Archives, Georgia State University Library.

FIG. 27. Muhammad Ali drew this picture the day of his fight with Quarry. It features the referee stopping the fight as Georgia governor Lester Maddox runs in from the top right, pickax in hand, demanding that the fight be stopped. Image courtesy of the Muhammad Ali Center, Louisville KY. Original work donated to the Muhammad Ali Center by the LeRoy Neiman and Janet Byrne Neiman Foundation.

FIG. 28. The day of Ali's fight with Quarry, Ali held a drawing contest between his father and artist LeRoy Neiman. His father, Cassius Clay, Sr., drew a landscape based on the backyard at Leroy Johnson's lake house, where the camp was staying. Ali declared Neiman the winner, and Clay stormed out in disgust, but Neiman saved the drawing. Image courtesy of the Muhammad Ali Center, Louisville KY. Original work donated to the Muhammad Ali Center by the LeRoy Neiman and Janet Byrne Neiman Foundation.

FIG. 29. (ABOVE) The cover of the program sold at the Ali-Quarry fight, October 26, 1970. Image in the public domain.

FIG. 30. (OPPOSITE TOP) Ali hits Quarry with a hard right hand at Atlanta's Municipal Auditorium as fans and reporters look on. Photo courtesy of the Associated Press.

FIG. 31. Ali and Quarry sign the contract for their Atlanta fight, with Leroy Johnson sitting between them. Photo courtesy of the Associated Press.

WJR
BAN
abc
WINS

FIG. 32. Muhammad Ali arrives to appeal his draft classification on March 17, 1966, which would ultimately lead to his refusal of draft induction. He stops briefly to greet a friend and play to reporters and a supportive crowd. Behind him, in a dark coat and hat, is his attorney, Edward Jocko, of New York. Photo courtesy of the Associated Press.

4. THE POLITICS OF RACE (AND BOXING)

JANUARY TO JULY, 1970

As 1970 began, Massell and Jackson were sworn in as Atlanta's executives, and five Black aldermen sat on a council that had never before seen such representation. Massell appointed two of the newcomers, Ira Jackson and Joel Stokes, to chairmanships of the vital Building and Finance Committees, respectively. Veteran alderman Q. V. Williamson was appointed to head the Police Committee, a particularly important gesture, if only as a symbol, in the wake of the police brutality scandals that plagued 1969.[1]

Blocks away at the statehouse, Leroy Johnson attempted to attach a rider to an education bill requiring the teaching of Black history in all public high schools in Georgia. But the problems with Georgia public education were roiling on other fronts besides Johnson's ill-fated effort to get Black history into the curriculum. A federal court order mandated that Atlanta's city schools develop a plan for teacher transfers to achieve a measure of racial balance in the public school system, and white locals were incensed. The plan was supposed to be submitted Monday, January 12. On Friday, January 9, thousands of white students stayed out of school, and roughly three thousand of them marched to the state capitol in protest. Some held a sit-in in the capitol building; others gathered at the old Atlanta post office. Lester Maddox held a press conference praising the students and urging a further boycott of public schools until the court order was rescinded. The order was a "criminal action by the government against American children and their teachers and parents," so Maddox was "asking that black and white teachers quit teaching until constitutional freedom of choice has been restored." He praised the student protesters and promised, "I will support your march anywhere and anytime." The students met with Maddox, Massell, and U.S. District Court judge Frank Hooper, who had been in charge of supervising Atlanta's school desegregation for twelve years, before going home and vowing to continue the protests the following week.[2]

Of course, the court order wasn't simply caprice. Teaching and administrative units at Atlanta's public schools were still starkly segregated. Maddox's encouragement of the protests was criticized by many white public officials, most of whom were not fans of the teacher transfer order but feared the implications of siding with a protest clearly racialized in its intent. The NAACP was more genuine, denouncing Maddox and supporting the order. John Lewis watched the protesters up close inside the capitol, arguing, "If this was a civil rights march or a peace demonstration, it wouldn't be allowed." He was right, and a portion of the protesters and all of Maddox's allies opposed teacher transfer for decidedly racist reasons. But the issue was not as simple as that. Many of the students repeated, "We don't want to lose our teachers," which was a perfectly reasonable lament. Among those supporting the protest was James Bentley, state comptroller and Republican gubernatorial candidate. "I have seen hundreds upon hundreds of clean, decent young people parade around the Capitol grounds in almost zero [degree] weather, literally begging to preserve their schools and continue their education uninterrupted. It was not a parade of demagogues nor was it a series of hippies, militants or radicals," he said. Bentley supported the "parade of desperate and hurt young people." It was the first protest during his time in government that "I have wanted to join."[3]

For many Black Atlantans, Bentley's statement was a revisionist insult. They expected racist rhetoric from Maddox and his allies. But Bentley had been seen as reasonable and fair-minded. Now he was using barely coded rhetoric to describe "clean, decent young people," the white protesters, who were far superior to "hippies, militants or radicals." In a state that had experienced so many meaningful protests for racial justice, this was the only one he had considered joining. Johnson, like everyone else in Black city leadership, supported the teacher transfer order and saw Bentley's duplicity as the most galling part of the January protest. "Where is the Jimmy Bentley of yesteryears?" Johnson asked. "The Jimmy

Bentley who met with us, who sought our counsel, and who committed himself to help black people in this state?" He wondered, in a seeming threat to the gubernatorial candidate, "if you are part of that political philosophy which believes that you can win a political office in the south without the black vote. If so, you are destined for a sad awakening." Johnson, like most of Black Atlanta, saw faculty desegregation as a necessary step to fix inequality in the schools. "The governor has acted irresponsibly in this area and has offered no leadership at all," and he couldn't be shamed by public statements because he had built his career on race-baiting politics. But Bentley, Johnson reasoned, was someone who might feel that pressure.[4]

Bentley, for his part, was opposed to mandating ratios of Black and white teachers that would send instructors on "random and arbitrary assignment anywhere within the system." One of the most prominent Black voices agreeing with him was that of the *Atlanta Daily World*. The paper argued that while there needed to be some percentage plan to create an integrated system, white parents preferred white teachers for their children and Black parents preferred Black teachers. The *World* suggested that the ratio system, in which 53 percent of teachers were Black and 47 percent were white, be maintained, "but let the superintendent and the Board of Education say which teacher should be placed at a given school." It would give teachers more say in where they would teach and allow the system to allocate new hires to unequal schools to create racial balance. Bentley's criticism was fair, the paper reasoned, and Johnson's criticism was a political ploy. Bentley "had the support of the great majority of our people" when he last sought election, the *World* claimed, and he "is the same man now that he was when he ran for office."[5] Such was common practice for the *World*. The paper's leader, C. A. Scott, was a staunch Republican, a Nixon supporter who led his paper to broadly oppose the sit-ins early in the decade. Scott was usually in line with the old guard of Atlanta's Black leadership, but there was a new guard in place, and his editorial policy on teacher desegregation was out of step with Black opinion. His conservatism resulted in the *World* being overtaken in popularity by two competitors, the *Atlanta Inquirer* and the *Atlanta Voice*, both of which adamantly supported teacher desegregation.[6]

More pragmatically, supporting Bentley against Johnson seemed like a tactical error. The comptroller general had been a Democrat before switching parties after the 1968 Democratic National Convention, after the protests in Chicago, after the Civil Rights Act and Voting Rights Act had been authored by a Democratic president, after his state had voted for George Wallace in the 1968 election. Later in the election cycle he ran television ads showing an empty school bus while an ominous voice told potential voters, "Last year this bus went to only one neighborhood; this year it will go to two." Whatever racial liberalism Bentley may have been known for in the past was, by 1970, largely gone.[7]

When Maddox gave his January State of the State address in the midst of the controversy, he claimed that "public education in Georgia and elsewhere in America has fallen under the strong arm of a federal police state which demands that we surrender our children and grandchildren, their teachers and their schools and our communities, as outlined by the Communist enemies of our children and America." The inflammatory statement led Johnson, along with Black representatives John Hood and Bobby Hill, to walk out of the chamber in protest. "It was more than I could stomach," said Johnson. Black legislators had a responsibility "to start attacking these fellows" like Maddox and Bentley "immediately when they attack our interests." He followed his walkout by writing a public letter to Bentley expressing his disappointment "in your observations, your attitude and your views." Maddox was no better; he "has acted irresponsibly in this area" and had shown no leadership, but Johnson was "greatly surprised" that Bentley had, "for obvious political reasons, offered to show no leadership" either.[8]

But Bentley would ultimately have his way. In February the state senate passed a bill to prevent busing for racial equality and banned the transfer of teachers to different schools to meet racial quotas.[9] Johnson was among its loudest opponents, but he was, in many ways, swimming upstream. In the middle of school and other racial controversies, Maddox traveled to Washington where, after a confrontation with Charles Diggs, he called the Black Michigan congressman an "ass and a baboon." The governor "continues to be the laughing stock of America and a constant source of embarrassment for every decent Georgian—white and black," said new vice mayor Maynard Jackson. Johnson echoed the sentiment, calling the remarks "extremely disgusting, distasteful and unrepresentative of any person who holds as high an office as governor of a state."

Their voices were part of a loud chorus of leading Black Atlantans who excoriated Maddox for his open, unapologetic racism.[10]

At the same time, leading Black Atlantans were experiencing more substantive victories. The city further enmeshed itself in the boxing world when a group of businessmen, led by white attorney and entrepreneur Alan Leigh Baier, held a press conference announcing that they had purchased the contract of young Black heavyweight and Georgia native Vernon Beale from trainer Angelo Dundee. Baier was joined by Azira Gonzalez Hill, a nurse, civil rights activist, and wife of Atlanta Life's Jesse Hill; Dr. Clinton E. Warner, a prominent Black surgeon in the city; and Herman J. Russell, a contractor and property developer whose foray into boxing would only whet his appetite for participation in sports—an appetite he would feed two years later when he joined the ownership group of the National Hockey League's Atlanta Flames. But back in February 1970 Russell appeared with Baier and Beale at the press conference. Baier acknowledged controversies surrounding the sport but claimed that the group's effort was "an attempt by honest businessmen to retain the good and attempt to remove the bad." The sport itself was worthy. "We think that what is needed is for more good businessmen genuinely interested in America's youth to get involved at the management and control level." Beale would continue to train in Miami with Dundee to ensure him the best chance to succeed.[11]

Beale was a Georgian who had served as a sparring partner for Jimmy Ellis and was undefeated in three professional fights, all of them by knockout, but after signing with the Atlanta group he lost his next two fights. Beale would not box professionally again for more than three years. When he returned to the ring in 1973, he did so at Atlanta's Municipal Auditorium, where he suffered a technical knockout in the fourth round. He fought again later that month on another Municipal Auditorium card and won that contest in a split decision, but his career was effectively over.[12] Still, the effort of Atlanta businessmen to buy into the fight game demonstrated that the city seeking to be major league in so many team sports was also eager to be major league in combat sports. The signing was, for *Atlanta Inquirer* columnist D. L. Stanley, "as welcome as the flowers in May." Failed as it was, the Beale purchase proved there was an appetite in Atlanta to be a part of boxing.

Also in February, far from Atlanta, in Harrisburg, Pennsylvania, a group of legislators petitioned the state athletic commission to grant Muhammad Ali a boxing license and sanction a bout between Ali and heavyweight champion Joe Frazier. They argued that the license would "correct the injustice" against Ali. It would also make a lot of money, and legislators promised to designate part of the proceeds to higher education in Pennsylvania. It was a common strategy for those attempting to bring an Ali fight to their area, but the proposal was ultimately rejected.[13]

It wasn't the first time an attempt had been made. Publicist Harold Conrad had approached twenty-eight states beginning in 1968 about the possibility of Ali receiving a license, but each time authorities turned him down. Maine's governor, John Reed, claimed that Ali "should be held in utter contempt by every patriotic American." With plenty of Maine citizens fighting in Vietnam, he was sure that his voters wouldn't "want our state to be used to further the ambitions and gains of an individual of Ali's character."[14] Montana seemed like a possibility, with authorities telling Conrad that a fight might be sanctioned if he supplied bribes to several legislators—bribes Conrad was unable or unwilling to produce. His one brush with success had come in California, where the state athletic commission seemed to have the votes to license the former champion, but when California's governor, Ronald Reagan, got word of the potential decision, he immediately shut it down. "That draft dodger will never fight in my state, period," he said. Boxing officials in Nevada similarly agreed to license Ali, but Las Vegas hotels, operated by the mob, exercised a different kind of veto. Then there was Conrad's ill-fated attempt to secure a venue in the small Black town of Boley, Oklahoma, population 720, a compromise move after political pressure stopped an effort in Tulsa.[15] Herbert Muhammad, meanwhile, almost had an agreement in place with an Arizona Indian reservation, but the tribal council ultimately canceled the deal, as "it would desecrate the land some of our brave boys have walked on."[16]

Ali, meanwhile, was lecturing across the country, attempting to keep himself afloat. Gene Kilroy remembered traveling to different college campuses. "We'd go there, he'd get paid, and then we'd go right to Western Union and send money to his mom and his dad in Louisville." As members of the Pennsylvania legislature were requesting a boxing license for him, Ali gave a speech in Allentown at Muhlenberg College. A group of Black students wearing dashikis interrupted his talk to criticize the former champ for buying an expensive home in Pennsylvania's exclusive Main Line region outside of Philadelphia. He told them in response, "You n——s give me more trouble than whites." He said later, "If I'd been closer I would have knocked one of them down." After the confrontation, some one hundred students, both Black and white, left the auditorium. Ali exited the venue under the guard of six policemen. He told the *National Enquirer* that he was angry and frustrated about being heckled. He apologized, telling the magazine that he would not normally use such language. "But when one of them called me an Uncle Tom—me of all people—I lost control."[17]

Things went more smoothly elsewhere. In Kingston, New York, he told his audience that integration was a false goal for Black equality. "I believe in total separation," he argued. "Some people think integration is a solution to the problem. Some think one day after white and black marry each other, they'll be the same color. Some fools actually believe this. They'll be waiting a long, long time." To nodding heads and cries of "amen" and "right on," he told the group, largely composed of students from Kingston High School and Ulster County Community College, "The truth shall make you free, not integration, not Lincoln and not open housing." Marion Jackson, sports editor of the *Atlanta Daily World*, covered the speech extensively. He explained that Ali was his friend, but he did not intend to make his description personal. Jackson was not a member of the Nation of Islam, but he had "sincere admiration for some of the principles of the Black Muslims." Ali, "who has a slave name of Cassius Clay, is now a namesake of Jack Johnson," not allowed to leave the country, constantly under indictment and suspicion, demonstrating "America's chauvinism, prejudice, despair, segregation, and degeneration." He noted that when Ali was Cassius Clay, when he was an up-and-coming fighter in Louisville, "Southern white men backed the handsome youngster in the fight game." But "today racial amity eludes him."[18]

The *World* was no bastion of radicalism, but the way its sports editor framed the former champion was fundamentally different from the way Ali was framed in the paper's white counterpart. In the *World*, "Clay" was Ali's slave name; he was a victim of racial animus who preached an important message to Black youth around the country, earning far less than he once made for a championship fight. His conscientious objection was perfectly in keeping with his religious faith, and the punishment he received belied nothing but prejudice.[19] The story that readers of the *World* received was virtually a mirror image of the one presented in the *Atlanta Constitution*.

The *World* also covered, for example, *The Great White Hope*, a film from 20th Century Fox based on the play that had premiered three years earlier. The film starred James Earl Jones and depicted a fictionalized version of Johnson's life and relationship with his first wife, Etta Terry Duryea. Both Jones and his costar Jane Alexander would be nominated for Academy Awards, but the film was not received well in the white South. The *World*, however, clearly saw the plight of Ali in the portrayal of Johnson. The paper published pictures of Ali visiting the set with Jones, explaining that Johnson was "the Black champion who was also stripped of his title over fifty years ago for reasons having nothing whatsoever to do with his acting in the ring." For the sports editors of the *World*, the film was a story of historical racism, but also one that represented a current version of it in the person of Ali.[20] It was a markedly different depiction of race critique than the politics editors presented several pages away when defending Bentley against teacher desegregation.

Ali had already seen the stage performance, which starred Jones as the main character, and also saw himself in the depiction. He had befriended Jones during the play's Broadway run, telling him, "You replace the issue of the white women with the issue of religion and the war, and this is my story." When asked later that year if he saw himself as a modern Jack Johnson, Ali said, "Our beliefs are different, but in many ways our lives are familiar." He had a point. "For three years, they don't let me fight and then they tell me in six weeks to get ready. Johnson was all out of shape and people were sure he would get beat. It will be just the same for me."[21]

In the world of actual boxing, Joe Frazier had defeated Jimmy Ellis, and observers worried that there were no more legitimate challengers to his throne. Ellis had been the WBA heavyweight champion since winning the tournament held after Ali vacated the title. Frazier had not participated in that tournament, but was recognized as the champion in most places, particularly after knocking out Buster Mathis in March 1968. When he won a technical knockout against Ellis in February 1970, there was no longer a doubt about Frazier's supremacy. There was, explained the *Norfolk Journal and Guide*'s Cal Jacox, "nobody for Frazier to fight worthy of the fans' interest and the promoter's time." Frazier had the talent "to boost the still sagging prestige of boxing," but without a viable opponent, that boost was unlikely to come. The obvious opponent, of course, was Ali, "but, alas, the prospect of such a classic battle appears to be non-existent in view of Clay's seemingly permanent incarceration on the sidelines." Jacox, like everyone else in the Black press, wanted that seemingly permanent incarceration to end, but unlike the majority of writers in the Black press, he still referred to the former champion as Cassius Clay. The *Journal and Guide* was a Southern paper similar to the *Atlanta Daily World*, founded by P. B. Young, a conservative advocate of the Booker T. Washington accommodationist philosophy. Young had died years earlier, in 1962, but the paper was still largely representative of the same cautious strategy. Advocating for Ali while still calling him Clay gave the paper a measure of cover were any protest from white quarters to come its way.[22]

The Black press, however, whatever an individual paper's bent, understood that all such discussions of boxing reduced to a common denominator of race. "If, as Freudian theory insists, sadists, paranoids and, in fact, the mass human collective unconscious gets a rewarding bang out of watching unmitigated brutality," wrote the *Pittsburgh Courier*'s Ric Roberts, "the terrible beating dished out by Joe Frazier, at the expense of Jimmy Ellis, was joy indeed!" When the fighter dishing out that punishment was Jack Dempsey, Rocky Marciano, or another white fighter, at least. It drove fans' bloodlust, leading them to pay top dollar for ringside seats. "Yet, when the wielder of the red axe, the fistic wrecker, happens to be a black man, human sociopathology enters the picture." Roberts cited behaviorists like Jean Veneuse, Frantz Fanon, and Carl Jung to note that "a big, 'bad' black athlete, on a rampage, subjects white males to traumatic convictions of their own inferiority." It had happened when Joe Louis pummeled Max Baer, leading a *New York Sun* columnist to claim that "there's something of the jungle in Louis," and it was true of Joe Frazier. For Roberts, Muhammad Ali's popularity and world renown came specifically because he never overwhelmed white audiences with sheer punching power. He talked and danced and proved dominant without the sheer brutality of Frazier. "The big, bad athlete has long been eroticized. They symbolize the super biological." Roberts cited Jack Johnson as an example, a fighter who "exuded both super sexuality and black supremacy," and ultimately courted his own downfall because of the threat he presented to white people's assumptions about themselves. "To some whites, rape and Negro are identical. Frazier's destruction of Ellis merely increases belief, by many behaviorists, that the animal powers of black men are hallucinating." And that mindset had real-world consequences in the sport, as organizations from the World Boxing Association to the Associated Press tended to overrate white contenders and underrate Black fighters who posed a threat to assumptions of white supremacy. "What white America demands in her black champions is a brilliant, powerful body, and a dull bestial mind," explained Eldridge Cleaver, "a tiger in the ring and a pussycat outside the ring." Johnson and Ali both, in their own ways, behaved counter to those demands.[23]

Roberts was right. Boxing had come of age in the era of social Darwinism, wherein encounters in the ring were seen as melodramatic allegories of survival of the fittest. When white champions dominated the sport, there was, even for those who hadn't read Herbert Spencer or William Graham Sumner, an understanding of white physical dominance that created a pride of place in many white fans. It was a white pride of place only exacerbated by the longstanding association between Black bodies and physicality, an association dating back to the earliest days of slavery, when valuations of Black lives rested almost solely on physical prowess and capacity for work. The end of slavery in the decades before boxing exploded in popularity did not diminish those associations among white sports fans, nor among white citizens in general. Black athletes, then, when they were celebrated, were celebrated for the same physical prowess that would formerly have fetched a high price at auction. More often that prowess was interpreted as a threat. Heavyweight boxing had been dominated by Black athletes since the retirement of Rocky Marciano, but the assumptions that had long guided white opinions on both sports and race still remained.[24]

After the Frazier fight with Ellis, Ali said publicly that he had retired, and had even offered to give the belt he still held to the winner of that contest. In a speech at Michigan State University the former champ told students that he was "through with boxing." He still took his shot at Frazier, saying, "Frazier showed me nothing in the fight with Ellis. All he did was beat my former sparring partner." But digs at Frazier aside, he was clear that he had retired. The WBA and WBC had stripped him of the title, but *Ring Magazine* had, through the last three years, held firm in referring to Ali as the champion. After Frazier's destruction of Jimmy Ellis and Ali's claim of retirement, however, *Ring* finally announced that the magazine would recognize Frazier as heavyweight champion.[25]

That particular national controversy finally settled, another more local conflagration was developing in Atlanta. As spring began so too did a city employee strike that left Atlanta crippled. The American Federation of State, County and Municipal Employees (AFSCME) took part in a general strike on March 17 to demonstrate for pay raises, and members soon afterward voted for a full strike after raise requests were rejected by the board of aldermen. This was not a wildcat strike, as had been a similar effort in 1968, and the participation of the local union demonstrated a strong front—a decided shift from the previous effort wherein AFSCME declined to participate. Another difference between the 1970 and 1968 efforts was that Black leadership did not provide the same virtually unanimous support the second time around. Massell argued that the requested raises couldn't happen without funding from the state legislature; Atlanta didn't have the $2.5 million that the pay increase for 8,000 city employees would cost. And so the union struck. Members wanted to boost the minimum wage from $1.67 per hour to $2.13 per hour and have a baseline $5,000 life insurance policy included without charge to employees. Massell took a hard line in response, threatening to fire anyone who didn't return to work. It wasn't an idle threat; at the end of the strike's first week he fired 1,400 city employees. He heightened the city's police presence and worked with Governor Maddox to ready the national guard in case there was violence by the strikers.[26]

At the end of March the strike was two weeks old, garbage was piled up and festering all over the city, and negotiations seemed at a standstill. It was Johnson, a pro-union Democrat who was also allied with Massell, who brokered talks between the two sides. Negotiations failed, but after a third week of work stoppage, Johnson was still trying to concoct a deal. He and other Black leaders like Jesse Hill and Martin Luther King, Sr., had supported Massell for mayor and didn't want to damage that relationship by challenging him. It was a source of frustration for AFSCME leadership, which complained of the lack of support from Black leaders like Hill, King, Sr., and Johnson. "Sam called in his Toms," *The*

Great Speckled Bird wrote of Massell, singling out "State Senator Leroy Johnson, Sam Williams, Martin Luther King Sr. and Jesse Hill—who sowed more confusion among the strikers, urging them to compromise and respond to the city's 'concessions.'" On April 7 Johnson met with Massell and SCLC president Ralph Abernathy, who had pledged his organization's support for workers while still publicly backing Massell, and convinced the city to make concessions. As they met, hundreds of workers held a candlelight march through the city, some holding "I Am a Man" signs that mimicked those of the 1968 Memphis garbage workers during the tumult that ultimately witnessed the assassination of Martin Luther King, Jr. "The city has moved from a point it said it wouldn't, to a place beneficial to the lowest paid employees," said a hopeful Johnson. "Now it's time for the union to give a little." It was an effort to help end the deadlock, but one that was clearly in favor of Massell and the city coffers. Johnson even participated in a televised debate on the subject with the SCLC's Joe Boone, who supported the strike.[27]

It was the kind of compromise that typified Atlanta's Black leadership class, one that frustrated striking workers. For Gene Guerrero, "Leroy Johnson, Rev. King Sr., and Joel Stokes functioned in such a way as to sabotage the strike at several important points." Those leaders were usually sympathetic to campaigns to support Black citizens more broadly, Guerrero argued, but their class made them more reluctant to support union activism. Hosea Williams remembered that Black power brokers "made it plain that we were not anti–City Hall nor were we pro–labor union, that we were committed to helping the poor city workers." They were, Johnson among them, "handkerchief headed n——s," wolves in sheep's clothing. As William Seth LaShier has explained, racial solidarity, "at times, helped paper over class divisions that otherwise may have prevented black community leaders from supporting workplace struggles. On other occasions, however, black middle-class reformers interpreted protests by black workers as damaging to the black community." As if to demonstrate that very interpretation, late in the strike, the Fulton County Citizens Democratic Club, one such Black leadership group, appointed Johnson to investigate the strike, as if the issues hadn't been clear over the proceeding weeks. "The last minute interest of the local civic groups and politicians," says LaShier, "changed nothing."[28]

The city's small minority of Black Republicans were frustrated with Black Democrats' lack of "both rhetoric and action" in relation to the strike. They charged that had Republican mayoral candidate Rodney Cook been elected over Massell, and had he behaved during the strike as Massell had behaved, Black leaders would have been screaming that he was "'racist' and 'anti-Negro.'" It was fair criticism, but there were Black leaders who supported the strike and criticized Massell. Ralph Abernathy uncompromisingly backed the workers, just as he had in 1968, as did Hosea Williams and Lonnie King, president of the Atlanta NAACP. So too did the Metropolitan Atlanta Summit Leadership Conference, the Atlanta Ministerial Alliance, Tenants United for Fairness, and other more rights-oriented organizations. The *Atlanta Inquirer* covered the strike assiduously, telling its readers that public service workers "perform services that are vital. They have asked little in return." They did jobs "that have to be done for a public that thinks they are satisfied, a public that often fails to show any kind of gratitude and a public that expects them to cash loyalty and pride in their jobs at the stores." The paper portrayed the strike as the inevitable consequence of Sunbelt politics and the impetus of Atlanta to invite industry to the area. "Perhaps it thought very little of the coming of unions with that industry." But think about it the city would have to, else the AFSCME strike would be the opening salvo of a series of labor actions across Atlanta.[29]

Massell could not make unilateral decisions about wage increases, of course, and the striking workers hoped to receive more support from the board of aldermen. Though five Black aldermen were on the board, it was still a decidedly white conservative body. Joel Stokes, one of the Black aldermen, chaired the finance committee, making him a vital part of the union's strategy. But Stokes was a bank executive at Citizens Trust and a member of the Black elite. He made an effort to continue negotiations, but remained adamant that the city did not have the funds to meet union demands.[30]

Many workers understood that while Black leadership demonstrated concern for the employees, it was less interested in AFSCME's success or the success of unionism more broadly. When Johnson appeared at one union rally, the crowd booed and chanted "Super Tom" and "Massell ass-kisser." Johnson emphasized that the strike was an economic issue, not one of civil rights, as did others, like Martin Luther King, Sr., even though three-quarters of the municipal employees were Black. Both Johnson and King wanted better wages for workers, but they argued that framing the strike as a race issue created an unwillingness to engage in compromise necessary in labor negotiations. Many strikers castigated Johnson as a sellout for not depicting the conflict racially, but his efforts to increase worker wages and negotiate an end to the standoff earned him new respect from many white and Black leaders. Still, when striking Black employees marched from Abernathy's West Hunter Street Baptist Church to government buildings downtown, Johnson wasn't among them, and he was seen by many to be on the wrong side of the issue. When Abernathy and other SCLC leaders met with Massell, Johnson was sitting on Massell's side of the negotiating table. At a meeting of some strike leaders with Black officials at the Butler Street YMCA, Johnson updated everyone on the city's offers and the union's demands. He acted as a neutral arbiter, but his efforts were met with boos and catcalls by several of the strikers, at least one of whom made threats against the senator. The conservative *Atlanta Daily World* framed Johnson as a hardworking consensus-builder trying to help misguided strikers who were working against their own best interest. The paper worried about boycotts of downtown businesses. Consensus among Black elected officials was the only way through the crisis. "It is most illogical for our people to get or let anyone put them in a position of opposing Mayor Massell," editors claimed. The paper wanted everyone to return to work while negotiations continued. Johnson wasn't necessarily saying that, but his role in brokering a deal between the two sides, despite the racial peril it courted, was at least noticed by the press. When the strike finally ended in late April after thirty-six long days, with the striking workers getting a 4.3 percent pay raise, Johnson earned much of the credit from the media, the city, and the union for mediating between both sides.[31]

That credit, however, did not come from workers themselves, who were frustrated by the delay, the compromise, and the failure to get everything they felt they deserved. Hosea Williams interpreted the deal as a "selling out of Atlanta's city employees," a conspiracy by Johnson and other Black leaders to curry favor with Massell and City Hall. LaShier characterizes the settlement as "all but a complete victory for Massell."[32] The strike was over and a pay raise for municipal workers was assured, but the tumult both exemplified and exacerbated the rift between the majority of Black Atlantans and the leadership class that often claimed to speak for them.

Johnson, meanwhile, was using momentum from the strike's conclusion to spread his political capital liberally. In May he joined Maynard Jackson to lambast discrimination in city hiring. Johnson wanted a "blue ribbon panel" to study personnel decisions. Among the problems was presumed police department discrimination against Black officers. Johnson and ally Jesse Hill, representing the Atlanta Summit Leadership Conference, spoke before a meeting of the Aldermanic Police Committee, urging more hires of Black law enforcement in leadership positions. "Senator Johnson, along with myself, Reverend Martin Luther King, Sr., and Reverend Samuel W. Williams," remembered Hill, "were always on the point in Atlanta on issues that impacted the lives of African-Americans for good. We were kind of like a trouble-shooting group." After Hill and Johnson met with Massell, police chief Jenkins, and Police Committee chair Williamson, the mayor and chief agreed to make new hires from sergeant to superintendent. At the time, there was one Black captain, one acting captain, five lieutenants, and four sergeants in the entire force, with no superintendents at all. Johnson told the public aldermanic meeting, "It is felt by far too many policemen that under the present method of promotion, one must either be the 'Chief's Boy' or the superintendent's bosom friend in order to be elevated in the department." And that would never be Black officers. By creating representation in leadership, many of those problems could be avoided.[33]

It was legitimate progress, but Johnson would remain a lightning rod in the Black community. He had clashed before with the MASLC and the SCLC, led by Hosea Williams, and he would do so again in August as election season ramped up. Williams had been one of the chief protest organizers for Martin Luther King, Jr. A World War II veteran from the small town of Attapulgus, Georgia, Williams had joined the SCLC executive board in 1962 while working as president of the Southeastern Georgia Crusade for Voters in Savannah. He had come to rights work after being severely beaten for drinking from a white Savannah water fountain after returning home from the war. From Savannah he moved to St. Augustine, Florida, then to Selma, Alabama, where he, along with SNCC leader John Lewis, organized and led the Selma to Montgomery

March. He joined King in Chicago in 1966, then returned South to help lead the Poor People's Campaign. Williams was in Memphis for the sanitation workers' strike and at the Lorraine Motel when King was assassinated, and he became executive director of the SCLC after King's death. Williams was decidedly outside the inner circle of Atlanta power brokers and was regularly frustrated with what he interpreted as their capitulation. His militancy gave him the nickname "the wild man of Atlanta."[34] His emphasis on direct confrontation made him "a thorn in the sides of both the black and white power structures in Atlanta," explains Alton Hornsby, but so too did his routine denunciations of "the selfishness and timidity of middle-class blacks as well as the racism of whites." He clearly understood the city's class divide, to say nothing of the division between outsider rights activists and insider negotiators, and consistently sided with the agitators, putting him in semiregular conflict with Johnson, though the two at times seemed to hold at least a begrudging respect for one another.[35]

But when Johnson called a meeting at the Holiday Inn in downtown Atlanta to poll people from around the state as to the strongest Black candidates for that year's elections, Williams led a picket outside the building against Johnson for "selling people out," largely because of his support for gubernatorial candidate and former governor Carl Sanders. Williams claimed that white candidates paid Johnson $42,000 for his endorsements, which Johnson categorically denied and for which no evidence exists. The senator was frustrated by Williams's grandstanding. "Somehow or other," he said, "black people have got to learn to disagree with each other."[36] Or to disagree with each other responsibly. Really, Williams's critique of Johnson was a frustration with the necessary compromises of governing, something Williams had never done. Pragmatists had long been critiqued by idealists, even as those unwilling to negotiate usually sat on the sidelines without making decisions. Or perhaps to use a more appropriate metaphor, Johnson was in the ring, which made him more vulnerable, while Williams was screaming from the grandstand.

That is not to say that Williams was wrong in his criticism. Johnson had come under fire in 1968 when the NAACP tried to unseat him in that year's election because Johnson had accepted a post as a Georgia delegate to the Democratic National Convention, appointed by Lester Maddox. Johnson had won that fight, but it demonstrated his willingness to court controversy in aid of the compromise and political horse trading required of state politicians.[37] Johnson was, in fact, supporting the gubernatorial candidacy of Sanders, but he had also endorsed Mike Padgett, a candidate for comptroller who had been trained by Augusta segregationist Roy Harris. It was relatively easy for Johnson to defend his support for Sanders, a racial liberal. Padgett, for many Black Atlantans, was a bridge too far, even if political expediency necessitated the move.[38]

When the Fulton County Democratic Party held its convention in late March, Johnson was among the keynote speakers, as was Sanders, who the *Atlanta Daily World* explained was "instrumental in founding the Fulton County Democratic Party."[39] Sanders was a lawyer who had previously served as governor. He had collaborated with real estate developer Tom Cousins to bring the NBA's Hawks to Atlanta in 1968, using as one of his chief arguments that a new basketball arena in downtown Atlanta could draw the 1972 Democratic National Convention to the city. He was, in a sense, the model for using sports as a form of politics, or for using sports to help generate political relevance. Johnson's support of the former governor for a return to office seemed a natural fit, despite Williams's protests.[40]

Meanwhile Muhammad Ali reasserted in the May edition of *Esquire* that he had no plans to resume his fighting career. "I want to be the first black champion that got out that didn't get whipped," he said. He claimed the only reason he boxed was because of his upbringing, that he didn't really like doing it. Mirroring the social Darwinist concerns of Ric Roberts, he argued that "fighters are just brutes that come to entertain the rich white people." When two Black boxers competed in front of a predominantly white crowd, they were "just like two slaves in that ring." Now that he had converted to the Nation of Islam, he worried that fighting would give someone a concussion or do "something terrible to a fellow human being just for a little old check that the government takes 90 percent of, anyway." He claimed that now "my job is freedom, justice and equality for black folks" instead of punching people for a living. "I don't care what they do to me—jail me, shoot me, I don't care. I just want it to go down in history that I didn't sell out or Uncle Tom when I got famous." He did say that he would fight exhibitions with Joe Frazier for charity to help alleviate poverty, but only to "use our fame for freedom."[41]

But he wasn't completely over the sport. "I was too good," he asserted, "and that's why they had to get rid of me. That's why they tried to take the heavyweight championship away from me." The people understood that, he claimed. While the leaders of boxing and the leaders of the country were against him, attempting to sabotage him at every turn, the people were with him. It was a scattershot, disorganized essay. In one paragraph he defended the Nation of Islam and its desire for separatism; in the next he recited some of his poetry. He defended the Black Panthers before moving into a discourse on the rules of boxing and how they should change. And even with his claimed satisfaction with being away—his insistence that he would never return—he was still the playful Ali. "What if," he asked, "Muhammad Ali, who used to be known as Cassius Clay, came back and brought the drama back with him? You think that wouldn't fill Madison Square Garden?" He closed his screed with lyrics from *Buck White*:

> You've had us in your lock, tight as any cage,
> And now you're actin' shocked, 'cause we're in a rage;
> Us on the bottom, with you on top,
> That's just a game that we aim to stop.
> That's all over now, Mighty Whitey. That's all over now.[42]

At the same time, his faith was not the same as formal NOI membership. Ali had been defrocked in 1969. In May 1970, when a reporter from *Jet* magazine asked him about his affiliation with the sect, an angry Ali refused to talk. "Religious matters are not for publication," he told them.[43] He was more willing to talk about the suspension two months later to *Black Scholar* magazine, framing his punishment as a demonstration of the faith's virtue. "This is what makes the Honorable Elijah Muhammad so great," he said. "There's no favoritism. This is what destroys more religions and more movements: The leader has a couple of people he'll let do a few things because they are famous or have a lot of money and the rest of the followers are punished." But Muhammad wasn't like that, according to Ali; everyone was treated equally.[44] The statement was obviously untrue, and Ali had received overt and obvious favoritism because he was rich and famous. Such statements, however, were a way, at least in theory, to get back in the good graces of the NOI. Ali was devastated by his suspension from the faith, just as Malcolm had been five years prior. Without his boxing career or membership in his church, he felt he had fallen as low as he could go.[45]

Even if he was claiming retirement, however, Ali was supported by many. Speaking from South Africa, Arthur Ashe told reporters that he supported Ali's claim of conscientious objector status.[46] Ali traveled to Pittsburgh that month, where he was feted around town, touring the Hill District and Homewood, visiting the Children's Hospital, and appearing at a testimonial dinner where fawning guests watched films of his fights with Sonny Liston and Floyd Patterson. While there was some criticism of Ali, he remained inordinately popular in Black circles.[47]

It was also in May that the SCLC announced that it would work to get Ali reinstated with the WBA. Joe Peters, the SCLC's sports project director, gave a press conference at Ali's Philadelphia home. He had spoken with Coretta Scott King, "and she said she would do everything possible to help get Ali's license back." The organization was in Philadelphia for its International Freedom Games, held to honor its founder and to raise money for SCLC projects. Ali planned to participate in the games as a guest attraction at the request of King's widow. Peters hoped that if the reinstatement campaign was successful the boxer would fight some benefit bouts to raise money for the organization. Ali, for his part, claimed that the initiative was not his idea. "It's been so long since they took my title away that I just don't think much about it anymore."[48]

It was easier for the group to make such stands because the public was turning against the war. In late April 1970 Nixon had authorized the use of ground forces in Cambodia. Days later four students were killed by National Guardsmen at an anti-Vietnam protest at Kent State University. Two weeks after that the Mississippi State Police killed two student protesters at Jackson State College. While there was the inevitable vocal support for law enforcement among many conservatives, a majority watched in horror as Vietnam-related deaths began at home. In that context Ali's stand looked far more prescient in the mainstream, even the white mainstream, than it had previously.[49]

The next month Gloster B. Current, director of branches and field administration for the NAACP, echoed Peters's statements. He claimed that Ali was "victimized by a dual standard of justice" because he was "black and a member of a sect about which most Americans are uninformed." Ali should be able to fight pending his appeal, Current argued. "The time has come for decent Americans, black and white, to speak out in his defense."[50]

That kind of institutional support could provide its own momentum. In June *Sports Illustrated* presented a profile of Bill Russell, whom the magazine named the most dominant athlete of the 1960s. Russell claimed that he didn't think he deserved the award. "That honor can only belong to Muhammad Ali," said Russell. "In fact, of all the athletes I have known, he is the one I would most prefer to have my sons look up to." All kinds of people claimed to believe in something, "but Ali has supported his faith at great financial loss to himself."[51]

And that meant something, particularly to people outside of the United States. Tijuana, Mexico, for example, wanted to host a fight, but the State Department refused to grant Ali permission to travel over the border. The same problem arose with a potential fight in Japan. In April the boxing commission in Ontario agreed to license Ali to fight Frazier in Maple Leaf Gardens, which prompted a hearing by the Fifth Circuit Court of Appeals in New Orleans as to whether the fight could take place. Judge John Minor Wisdom obviously couldn't overturn the decisions of Canadian boxing commissions, but among the terms of Ali's criminal conviction for draft evasion was a mandate that he not leave the country. If his bail could be extended to Canada for a twenty-four hour period, then the fight was on. Ali's attorney, Chauncey Eskridge, requested permission from Supreme Court justice Hugo Black for Ali to visit Toronto for eighteen hours to fight Joe Frazier, claiming that as much as 70 percent of television rights fees could be used as bond for the fighter's return. An angry Ali claimed he was going to fire the lawyer. "I told him I'm not interested and they're not going to let me leave the country anyway, but he went ahead." He was frustrated that "people everywhere are trying to get me a license, but I tell them all I'm not interested." He claimed that his lawyer was "out for the money, and he's owed a lot of back salary. The price of justice is high." That was true, but Ali's statements about not being interested in fighting again seemed less so. He had criticized Frazier; he had hosted the SCLC for its press conference advocating his reinstatement. Most seemed to think he was hedging against an outcome that would probably not go his way. "Fat chance of his firing Chauncey Eskridge or turning down a crack at Frazier if the opportunity presents itself," figured the Baltimore *Afro-American*.[52]

But the opportunity did not present itself. Black denied Eskridge's application, arguing that Ali would not be subject to extradition from Canada. Even if federal marshals accompanied him, then, the trip presented an unacceptable risk. The fight in Toronto would not take place.[53] Still, Eskridge wasn't done. He tried again with Supreme Court justice William O. Douglas, but as he was unavailable, the new petition went to the entire court. Eskridge noted that Abbie Hoffman, appealing a five-year sentence for his role in protests at the 1968 Democratic National Convention, had been allowed to travel to Cuba for twenty-six days, making it seem as though a fundamentally different standard was being applied to Ali.[54]

The *Afro-American* was frustrated with Black's decision. Ali "deserves the chance to go to Toronto, Canada, for the fight that has been arranged for that country," but he should also be permitted to fight in the United States. Ali's original petition was rejected because he claimed to be a minister after other avenues failed, but "a lot of ministers make their living, or enhance it in other work." The paper was also angry about the government's wiretaps of the former champion. But all such realities were angels dancing on the head of a pin. Ali "had every right to a deferment," the paper argued. "It is not any state's business to decide the legitimacy of a religion nor to determine who is a minister within that faith."[55]

Though Black had ruled against allowing Ali to travel to Canada, in other ways the Supreme Court's thinking seemed to jibe with that of the *Afro-American*. A June decision by the court exempted from the draft those who opposed war on ethical or moral grounds, even if that belief wasn't based on the teachings of a specific religious faith. That mattered for Ali, because while he did base his conscientious objection on his Black Muslim faith, the U.S. Court of Appeals that ruled against him mentioned in its decision that it did not doubt Ali's sincere objection to war. Instead the court had ruled that the Nation of Islam was a political and racial group rather than a religion. If the standard for conscientious objection included general moral objection, the courts had already admitted that Ali met that standard. Brad Pye, sports editor for the *Los Angeles Sentinel*, reasoned that the decision "virtually makes Muhammad Ali's freedom a matter of course."[56]

The case emanated from Ali's hometown. Draft Board 47 in Louisville, which had heard Ali's case, had refused to consider the conscientious objector status of Joseph Mulloy, an organizer for the Southern Conference Educational Fund, a Louisville-based organization that worked throughout the South to fight racism, poverty, and war. He was given a five-year prison sentence and fined $10,000, just like Ali. But a unanimous Supreme Court reversed the decision, ruling that moral objection was legitimate. Mulloy and four other SCEF workers had been charged in 1967 with sedition after an attempt to stop strip-mining in Pike County, Kentucky, an act that he believed prejudiced the board. Despite the claims of the SCEF, though, the Supreme Court did not rule on the incompetence or corruption of Draft Board 47.[57]

Even though a ruling on Ali's case wasn't expected until 1971, the conscientious objector decisions boosted Eskridge's confidence. "This gets us one step closer to freedom," Ali's lawyer said. "We're acting on it now. We also have a couple other actions underway that should have decisions soon." Among those was the petition before the Supreme Court to undo Black's ruling and allow Ali to travel to Toronto. Another legal action in New York charged the state's boxing commission with discrimination, citing past instances of the commission issuing licenses to others with criminal records. Eskridge reminded reporters that when Ali first applied for conscientious objector status, Kentucky's state hearing officer Lawrence Grauman had approved. The Justice Department advised the Kentucky draft board to hold the line against Ali, claiming the Nation of Islam was not a religion. Then there was the questionable admissibility of the government's wiretaps. The hope was that the several different instances of discrimination would convince a full Supreme Court to allow Ali to travel to Toronto.[58]

Again the *Afro-American* was in total agreement. Ali's conviction and the slow pace of adjudicating his legal actions stemmed "from racism and the dislike of the Black Muslims." Ali deserved better from his government. He had done things "that no other black boxer ever had accomplished." His objection to the war "was a courageous thing. He still is a hero among most black and some white Americans and to millions of peoples outside the borders of this country." Court delays were themselves further penalties against a man who deserved none of them. "Enough time has been wasted," the *Afro-American* editorial closed. "This newspaper, once again, urges immediate court action. Justice delayed is justice subverted." The *Michigan Chronicle* had a similar response to the new conscientious objector rulings by the court, arguing that the former champ's case "certainly should be reviewed and overturned because of it."[59] The papers weren't making constitutional claims. They were making a social case that the courage of a race hero merited, if nothing else, a speedy trial, and even more, the benefit of the doubt. But whatever the argument, it was clear that momentum was on Ali's side.

Or so it seemed. A unanimous Supreme Court soon sided with Hugo Black's original decision and denied Ali the ability to travel to Toronto to fight Frazier. Even traditionally conservative outlets like the *Michigan Catholic* saw a measure of hypocrisy in the conflicting rulings. The paper "burns no candles for professional prize fighting" and "we care little more for the violent doctrines of the Black Muslims," but the fact remained that in a free country anyone was allowed to believe in them. The paper described the cases of many who were able to maintain their employment while their cases were on appeal, but all such examples "involve Americans with white skin. Is it possible that Mr. Ali is the wrong color for the same kind of equal justice?"[60]

Philadelphia civil rights attorney Cecil B. Moore gave a speech decrying a boxing system that allowed Jack Dempsey, whom he claimed dodged the draft in World War I, to fight and thrive, while calling Ali a criminal.[61] For the *Chicago Defender*'s Doc Young, the whole thing was a monumental tragedy. He supported Ali's moral stance, but did note that if he had enlisted, he would have been able to keep his title, have big-money fights, and would not "have come any closer to the Viet Cong than the Empire State Building is now." The constant efforts of his lawyers and Ali's claims that he was retired and uninterested in fighting anymore "sounded like a terrible piece of blues, the unfinished symphony of a man who didn't know whether he wanted to go or stay."[62]

The *Los Angeles Sentinel*'s Brad Pye was less equivocal. Ali should have been able to fight and should be able to fight now. He was frustrated that the loudest voices opposed to the boxer's reinstatement came from the American Legion. "Where are these American Legionnaires, when blacks are fighting to have their black brothers buried in some national cemeteries in the South?" he asked. They were silent, as surely they would be when Ali fought again. "And when that day comes, America will again have to hang its head in shame for its disgraceful treatment of one of the greatest black Americans of all time." The following month, Pye continued his attack on the Legion, comparing its protests against Ali with the group's silence in the case of Poindexter E. Williams, a black serviceman killed in Vietnam who was refused burial in an all-white cemetery in Fort Pierce, Florida. The plot had been given to his mother by a white woman, but the cemetery's board refused the interment. The Legion lodged no protests against the cemetery for dishonoring a veteran killed in combat, because the combatant himself was Black. Neither did the Veterans of Foreign Wars nor Disabled American Veterans, two other groups loudly opposed to Ali's return to the ring.[63]

The Legionnaires had issued a public resolution in May denouncing "a small portion of misguided young men" who had "refused to serve their nation, and have elected to evade their military obligation." The organization was also opposed to "certain individuals and groups" that "have aided and assisted these draft evaders and deserters from our Armed Forces." The resolution didn't specifically mention Ali, but he was the most famous of those "misguided young men" and the resolution appeared as promoters were seeking to create an Ali fight and the Black press was defending his right to do so. The Legion even sent a copy of the resolution to *Ring Magazine*, just in case the news cycle itself hadn't made its target clear.[64]

Back in Georgia, the focus that summer—of those in the state and of those in the nation—shifted from Atlanta to Augusta as a racial uprising and violent police response reminded everyone that for all of Georgia's curated reputation for moderation, it was still the Deep South, with all of the racial baggage of the Deep South. The uprising didn't spread to Atlanta, but it magnified racial tension in the state and modified the image of what many outside the region had previously seen as something of a Southern oasis.

Prompted by the suspicious March 28 death of Charles Oatman, a sixteen-year-old, Black, mentally challenged student arrested for the murder of his niece, in police custody, the Augusta uprising brought renewed racial scrutiny to Georgia. The police originally claimed that Oatman had fallen off his bunk—a story that seemed ludicrous. He had wounds all over his body, including deep gashes in his back from whippings with a strap and cigarette burns on his skin. So the story changed.

Police scapegoated two juvenile prisoners for murdering Oatman.[65] Those charges, too, appeared suspect, as the cursory investigation that led to them seemed a convenient excuse for what the public saw clearly as overt police violence against a prisoner who was being unjustly held in the first place, or, failing that, as gross negligence on the part of guards at the county jail. A potential police cover-up only exacerbated Black frustration in Augusta over unemployment and unequal employment, poor housing, and a variety of social injustices—many of them at the hands of law enforcement—ravaging both the town and the county that surrounded it. Richmond County had vastly unequal education and led the nation in school dropouts. "Racism in Augusta is as much a part of the local ambiance as the oppressive heat and the wisteria and azaleas and the honey-suckled air," one report explained. "Racism has seeped into the very pores of the city." The structural inequality in Augusta laid the ground for the uprising to come. The conflagration included chaotic protests, the burning of the state flag, and eventually retributive police brutality. Officers killed six protesters.[66]

The burning of the state flag was significant. It was a symbolic denunciation of white state leadership, but it was more than that. The Georgia state flag had been changed in 1956 by legislative fiat, adding the Confederate battle flag prominently to the state design. The alteration was an overt reaction to the Supreme Court's *Brown v. Board of Education* decision and the nascent civil rights movement developing in its wake, a grand symbol of massive resistance that would fly over the capitol and all state buildings, reminding everyone that Georgia stood for white supremacy. By 1970 defenders of the Confederate version of Georgia's flag attempted to make an argument that the Lost Cause iconography wasn't a response to civil rights but instead was a change in preparation for the centennial of the Civil War, but it was an argument that fell flat, reverse engineered to absolve its creators of the racism that underlay the effort. It was that flag, bright with Confederate symbolism, that would fly over all of the sporting events in Georgia, and it was that flag that the Augusta protesters would burn.[67]

And police officers would respond by shooting, indiscriminately, at people protesting and at those simply on the street. The police made dozens if not hundreds of arrests. The GBI report on the incident claimed, without evidence, that the police were under sniper fire. It was another in a long line of cover-ups that had begun with the murder of Oatman. Three police officers quit the force that night in protest. At the end of the uprising six Black protesters were dead and sixty more injured. All six victims were unarmed and had been shot in the back. More than twenty others suffered gunshot wounds at the hands of the police.[68]

Lester Maddox had, the day after the uprising, sent in the National Guard. "They're going in with live ammunition," he said. "We're not going to tolerate anarchy in this state." He blamed a "communist conspiracy" for the violence. But against his wishes, on September 1, a federal grand jury in Augusta indicted two white police officers, one for murder and the other for shooting and wounding an unarmed man during the May protest. But in the months that followed courts also convicted the juveniles accused of Oatman's murder, along with more than one hundred protesters. The police captain in charge of the massacre was promoted to chief, and the bigotry at the heart of the Augusta uprising continued.[69] That bigotry stood as a scarlet letter on the chest of a state that had presented itself as a moderate alternative to its Southern counterparts, one with integrated professional sports and Fortune 500 corporations. As the nation watched the violence in Augusta, Atlanta boosters wrung their hands at the possible undoing of the hard-won results of their propaganda campaigns.

While the conflict in Augusta was ongoing, Maynard Jackson was declaring a "full scale war against narcotics addiction" in Atlanta, and against heroin addiction in particular. It was a problem that had ravaged the city's Black population, "but this plague can no longer be quarantined in the ghettoes." He wanted rehabilitation, research, and educational programs to stem a problem that was becoming an "epidemic" in poor neighborhoods across Atlanta.[70] It was a war that wouldn't accomplish a great deal, but it was significant in that it directed the attention of municipal government toward a virus that had infiltrated the working classes while those in power were busy with other issues.

And those issues inevitably redounded to white supremacy. In 1970 Maddox wrote a brief essay he called "Epitaph of World's Greatest Free Republic," which he used as a stump speech for much of the year. "Here lie the remains of the United States of America," he wrote, describing a country that started strong, but later "turned from God." The people "surrendered public education, but a million times more important, they surrendered their children—America's most precious resource—to a federal 'police state' which acted without constitutional authority in stealing away the rights and freedoms of America's children and their parents." Ultimately, "communism and socialism replaced capitalism and freedom," and "human dignity and personal initiative were gradually eroded and replaced with government handout programs until, finally, everybody was getting a government paycheck and there was nobody working to produce the needed wealth." It was a racist screed only slightly veiled by a delusional patriotism, standing against integration more than a decade and a half after *Brown v. Board of Education*, portraying welfare as evil and a harbinger of communist influence. Such was the leadership of the state and the mindset of those who voted for it. The following year Maddox would record his "Epitaph" as the closing track on his *God, Family and Country* album.[71]

It was, in a sense, poorly timed. In the summer Maddox's troubled son was released from probation for a previous offense, then was almost immediately arrested again on a charge of attempted burglary. Because his last name was Maddox, he was given a sweetheart sentence of one day in jail each weekend for six months and another round of probation. It was, to J. Lowell Ware, editor and publisher of the *Atlanta Voice*, an insult to those who received much harsher sentences for much lesser crimes. The penalty also served as a glaring irony for the "standard bearer of 'law and order.'" For the elder Maddox, anyone who disagreed with him was a "communist." Anyone who supported Black rights "is anti-Christ." A frustrated Ware explained that Maddox "talks about law breakers, forgetting how he got to be governor." Lighter sentences, of course, would probably be a value added to most convicted of crimes, but they would not receive them. "They don't have an unelected governor for a father." It "all adds up to Georgia's past, where history tells us this state was settled by thieves and prostitutes. . . . Times haven't changed, have they?"[72]

5. THE POLITICS OF BOXING (AND RACE)

AUGUST TO SEPTEMBER, 1970

With the proposed Toronto fight off because of Ali's inability to leave the country, promoters in Detroit sought to bring the bout just south of the Canadian border. Those attempting the feat were Lou Handler, a former referee; Jerome Cavanagh, former Detroit mayor; and columnist Edgar "Doc" Greene. Their efforts were fraught. Greene was fired from the *Detroit News* for his involvement in the promotion—his editor, Martin Hayden, worried that bringing Ali to Detroit would cause a race riot. It would "not be in the best interests of Detroit," Hayden said. The city's Black newspaper, the *Michigan Chronicle*, described the reaction of Hayden and the *Detroit News* as "merely a surfacing of inbred white hostility to blacks and symptomatic of the overall double standard by which blacks and whites are judged by their fellow man." For his part, Michigan governor William Milliken claimed that while he wanted no part in the process, he would not stand in the way if the state's boxing commissioner, Chuck Davey, approved the fight. But with the reaction of the *Detroit News*, any hope of Davey agreeing seemed slim at best. Davey himself was a former professional boxer who had previously said that he saw nothing wrong with an Ali fight in Detroit. "Yet the bigots who control the industry have yet to give their sanction," explained the *Los Angeles Sentinel*. "It seems strange that Ali is going to have to live with this incessant persecution all of the rest of his professional life simply because he chose to follow the teachings of his religion." But he was going to have to live with it, at least in Detroit, as in mid-July the Michigan Boxing Commission rejected the possibility of a fight.[1]

Promoters made another effort for an Ali-Frazier matchup in Tacoma, Washington, but were rejected by the local athletic commission. Among the witnesses in that hearing was Charles P. Larsen, a pathologist and, more importantly, a former president of the World Boxing Association. "We have for many years committed a great injustice against Mr. Clay," he told the body, using as an example doctors convicted of crimes who were able to continue practicing medicine until their final appeals had been exhausted. The lawyer for the promoters made the same case about attorneys who were able to continue practicing until full disbarment proceedings had run their course. Though Ali's supporters saw the rejection decision as "unmitigated bigotry," the two-to-one vote of the athletic commission ensured that there would be no Ali-Frazier fight in Tacoma.[2]

Among the comparisons the Black press used to bolster Ali's chance at a return was that of Dennis McLain, a white Major League baseball player given a six-month suspension for betting on baseball and even financing a bookmaking operation. McLain was reinstated and returned to baseball in early July, as Ali's attempts to return to his own sport continued. "The black and white of it is," the *Michigan Chronicle* explained, "that Ali is continuing to be harshly punished because of moral conviction, while Dennis McLain was only mildly chastised for lack of it." The *Los Angeles Sentinel*'s Brad Pye pointed to famed pediatrician Dr. Benjamin Spock, who encouraged young men to burn their draft cards and refuse to fight in Vietnam, and who was allowed to continue his practice until his case in court came to an end.[3]

The double standard was, for *Chronicle* columnist Nadine Brown, built on white supremacy. "These people, this white racist society, have no intention of allowing blacks to obtain anything constructive," she said in response to Ali's failure to get a boxing license. White men could refuse induction into the military for whatever reason they wanted, but those in government "don't respect a black man's right to worship as he chooses. As far as they are concerned, the Nation of Islam is non-existent."[4] That wasn't true, of course. The Nation of Islam was all too existent for the federal government; it just wasn't a religion in the government's eyes. The problem for Ali was not a governmental lack of recognition of his religion, but a governmental rejection of it. Brown's larger conclusion that racism was at the heart of such decisions, however, seemed difficult to refute.

For his part, in early July, Joe Frazier was publicly saying that he wanted a fight with Ali. His manager was arranging a match with Bob Foster, the light heavyweight champion who previously defended his title in Atlanta, but Frazier didn't want it. "If I don't fight Ali this year, there will be no title defense in 1970," he said. Frazier would devote himself full-time to his music career; he even planned to start his own record label. The only contest that could make him delay those plans was one with Ali.[5] It was a stance he would later change, but as of July, with the Supreme Court decisions and the push by promoters to make a fight happen, Frazier's focus was squarely on the former champion.

While the debates continued, Jerry Quarry was still boxing. In June he defeated previously unbeaten Mac Foster, the top-ranked contender for the heavyweight title, in Madison Square Garden with a sixth-round technical knockout. It had been a year since his loss to Joe Frazier; he had in that time amassed four more victories and one loss, to George Chuvalo in December. His defeat of Foster, combined with those intervening wins, catapulted him back into championship contention.[6] His victory also affected Sonny Liston, who had bet $10,000 on the fight, losing it all after choosing Foster. His resulting financial desperation led Liston to one final fight with Chuck Wepner, in which he made only $13,000. The career of the former champion who had originally ceded the title to Ali was over.[7]

That month Muhammad Ali gave an interview to *The Black Scholar* magazine. "What's wrong with me going to jail for something I believe in?" he asked. "Boys are dying in Vietnam for something they don't believe." Among those who could actually limit that death were athletes and entertainers, he claimed, referencing his meeting with Black athletes two years prior. He argued that all of them needed to take "a walk through the ghetto" and tell white America, "We're with these people and we ain't going to sell out anymore."[8]

Harold Conrad, meanwhile, was hoping that despite such interviews, which clearly hurt his chances, Ali would be boxing again soon. Conrad's next attempt to get his fighter licensed was in Mississippi. Ali was not popular among white leaders in one of the most notoriously racist places in America, but Conrad and Gene Kilroy were able to convince both the governor and the mayor of Jackson of the benefit of an Ali fight to the state's coffers and reputation. "I met with Governor John Bell Williams,"

Kilroy remembered. "They had had a big flood down there, so we agreed that if they gave Ali a license, we'd donate the live gate to the state of Mississippi for the flood victims" through the Salvation Army, and with that managed to get approval. When white Mississippians heard about the deal, however, they erupted. Led by the American Legion, an angry backlash caused the governor to renege on the deal, Williams publicly denying the existence of a Mississippi boxing license for Ali, even though it had already been issued, and assuring his white supporters that no Ali fight would happen in the state. It wouldn't.[9]

"It was almost as if Muhammad was radioactive," remembered Angelo Dundee. "Every time a license was granted he suddenly became untouchable." It happened in Mississippi, and it happened everywhere. "The American Legion, the Veterans of Foreign Wars, and White Citizen[s] Councils lined up to proclaim that they would boycott any fight of Muhammad Ali's and would shut down any arena that dared to stage such a fight."[10]

Conrad's next real attempt was for a charity bout in Charleston, South Carolina, in July 1970, wherein Ali would spar three rounds each with two different opponents. The contract had actually been signed in May. It wouldn't provide the fighter's much-needed payday, as proceeds would go to underprivileged children, but it would get him back in a ring. Ali had even flown to Charleston in preparation. Alas, the Charleston County Council voted unanimously to refuse the contract for use of the four-thousand-seat arena after the mayor received a phone call from segregationist congressman L. Mendel Rivers, who exploded that the city was "letting that draft-dodging black sonofabitch fight in my hometown." Ali went to the arena only to find that the long line at the ticket window was composed of people there not to buy, but to wait for refunds. Another neighboring state, Georgia, had also tried and failed to bring Ali to the ring.[11] Still, it was significant that in the absence of availability in other parts of the country, Conrad had, at least briefly, turned his attention to the South—a region that, because of its long Jim Crow history, had not been able to secure many professional sports, save Minor League Baseball, and therefore didn't have state athletic commissions to revoke Ali's license to fight.

When the efforts in Mississippi and South Carolina failed, attention returned to more traditional boxing venues. In early August a group of prominent Black leaders in Detroit publicly urged Governor Milliken and boxing commissioner Davey to reverse the decision stopping a fight between Ali and Frazier in the city. Speaking for the group, circuit court judge Charles Farmer reasoned that the decision was not only unfair to Ali, but that "it acts to wash away the bridge of racial and religious understanding we have tried to build." And there was no racial and religious understanding in the boxing commission's decision. "If Muhammad Ali were not black and not a Muslim, he would not now be suffering the restrictions applied against him." Congressmen John Conyers and Charles Diggs signed the statement, as did a variety of councilmen, judges, union leaders, and NAACP officials. The group would not take legal action to force the issue, but wanted instead to create a groundswell of support that Milliken and Davey couldn't ignore.[12] Milliken seemed, once again, close to agreeing, but again white public pressure stopped any forward momentum. The *Detroit Free Press* claimed that "approving a fight for Clay would appear to the public to be approving of his way of life." No white politician wanted to appear to be doing that. There would be no fight for Ali in Michigan.[13]

Back in Atlanta, racial tensions remained even higher. In early August two white policemen shot and killed an unarmed fifteen-year-old, Andre Moore, in Summerhill, the site of so much tension the previous year. The two officers were investigating a robbery, questioning a suspect at the corner of Fraser and Connally streets. Moore arrived and told them that the supposed suspect had done nothing wrong. The policemen asked his age, and, discovering he was fifteen, told him he was under arrest for violating curfew. Moore began running home to avoid arrest, so the officers shot him in the back. The furor that arose as a response led to a march on City Hall, where Maynard Jackson and police committee chair Q. V. Williamson met them and promised that "justice will be done." Several Black groups, including attorneys for Moore's mother, attempted to swear out warrants for the officers' arrests. For those who knew the teenager, the murder was devastating; for those who didn't, the murder was a more violent example of police harassment practiced in Black neighborhoods like Summerhill every day, giving lie to the myth of racial egalitarianism that Atlanta had created for itself.[14]

If racial egalitarianism was a myth, then the officers facing justice in local courts was unlikely. Black leaders argued that not only should the two policemen be held to account, but that they should be charged federally. "So far as I'm able to ascertain," said Reverend Samuel W. Williams at an NAACP press conference following the murder, "not a single conviction has come from a Grand Jury of policemen killing black folks." The angry residents of Summerhill, meanwhile, couldn't release their frustration at press conferences, and tensions in the neighborhood threatened to boil over, as they had in 1969. Mayor Massell met with residents to try to quell the tension, but it was, in the words of one resident, a "total failure." Mattie Ansley, chair of the Summerhill Nonviolent Coordinating Committee, was frustrated that "there's just not much justice when it comes down to the way the white man treats blacks," but she and her organization would try to create constructive outlets for hurting residents. "I really don't know how long we can hold the young back," she said, "maybe a week, maybe a month, maybe six months."[15]

The simmering frustration ensured that the 1970 elections would be more hotly contested than ever. In August Johnson held a series of meetings with Black state leaders to gauge their preferences for candidates. More than twenty-four counties were represented under the auspices of Johnson's Georgia Association of Citizens Democratic Clubs, as the organization wanted as much input as possible before considering endorsements for major offices. It seemed an understandable mission, but even that caused controversy. Black lieutenant gubernatorial candidate D. F. Glover accused Johnson and his allies of advocating against his candidacy. It was possible, he figured, that Johnson was on the payroll of Carl Sanders, or at least accepting money from him. Glover claimed that he was the only one who could remedy the public school desegregation crisis and racial unrest in the counties, but if Black leaders like Johnson worked against him—and, went the conceit, colluded with white power brokers to do so—he would never get the chance to essentially save Black voters from themselves.[16]

Johnson's reputation for compromise and back-room dealmaking led to regular charges like Glover's, that he was a corrupt politician working against the best interests of Black Georgia for his own political gain. The charge that he worked against the interests of Black Georgia was decidedly false, but he was most certainly a dealmaker who looked out for his own. And while it could create controversies among his base in the context of elections and legislation, in other areas it was an unqualified asset. Horse trading, for Johnson, was always necessary, whether in politics, business, or both, and it was that penchant that would bring the Atlanta politician and the Louisville boxer together. As historian Johnny Smith has explained, "Johnson had never promoted a boxing match before, but he knew the art of promotion." Johnson was aware that Ali was looking for a home for his comeback fight. He had watched as efforts in Florida, Mississippi, and South Carolina failed. In August he received a telephone call from Robert Kassel, head of Sports Action, Inc., inquiring about the possibility of an Ali fight in Atlanta. Sports Action was a New York promotion company that Kassel had founded with Bob Arum and Michael N. Malitz in 1967 to present the WBA heavyweight elimination tournament to replace Ali as champion. And now the company, with Malitz as president and Kassel as vice president, wanted to be in the business of Ali's return.[17]

Kassel had gone to college at Emory. His first wife was from Atlanta. "I went to the office one day and thought, it sounds weird to try the South," he remembered. "It wouldn't be very likely. But what the hell." He called his father-in-law, Harry Pett, and asked him who might be able to make an Ali fight happen. "The man to see about that is Leroy Johnson," his father-in-law told him. Pett, the president of Pett's Spice Products, was from New England but had moved to Atlanta in 1953. He called Johnson on Kassel's behalf, promising Johnson and his team the live gate if they could make an Ali fight happen. Johnson seemed interested but wasn't sure about the legality. He promised to get back to Pett. When he found that "there was no state law on the books governing the sport of boxing," that "the question of whether or not a person got a license to fight addressed itself to each municipality," he felt confident. "I called Pett and said, 'Look, I can get him a license to fight in Georgia,' because I knew that the only legal body to make that decision was the mayor of Atlanta and the Board of Aldermen." Johnson also knew that he had helped get Massell elected, as well as several members of the board.[18]

Kassel flew to Atlanta and met with Johnson in a motel room, where within an hour they cut a deal. Kassel was worried about Lester Maddox, but Johnson was unfazed. "I'll take care of that," he told him. Johnson's first move was to create a new corporation, House of Sports, Incorporated, with ally Jesse Hill and Pett, who served as House of Sports vice president. Hill, for his part, had been frustrated by Ali's ban from its inception. He had long supported civil rights causes and saw the suspension as an injustice, and when an opportunity came to help remedy the wrong, Hill devoted himself to the cause. Under the auspices of the new corporation, Johnson and Hill went with a fight proposal to the board of aldermen, hoping to use Municipal Auditorium on October 26 to host an Ali fight with Joe Frazier. Kassel, through Sports Action's parent company, Tennis Unlimited, would finance publicity, fighter guarantees, and training camps, along with taking on promotion for ancillary rights to whatever bout materialized. They would collect the closed-circuit revenue and leave the rest for Johnson and the city.[19]

But first, Johnson visited Massell. "Sam, I want to bring Muhammad Ali here to fight."

Massell did a double take. "You want to bring who to do what? Leroy, I don't need to take all those brickbats on something like that."

But Johnson was quietly insistent. "Sam, I need your help. I can't do this without you."

Massell was silent for a moment. Then, "If anyone else had come in here and asked me for that, I'd of told him to go straight to hell. But you I can't tell no."[20] Massell was no fan of boxing, but he was sympathetic to the argument that an Ali fight would be good for the city. The mayor had been an appeal agent for the selective service during World War II and understood the regulations governing conscientious objectors. He could understand Ali's position and was willing to give Johnson a shot to make it happen. He also responded to Johnson's pitch that the fight would be a showcase for "the city too busy to hate." Atlanta could demonstrate itself to be sophisticated, racially moderate—to undo some of the negative racial publicity it had received over the last two years. Atlanta was, journalist Scott Freeman reasoned years later, "the only city in America with enough black political power to put Ali back in the ring." And Johnson's successful effort "would mark the first time the city's black leaders flexed their political muscle in the post–civil rights movement era."[21]

The governor had already gone on record as being opposed to a possible fight, claiming it to be "phooey," but Maddox had no power to stop it. Georgia had no boxing commission, and there was no significant legal hurdle to staging an Ali match. If the aldermen agreed, any remaining barrier would disappear. Johnson argued that if Paul Jones, promoter of

Georgia Championship Wrestling, headquartered in Atlanta, brought in Ali as a special guest referee for one of his wrestling matches, no one would or could stand in his way. Bringing the former champion to box was not much different. "In both cases, Clay is performing inside a ring."[22]

Paul Jones, the stage name of retired wrestler Andrew Lutzi, founded Georgia Championship Wrestling in 1944 as the public-facing name of ABC Booking. The company ran professional wrestling shows every Friday night at Municipal Auditorium for decades and eventually purchased the local Sports Arena on Chester Avenue. In early 1972 the company would begin its influential television program, *Big Time Wrestling*, but it was able to survive for years without a television program because of its consistent popularity in the city and its willingness to bring in celebrities for roles like special guest referee. GCW's popularity helped make many wrestling stars, but it also helped finance and maintain buildings like the Sports Arena and Municipal Auditorium—buildings that would be essential for the city's international boxing debut.[23]

Still, the governor couldn't be completely ignored. Johnson met Maddox in his office in the capitol. He knew that the governor's son had recently been arrested for burglary, and the trial judge had let him off while explaining that everyone deserved a second chance. "When I met with the governor," Johnson remembered, "I said to him, 'Everyone deserves a second chance. That's what I'm trying to get for Ali.'" It was a message with immediate relevance for Maddox. At the end of the meeting, the governor turned to Johnson. "Senator," he said, "on with the fight."[24] Andrew Young interpreted the governor's acquiescence as speaking "to a different image of Lester Maddox than most people have." He gave Maddox credit for working with Black officials on Atlanta's public transportation system, the Georgia World Congress Center, and the Ali fight. Maddox, upon entering the governor's chair, hired and promoted Black officials; he developed an early release program for the state's prisons. He hadn't stopped being racist, and would turn on Johnson and Ali soon enough, but for the moment a potential bout in Atlanta had gubernatorial support.[25]

Maddox, of course, was not the only white Georgian who hadn't stopped being racist. The same white newspapers in the city reporting on the negotiations were also running advertising for a Ku Klux Klan rally and cross lighting at Stone Mountain, where such meetings had been held for decades. In May 1970 the movie theater at the Peachtree Battle Shopping Center began showing D. W. Griffith's *Birth of a Nation*, including in its advertising that the Ku Klux Klan was featured in the film. And neither the people who would attend the film nor those who would attend the cross lighting wanted an Ali fight. They denounced the decision and even shot out a window at Johnson's house.[26]

Atlanta's Municipal Auditorium had never hosted a Klan rally. It was completed in 1909 as a showcase for big events in the city, part of that early striving for national relevancy. It had hosted the opera, and even featured a bust of Enrico Caruso; it had hosted tennis matches and the circus. But the most common event in the auditorium was Paul Jones's Friday night professional wrestling. It was, for Bert Sugar, "an old arena with pillars that looked like something out of *Gone with the Wind*." And it was the venue Johnson hoped to use to host Ali's return to the ring.[27]

When the aldermen responded positively to Johnson, the possibility of a fight became reality. "People think now that the Supreme Court decision is what allowed Ali to fight," remembered Harold Conrad, "but that didn't come until later. All it took was politics and money and three years of trying until we worked things out in Georgia." Jesse Outlar, *Constitution* sports editor, contacted Joe Frazier's manager, Yancey "Yank" Durham, who was in Nevada with the champion for a performance of his band, Joe Frazier and the Knockouts. Durham doubted the veracity of the Atlanta claim. "It's a lie," he said. "We aren't even dickering with Clay." But he did say that in the case that Ali actually was able to get a Georgia license to fight, "Frazier will fight him." Just as dubious was Bruce Wright of Philadelphia's Cloverlay, Incorporated, which promoted all of Frazier's fights. "I refuse to believe it," he said. "We've been through this before." But just like Durham, Wright conceded that if Ali really was licensed in Georgia, Frazier would fight him. Johnson had not bothered to contact the Frazier camp, but he had used his political connections to overcome a barrier that none of the more experienced sports promoters had been able to surmount. Outlar was certain that Frazier would sign a contract for the fight: "You simply don't reject a million dollar deal." That was yet to be seen, and Municipal Auditorium only had capacity for five thousand spectators, but the hardest part seemed to be over. "You don't ordinarily channel Sen. Leroy Johnson in a mental bracket with the late Tex Rickard and Mike Jacobs," Outlar wrote, "but he emerged Thursday as fight promoter of the decade."[28]

Thus it was, as Gerald Early has explained, that Ali received a Georgia boxing license, "something made possible by the very civil rights movement, the push for integration that, as a Black Muslim, Ali condemned."[29] While Johnson's political acumen technically won the day for the former champion, Early is right that without the integrationist efforts of the Southern movement, Johnson would never have been in a position to make such a deal and Maddox would have been in no position to allow it to happen. That the Nation of Islam bemoaned the movement as counterproductive added irony to the announcement—an irony that would have been more pronounced had Ali not been suspended from the faith at the time.

Johnson's announcement that Ali was eligible to fight in Atlanta sent a shock wave through the country. He had solved all the legal problems associated with the bout; he had even convinced Maddox, reluctantly, that the possible fight was not "phooey" after all. "We're all entitled to our mistakes," said Maddox. "This is the way I see it. I see nothing wrong with him fighting here." It was a capitulation, however temporary, that demonstrated Johnson's political acumen. "We have everything but the two fighters' signatures on the contracts," Johnson told the media. But while the hardest part was done, there were still hard parts remaining. Frazier, for example, had a verbal commitment to fight light heavyweight champion Bob Foster on October 21 in Detroit. The promoter for that fight died in early August, leaving that potential bout in limbo, but the Michigan Boxing Commission, fearing that it had squandered its opportunity, claimed that an Ali-Frazier fight had already been set up in Detroit for September 21, that commission approval had only been waiting on a resolution of ancillary rights fees paid to the state.[30]

But those were angels dancing on the heads of pins for so many Atlanta boosters. Johnson's press conference featured many of his longtime allies. Martin Luther King, Sr., Q. V. Williamson, and Marvin Arrington joined Maynard Jackson at the press conference. "It was a striking scene," explains Johnny Smith, "a picture of southern black unity in triumph." Not only would Ali fight in Atlanta, but a portion of the proceeds would go to battling the drug epidemic in the city. "It is obvious that Atlanta is full of people too busy to hate," said Johnson at the press conference. "This city has the capacity of becoming the finest city in the nation." Ali himself arrived after the announcement had been made. He was overweight but happy that he was going to be able to fight again. Jackson was effusive. "I want you to know how much we enjoy having you in the city," he told the champ.[31]

It was a press conference hard won in negotiations with the city, and it was also hard won in negotiations with the main attraction. When Johnson called Ali and told him that he could get a boxing license in Atlanta, Ali was skeptical. He had been burned so many times before. He had even been burned in Georgia, reminding Johnson of the Macon debacle. Johnson told him that it had been tried "in Georgia, but not in Atlanta." Pett and Hill began calling Ali's manager, but Johnson called Ali himself every day. The former champ finally decided to fly south to meet with the group after encouragement from his wife, Belinda. She was six months pregnant at the time and had previously had a child prematurely who lived for only half an hour, so Ali was eager to accommodate her and reduce her stress as much as possible.[32]

When he arrived in Atlanta a group was waiting for him at the airport. Johnson and Hill were joined by Maynard Jackson, along with Pett and Kassel, Sports Action's Mike Malitz, and publicist Harold Conrad. Ali knew, however, that mayoral approval was the linchpin of the deal and asked where Massell was. Jackson told him he was waiting at the hotel, but he wasn't. Johnson and Pett attempted to placate a worried Ali in his room at Paschal's Motor Hotel, explaining that Johnson could easily outmaneuver Maddox and had largely been responsible for putting Massell in office. "I know it looks like the same as what you've gone through before," Pett told him. "But there's something here missing in all the other packages promoters tried to put together. In Atlanta, there's black political power. The largest organized political power in the city is black."[33]

Paschal's itself was an Atlanta institution. Founded in 1947, the hotel and restaurant became an important hub of the civil rights movement, a place where leaders met to discuss strategy and tactics. But it was, moreover, a place of convergence where both the Black elite and Black working class came to eat. It was also where the former champion converged with the current mayor, as finally Massell arrived, welcoming Ali and assuring the group that he supported a fight in the city. But when it was time to go down to the press conference, Massell claimed to have another appointment. He wouldn't appear. "If you need me," he told them, "I'll be in my office." The group protested, but Massell refused. And if Massell wouldn't appear, Ali didn't think he should appear either, fearing that the event would make him look desperate and weak. So when the team got down to the press conference, Johnson called him and left the open phone line next to the platform so Ali could hear what was happening from his hotel room. Ali heard all the big names and Black leaders in the room, then changed his mind and decided to go down. As he walked into the press conference, Ali and Johnson and everyone else on the platform assumed that the fight would be against Joe Frazier. But even though that contest wouldn't materialize, the fight was on.[34]

Later, Johnson told journalist Stephen Lesher, "Now that's the way it works in this game." You called in favors, you made deals. "I've been accused of taking $50,000 under the table to help Massell get elected. But look, I'll make over three times that just from this fight that dropped in my lap out of the blue." Of course, not everyone could be allies. But "most of my enemies are guilty of Reconstruction thinking; they think that a politician—especially a black politician—only does something when you cross his palm with silver. What they don't understand is that when I support a man for an office, I want entry to that office, not money." Being able to talk to officials, to call in favors, to take advantage of relationships—those were the ways to make progress for Black Georgians. "I want to influence policy, I want to get blacks into key jobs and, yes, I want a voice in deciding who those blacks will be."[35]

While Ali's return to boxing was a direct result of Johnson's ability to call in favors and "the political peculiarities of Atlanta," as Michael Ezra has explained, it also came about "indirectly as a result of growing public sympathy for him" and against the Vietnam War, at least in areas outside the South. The *Atlanta Constitution*, for its part, was excited about the prospect of an Ali fight in Atlanta. "Our view is that he deserves no special treatment from his draft board or in the courts. But his boxing ability is something else."[36] The *Atlanta Daily World* was even more excited. After the announcement of the fight, the *World* republished a photo from years earlier when Ali, then the champion, visited Atlanta. In the photo he was playing around with local policemen on Auburn Avenue, pretending to challenge one of them to a fight as an interested crowd looked on.[37] It was a marked difference from the usual picture of adversarial positions between policemen and Black men with a crowd of onlookers, and one that was cause for celebration more than consternation.

WSB television news took to the street to ask a series of white residents downtown what they thought about the prospect of an Ali fight. The results were mixed. Some thought it would be a boon to the city and increase its national standing, while others preferred that it not happen because they didn't agree with Ali's draft stance. It was, then, for many white Atlanta residents, a question of priorities. None of those worried about the possibility of a fight considered the city's status as a major league sports city, and none of those welcoming the fight considered Ali's position on Vietnam. The two factors were in no way mutually exclusive, but in the early days of the announcement, white residents seemed to gauge their opinions by one or the other.[38]

Maddox, meanwhile, was less sanguine than Johnson, the *World*, or the man on the street. Despite his earlier endorsement, days later he changed his mind, claiming that he hadn't been aware of Ali's conviction for refusing induction into the army. In reality, he had learned from angry white constituents throughout the state how upset they were at his willingness to go along with the bout, so he changed his public position to keep in line with his political base. Johnson brushed off the governor's change of heart. Maddox was "a man of great compassion, and I'm certain he meant the kind things he said about giving Mr. Clay the opportunity to redeem himself" in his earlier comments. Of course, Maddox had known about Ali's draft status all along, and he wasn't a man of great compassion, but those were minor details. His opposition to the fight could do nothing to stop it.[39]

More pressing for Johnson was his negotiation with Frazier's camp. He claimed that he had sent copies of Ali's license and permission to use Municipal Auditorium to Frazier's lawyers. "We expect the contracts to be negotiated and agreed upon as quickly as possible," he said. But Yank Durham claimed that he had not had any contact with Johnson or his House of Sports, and that Frazier was still slated to fight Bob Foster.[40] Even with permits, "that evidence doesn't mean a thing because I've seen it twice before only to see them withdrawn when we called the boxing commissions for confirmation." Durham also assumed that the governor controlled boxing in every state. When reporters told him that wasn't the case in Georgia, he responded by asking, "Doesn't the governor control the state police? Well, if the state police appeared at the arena on the night of the fight, wouldn't that hurt the gate?" He had a commitment to the World Boxing Association and a commitment to Bob Foster, and he wasn't interested in staging a Frazier-Ali fight in Atlanta in October. It would cost $30,000 to train for the fight, so "the promise of money isn't important. Money in hand is." Neither Durham nor Frazier would even consider a deal "until we knew the governor approved."[41]

It seemed like a hard pass from the Frazier camp, but the city didn't give up. Dick Cecil, vice president of the Atlanta Braves, offered Atlanta Stadium as a larger venue after receiving permission from the stadium authority. Johnson traveled to Philadelphia to meet with Durham and Frazier in August, and he was guardedly optimistic about the prospects. "We are going to lend what helping hand we can in getting the contract signed," he told reporters, noting that having a choice of sites would only boost the offer.[42]

Though House of Sports still held out hope, or at least a public-facing confidence, that Ali-Frazier would take place in Atlanta, by August 20 it was clear that the odds were against it happening. Durham told the *New York Times* that "we're not interested in Cassius Clay until we see that he gets in the ring." As a remedy, Johnson announced that he would stage exhibition bouts with Ali prior to some legitimate fight on October 26, with an opponent to be determined, but one that Johnson assured reporters would be a "ranking heavyweight." One of the possibilities was Argentine Oscar Bonavena, ranked as the WBA's top contender, who admitted that he was flying to Miami to discuss the offer. Bonavena had lost to Frazier twice, but had competed well and kept Frazier from knocking him out. He claimed that his brother was already in Miami negotiating for a minimum guarantee of $100,000. Those negotiations, however, were not with House of Sports; in lieu of getting Frazier, Johnson ceded control of choosing an opponent to Kassel's Sports Action, which negotiated with Bonavena.[43]

Whoever the opponent would ultimately be, Johnson and others saw the possibility of an Ali fight not simply as a spectacle, but as an opportunity to make Atlanta a destination for championship boxing. In the late 1960s the city had been obsessed with bolstering its reputation through the acquisition of professional sports franchises like the Braves, Falcons, and Hawks. Boxing had no franchises, but it brought with it the same kinds of reputational advantages, and featuring a controversial activist fighter like Ali would only help enhance Atlanta's image as a city too busy to hate, despite the real racial problems hiding under the surface of such slogans. *Constitution* sports editor Jesse Outlar proposed making the October Atlanta fight a semifinal of sorts, with Ali fighting one opponent in Atlanta while Frazier fought Bob Foster in Detroit. Then the two could meet each other after those bouts back in Atlanta for the championship. Johnson, realizing that Ali-Frazier would probably not happen in October, latched onto the idea as a real possibility.[44]

His efforts were taking place during a difficult campaign season, wherein a contested gubernatorial race captured the attention of many. It was the election to replace Lester Maddox, and a variety of hopefuls wanted to take the mantle from him. The most prominent Democratic candidates in the race were former governor and Atlanta Hawks owner Carl Sanders, endorsed by Johnson and running a relatively progressive campaign, and peanut farmer and former state senator Jimmy Carter, who would, over the course of the campaign, make a play for supporters of Maddox by moving temporarily to the racial right. Sanders and Carter, however, were not alone. Johnson's support for Carl Sanders for the position and his efforts to secure the Ali fight through a private company gave the Black candidate, C. B. King, an Albany lawyer, an avenue to attack. For King, Johnson and fellow Black state representative Ben Brown were "political prostitutes who have forgotten the reason why black people should come together." It was vague criticism, to be sure. His principal frustration was simply that both Johnson and Brown were supporting Sanders. "The Johnsons and the Browns are saying we got to go with a winner. We've been taken by that before. But winning ain't been winning for us."[45] If there was a substantial argument below the rhetoric, it was that Black leaders siding with a white candidate when a Black candidate was in the race was a form of race traitorism. Johnson, for his part, ignored King's attack. Still, the brief controversy demonstrated the complicated racial politics of the city where Ali would fight. King was attacking Black elected officials for supporting a white liberal, and attacking that white liberal as well. He wasn't attacking the more conservative white candidate, Jimmy Carter, not because he didn't oppose some of Carter's more problematic racial stances, but because he knew that the opportunity to peel voters from the front-runners lay with those who supported Sanders.

Atlanta Journal political editor Steve Ball noted that the contest among Black power brokers was more than theoretical. Johnson "has been the single most powerful black voice, politically speaking, in Georgia," and he was supporting Sanders. "If Sanders breaks even with King, or does better than King among blacks" in the Democratic primary, "Johnson solidifies his position of power." If that didn't happen, however, "King automatically steps into a powerful bargaining position." The balance of Black political power in Atlanta was on the line.[46]

There was legitimate concern from King and others about Johnson's support for Sanders. When the former governor left office in 1966, he was known as a moderate who had supported Lyndon Johnson and refused to fight federal school desegregation orders, but in 1970, facing pressure from the right from Carter and assuming he would lose much of the Black primary vote to King, Sanders began campaigning on "law and order," returning schools to local control, and expelling students participating in protests. Georgia had abandoned its long Democratic tradition in 1964 to vote for Republican Barry Goldwater, then put Maddox in the governor's mansion in 1966, then gave its electoral college votes to George Wallace in 1968. The political winds were blowing in the direction of reactionary racial stances in Georgia.[47]

Sports, for better or worse, were an integral part of the governor's race that year. Sanders was not only a white racial moderate, but he also owned the Blackest of Atlanta's professional sports teams, the NBA's Hawks. Early in the summer the Carter campaign released a series of anonymous flyers designed to attack its opponent, one featuring Sanders being doused with champagne by two large Black men. It was a photo common to those involved in professional sports. The Hawks celebrated a division championship by pouring champagne over the heads of teammates, team personnel, and owners. Such was the shorthand of professional athletics, but Georgians outside of the city had yet to learn that language. The Hawks celebration picture became known as the "champagne shampoo," demonstrating Sanders's wealth, his association with alcohol, and, most importantly, his association with Blackness. The flyer joined others that highlighted Sanders's connection with Julian Bond, the fact that Sanders had attended the funeral of Martin Luther King,

Jr., and Sanders's opposition to George Wallace.[48] It was an effort to use Black sports to convince white Georgia that Carter's opponent was not an advocate of white interests. Professional basketball was in the same category as Julian Bond or Martin Luther King. Black sport, the Carter campaign seemed to be saying in the months before the Ali fight, was an affront to white values.

Meanwhile, in the midst of fight negotiations and the racial provocations of gubernatorial politics, Ali's wife, Belinda, gave birth to premature twin daughters, both of them less than three pounds. His wife was in critical condition in a Philadelphia hospital, and the twins, Reeshemah and Jamillah, were struggling as well, only adding to the former champion's stress. Belinda, though, soon recovered, and the twins were in incubators and doing as well as possible for children with such low birth weights.[49]

The survival of the twins was still a questionable prospect a week later, but Ali's sporting difficulties were beginning to ease. On August 28 Johnson's House of Sports, in conjunction with Tennis Unlimited and Sports Action, announced that Ali would spar in two four-round exhibition bouts at Morehouse College on September 2. Rufus Brassell, a young fighter with three professional fights, including a knockout loss to Jerry Quarry, and Johnny Hudgins, a journeyman boxer who, like Ali, was based in Miami, would be his opponents. Johnson and Jesse Hill worried that if Ali appeared at Municipal Auditorium as his first fight in Atlanta, "then the Ku Klux Klan and the White Citizen's Council would come in and tear up the place." So Johnson called Morehouse president Hugh Gloster, assuming that holding an exhibition at a Black college "would insulate us from the possibility of an eruption from the Ku Klux Klan and other whites." Gloster was eager to oblige, understanding after the protests on his campus that students would overwhelmingly support the return of a Black Power icon at the college.[50]

The Morehouse gymnasium—the Samuel H. Archer Health and Physical Education Building—sat three thousand people, and the promoters were confident that the building would be at capacity. The last distinguished visitor that the gymnasium hosted was Ethiopian emperor Haile Selassie months prior. At the press conference announcing the exhibitions, Mike Malitz maintained his hope that Ali's official opponent in

October would be Frazier, but for the first time noted that if that option failed, another possibility could be California's Jerry Quarry.[51]

Any time Ali was in the ring was exciting, but the white *Atlanta Constitution* was loath to report that Brassell and Hudgins were "a couple of sparring partners who will be wearing headgear and who apparently are so obscure that the promoters do not know their ring records." The paper, however, wasn't naive. Its sportswriters understood that the reason for the exhibitions was to demonstrate to the Frazier camp Ali's ability to fight in Atlanta. The Morehouse gym sat three thousand, but the contests would be directed to an audience of one.[52]

It was an audience that would need convincing. "If there is any place where there is tolerance and good will, then it is Atlanta," Johnson said the day before the exhibitions. Ali seemed to agree. "I am not surprised that Atlanta is where I am permitted to return to the ring," he told reporters. "I have always admired the South because people here are truthful. You know where you stand. Up North, people say things they don't mean." Honesty and goodwill, however, were often mutually exclusive. As promoters readied the city for the September exhibitions, the local district of the American Legion castigated Ali and the possibility of him boxing in Georgia, as did the Veterans of Foreign Wars. The Legionnaires sent a petition to Maddox and city officials urging them to step in.[53] The Legion knew that Atlanta may have been a place of tolerance and goodwill, but it was also a place with majority support for the conflict in Vietnam and a longstanding suspicion of outsiders that the group tried to leverage to keep Ali from the ring.

The *World*'s Marion Jackson was disgusted by the Legion and what he called "the sordid and cancerous sickness in American civic, community and political structure, along with flag-waving veterans and patriotic societies, along with the anguished mob psychology, embellished by their intellectual futility in deploying integration" that "has somehow used him [Ali] as a symbol of their wait and delay tactics against a unitary school system in the USA." And they were waiting and delaying with his return to boxing. "Can Star-Spangled Americans forget so quickly, and ignore in smugness and inhumanity that all people don't conform?" Ali, after all, was a boxer, lecturer, poet, and champion of human rights, and also "a friend of the common everyday people." He "mingles with the avenue boys and the ghetto inhabitants, who are almost devoid of hope, and is a tremendous inspirational force for the deprived, degraded and the devastated of our society, who find no panacea in sloganisms."[54]

Ali was all those things, but he was also a polymath. Before his Morehouse exhibition, he announced that he would star for a second time in *Buck White*. This time the play would tour the country, focusing on college audiences, beginning October 1. The revival would give Ali a chance to spread his political message and earn income as a hedge against any potential failure in Johnson's effort to produce a fight for him in Atlanta. The tour would take place only if the opportunity to box once again turned into a mirage.[55]

As part of his time in Atlanta, Ali attended events with the Southern Christian Leadership Conference and other groups, spending time with Coretta Scott King and her children, along with other civil rights leaders.[56] And then, on September 2, Ali finally returned to the ring, fighting an exhibition against three fighters. "The roof did not fall in," *Sports Illustrated* reported. "No one threw a bomb. Fire and brimstone did not rain down from heaven and no one was turned into a pillar of salt. There wasn't even a picket outside the Morehouse College gym in Atlanta—just a pretty girl distributing election campaign pamphlets."[57] Brassell and Hudgins ultimately got two rounds apiece before Ali sparred with Philadelphia's George Hill for four rounds. Hill was another young fighter based in Philadelphia, with two wins, one loss, and two draws in five professional fights. An estimated 2,700 fans crowded into a hot gymnasium without air conditioning and thrilled to see a Muhammad Ali who looked surprisingly similar to the fighter they had last seen three years prior. "I never heard no sound come from humans like what they gave [Ali]," Drew "Bundini" Brown remembered. Ali largely played defense against Brassell and Hudgins, diving and weaving away from their lunging attempts at his head. Neither fighter ever hit it. It was in his third fight with Hill that Ali showcased his offense to the appreciative crowd. In his second round against Hill, his sixth of the night, Ali found himself backed into a corner before erupting with a flurry of punches that pushed Hill to the center of the ring. Even as the crowd went crazy, Ali let up; this was a glorified workout, and he had no intention of knocking anyone out. Still, that didn't stop him from matching that strike rate in his seventh total round. In his corner Ali admitted that he was tired, and that he needn't go farther because it was an exhibition. Bundini Brown fumed. "This ain't no goddam exhibition, n——. This the Resurrection!" Ali had been through so much to get to this point, and now "them people out there, they bringin' you back to life." Brown was pushed in part by Harold Conrad, who was coordinating the filming of the exhibition for ABC's *Wide World of Sports*. Conrad had told Brown halfway through the exhibition that the crew was going to stop filming, because the fight was not exciting and Ali looked somewhat lackluster. So Brown reminded Ali that "the Government's ready to bury your ass underneath the jail. But they come to dig you out the grave. Tired? When you spendin' them five years in jail you get tired. Not now, Champ, not now! Now's your Resurrection Day! Straighten up!" In the eighth round, even though the crowd was howling for a knockout, Ali instead began his signature shuffle, dancing around Hill and giving the fans the next best thing to a fighter on the canvas.[58]

"Thus were confounded a horde of timid politicians in some 70 communities from one end of the U.S. to the other," said *Sports Illustrated*, noting the fear of offended veterans' organizations and other advocacy groups. "Despite the efforts of scores of promoters and would-be promoters, skilled and unskilled alike, no community would sit still for an Ali match." There were as many reasons given for refusing an Ali fight as there were attempts to make one, but all boiled down to "the timorousness of politicians, the noisy professional patriotism of various groups and occasional promotional ineptitude." Ali had come closest in Detroit and Houston, where contracts had been signed, but ultimately voided through political pressure. But then came Atlanta, "the South's most socially sophisticated and least racially torn big city."[59]

Ali was generally satisfied with his performance, but "I'm not in shape," he told reporters after the fights. "In eight weeks I will come into the ring ready at 210." He fought that night at 220, down from 235 at his original introductory press conference, but there was still more work to do. Target weight or not, however, his effort was spellbinding to most, all the more so because his three-year absence from the ring was compounded in an arena without air conditioning on a hot September night in the South. While his opponent for eight weeks away had not yet been formally established, it seemed that Jerry Quarry was the most likely option, as Quarry had defeated Mac Foster earlier in 1970 to become the number-one heavyweight contender. Ali provided a tell to that effect when asked about how he would have fared against Frazier that night at Morehouse. He admitted that he would have been flat-footed after eight rounds, "but back when I was fighting, neither Frazier nor Quarry would give me much trouble." Rufus Brassell reminded reporters after the bout that he had fought Jerry Quarry, and though Quarry had knocked him out in the second round, Brassell had taken him down in the first. "I believe Muhammad could have whipped Quarry tonight," he said. "And with the proper work, he will be more than enough for Frazier."[60]

He was more than enough for the crowd assembled at Morehouse, too, which thrilled to every Ali shuffle and punch. "I was a junior when Ali boxed here," remembered student Alvin Darden. "You couldn't get into the gym; it was packed. At the time, among Morehouse students, there was enormous interest in Afro-American consciousness and pride. That's why we loved Ali. He was fighting for his liberation." It was for Darden and his fellow students "a metaphor for what we were going through. So it wasn't just a boxer in our gym. It was part of a movement."[61] Along with the students, Martin Luther King, Sr., was there, as were members of the King family. Perhaps more importantly, there was no racist picket or protest. Ali had proved himself capable of professional boxing again, but Atlanta had proven itself, as well.[62]

While his opponents wore headgear, Ali declined, "because that's the way you tell if you took any good head shots." His trainer Angelo Dundee was perhaps more impressed than anyone in the scorching arena. "For any other heavyweight in history it would take them six months to return from a three-year layoff and perform as Ali did tonight," he said. "Dempsey, Tunney, Louis, all of them. This man here is truly a remarkable athlete."[63]

The Baltimore *Afro-American* was grateful Ali had the opportunity. He fought eight rounds "and the sky didn't fall in at all." Though Atlanta was not usually the source of positive racial news, "the nation, when it returns to a more sane period and a less repressive mood, may find itself owing Atlanta and Georgia officials a vote of appreciation for having the wisdom and courage to restore to Ali his right to fight." The paper credited "the rising political influence of black citizens in Atlanta" as making the former champ's return a possibility. "A lot of athletic commissions, a number of state and local officials and a lot of super-patriots and reactionaries may be forced to take another look at themselves in [the] face of Atlanta's action." The paper's Sam Lacy described Georgia's licensing of Ali as a "re-emancipation," one made all the more significant because it happened "in the heart of Dixie," in "this one-time stronghold of Confederate philosophy." Of course, that licensing was less a product of a change in white southern ideology and more the work of Leroy Johnson and Jesse Hill, whom the *Afro* credited with the heavy lifting of making the exhibition happen. At ringside in the Morehouse gymnasium were Kassel and Malitz, as well as Richard Cecil, vice president of the Atlanta Braves, and wrestling promoter Paul Jones, who held the license for Municipal Auditorium—a sign to many that Ali would have another official bout in the city.[64]

It was also at least a tentative sign that the political winds might be shifting. Ali's exhibition at Morehouse took place as the new school year was getting underway. As of the onset of the previous school year, 117 of Atlanta's 154 public schools remained segregated, with 80 percent of the students still learning in single-race classrooms. In January 1970 the U.S. District Court in Atlanta ordered the desegregation of teachers in the city's public schools, then in February it ordered that Black students wanting to attend majority-white schools be provided free transportation. As Ali was sparring at Morehouse, Black students began attending the public school of their choice for the first time. The new orders accelerated white flight from the school system, meaning that most of the city's schools, despite the image Atlanta had developed for itself, remained segregated. But Black student choice did create a situation wherein, for the first time, a greater percentage of Black students than white students learned in integrated settings.[65]

The day after the Morehouse exhibition, Johnson was again off to Philadelphia to negotiate with the Frazier team. At the airport, national reporters who had gathered for the exhibition rounds asked him about Atlanta's willingness to host such a bout. "I think it all goes back to Ralph McGill," Johnson said of the former editor of the *Atlanta Constitution*, a racial moderate who had stumped for comparatively liberal positions on desegregation. "He taught whites and blacks to get along with each other. There have been some demonstrations here, but black and white leaders have had sense enough to sit down with each other and let the conference table resolve our difficulties." While there was some truth in

Johnson's statement, the tumult of the previous decade had demonstrated that it was more pomp than circumstance. But the brave face he wore was one of a politician and promoter. "We've made greater progress in Atlanta than any other city in the South in the past 10 years."[66]

To be sure, there had been progress. Just over a week later, on September 12, Eddie McAshan became the first Black quarterback to play for Georgia Tech when the Yellow Jackets hosted South Carolina. It was, for the *Atlanta Inquirer*, "a date of great significance in the history of football." The *Atlanta Daily World* also covered the milestone game as Tech defeated the Gamecocks 30–23, McAshan completing 20 of 36 passes for 202 yards. "Never before had a Negro quarterbacked a SEC team, and like the Cassius Clay or Muhammad Ali exhibition, it happened in of all places Atlanta." That wasn't exactly true, as Georgia Tech had left the Southeastern Conference in 1964 and was playing as an independent, but McAshan was the first Black quarterback of a team associated with the SEC, and only the second Black quarterback to play for a traditionally white team in the South, after Wake Forest's Freddie Summers in 1967. The *World* described the "sometimes dubious trademark of Georgia's Capitol [*sic*] City being the 'New York of the South,'" and argued that "strange as it seems, McAshan and Ali may have proved the point."[67] Even in the seminal breaking of a legitimate racial barrier in a football-mad region of the country, Ali's exhibition bout was, for Black audiences, a measuring stick by which such events were judged.

The same day McAshan started at quarterback for Tech, Ali's Morehouse exhibition was broadcast nationally on ABC's *Wide World of Sports*, with Howard Cosell and Ali providing commentary. Atlanta that day presented to the nation a Black major college quarterback and the first nationally broadcast boxing rounds in three years for the most controversial athlete in the world. Though racial controversy still roiled the city and state, the presentations of Ali and McAshan gave the impression of a progressive city willing to countenance racial equality in a way that the rest of the South was not. That was, if not really accurate, the kind of image the city hoped to cultivate; it was a decided public relations coup for Atlanta.[68]

So Ali's return to the ring at Morehouse was a success by every measurable standard. The only hiccup on the night was when Ali's cornerman, Bundini Brown, admitted that there was still more work to be done before a sanctioned professional fight. "All we need now is more gas in the tank," he told reporters. "You can't become a soldier until you go to basic training."[69] It was the kind of clichéd athletic argot used in many settings and many sports, but when describing a fighter who had been out for three years specifically because of his refusal to become a soldier and to attend basic training, it only gave the media another opportunity to rehash the reasons the former champ was in the Morehouse gymnasium rather than Madison Square Garden. Still, Ali had proven his mettle; the countdown to a real fight was on.

But it was a countdown that wouldn't include Joe Frazier. Yank Durham explained to Johnson on his Philadelphia visit that Frazier's contract with Bob Foster for a fight in November was already signed. Only two days after Ali had stepped out of the ring in Atlanta, Johnson admitted to journalists that the Frazier fight was out, at least for October.[70] Instead, five days later, Kassel announced in New York that Ali's opponent for the October 26 Atlanta fight would be Jerry Quarry, *Ring Magazine*'s number-one contender and the WBA's third-ranked contender. The California fighter had a professional record of thirty-seven wins, five losses, and four draws. The contract was signed at a public news conference at Manhattan's Hotel Brookshire on September 10. As Kassel remembered it, Hal Conrad was the one who suggested, "'Let's get a white hope.' So that's why we went after Quarry." It would be the first time that Ali fought a white opponent on American soil since defeating George Logan in 1962, the year Johnson won his seat in the Georgia state senate, only adding to the racialized climate surrounding the bout, which featured a brash Black Muslim fighting in a Deep South state run by Lester Maddox. It was also the first time Ali would fight a younger opponent. "If one had wished to arrange the ingredients of Ali's return to the ring according to a recipe of racial melodrama," wrote Jack Richardson in *Harper's*, "Quarry was the perfect choice."[71]

Johnson was there as the two boxers signed a contract for the fight, to be held at Municipal Auditorium. While Atlanta Stadium had been held out as a possible venue for Ali-Frazier, Quarry, despite his legitimacy as a contender, was not the kind of name that could fill tens of thousands of seats. "I always knew it was going to happen someday," Ali told reporters at the signing event. He saw his Georgia boxing license as "a personal victory," but publicly worried about his readiness. "What champion ever stayed out of the ring for three years and then had to get ready in six weeks?" he asked. "It's gonna be tough and maybe I can't do it."[72]

Most, however, assumed that he could. Durham still didn't believe that the fight would actually take place, but he hoped that it would. Assuming Ali defeated Quarry, Durham told reporters that Frazier would fight him "any place in the United States he can get a license." Frazier said the same, "including Atlanta." For Johnson it was a lifeline that made up for the disappointment of not starting with Frazier, maintaining the possibility of turning the city into a boxing mecca, the Madison Square Garden of the South.[73]

Atlanta had never hosted a fight like that of Ali and Quarry before, but its interest in battles between Black champions and Great White Hopes was not entirely new. When Jack Johnson faced Jim Jeffries in 1910, more than ten thousand people waited outside the offices of the *Atlanta Journal*, listening for results from Nevada. At various venues around the city, announcers receiving the information would call the fight from notes as they came in by telegraph. At the Atlanta Crackers baseball game, updates on the fight were announced each half inning. Black Atlanta held an announcing gathering at the People's Tabernacle, with a barbecue and speeches by prominent city leaders. "Atlanta," the *Constitution* reported, "has gone crazy over the Jeffries-Johnson fight." When Johnson defeated the White Hope, the *Journal* mocked him with a picture of Jeffries accosted by an ink bottle labeled "Johnson."[74]

The Johnson-Jeffries fight would be significant beyond just Atlanta. It created the search for the Great White Hope, a search that would remain in boxing through the rest of the century. Tex Rickard promoted the fight specifically along racial lines, knowing that calling Jeffries the "Hope of the White Race" and Johnson the "Negroes' Deliverer" would draw fan interest and revenue. "Quite conceivably," argues Randy Roberts, "there had never been a more important athletic event in American history" than the Johnson-Jeffries bout. Jeffries, for his part, understood his role. "That portion of the white race that has been looking to me to defend its athletic superiority," he said, "may feel assured that I am fit to do my very best." Jim Corbett, who had defeated John L. Sullivan in 1892 on the same card that featured George "Little Chocolate" Dixon and Jack Skelly, was in Jeffries's corner. An arch white supremacist, Corbett hated

Johnson and spent the bulk of the fight screaming racist epithets in a failed bid to fluster Jeffries's opponent.[75]

The bout would give lie to much of the social Darwinist rhetoric that dominated boxing narratives at the time, but it would also have real-world consequences for many, particularly in Georgia and surrounding areas. In Uvalda, Georgia, Black construction workers celebrating Johnson's victory were attacked by a group of angry whites who marched on the construction camp and shot eight of the Black revelers, killing three. In Greenwood, South Carolina, just over the Georgia border, several whites attacked Black residents in response to the fight, sparking fear in the city and ensuring that no Black resident would celebrate or even publicly discuss Johnson's win. There were other casualties in Houston, Little Rock, Roanoke, Norfolk, New Orleans, Baltimore, and Chattanooga. But it wasn't just the South: racial violence in response to the fight happened in Cincinnati, Los Angeles, Boston, Washington, New York, and St. Louis. Jeffries had fallen in the fifteenth round, but so many others fell in the days after the crowd in Reno had gone home. Meanwhile, municipalities across the country—Atlanta among them—banned showings of the fight in local movie theaters. Mayor Robert Maddox and police commissioner Carlos Mason argued that showing the fight "could serve no good purpose," despite the interest shown by the city before Johnson's victory.[76]

Now Atlanta had a new racial boxing melodrama to consume, and Ali, playing the Jack Johnson role, knew that he was taking a substantial risk. He understood that if he lost to Quarry "everything would change," explains Jonathan Eig. "He understood that the safer move would have been to retire. He would have gone out on top, undefeated. He would have won the respect of Elijah Muhammad. He would have completed his martyrdom by sacrificing his career. He would have been remembered forever as a champion." And he was taking that risk alone. He complained during his training of loneliness after his time being feted by college students and antiwar activists. "We'd all have sessions on what we was gonna talk about and dinner was then planned in the hall, and we'd go to the student union buildin' and have the meetin' and they'd ask me questions, all the boys and girls, black and white," he said. "Now I'm just all by myself." Ali was taking the difficult path. That was what made him Ali. "Nobody has to tell me this is serious business," he said. "If I lose I'll be in jail for the rest of my life. If I lose I will not be free. I'll have to listen to all this about how I was a bum, I was fat, I joined the wrong movement, they misled me. So I'm fighting for my freedom." Meanwhile, were Quarry to win, everything was in front of him. "Quarry'll be a movie star," said Ali. "By beating me, he'll be so valuable. He'll be in big cinemas, probably playing in a top Western, the man who defeated Muhammad Ali. Like the man who shot Liberty Valance. He'll be a great man."[77]

At the press conference announcing the bout with Quarry, Ali described letters and calls from fans expressing worry about the failures of former boxing returns after long layoffs and retirements. And then there were "those people who say I was overrated before, and that Jerry Quarry will prove it now. All this leaves no time for poems, jokes and gimmicks." He held no anger, or claimed to hold no anger, against "the commissioners, or the American Legion, or the Foreign Legion, or all those arena owners. They did what they thought was right according to their beliefs." Some fights you lose, and real athletes didn't get mad over losses. "Whatever Allah wills is gonna happen, and I just try to please Allah, even if it means this man's law is broken, or this man's gonna put me on the firin' squad."[78] The dedication to his faith was all the more admirable to observers as it was practiced even after Elijah Muhammad's suspension. He was experiencing two simultaneous exiles, one from his profession and another from his church, but his training ensured that one of those absences would end in the coming weeks and his faith ensured that the other was never really gone.

Columnist Robert Lipsyte was glad for the return. Boxing had been boring since Ali went away. His fights were not memorable epics, but "the build-ups to those fights" made the sport relevant and interesting. "The star is back, he is reborn, and boxing will have some bright days."[79]

Or he hoped it would. The buildup to the fight included constant questions about whether or not it would even take place. Though Lester Maddox was powerless to stop the Morehouse exhibition, he did have an option that he didn't realize. The city's "Rules and Regulations Governing all Boxing Contests in the City of Atlanta" had been written in the late nineteenth century. Section 28 said that "no mixed bouts shall be permitted between white and black contestants in the city of Atlanta."

When Johnson learned of the regulation, and knowing that Quarry was locked in as Ali's opponent, he again went to the aldermen, convincing them to quietly remove the provision for its inconsistency with the Civil Rights Act of 1964 and the Fourteenth Amendment.[80]

There were still, however, other potential issues. Kassel had bought out his Sports Action cofounder, Bob Arum, earlier in 1970, and after the Morehouse exhibition and the announcement of the Quarry fight, Arum announced that he was suing Kassel over the original sale. Arum also contacted Johnson and tried to convince him to break his relationship with Sports Action and instead join a new organization that Arum was planning. Arum was close with Chris Dundee, Angelo's brother, and the two also approached Quarry, trying to convince him to stall the Atlanta fight while Arum and the younger Dundee sought a Florida license allowing Ali and Quarry to box in Miami. Both Johnson and Quarry demurred, but Kassel had further troubles. He had difficulty securing letters of credit from at least one New York bank that was worried about being associated with the fight. Several sponsors turned down radio rights, fearing that their companies would be branded un-American as a result. The letters of credit would eventually arrive, and the fight, which featured a redemption story and a race story being monetized in a growing metropolis, was one of the most quintessentially American events ever held, but the problems demonstrated that Southern bigotry was not the only potential impediment to Ali's return to the ring.[81]

Meanwhile, Herbert Muhammad, Ali's former manager and son of Elijah Muhammad, began appearing again after the exhibition. He stayed in the background, as Ali was still suspended from the faith, but it was clear that with all of the financial wrangling that resulted in the former champion's return to the ring, the Black Muslims saw restoring their end of the relationship with Ali as a good idea, one that could be as lucrative for them as it was for Kassel and Johnson.[82]

A week after the Morehouse exhibition, the Democratic Party held its gubernatorial primary, with Sanders soundly defeating C. B. King, even among Black voters. The win for Sanders was also interpreted locally as a win for Johnson, who had marshaled the support of the Black community for Sanders over the Black candidate. "Like Muhammad Ali, whom he brought to Atlanta," wrote *Journal* political editor Steve Ball, "State Sen. Leroy Johnson has the habit of making good on his boasts."

Despite attacks from King, Hosea Williams, and other more radical Black leaders, Johnson demonstrated that he was the leading political power broker among Georgia's Black voters. It was clear, of course, that Johnson wasn't the only reason for Sanders's African American support. Sanders had served the Black population reasonably well in his first stint in the governor's mansion, and he had also been endorsed by insurance magnate Jesse Hill, educator Benjamin Mays, and professor Clarence A. Bacote. But King had support from Julian Bond and Coretta Scott King. Sanders's victory among Black voters only bolstered the influence of Johnson, whom most saw as both the largest influence on that victory and a winner in his own right. If the governor's race had taken place only in Atlanta, Sanders would have become the Democratic nominee, but in the wake of racial controversy, the rural white part of the state would side with Carter, a rural white man who had campaigned on his ideological proximity to Maddox, leaving no one with more than 50 percent of the vote.[83]

A runoff between Sanders and Carter would take place two weeks later, causing consternation among Black leaders in Atlanta concerning Carter's race-baiting campaign and the infamous "champagne shampoo" flyer that played to the bigotry of rural white voters. Johnson was a prominent fixture in an advertisement running in the *Atlanta Daily World* denouncing Carter as saying, "I don't need a single black vote to win." Carter was supported by notorious racists like former governor Marvin Griffin and Roy V. Harris, former speaker of the Georgia House of Representatives. Sanders, Johnson's ad said, wanted the vote of every Georgian, whether Black or white. Johnson's signature on the public endorsement was joined by those of Mays, Bacote, Martin Luther King, Sr., and other prominent leaders. Carter, however, was right. Rural white voters outnumbered Black urbanites, and the peanut farmer took the nomination and began his rise to political prominence.[84]

Johnson was pitching himself as the moral voice of politics in Georgia and also as the de facto leader of boxing promotion in the state, even though the sport had experienced its own problems with morality over the years. After the primary Johnson publicly announced that he had a commitment from Ali that even though he would not be fighting for the title in October, when he did eventually fight Frazier, he would do so in Atlanta. "Let me repeat, we WILL sponsor the fight—here in Atlanta—

probably around the first of the year." Johnson lauded the city's influence. "We had the foresight and courage and the human compassion to grant Mr. Clay a license first. We put him back in the ring first. When other states and cities refused him, we didn't." Besides, he said, Ali had given his word that he would fight Frazier in Atlanta. "We will sponsor his title fight because Mr. Clay is an honorable man."[85]

Johnson's was the language of an experienced political operative. He knew that he was speaking to a predominantly white audience and used the champion's former name as part of a strategy to mollify those who would otherwise rankle at hearing the name Muhammad Ali. No such convention would convince recalcitrant racists of the worth of an Ali match being held in Atlanta, of course, but it would ensure that insult wasn't added to injury. It was, in a sense, a display of the double consciousness of W.E.B. Du Bois, the savvy Black pol understanding how to speak to white audiences in a manner that made his own life easier and helped ensure that the fight he had worked so hard to secure would continue.

The *New York Times* always referred to Ali by his chosen name, using Cassius Clay only when quoting white Southerners who refused to acknowledge it, while the *Atlanta Constitution* used Clay far more than Ali as a moniker, and often used both interchangeably. It was a decidedly different media presentation, one that demonstrated the difference in white Southern thinking about Black religion and activism. The refusal to use Ali's chosen name could, theoretically, be the result of Elijah Muhammad's ban of the fighter from the Nation of Islam and the reclaiming of his name. In reality, however, white Southerners used Ali's birth name as a public refusal to acknowledge the legitimacy of his faith. "My name is Muhammad Ali, not Cassius Clay," an angry Ali told reporters while training in Miami for the fight, "and it's surprising how many blacks still call me Cassius. The white people, who really can't stand it, never make that mistake." But he would find in Atlanta that they did, and they did so intentionally.[86]

It wasn't just Atlanta. The *New York Amsterdam News*'s Dick Edwards took the white New York dailies and their sports columnists to task for referring to Ali as Cassius Clay, for excoriating the state boxing commission for reinstating the fighter's license, and for supporting the American Legion protests against the Ali-Quarry fight. "Your prejudice shows," he told them, noting that Ali's fight was attracting more attention and more money than Frazier's comparable fight against Bob Foster in Detroit. "Really old boy," he told New York's white sportswriters, "you have the shock of your life coming." In another editorial the *Amsterdam News* pointed out that Sugar Ray Robinson's birth name was Walker Smith, and Jersey Joe Walcott's was Arnold Cream, and no one felt the need to ignore their chosen name. It was "a picayune gesture," one that demonstrated that intransigent sportswriters were "being smalltime."[87]

The announcement of a potential second fight in Atlanta was anything but smalltime. It was also something of a preemptive attack. Earlier that day, September 14, a federal district judge in the New York lawsuit brought by the NAACP's Legal Defense Fund overturned a 1969 ruling by the New York State Athletic Commission and granted Ali the right to fight in New York. The commission had "denied Ali his rights under the 14th Amendment to equal protection," wrote Judge Walter R. Mansfield, and had done so in an "arbitrary and unreasonable" manner. It was a ruling long overdue, the *New York Amsterdam News* reasoned, pointing out that since Ali's suspension, the state's boxing commission had granted or renewed licenses to at least 244 men with criminal convictions ranging from extortion to second-degree murder. That information was courtesy of Legal Defense Fund attorney Ann Wagner, who had researched each instance of criminal licensing. Ninety of those licenses had been given to applicants with rape, sodomy, robbery, or murder convictions. Wagner even found fifteen cases of fighters with military crimes on their records being given New York licenses. Given that information, Mansfield ruled that the commission's denial of Ali's license "appears on its face to be an intentional, arbitrary, and unreasonable discrimination against plaintiff, not the even-handed administration of the law which the Fourteenth Amendment requires."[88]

The decision was controversial, to be sure. Nat Fleischer, editor of *Ring Magazine*, acknowledged that Ali had many supporters, but the New York commission had never "issued a boxer's license to any man out on bail on a felony charge." The conflict in Vietnam was unpopular, but "Clay has been sniding the United States and its efforts to advance and protect the freedom of the world," Fleischer claimed. It was the language of the American Legion, and not particularly substantive. But Fleischer's more meaningful concern was that "the Mansfield decision reduced the New York Commission to an innocuous appendage of the state's payroll." The intent of New York law was not to make the commission chairman a "rubber stamp" for government concerns. In a letter to the editor Fleischer published in the same edition of *Ring*, a correspondent made the case that Mansfield's decision demonstrated "that only rich men can in effect defer justice by appeals ad infinitum" while "a poor man would have been in the pokey long ago."[89] They were much better arguments than the early patriotic grandstanding, and Fleischer's opinion was shared by athletic commissioners across the country who had denied Ali a license over the previous three years, but they were whispers in a rainstorm after the momentum provided by Atlanta's licensing and Mansfield's decision.

In response to the verdict Ali's lawyer, Michael Meltsner, said that "every effort" would be made to create a fight for the former champion in New York, and, for its part, Madison Square Garden "has plans for Cassius Clay." In its own response to the ruling the state athletic commission announced that it would consider Ali's application when it arrived. So Johnson pounced, as he had done in so many different political situations, knowing as he did that when people thought of major championship fights, they thought of Madison Square Garden, not Atlanta Municipal Auditorium.[90]

His efforts had supporters outside of the city. The *Los Angeles Sentinel*'s Brad Pye noted that Atlanta was the only city that had licensed Ali. "And this writer would like for Ali to tell the New York State Athletic Commission and all the other commissions—except the one in Atlanta—what to do with their licenses." He argued that since, "when nobody else wanted Ali, Atlanta took him in," then "Ali should demand that all of his future fights be held in Atlanta."[91] It was, in its way, a reasonable request, but most outside the Johnson household knew that any such demand was far-fetched, at best, and didn't take into account the ancillary racial problems in the city and state that would make Atlanta inhospitable as a long-term home.

For Ali's part, he was happy about the ruling but claimed not to be overly concerned. "I'm busy getting ready for Quarry," he said. "I can't have too many things on my mind."[92] Johnson, however, knew he was now in a race with New York and other states that would surely follow New York's lead. He was able to secure the October 26 contest largely because there was no competition. The only chance he had against more established boxing states, he assumed, was to come out swinging.

Back in Atlanta, securing a training venue for the fighters became paramount. Because the city did not have a traditional boxing arena, Johnson rented the Sports Arena at 310 Chester Ave. SE, operated by Paul Jones's ABC Booking, to serve as the training headquarters for both Ali and Quarry when they finally arrived in the city.[93] It was not a well-appointed venue, but it was one with a long history. A twenty-year-old Elvis Presley had played the building, as had Jerry Lee Lewis, the Allman Brothers, and the Grateful Dead. It was probably best known as a professional wrestling venue, where Classy Freddie Blassie and Haystacks Calhoun had run the ropes to enthralled crowds, helping grow the legend of Georgia Championship Wrestling.[94] The city's board of aldermen began preparing for the fight as well, passing an amendment to the city's code of ordinances "to provide for fire protection at boxing, sparring, or wrestling matches or exhibitions."[95] For those hungry to see Ali fight sooner than late October, local drive-ins began showing *The Super Fight* in theaters in late September. Around the same time, *The Great White Hope*, starring James Earl Jones, finally debuted in New York, though it was uncertain when or whether it would get a showing at theaters in Atlanta.[96]

In late September, before coming north to Atlanta, Ali held a public workout at Miami's Fifth Street Gym, an inauspicious venue above a local drugstore. There were heavy bags and a ring, no air conditioning, perfumed by the sweat and hope of would-be contenders waiting for a shot. It was where Ali would conduct his pre-fight camp with trainer Angelo Dundee. Ali weighed 225 pounds, 10 more than his newly revised goal of 215 for the Quarry fight, but he seemed more serious, less brash than he had previously. "I've worked so hard, so seriously," he told reporters. "No more big-mouthing." When a local's punching on the heavy bag was distracting Ali in the ring, the former champ had him removed, which led to a confrontation that forced both fighters to be restrained lest a real fight break out. In an interview after his workout, Ali praised Elijah Muhammad, but other than that refused to talk about religion or Vietnam. He was, it seemed, a different Ali, one prepared for the challenges that faced him. "Many people said I was finished and it was all over for me," he said, noting that if fighters like Joe Louis, Jack Dempsey, or Rocky Marciano had a layoff of one year, they would have refused to fight again. Ali was trying to fight after three years away. "It's like a dead man rising, I tell you. There were young people who didn't get to see me six years ago. It's just like stepping back in time."[97]

It was also stepping back into the often seedy world of boxing finance. The Atlanta fight guaranteed Ali $200,000 against 42.5 percent of revenues and Quarry $150,000, or 22.5 percent of revenues.[98] An additional $50,000, Johnson announced, would be donated to the "fight against drugs in Atlanta." Tickets would cost $100 for a ringside seat, with graded pricing beyond ringside at $50, $25, and $15 for the remaining seats in the roughly five-thousand-seat auditorium. For those who couldn't get in and for others around the country, the fight would be broadcast on closed-circuit television; it would also appear live via satellite in Europe, South America, and Asia. By early October more than nine hundred thousand seats had been booked in venues across the United States and Canada.[99]

To appear on closed-circuit television in Madison Square Garden, Ali had to have a New York boxing license. There was much money to be made in the New York closed-circuit market, so the application continued, supported by Johnson and House of Sports. That meant that Johnson's organization was in the difficult position of helping secure the possibility of Ali fighting his pending bout with Frazier in New York to make his preliminary fight with Quarry more profitable in Atlanta. Though the effort sowed the seeds of Atlanta's own demise for a championship fight in 1971, the New York State Athletic Commission, on September 28, voted unanimously to issue Ali a boxing license, immediately opening the door to closed-circuit revenue for the former champ's fight in Atlanta and keeping it open for a future Ali fight in the Garden. It was a win, but Ali was humble in victory. When reporters asked him if he still considered himself the champion after getting his New York license, for the first time he admitted, "I'm just a former champion trying to get the title. I said I was retired, and Frazier won the title."[100]

Johnson's plan to use fight profits to contribute to drug abuse programs was partially an effort to grease the wheels of government, but it wasn't only pragmatic. That month Johnson joined with other Black lawyers and lawmakers to create the nonprofit Awareness, Ltd., to help youth drug addicts after their release from drug treatment centers. The group planned to purchase a farm where those released could live and work until they were ready to ease back into society. The farm would include a psychiatric staff and treatment along with agricultural training. The thinking was that most drug addicts came from urban centers, and farm life, which combined clean air and hard work, "where progress can be measured by the weight of cattle and lushness of crops," could better and more quickly rehabilitate those waiting to return to city life. Johnson, who had long been a member of the Juvenile Court Law Study Commission and had heard testimony from both experts in the field and addicts themselves, would serve as president of Awareness, Ltd.[101]

The fight itself, meanwhile, served as a magnet for boxing interest around the city and state. In September the Atlanta Association of Life Underwriters invited Chuck Davey to speak to them. Davey was an insurance executive from Detroit, but he was also the chairman of the Michigan State Boxing Commission, an ally of Joe Frazier, and a contender for recruiting the potential Frazier-Ali bout to his city. Davey's talk to his fellow insurance men was less about underwriting and more about boxing. He assured his audience that Frazier would handle Ali easily, and would have done so even if the former champion hadn't been away from the game for more than three years. One fight with Jerry Quarry was not preparation enough for someone with the talent of Frazier, who would "go down as one of the truly great heavyweight champions of our time." Davey proposed ideas for Ali's potential strategy, but he knew, of course, that Ali would not be influenced by his suggestions. "He's going to do what he wants to do," Davey said of Ali. "He listens to nobody."[102]

But Ali could do what he wanted only if the powers that be cooperated, and as the fighter trained, Lester Maddox made one last attempt to stop the fight, publicly calling on Massell and other city officials to step in and cancel the match. "We shouldn't let him fight for money if he won't fight for his country," he said, reprising his former arguments. Maddox knew that he had no power to stop the bout; the move was largely an effort by the racist politician to reaffirm his position against Ali. It was also a ploy to curry favor with local veterans' groups who had pressured Maddox to oppose the fight. The event, the governor claimed, "would be an affront" to those killed and wounded in Vietnam. The governor even promised to raise $75,000 for an Atlanta drug-abuse treatment program if promoters agreed to stop the fight, one-upping Johnson's

$50,000 pledge. He claimed that Johnson's promise of the drug money was a "bribe." Besides, "what good is $50,000 when you honor a man who has denounced the military?"[103]

Massell treated Maddox's opposition as a joke. "Who'll make it $100,000?" he asked, reminding reporters that Maddox had no legal authority to stop the bout. Johnson, however, who had a far greater stake in the game, saw a bigger problem with the governor's grandstanding. "He is playing right into the hands of the New York crowd that wants to take the fight from Atlanta and wants to hold the championship fight between Clay and Joe Frazier in New York." That was the real fear. Though Maddox claimed to have asked Georgia attorney general Arthur Bolton to see if there was any state law that would allow him to block the Quarry fight, no one believed that such a law existed. When Bolton announced that it didn't, Maddox said that he hoped "public indignation will stop it. I think Atlanta will suffer if this fight takes place," he said, "and I think it will hurt Georgia. I plan to encourage all the peaceful opposition I can encourage." But it was actually Maddox who was hurting the state. If the reactionary governor continued to rail against Ali, the likelihood that the former champion would fight Frazier in Atlanta, where leadership was hostile to him, was not good. "We deserve the fight in Atlanta," Johnson said of Ali's potential Quarry follow-up with Frazier. "I hope the governor reconsiders his position."[104]

The battle between Maddox and Johnson was largely performative. After his press conference Maddox called Johnson and scheduled a meeting, wherein he explained that he wasn't actually going to make an effort to stop the fight. Maddox was running for lieutenant governor, a position that carried much power in Georgia, power that the legislature had considered limiting in recent years. Maddox knew that offending Johnson over a battle he knew he couldn't win would only hurt his future political prospects, when he would need allies in the statehouse.[105]

Still, there were potential stakes even for the Quarry bout after New York issued Ali a boxing license. The *Los Angeles Sentinel*'s Pye wondered whether the Ali-Quarry match would be moved to Madison Square Garden in the wake of Maddox's interference. Ali, Pye claimed, was willing to move the fight if necessary, but Massell's support was definitely valuable. "I wouldn't want to think what will happen to race relations in Atlanta if Gov. Maddox is successful in his ax-wielding antics again this time." For Cal Jacox of the *Norfolk Journal and Guide*, promoters "could find themselves hung on the horns of a dilemma if the governor forces them to shift the site from Atlanta to New York's Madison Square Garden where they just might not come up with that million dollar gate they're looking for on such short notice."[106] Michigan saw an opportunity, as well. State boxing commissioner Davey claimed that Ali had never been barred from fighting in Detroit. Instead, he argued that "the shakiness of the promotion" actually "forced the earlier cancellation." The city would be "glad to have Clay meet the winner of the Joe Frazier–Bob Foster fight." It was a patently untrue statement, but it demonstrated that as went New York, so went everyone else, which only created more competition for Johnson and Atlanta when it came to securing Ali for the city.[107]

Constitution columnist Hal Gulliver was among many who saw through the governor's ploy. "You may not like Clay's beliefs or his battle with his draft board," he argued. "But that's not much of a reason to try to keep Clay from practicing his livelihood. Why, to do that would be like saying that a man shouldn't run a restaurant or sell fried chicken because you didn't happen to agree with his political beliefs." It was an effective shot across the bow at a governor who had earned his reputation as a recalcitrant segregationist owner of a chicken restaurant. When the city's white media was taking the side of Ali over and against that of the governor, the prospects that the fight would come off seemed stronger than ever.[108]

6. RETURN OF THE KING

OCTOBER 1970

Among the reporters trailing Ali in the leadup to his reemergence was *Sports Illustrated*'s Mark Kram, who described the Fifth Street Gym in Miami Beach that was Ali's home base before he moved to Atlanta in the weeks before the fight: the "thin coat of dust on the windows, the dirt neatly piled in corners, that smell of dead dreams." The old promotional posters on the wall, the American flag, and the face of Angelo Dundee, who had been with Ali for most of his professional career, a face "of weariness, of too many nights in too many corners in too many faraway places." Sitting there in the middle of it was Ali, considering the rapid turn his life had taken. "I never thought I'd be back again," he told Kram, "here again. Back in my old life again. All those years." When he got in the ring, however, everyone in the gym claimed that the former champion hadn't lost a step. He was the only fighter at Fifth Street who didn't wear gloves when using the heavy bag. He leaned on the ropes and let his sparring partners attack his body to prepare for Quarry's punching power. "He's human," said the gym's Ollie Wilson, "but hey—maybe he ain't."[1]

When the gym work was done for the day, Ali retreated to a "small, dim hotel on the ocean, an obscure Jewish retreat during religious holidays where old women sit rocking and looking on the porch and others sit nodding in a half-sleep in the lobby." He made himself dinner; he prayed facing east three times a day; he stared at a picture taped to a bedroom mirror of himself before his second fight with Sonny Liston. "That's when I was at my top condition," he said.[2]

The night before Ali was scheduled to go north to Georgia, he received a package, opened by his sparring partner, with a headless black chihuahua. "We know how to handle black draft-dodging dogs in Georgia," the note said. "Stay out of Atlanta." A small Confederate flag drawn on the paper added a fitting exclamation point to the message.[3]

Earlier that day he had been sparring with Blue Lewis, who was tagging Ali with shots to the body. The work was in preparation for what the team assumed would be Quarry's plan, but the last of Lewis's shots dropped the former champion. When they got him back to the locker room, Dundee, Bundini Brown, and others all worried that he could have a broken rib, but they knew they couldn't call off the fight. "If we postpone, God knows when we'll get this far again," said someone in the room. "We got to keep it out of the newspapers." They knew, of course, that in the incestuous world of boxing, news of potential injury would make it to Quarry's camp, but if it wasn't the subject of larger public concern, then the match would be able to continue.[4]

That day Ali also submitted a deposition in a lawsuit filed against him by Murray Worner, producer of the mythical Ali-Marciano superfight. When Worner had Marciano win the bout for American audiences, Ali told fans that it was "a Hollywood fake," and the producer sued him for defamation.[5] Race, boxing, and business, the elements that had dominated so much of Ali's life, now coalesced as he prepared to travel to Atlanta.

Quarry, meanwhile, conducted his pre-fight camp in Gilman Hot Springs, California. He arrived in Atlanta on October 13, having sparred eighty rounds and run one hundred miles. Ali would arrive from Miami the following day. Quarry said he had watched Ali's Morehouse exhibition. "He didn't appear to be in too good shape then," he said, "but I'm sure he'll be in shape when he meets me." He admitted that he didn't know whether or not he would have been able to come back after a years-long layoff, as Ali had. It was impressive, but Quarry was still confident he would win the contest. He brought a sparring partner with him to Georgia, one who hopefully mimicked what the former champion would do. "Atlanta being sort of out of the way so far as boxing is concerned, we didn't figure that we would have found a sparring partner here," he told reporters. "But I like being here. It's a pleasant change from always going to the same cities."[6]

Quarry was joined in Atlanta by his two brothers and his father. His nineteen-year-old brother Mike, an undefeated light heavyweight, served as one of Jerry's sparring partners, too, Ali's opponent explaining that sparring with light heavyweights forced him to react to speed.

Quarry knew that Ali would have an eight-inch reach advantage, but the brothers described a strategy of compensating for the difference. "Clay has a habit of leaning way back when a right hand is thrown at his head," Mike told reporters. "But Jerry is going to follow that with a left hook to the body which is going to bring Clay back in range for another right." The other potential problem for Quarry was his temper, which had in the past led him to impulsive moves into contact. "That used to be true but no more," the fighter said. "Maturity cured it."[7] To prepare for his opportunity, Quarry attempted to settle his mind with hypnosis. Jimmy Grippo, a hypnotist who had worked with several other athletes, had Quarry project himself as the winner of the fight. But there were ripples in the boxer's hypnotic calm. He had recently broken with longtime trainer Johnny Flores, making his abbreviated training camp in Gilman Hot Springs a new experience for Quarry.[8]

When Ali arrived in Atlanta, he was met at the airport by Johnson and Harry Pett, along with a delegation of others who followed behind them. Before he left Miami, Ali had told reporters that "I ain't gonna lose to no white hope." But after appearing in Georgia, Ali was decidedly more tranquil. He was surprised Quarry didn't defeat Frazier. He would do his best in the fight. He was in good condition; he weighed 214 pounds, two less than when he fought Sonny Liston the first time. He stood in a green velvet vest and bell-bottoms, flanked by Dundee, trainer Drew "Bundini" Brown, his father, and his brother. Brown had spent time traveling at sea, where he picked up the Hindi name Bundini. He had worked for Sugar Ray Robinson at one point, and he had come into Clay's orbit in March 1963, sent by Robinson and imposing himself on the fighter the day of his bout with Doug Jones. He became Clay's hype man and assistant trainer, a cornerman there to keep his fighter upbeat and ready. And Ali was ready; he was confident. "I'm faster now and much stronger than when I quit," he told reporters. He was confident, but he was calm. Gone was the loud, boasting champion who ran down his opponents. He was a fighter grateful to be fighting. "I'm more mentally ready for this fight because of the atmosphere." The atmosphere of Atlanta. The atmosphere of acceptance from the boxing community. The atmosphere of possibility.[9]

His new maturity was perhaps prompted, at least in part, by the fact that his twin daughters were still in incubators in Philadelphia and would need to remain there for another month. In a public sparring session in preparation for the fight, he was asked about his famous poetry taunting opposing fighters. Did he have any rhymes to threaten Quarry? "Maaaan, I ain't got no poetry. I used to have, but I ain't got it no more." A group of kids there to watch the workout looked in awe at the former champ. "It's a hard way to make a living," he told them. "Stay in school. I've been at this sixteen years now." That is not to say that Ali wasn't confident. He was sure of himself, convincing those assembled that he was ready, that he was going to dance, that he was "fast and quick and strong."[10]

There may have been other reasons for his quieter approach. Ali was staying at Leroy Johnson's lakeside vacation home in the Atlanta suburbs during his time in the city, with Johnson's sister cooking for the team. Dundee and Brown argued against it, reminding the fighter that he had always stayed in an urban setting before a fight, but Ali wanted something different. One night, soon after his arrival, he awoke to gunshots, followed quickly by the ringing of the telephone. "N——, if you don't leave Atlanta tomorrow, you gonna die. You Viet Cong bastard! You draft-dodging bastard! We won't miss you the next time!" The Atlanta police received threatening letters; angry whites made threatening phone calls to Ali's wife in Philadelphia. It was a reminder that Ali and his team were, whatever the opportunity, still in the South. Ali's physician, Ferdie Pacheco, remembered that the gunshots were not an isolated occurrence. "We had police protection," he remembered, "but every night someone shot at the cottage."[11]

It happened during the day, as well. As Ali was shadowboxing on Johnson's back porch one day, shots rang out through the trees. He scrambled into the house and everyone there got on the floor. Three different voices screamed from the woods, calling Ali a "black sonofabitch" and a "draft dodging-bastard." One screamed, "Get out of Georgia!" Everyone in the house was scared, wondering what would happen next, worried that they had no weapons with which to defend themselves. Then another threatening phone call cut through the whispers on the floor of the house. Finally Ali's police detail, led by Lieutenant J. D. Hudson, arrived with a station wagon and guns, ready to spirit the group away. Hudson had been one of the original Black police officers in Atlanta, hired in 1948. He had lived through the days when Black patrolmen weren't allowed to arrest white suspects, when they were not allowed to use the locker room at the police station and had to change clothes at the Butler Street YMCA. He understood racial violence in Atlanta. On the drive Hudson told Ali that the department had received reports of a possible assassination attempt at the fight, but that the boxer had no reason to worry. They had it all under control; there would be extra security on the night of the bout.[12]

The threats were real. Kassel was not staying with Ali, but he too experienced intimidation. He had his wife and children stay with his father-in-law outside the city limits to keep them safe. Though the relationship between Ali and the Nation of Islam was strained at the time, Kassel claimed that "the Black Muslims had guys allocated to protect me. They didn't want anything to happen to me." The Black Muslims were on the minds of the Quarrys, as well. Jerry's father, Jack, claimed that the group "made like they were going to shoot Jerry down in the ring. That was the word that got back to us." Because of those rumors, the elder Quarry sat near the aisle in the arena during the fight, he said, "because if this became involved with a shooting or something, I wanted to be near to where I could get up and leave." The threat itself was obviously absurd, but the white family's fear, manufactured as it was, surely felt all too real in the heated racial climate of Atlanta.[13]

Even among the tense atmosphere, however, Ali always had time for levity. During his time at Johnson's lake house, the former champ relaxed with his father and artist LeRoy Neiman, renowned for his paintings and screenprints of athletes and athletic events. The fighter told his two companions that he was holding a "drawing championship." The two contestants sat at the kitchen table, with Ali in between them, sketching landscapes. Neiman drew a picture of Johnson's backyard while Clay, Sr., drew from his imagination. After roughly ten minutes, Ali yelled, "Stop!" It was, he said, "No contest. LeRoy is the Artist Champion of the World." While Neiman liked Clay's picture and attempted to shake his hand after the contest, Ali's hypercompetitive father stormed out of the room after losing.[14]

In the weeks before the fight, publicity also began for a new feature documentary scheduled for release in early November. Ali had signed a deal to participate in *a.k.a. Cassius Clay* the previous year. Depicting the fighter as a thinker and leader, it told the story of Ali's civil rights work and his membership in the NOI, leading to his boxing suspension. Released by United Artists, the documentary was produced by William Cayton and directed by Jim Jacobs, filmmakers who had been capturing aspects of Ali's career for years. The original plan was for the film to arrive in early 1971, but renewed interest because of the Quarry fight drove the studio to rush the movie to theaters.[15] It showed Ali singing in *Buck White*, speaking on a college campus, riling up a local crowd. Ali and Cus D'Amato argued about whether or not Ali could have defeated Joe Louis. Then there was Ali's biography, from Louisville to Rome to Madison Square Garden, and his conversion to the NOI. Ali and D'Amato analyzed several of his fights. After describing Ali's induction refusal and the plum assignment he would have received had he made the step forward in Houston, the film's narrator portrayed such treatment as a kind of bribe. "Muhammad Ali was accepting no soft touches at the expense of his ideas." The film closed by calling a champion "a species of hero, and a hero is nourished by misfortune. That is why he attracts legend."[16]

Ali attracted legend, to be sure, but no fighter had successfully come back from a three-year layoff, and the question for many was less about Ali's legacy and more about his immediate prospects. The *Constitution*'s George Cunningham was not confident. The history of boxing was littered with former heavyweight champions who attempted to come back after retirement. "Joe Louis couldn't do it," Cunningham wrote. "And neither could Jimmy Braddock, Jim Jeffries or Jim Corbett." And none of them had been out of the game for three and a half years. Cunningham asked Nat Fleischer, publisher of *Ring Magazine*, about Ali's chances—or rather Clay's chances. Fleischer, demonstrating the kind of bigotry Ali regularly experienced, refused to call the boxer by his chosen name. Fleischer gave Quarry a good chance to win, particularly if the fight went into late rounds. He had been impressed by the Morehouse exhibition and believed that the former champion would win, but "Quarry has better than a good chance." Almost no sports book had established betting lines for the fight as of October 18, though the line would eventually make Ali a 3.5 to 1 favorite.[17]

Black pundits were far more willing to make predictions. The *Chicago Defender* polled its readers, and they unanimously assumed that not only would Ali win his return bout, but that he would soon regain recognition as the world's heavyweight champion. The *Defender*'s Norman

Unger predicted Ali would win in six rounds or fewer. A selection of Philadelphia's Black boxing cognoscenti gave their opinions in the *Philadelphia Tribune*. They debated whether or not Ali could defeat Frazier, but everyone agreed that Ali would defeat Quarry. "Ali, even an out-of-shape Ali, has too much ring savvy for the likes of Quarry," said Sonny Liston's former trainer Willie Reddish. Quarry was the number-one-ranked heavyweight, but the gap between Ali and Frazier and everyone else made such numbers relatively meaningless for Black pundits who understood that, while young fighters like George Foreman were quickly rising through the ranks, the heavyweight division in 1970 consisted of two boxers.[18] The *Los Angeles Sentinel*'s Brad Pye had a similar take. "If Jerry Quarry were running for President rather than running for his life against Muhammad Ali he would have a better chance of winning in Watts than he will against Ali in Georgia."[19]

The *Tribune* handicapped the fight by noting that Ali was never, even before the layoff, a power puncher. He had an effective left jab and earned his knockouts by wearing down opponents with an accumulation of fast punches. He had always avoided hard body shots because of his speed and footwork. His biggest hill to climb in this fight, of course, would be the long layoff, the possibility of someone who boxed with so much movement tiring in late rounds. Quarry, for his part, often looked like a great fighter but struggled with consistency. His best weapon was his left hook and power in both hands. Quarry focused principally on the body of his opponents and often fought off the ropes, even moving to the ropes intentionally to give the illusion that he was retreating. He took a punch as well as anyone but sometimes tired in late rounds. The biggest unknown, besides the layoff, was Ali's seeming humility and unwillingness to showboat, boast, and belittle his opponent. If that was the fuel that he turned into energy, then what would its absence do for his return? If that was the way he prepared for fights, then was he really ready mentally for what was to come?[20]

Virtually everyone, however, was certain that the fight would draw the largest cash gate in Atlanta's history, even though Municipal Auditorium, as configured for the fight, only sat 4,300. More than 2,000 of those seats would cost one hundred dollars apiece. Almost a million seats in the United States and Canada would also be sold at 220 closed-circuit venues.[21]

One of those venues, after Ali finally received his New York license, would be Madison Square Garden, along with nineteen others in the New York metropolitan area, including Harlem's 369th Armory. Six theaters in Chicago would show the fight on closed-circuit television, as would twenty-six in Southern California. Among the Los Angeles venues was Dooto Music Center, owned and promoted by Dootsie Williams, the first Black promoter to present a closed-circuit broadcast of a major sporting event. "This may be Clay's last fight," he said, still worried that the former champ might have to go to prison, "but there's more interest in this fight than in any other fight we've had here." People were concerned about Ali's long layoff and whether he could overcome it, and they were worried about the controversy over staging the fight in the South. It created, at least in Williams's Los Angeles, "the most excitement of any fight in history."[22]

In Denver Joe Louis helped promote the closed-circuit broadcast. The Brown Bomber was staying in the city's Veterans Administration Hospital undergoing treatment for mental health issues, but the fifty-six-year-old was still in good condition, leaving on weekends to visit family and play golf. In healthier days in 1962 Louis had organized a fight card in Los Angeles that was headlined by Cassius Clay, and age and infirmity had not dampened his enthusiasm for Ali or boxing more broadly. Louis was associated with the International Boxing League, owned by Bill Daniels, who also owned the Denver Rocks amateur boxing team, and the two joined forces to promote the Ali-Quarry fight in the city. A spokesman for the VA said that the former champion's closed-circuit venture in Denver was the best therapy he could get. "No matter what the outcome of the fight, Joe Louis will still be the winner."[23]

That was cold comfort to the boxers. Quarry's plan was to work the body with what he called "the Marciano style lasagna punch," hoping it would take the wind from a fighter who hadn't competed for several years. He described his strategy as "Operation Breadbasket," fundamentally racializing the common nickname for a fighter's stomach.[24] Operation Breadbasket had been a 1962 creation of both the national SCLC and the group's local Atlanta chapter, an effort to confront income inequality by working for employment desegregation and the creation of new job opportunities for the city's Black workers. Led by King family friend Fred C. Bennette, Jr., Breadbasket used strategies like boycotts and buying campaigns to pressure businesses into fairer hiring practices. When Martin Luther King, Jr., turned his attention to Chicago in late 1965, so too did the Breadbasket program, and just as King widened the scope of his vision of racial justice, so did Breadbasket, working to bring greater access to banking, corporate boards, and other financial resources to Black Chicagoans. The leader of the operation was Jesse Jackson, who would replace Bennette as Operation Breadbasket's national director in 1967. The agency would change in his hands to focus in particular on supporting Black capitalism and entrepreneurship, gaining along the way a national reputation that made it prime fodder for Quarry and others. No one in the heated racial climate of 1970 would have missed Quarry's meaning.[25]

The fighters had October 19 off, but their representatives met that day to agree on the rules for the fight. Quarry's father, Jack, represented him, while Dundee represented Ali. Harold Conrad, representing Sports Action, was also present. Conrad was coordinating the promotion, a veteran of the game "who promotes more printed words daily than cousin Joseph wrote in all his novels." The fighters would use eight-ounce gloves. There would be two judges at ringside and a ten-point must scoring system. Neither the referee nor the judges would be from Georgia, and the identity of all would remain secret until the night of the fight. The one element not agreed upon was the size of the ring. While eighteen feet was a standard minimum, a twenty-foot ring would give Ali more room to maneuver. At the same time, the extra room would be more ground to cover for a fighter coming off a long layoff.[26]

Even more significant for Ali, the same day, October 19, his twin daughters, Reeshemah and Jamillah, finally left the Pennsylvania hospital where they had lived since their arrival in August. Weighing less than three pounds at birth, the two were now stable at just under five pounds and ready to go home.[27]

The following day, now confident that his daughters were safe, Ali did a telephonic press conference from the Sports Arena, where both fighters were training. Because Georgia Championship Wrestling usually used Municipal Auditorium for its Friday night shows, the Sports Arena's more common use as of 1970 was for square dancing; it even had wagon-wheel chandeliers and decorations to make one part of the arena look like a Western saloon. Reporters from twenty-five cities were on the call as the fighter held forth under the wagon wheels, despite a bad connection that the phone company struggled to remedy during the event. “This must be a plot to get me tired,” Ali quipped. When any of the reporters called him Clay, he calmly corrected them. Ali claimed to be at 209 pounds and that he would fight at 205. He had lost the weight by “drinking the juice of 20 or 30 carrots a day, eating a lot of raw beets and eating a lot of fresh vegetables right out of the garden.” One of the reporters attempted to goad him by saying that his diet was very similar to that of Georgia governor Lester Maddox. “I don’t know what he eats,” said Ali, refusing to take the bait.[28]

He complimented Quarry, claiming that his opponent was never hurt when losing to Frazier. He compared Quarry to Floyd Patterson, whom Cus D’Amato had guided to a heavyweight championship. It was a departure for a fighter who made his name by taunting his opponents and castigating their abilities in the ring. Joe Louis and Jersey Joe Walcott were on the phone as well, Louis doubtful that the comeback would be a success and Walcott supremely confident in Ali. Louis’s doubts didn’t bother Ali. “He doesn’t understand me,” the fighter said, “because I’m so much faster than he was.” Louis was a “flatfooted fighter who was not a dancing master. Joe just can’t imagine anyone was faster and better than he was, so he can’t predict me.” A joking Louis interrupted. “Watch it Clay, I’m listening to you.” Ali told reporters that he would prefer to fight Frazier, “but if he gets past Foster and I beat Quarry, we can settle it.” Frazier would be an easier fight than Quarry. “All he knows is to slug,” Ali said of Frazier. “It’s hard to sell these flat-footed, slow heavyweights to me. And anyway, he wears a homemade elimination belt.”[29]

When the former champ hung up the telephone, he spotted Walt Bellamy entering the arena. The Hawks center squared up with Ali for reporters, and the two talked briefly before the telephone rang again and Ali returned to answer more questions. He kept talking until Conrad quietly pointed out that Quarry was in the ring and ready to conduct his workout. Ali had no choice but to get off the line and let his opponent have his practice time.[30]

After Quarry’s sparring session, he took his turn with the teleconference’s spotty connection. He was bored, he said, tired of the repetitive nature of training. He knew all the moves of his sparring partners. “I make ’em miss almost anytime I want. I think I got hit with one jab today." Quarry was ready for the real thing. He assured reporters that he was prepared, that he would win the fight. He had no pain in his hands. He just wanted Ali.[31]

Quarry's confidence was noted, but Ali was the story. The following day, October 21, reporters flocked to the former champ's seven-round sparring session and again peppered him with questions, which Ali dutifully answered, largely without the bombast and insults of his previous life. Dundee also spoke to reporters and reiterated his confidence in his fighter. Yes, Ali kept his hands too low, but he had always done that. "How can you argue with an undefeated record?" Of course he was worried about the long layoff, but Ali was ready. The former champ teased a Frazier fight, then excused himself. "I'm going out and get some homemade, colored food," he told his white audience, smiling as he backed away.[32]

The hype made everyone interested in Ali's return. "Russia is interested not only in wars in the Near East and the Far East but in a battle that will take place next Monday in the Deep South." The *Constitution* reported that its offices were in an uproar as a call from Moscow came in: a Russian sports reporter asking about the fight. "There was no mention of capitalism versus communism," the paper joked with its readers. The Russian journalist asked how he could contact Cassius Clay—never referring to him as Ali—and the paper told him to try Johnson's senate office. "Ah, yes," said the voice from Moscow, "as in President Johnson." Russian representatives also called the office of mayor Sam Massell to ask about the fight. "The calls," the paper reported, "were not collect."[33]

The fighters, meanwhile, had their medical examinations on Wednesday at the Sports Arena, the first time in professional boxing that fighters had their medical examinations together. It gave the two a chance to talk, with Ali characteristically needling his opponent, attempting to rattle Quarry. But Quarry held his own, only showing noticeable frustration when one of Ali's sparring partners, Willie Johnson, yelled at him about calling an undertaker. Quarry told reporters that he "used to knock that guy out when I was a preliminary boy in the gym. He's nothing." And he wasn't worried about Ali's talk. "A guy does that when he's scared," Quarry told reporters. "And he's scared."[34]

When reporters asked Ali about being scared, he told them he had been scared before on airplanes when flying through thunderstorms.

But "I never worry about the fight. I worry about the flight on the way to the fight." But his rhetoric rarely got more bombastic than that. It was, the *New York Times* explained, part of a strategy "to avoid any statement or incident that might force the local or state government to cancel, or harass, his first fight in 3½ years," encouraged by Johnson. But the paper was clear that there was "no lack of confidence in his caution," and when his attention turned to Joe Frazier, he was far more willing to demonstrate the old bombast. He called Frazier "the new tramp . . . I mean champ." Ali smiled. "A man said to me, 'Joe Frazier's awful strong,' and I said, 'that's why they invented Ban Roll-On.'"[35]

Ali was going to have to "sidestep the fistic skill of his opponent," worried the *Atlanta Daily World*, but also "the silent lament of self-ordained oracles, fortune-tellers and soothsayers, that his haste in returning to the ring may lay him waste." Quarry had less to lose in the bout, and if the "Great White Hope" could pull off the upset, he "will be enthroned and enshrined in the market places of Caucasian supremacy." The fight had "stirred worldwide social, legal, political and race relations involvement to result in unprecedented interest among the masses" for a variety of reasons. Ali's layoff and the Ali-Frazier payoff if he were to win were parts of it, as was the fact that Quarry "is no bum." But even more than that, for the *World*, "the fight itself is redemptive for Ali, who has trudged the long and weary road of legalisms, without sanctuary in the snarling deceit and subterfuge of public opinion, for what he thought was right and just and which sinister forces used for evil and sinister discord and diversiveness [*sic*] in troubled times, when the bursting emergence of the Negro toward freedom and justice was unmercifully being defected back into the status quo."[36]

It was an important point. Ali's ability to overcome that sinister discord was partly the result of a broader trend away from public support for the war in Vietnam, but there had always been a racial element to that support. Vietnam was the first long-term military conflict the United States fought with a fully integrated military, making the racism it engendered fundamentally different from that of previous conflicts. In the world wars Black soldiers were relegated to inferior positions and largely kept away from the front based on white assumptions of Black inferiority. When the military was integrated, Black draftees were sent to war in greater numbers than the population would indicate, and they were often sent to the front in greater percentages, as well. When the Black press talked about sinister forces manufacturing consent for an immoral war, they were seeing victims in all nonwhite peoples involved in the fight—both the Vietnamese and the Black American servicemen called to duty, the majority of whom were unable to find deferments at the same rate as whites who found their draft numbers called.[37]

Ali, for his part, was just happy to be back in the ring. Many of the reporters gathered for the fight wanted to talk about his three-year absence, the consequences of his conscientious objection to the Vietnam conflict. Ali wouldn't take the bait. That was in the past, and he wouldn't reach his peak, he told them, until he was thirty. Some speculated that "because of his reputation as a pop-off and a draft dodger," the crowd would largely be rooting for Quarry at the fight. Quarry was also the next in a long line of Great White Hopes fighting in the capital of the Deep South. But Ali wouldn't take that bait, either. "I don't care if I'm the villain. It's not as bad here as Chicago or New York," he said of Atlanta. "Down here, you know where you stand. They're a bunch of hypocrites up North." Besides, there would be all kinds of people in the crowd. "One black man in New York bought $2,500 worth of tickets. There'll be people here from Mexico, Europe, Panama, all over. There'll be a lot of blacks in the crowd. A lot of 'em will come from right here in Atlanta. There are more blacks with money here than anywhere." That was true, despite the poverty that beset a large portion of Atlanta's Black population. But it wouldn't just be Black Atlanta rooting for him. "When I fight, everybody comes to see me," Ali said. "The Black Panthers, the pimps, all the chicks—everybody, all kinds. You watch. Monday there'll be people here from all over the world."[38]

One of those certainly not rooting for Ali was Lester Maddox. On October 22, four days before the fight, the governor called a press conference to read an official proclamation declaring Monday a day of mourning and ordering flags to be flown at half-staff on the day of the fight. He denounced Ali as a draft dodger. "I hope he gets beat in the first round," he told reporters, "flattened out . . . to the count of 30." He encouraged "the families of all prisoners of war and men who have died in all wars plus all veterans" to contact Atlanta officials to "express their indignation that this fight has been permitted to take place." His official proclamation was even more on the nose, using patriotism as a crib for racist politics. It declared, "To glorify an individual who has so callously forsaken his duty to his country represents an affront to every American who has answered the call and sacrificed to protect our great republic." Maddox urged Georgians to use the day of mourning to pray "that those who have lost loved ones for the cause of American freedom be spared any further affront to the memory of their loved ones and be comforted in their grief."[39]

Very few were buying it. Frank Miller, the Republican state senator from DeKalb County who was running against Maddox for lieutenant governor, rightly interpreted the move as a publicity stunt, a way to stand in the reflected light from Ali. "Maddox has declared a day of mourning for something he set up and started rolling in the first place," said Miller, reminding everyone that Maddox was an original supporter of the fight before feeling a change in the white political winds.[40]

"Ole Lester has about the same affection for Ali, that General Motors has for Ford," the *Chicago Defender*'s Norman Unger explained, but "that doesn't bother Muhammad a bit. It's a large part of the publicity. . . . And the more the merrier." Unger was right, of course. Maddox's antics only helped the gate and swelled the coffers of Ali and his Atlanta promoters. Cassius Clay, Sr., Muhammad Ali's father, found Maddox similarly ridiculous, but knew the value of such comments. "Don't you think he was aware of all the writers here? Don't you think he knew this would get him publicity everywhere?" he asked. "If my boy loses, Gov. Maddox will have a feast and give away fried chicken. And if Monday is a day of mourning, then I guess he will declare Tuesday a day of jubilee if my boy loses."[41]

Constitution sports editor Jesse Outlar couldn't have agreed more. "Maddox and others may consider it sheer heresy," he wrote, "but the fist fight scheduled Monday night at the auditorium is focusing more world attention on the city than any event since the original Battle of Atlanta." That was the kind of thing a governor should be endorsing. Besides, he argued, whatever anyone might think of conscientious objectors, "as Mayor Sam Massell informed a Moscow newsman via long distance Wednesday, Americans have the freedom to challenge laws in legal channels."[42]

Ali and his camp, however, were worried—about the fight being canceled, to be sure, but also about potential violence against the former champion spurred by the governor's rhetoric. The leader of Ali's police detail, J. D. Hudson, doubled the number of officers devoted to the boxer's security. With rumors that Maddox was planning to seek an injunction, Dundee and Ali looked to Johnson to assure them that the fight would take place. Johnson did. With the Reconstruction-era municipal law barring interracial boxing contests nullified, any potential threat was gone; Maddox's rhetoric was sound and fury signifying nothing.[43]

While Maddox was grandstanding at the state capitol, Ali was sparring six rounds in front of far more reporters at the Sports Arena. After his workout, he fielded far more questions than did Maddox, and without the bluster of either the governor or his former self. Ali was confident in his ability and his training, and he believed he would win. But absent were the proclamations of greatness and the taunting of his opponent that had brought him so much attention early in his career. He told reporters that he was enjoying his time in Atlanta. "You know when the fight was announced, people cocked their eyebrows and said, 'GEORGIA and LESTER MADDOX!' Let me tell you, Georgia's all right. When I ride around the red clay hills mornings at 4:30, people yell and say, 'Hi, Champ, hi good ol' boy,'" he said. "And Sen. Johnson and his people have figured those tickets down to the last seat. They got us this house in the country and filled it with steaks and all kinds of goodies." He also expressed his relief that "these Georgia reporters don't ask me tough questions like what's my religion and what meetings have I attended lately." The people of Georgia are nice, he said, not mentioning the gunshots and threatening phone calls at his temporary lodgings, "even the newsmen." As one reporter quipped, referring to Ali's praise of the press, "If Muhammad wasn't already on Gov. Maddox's unpreferred list, that remark would have earned him a spot."[44]

The newsmen did, however, ask Ali's father about such issues, wondering how he felt about his sons changing their names (Muhammad's brother Rahman Ali had also joined the NOI). Clay, Sr., was unfazed. "Bing Crosby did it," he said, "and so do most stars. There is an old Chinese saying that it is all right to change your name when you are 21."[45]

When it was Quarry's turn to talk, he discussed his June 1969 loss to Frazier, when he was knocked out in the seventh round. "I was disgusted," he told reporters, telling them that he had considered retirement after the loss. "I had something to prove in that fight and didn't. I thought I wouldn't get another shot at the title, and what's the use of fighting if you can't fight for the title?" In the previous year, 1968, he had lost to Jimmy Ellis in fifteen rounds in a fight during which he had reinjured his broken back. Still, he claimed that he had only been hurt in the ring one time, when Al Jones knocked him down in a fight in San Francisco. Quarry knocked out Jones two rounds later, but he still didn't remember the ten count. For this fight, the Ali fight, he was confident. After all, Ali wasn't a superhero; he was a man, "just like me. He puts on his pants one leg at a time."[46]

Quarry was also asked about Maddox's day of mourning. He brushed off news that Maddox hoped he would knock out Ali. "If Gov. Maddox wants to mourn, let him mourn," he said. "If he stops it now, both of us will go after him." That line of inquiry led to questions about Quarry's opinion of Ali's case. "I think that he should have served in the service," he said, "but that's his convictions, it's his business. I think it's unjust that they took his title away. A man should be allowed to fight as long as he's able to fight."[47]

That said, Quarry was not above engaging the racial dynamic of the bout. "The black man is yelling about prejudice," he said, "and what makes me mad is the government is afraid to do something about what they're doing. The black man is being prejudiced against the white man by those who don't want equality but superiority. But everybody's afraid to sock it to the black man."[48] Johnny Smith describes Quarry as part of the white conservative California contingent that had put Ronald Reagan in the governor's chair. He "tapped into the very tensions that drove 'white flight'—open housing, busing, affirmative action, and welfare for blacks."[49]

It was to be a busy sports weekend in Atlanta. Georgia Tech's football team was hosting Tulane on Saturday afternoon, and that night the Boston Celtics would play the Atlanta Hawks. On Sunday the NFL's Falcons were hosting the New Orleans Saints. Then on Monday night Ali would return to the ring. But for the week preceding those events, "the dingy old Sports Arena, corner of Chester Avenue and Old Flat Shoals off Memorial Drive, had been the headquarters for the world of boxing," declared Jesse Outlar. It was "an unlikely stop for the fight crowd," as the Saturday before the bout, after the fighters had concluded their training, workers were dismantling the ring to make space for square dancing later that night.[50]

But so too was Municipal Auditorium an unlikely stop. It was "an eyesore structure," a "ramshackle building the city outgrew years ago and hasn't replaced." But it "will serve as the stage for the greatest exposure of any event ever staged in the Southeast." Outlar was right. No matter who won the fight on Monday, Atlanta would certainly come out ahead. "By Tuesday morning the city will have been datelined by some 600 writers who will circulate upwards of three-quarters of a million words throughout the world about the fight that couldn't happen—except in Atlanta."[51]

On Friday Ali announced that he would not be making 205 pounds for his fight. He would, he explained, dance less and focus instead on power. His new goal would be 210 pounds, still a comparatively light total for the former champion. "The eyes of the whole world are going to be on Atlanta because of this fight," he said. "But that's only new for Quarry. I'm used to it." That said, he wasn't going to make a prediction. He had done that previously only to publicize his fights, he claimed. He compared his antics to those of Jack Johnson and professional wrestler Gorgeous George, a name well-known to the GCW fans who commonly attended Atlanta's arenas. A young Clay had watched one interview with Gorgeous George in which he promised, "If this bum beats me, I'll crawl across the ring and cut off my hair, but it's not gonna happen because I'm the greatest wrestler in the world." He understood that playing the heel created interest. "I was saying to myself, 'Man I want to see this fight. It don't matter who wins or loses; I want to be there to see what happens.'" It was a lesson he would carry with him into his own career. "Gorgeous George would go into a ring and they'd hate him. He had long, blond hair, a girl would hold his robe and he'd spray deodorant in his opponent's corner. That made folks angry, and they'd pay to see that bum whipped," said Ali admiringly. It had been a useful gimmick, but one he claimed that he didn't need anymore.[52]

For those not attending the Georgia Tech football game on Saturday, another option was to sit at home and watch ABC's *Wide World of Sports*, which, two days before Ali's return to the ring, showed the computerized superfight between Ali and Rocky Marciano—the version for American audiences wherein Marciano knocked out Ali in the thirteenth round. The film had completed its tour of more than three hundred theaters around the country and had been shown around the world to some five hundred million people. But now that its theatrical run was over, ABC took advantage of the attention Ali was garnering in Atlanta to broadcast the bout on its flagship sports program.[53]

Race underlay much of that attention: in public reaction to the superfight, in questions posed to Ali about his conscientious objector status, in Quarry's role as the Great White Hope, in the location of the fight in the Deep South. But it also appeared in more explicit ways. The day before the bout, for example, Quarry demanded that two of the fight's four assigned doctors be white, claiming that Black doctors in his corner would be prejudiced against him. "They would probably stop the fight for a scratch."[54]

In an informal poll of sportswriters covering the fight, the vast majority picked Ali to win. Or they picked Clay. Of the twenty-seven writers polled, sixteen chose Cassius Clay. Five said Ali. Three picked Quarry, and three others bowed out without a guess. It was not a strong vote of confidence in Quarry, but it also demonstrated the reluctance of the white press to use Ali's Muslim name. Still, despite their problematic relationship with the boxer's chosen name, the sportswriters saw the fight as significant. The *New York Post*'s Milton Gross, for example, predicted a Clay victory. "But this is more than a prize fight. It's part of the social condition of our times. It goes beyond the four ropes of the ring. There are overtones and undertones. It's part of the recognition of man . . . and the recognition of the Constitution." Jack Griffin of the *Chicago Sun-Times* compared Ali's return to the World Series or the Super Bowl. Even those who couldn't bring themselves to acknowledge Ali's faith were perfectly ready to acknowledge his importance and his meaning to the worlds of sports, culture, and politics. "It's got to be," said Griffin, "the biggest single sporting event on in the world."[55]

While the world expressed unwavering interest in Ali and his comeback, however, the one potential viewer with the most at stake, Joe Frazier, claimed not to be interested. "I could care less," said Frazier's manager, Yank Durham. "I speak for Joe and he isn't interested. I care less, he cares less." When asked about the chances for Ali to have a successful comeback, Durham said, "We're the champion and anybody's gonna hafta come to us." Did he think Ali would beat Quarry? "We're the champion and anybody's gonna hafta come to us." Professional jealousy of the media's focus on Ali was taking a toll.[56]

The day before the bout, the promoters planned a party for the press. Kassel wanted to host the event at the Playboy Club, but it was Sunday. To get the venue opened, he called Hugh Hefner. "I'll make you a deal," Hefner told Kassel. "You run a closed-circuit line into the Playboy Mansion, and I'll give you the club." Kassel asked his technical advisor if it was possible to run a closed-circuit broadcast into a private home. It was; he made the deal. Hefner got to watch the fight from his house, and "they opened the club and brought in all the bunnies. It was the wildest scene you ever saw."[57]

That evening, before the press debauchery at the Playboy Club, Ali and his entourage attended the downtown Lowes theater for a special screening of *a.k.a. Cassius Clay*, then strolled down Peachtree Street, "spiritual and legendary Southern thoroughfare," as Jack Richardson wrote for *Harper's*. "It was a Klansman's nightmare, a recrudescence of the worst excesses of the South's post-bellum years." Richardson saw real meaning in the stroll the night prior to Ali's return to the ring. It was "as though each step were a gentle appropriation of a moment in history, a casual reclamation of a cultural manner that had been kept, except for moments of entertainment, in the corners of our society for a hundred years. This was no peace march, no righteous group of protesters heading for annihilation." It was, instead, "sheer, black, street-corner ebullience out for a Sunday evening promenade." And it was Blackness "on high display in the very center of gone-with-the-wind country."[58]

José Torres described Ali talking and shadowboxing with the crowd that followed him down Peachtree. The group ended their stroll at the Hyatt Regency Hotel, marveling at the architecture and also at the sea of Black faces that occupied the hotel lobby. "Man, we own this place," said the former champion. Though the hotel bar had a dress code, it was forced to change the rules to accommodate the parade of Black fashion from around the country that had descended on Atlanta. When a reporter asked him about Maddox's day of mourning, Ali claimed not to know the meaning of the word. "You know, a sad day," the reporter said, "a *black* day." The champ was quick with a response. "Oh, that! Yes, *that* we gonna have."[59]

Finally the black day arrived. "It is the fight that nobody but Atlanta wanted," wrote the *Constitution*'s George Cunningham, "but it is one that all corners of the world want to know about."[60] Fans across Europe,

South America, Australia, and Asia would watch on television, along with roughly nine hundred thousand spectators at American closed-circuit venues. Even Soviet television purchased live rights to the fight, the first time the Communist nation did so for an American television product. As Outlar explained, the bout was not destined to become one of the legendary contests in the sport, but "from a sociological standpoint, there's no parallel and it would be no gross exaggeration to say that the world hasn't been so interested in a heavyweight bout since 1938," when Joe Louis defeated the German Max Schmeling.[61]

The weigh-ins took place that morning, largely a matter of ceremony in a heavyweight division that didn't require boxers to cut weight. Quarry stepped to the scale first: 197 pounds. "He is, indisputably, a tough-looking man," Jack Richardson explained. "If one had wished to arrange the ingredients of Ali's return to the ring according to a recipe of racial melodrama, Quarry was the perfect choice." Because of that look, "as unfair as it is, he remains in the mind as something sullen and angry, as the perfect White Hope as conjured forth by a black imagination."[62]

When Ali followed, he tipped the scales at 213.5 pounds, down 25 from the onset of his training six weeks earlier but not at his goal of 210. "Who is the champion of the world?" Ali screamed before stepping on the scales, and one sarcastic reporter shouted back, "Jerry Quarry!" Ali was in full form. "I got something for Quarry, and I got something for all of you!" he responded. "After tonight there will be no more Quarry." Just reaching the weigh-ins was a victory, of sorts, and Ali hugged his mother and signed autographs as the two walked out of the building to a waiting car. One of his fans pushed through the crowd. "Ali, baby," he screamed. "Tell me I should bet on you." Ali pointed at him. "Bet your house *and* lot." The fan smiled. "My man."[63]

After the weigh-ins Ali relaxed in Johnson's vacation cottage, a three-bedroom lake house surrounded by forest.[64] Or he tried to relax, despite phone calls from Hank Aaron, Willie Mays, Willis Reed, and Gale Sayers, and visits from a variety of well-wishers. None of them were radicals. They were athletes "who play the game, mind their own business, and do not get involved with the black movement," explained Budd Schulberg, "yet they are all with Ali, as if to say, 'You're doing it for all of us, baby!'"[65] It was a messy scene, with newspapers and boxing magazines strewn across the floor, beds unmade, and sports equipment of various kinds lying around. In the corner of the dining room was a large trunk marked MUHAMMAD ALI—THE KING. Filmmaker Jim Jacobs, director of *a.k.a. Cassius Clay*, projected an unreleased Jack Johnson documentary onto a sheet nailed to the living room wall, though Ali was constantly distracted by telephone calls. "I grew to love the Jack Johnson image," Ali later explained. "I wanted to be rough, tough, arrogant, the n——the white folks didn't like." Ali ate vegetables and lamb chops after the first reel of the film had finished, noting as he had earlier in the year that his life and Johnson's were similar. Johnson's fights were canceled for his supposed violations of the Mann Act; Ali's were canceled for his violation of draft laws. "Governor was involved in his fights, too." He noted the four days Johnson spent in jail and remembered, "I was in seven days for a traffic ticket." Both Ali and Johnson were defensive fighters; both taunted their opponents; both engaged the crowd at ringside. More importantly, both defied racial norms and both were punished for their defiance. Of course, Johnson dealt with social Darwinian assumptions among white fans in a country still decidedly in the throes of Jim Crow. As Art Evans explains, the dominant white concern in the early decades of the twentieth century was that "a black would permanently reign as champion; this situation they would not tolerate."[66] There was at least a begrudging toleration of Black champions by 1970, but Angelo Dundee never understood the comparison between his fighter and Johnson. He remembered Ali wanting to come to the ring as Johnson for the Quarry fight, but Dundee was incredulous. "You're in no way like Jack Johnson," he said. "You're not like Sugar Ray Robinson; you're not like Joe Louis. You're new, different. You're yourself, and they can't compare to you."[67]

Ali took a walk after his meal. He had regularly taken similar walks throughout his time at Johnson's cottage, which was just down the street from the home of Otis Redding. He had often stopped at Redding's house to relax and watch movies, but on fight day he met with fans in the neighborhood, returned to take a nap, then sang and sparred with Curtis Mayfield, who would sing the national anthem before the fight.[68]

During Ali's nap Bundini Brown explained to George Plimpton that an Ali victory that night was "medicine for everyone. He's sellin' *pride*. Medicine. And he sellin' it down here in Klan lan'. The ol' Slave Master is lettin' him rumble. He do everyone some good if he win." Their conversation was interrupted by Jesse Jackson, who had just entered wearing a large medallion depicting Martin Luther King, Jr. "He's a young prophet," Bundini said of Jackson. "Prophets recognize prophets. That's why he's here. This place is sort of a prophet place." Jackson came into the kitchen with Brown and Plimpton describing the meaning of the upcoming fight and Ali's forced layoff. "Martin Luther King had a saying: 'Truth crushed to the earth will rise again.' That's the black ethos. With Cassius Clay all we had was the hope, the psychological *longing* for his return. And it happened! In Georgia, of all places, and against a white man." For Jackson, "there are tremendous social implications" for that night's fight. "It doesn't mean that Quarry is a villain," he said, but Ali was definitely a hero. "He carries the same mantle that Joe Louis did against Max Schmeling, or Jesse Owens when he ran in Hitler's Berlin." Quarry wasn't a Nazi, of course, but Ali was fighting against both a physical opponent and a broader injustice at the same time. "In Atlanta, I have never sensed such electricity, such expectation in the streets. For the downtrodden, they need the high example—that their representatives, the symbol of their own difficulties, will win." Brown agreed, explaining that when Ali fought Frazier it would be for himself and for boxing, but tonight's fight was for the people.[69]

Bundini left to go talk to Ali, who was now awake and wanting companionship. The two began arguing about the fight, Ali saying that he didn't want it stopped because of a cut; that if there was significant bleeding, he would go for a quick knockout rather than playing the advantage. Brown thought that was crazy. "Think of the Quarry camp," he said. "Why, that man open a cut on you, and you think he say, 'Oh my goodness, what a terrible thing! I cut him! I got to hurry up and knock him out.'" Of course he wouldn't. Ali gave up the argument, put on pants, and moved from the bedroom, excited to see Jackson. Jim Jacobs had gone, but he had left the Jack Johnson film, and Ali put it back on, watching Johnson fight Jeffries. Ali also spent time drawing a picture: he was beating up Quarry as the referee was stopping the fight; meanwhile, Lester Maddox was running down the aisle screaming to stop it.[70] Outside, in the red clay driveway of Johnson's cottage, a fan in a green suede suit was showing off a custom-built Cadillac with telephones, black carpet, a stocked bar, and a television inside. He was hoping to sell it for $50,000. While Ferdie Pacheco and others in Ali's entourage marveled at the car, no one decided to buy.[71]

Finally, after the guests moved on, Ali left with his large entourage. The group traveled first to the Hyatt Regency, where Ali was supposed to meet with Coretta Scott King, but she was late, so the group moved from the Regency to Municipal Auditorium. As Ali walked to the auditorium's back entrance he stopped to shake hands with fans waiting for him. "You better get there early," he told them. "You might be too late." But when fans asked him to call the round, he demurred.[72]

Meanwhile, Harold Conrad, doing the actual work of promotion in lieu of novices like Johnson and Hill, was hustling to ensure that the fight would actually take place. Dundee had insisted on a twenty-foot ring, though the available ring at the venue was nineteen and a half feet. Conrad pleaded with Dundee to forgo those six inches, but the trainer was insistent. So Conrad scrambled to find a twenty-foot ring, finally locating one at the Norfolk Navy Yard in Virginia. After some negotiations, the Navy agreed to rush the ring to Georgia. It had arrived the Friday before the Monday contest, a seeming catastrophe avoided. But though Conrad had been assured that a ring crew would be on hand to set up the structure that weekend, a ring crew never materialized. So Conrad and an elderly auditorium employee who had worked at the venue for forty years spent the weekend putting the ring together—a vital task not only because it was the playing field for the fighters but because seating couldn't be set up and mapped until the ring was in place. The auditorium employee was working on the ring into Sunday night while Conrad and Pacheco, Ali's doctor, were opening folding chairs and putting them in position around the ring. By Monday the task seemed to be done; ringside press credentials had been distributed. But Conrad soon realized that without a cross cable to support the structure from below, the ring would collapse. "Can you imagine what Jesse Jackson, what all the brothers would think if that ring collapsed?" asked Conrad. "They'd be sure it was sabotage—the Klan and the White Citizens' Council getting even with Clay. It could start a riot." At the last minute he secured a cross cable and got it in place.[73]

Still there were other problems. Kassel later claimed that on the day of the fight he was served with an injunction to stop the contest by a federal district court judge. "I stuck it in my pocket and walked away like nothing happened," he remembered.[74] "Atlanta has not had a fight of any major proportions since 1939," journalist and former boxer José

Torres explained, and it showed. In the minutes before preliminary fights began, organizers realized that they had not made arrangements for corner stools for the fighters between rounds. As the first bout began, an official ran to a downtown hardware store, purchased two stools, and brought them to the ring. The $3.98 price tags were still on the stools as the weary fighters sat down. They were finally there, at least. The fight would go on, but just barely. "Usually we have an experienced staff we can count on," said a frustrated Conrad. "Here it was big talk and no action."[75]

Outside the auditorium, however, there was plenty of action. Delta, which made its home base in Atlanta, advertised flights from Los Angeles, Detroit, New York, and Chicago for the fight in the cities' Black newspapers, offering a $53.05 package for fans to get a ticket to the match and three days and two nights in "first class accommodations in a top Atlanta hotel." All a fan needed to do was purchase a Delta ticket.[76] Those already in Atlanta could view the closed-circuit showing at the Sports Arena, site of the competitors' training regimes, for ten dollars per person. There was originally a blackout in Atlanta, but Jesse Hill explained that they decided to make the Sports Arena available for closed-circuit broadcast because the only seats remaining for the live event cost one hundred dollars, a price that most Atlantans couldn't afford.[77]

The *Los Angeles Sentinel* sent both A. S. "Doc" Young and Brad Pye to cover the fight at ringside. Pye reported on throngs of Black fans from Los Angeles, New York, and Philadelphia taking advantage of Delta's fight promotion. One commentator claimed it was "the biggest black turnout in Atlanta since the funeral of the late Dr. Martin Luther King Jr." Pye described thousands of Black visitors filling the Hyatt Regency hotel, people "with names like J.C., Sundown, Snake, Black Buddha, Cross-Eyed Taylor, and others some people label pimps, boosters, dope pushers and all the other kinds of funny sounding names—low and high society folks." They were dressed in "Bonnie & Clyde outfits, Frank Netti suits and reptile shoes. All sorts of mink, leather, rubber and velvet costumes." As one visitor marveled, "Sitting in the lobby of the Regency Hyatt House in Atlanta was like watching a costume ball." Pye claimed to have overheard one reveler say, "Man, they didn't give us the 40 acres and a mule they promised when they turned us loose. But now we own 80 acres and custom-made El Dorados."[78] Bert Sugar later remembered that the gathering was "the greatest collection of black money and black power ever assembled until that time. Right in the heart of the Old Confederacy, it was *Gone With the Wind* turned upside-down." *Harper's* Jack Richardson had a similar take, noting that as Ali's fans filtered out into the cool Atlanta night, "one knew that there was a new tempo in town that was much more devastating to Old South rhythms than the gospel cadence of a freedom march."[79]

It created, at times, a culture clash. A portion of that throng had come from Harlem, brought by basketball legend and drug trafficker Pee Wee Kirkland, who had purchased five hundred tickets and brought hundreds of Harlemites, many of them armed with concealed handguns, down to Atlanta in a caravan of cars. Boxing journalist Budd Schulberg saw the crowd at the Hyatt and noticed that the hotel's bartender "was a real white cracker. I thought he was going to have a heart attack when these hustlers came in and put wads of money on the bar, hundreds and hundreds of dollars." The Harlemites loved every minute of it, acting as if "they'd been waiting for this moment, waiting for the day when black men and women could strut arrogantly across a southern city," writes Jonathan Eig, "taking Ali's swagger and making it their own."[80] The bartender told Richardson that "we've had plenty of blacks staying here before, but, you know, they wore normal suits, talked quiet, had one drink and were gone." There had even been a civil rights convention at the hotel and "you hardly noticed them. But these—it's like a lot of bombs going off."[81]

"In what used to be the never, never land of Oz, the escape retreat for Americans, professional athletes were refreshing characters who sprouted intriguing dialogue and entertained," wrote Al Thomy. "That was before they were shaven and shorn with square haircuts and given attaché cases, meshed into the work-a-day crowd and told to say the right things about their enemies and the world in general." But "suddenly out of this maze of the civilized jungle the city of Atlanta is treated to a rebirth of boxing, a sport born in the illegitimacy of wharfs and back alleys." For the week leading up to the fight, "Atlantans have been offered a nostalgic street scene from the past, a satirical sketch" that "brought all the ingredients of lovable slapstick and the naked con artistry dished out before press agents became public relations directors."[82]

The Hyatt Regency, which hosted so much of that slapstick, had opened on May 1, 1967, the most cosmopolitan hotel in Atlanta. Stars from Aretha

Franklin to John Wayne had stayed there. Richard Nixon stayed there. It hosted the SCLC's annual meeting. Martin Luther King, Jr., called it the "Hotel of Hope." The Hyatt Regency was designed by architect John Portman and was the first building to incorporate his trademark atrium with glass elevators, which allowed riders to look down on the well-appointed lobby and allowed those in the lobby to watch the riders traveling up the building's twenty-three floors. It was a hotel, Richardson explained, "that intends to make its guests feel that they are in a great launching pad with their rooms somewhere in outer space. One looks up several hundred feet to a glass-domed roof, the rising emptiness broken only by the balcony railings on each floor." Bert Sugar remembered watching Ali in the elevator, "and they were cheering him. It was like some scene from a sci-fi movie: The god was rising and the people were cheering. It was *1984*-ish in 1970." Leroy Johnson remembered that the reaction of visitors upon seeing the elevators was "God damn!" So for the weekend, "that atrium got the name of 'God damn.' They would come in and say, 'Did you see the God damn . . . ?'"[83]

That the fight was a decidedly Black event in Atlanta was significant. Richardson, writing in *Harper's*, described Quarry's "pale, hard, sullen, lower-class face" that "would seem most apposite peeping out from behind a police visor." The challenger was "sullen and angry," the embodiment of what Black fans imagined when they envisioned a Great White Hope. In the face of what many interpreted as Ali's mistreatment at the hands of white authority, it was Black fans who relished the presence of a Great White Hope, a stand-in for that authority on whom Ali could take out three years of frustration and in the process provide a measure of catharsis for all the other Black frustrations generated by white authority.[84]

Soon, however, the crowd would leave the Hyatt Regency and make the short trip several blocks through downtown to the arena. Municipal Auditorium, Richardson explained, "looks as though it were constructed to hold a good-sized PTA meeting. In its better days Caruso once sang within its walls, but now all it has left is a certain run-down, functional sincerity." But that night Municipal Auditorium was something more. "The throng mills about, eyeing itself with admiration," wrote Richardson. "Back and forth move coiffures that would have dwarfed the wigs at Versailles." The show was outside of the ring as much as within it.

"Everything is black and dazzling, and one imagines that, if Ali should lose, all the colors would fade away and the city of Atlanta would be still except for the wailing sound of Cadillacs changing into pumpkins."[85]

The celebrities at Municipal Auditorium to watch Ali's return were legion: Bill Cosby, Hank Aaron, Diana Ross, Stepin Fetchit, and former lightweight champion Ike Williams. Then there were future celebrities, like Los Angeles attorney Johnnie Cochran. Heavyweight Jimmy Ellis, who had been knocked out by Frazier and had won a decision against Quarry earlier in his career, was also on hand to watch the fight. So were Whitney Young, Coretta Scott King, Donn Clendenon, Julian Bond, Jesse Jackson, Ralph Abernathy, Harry Belafonte, Clarence Williams, and Sidney Poitier.[86] Jackson, in particular, attempted to sum up the meaning of the fight to the country's Black population. "If he loses tonight it will mean, symbolically, that the forces of blind patriotism are right, that dissent is wrong; that protest means you don't love the country, this fight is Love-it-or-leave-it vs. Love-it-and-change-it." But perhaps the biggest celebrity other than Ali was Leroy Johnson, who received a standing ovation from the crowd for making the fight in Atlanta happen.[87]

Among the names of celebrities at ringside, Fetchit's stood out. Stepin Fetchit was the stage name of Lincoln Perry, first publicly associated with Ali before the champion's rematch with Sonny Liston, a seemingly incongruous pairing of a radical separatist and paragon of Black pride and an actor best known for minstrel-show caricatures of Blackness. But their friendship, unlikely as it was, remained, and Fetchit was there with his fellow celebrities and the pimps and hustlers who joined them for the event.[88]

It was a gathering that, for all Ali's radicalism, would take place under the bold Confederate iconography of the Georgia state flag, flown at half-staff on Maddox's orders for the official day of mourning. It was a powerful visual: a Confederate flag lowered in protest over Ali's presence, flying in front of a building where a large celebration of Black fans, Black celebrities, and Black wealth had congregated to celebrate the end of a suspension that most interpreted as having racial motives. The Confederate flag remained halfway down the flagpole that night because of a government decree, but it may as well have been because of Black will.

Security for the fight was incredibly tight, partly because of the celebrity presence but mostly because of fears of potential white saboteurs.

Maddox's "inflammatory statements about the fight" led to an abundance of caution as to "persons working in and around" the arena. Plainclothes detectives searched the building diligently before it opened. Police admitted no specific threat, but conditions were such that an abundance of caution was the order of the day.[89]

The dangers, it seemed, weren't only in Atlanta. The night of the fight, a bomb threat was made against Ali's home in Philadelphia, where his wife Belinda was still staying with their young twins. "Ali won, you lose," said a mysterious voice on the telephone. "The bomb goes off at midnight." Though she assumed it was a hoax, she still called her husband in Atlanta, who in turn called the Philadelphia police. They spoke with Ali and told him not to worry; it was just an effort at intimidation, but they would take it seriously and ensure the safety of his home and his wife. They moved Belinda and the children to an apartment for the night, and the city's bomb squad checked the house the following day, finding nothing.[90]

The program sold at Municipal Auditorium featured a reproduction of a limited-edition poster by LeRoy Neiman, only five hundred of which were printed in honor of Ali's return to the ring. The program's opening page—a full-page biography of Leroy Johnson—made it clear who the prime mover of the fight was. Another page trumpeted Atlanta's progressivism and its intersection with high-stakes athletics. It was a city too busy to hate, with a Protestant white majority but a Jewish mayor and Black vice mayor. "But perhaps the clearest demonstration that concepts like reasonableness and fair play are more pervasive in Atlanta than transient passions will come tonight." It was Atlanta that would host Muhammad Ali, who had been stripped of his title "by a willful band of men who don't agree with his religion or with his political views." The program claimed that seventy-two cities had previously turned down the former champion. But then came Johnson and Robert Kassel to save the day. Johnson secured the mayor's support, then met in a closed-door meeting with the Athletic and Building Committee of the board of aldermen, winning Ali a license to fight and a permit to hold a bout in Municipal Auditorium. There were plenty of "doubting Thomases," but Johnson had pulled off the miracle. More than eight hundred thousand people would see the fight, the program claimed. "But they will be seeing not only one of the most important sporting events of the decade, but a city and its people as well—a city and people just too busy to hate."[91]

The program included a biographical sketch of the competitors, as well. "No other heavyweight in modern or even ancient times has created more stir than this 28-year old" Muhammad Ali, it told attendees. There had been times in Quarry's career when the fighter had wanted to quit, "but always, not just for money, he came back for another try because Jerry is proud and knows he can fight." Mirroring the Black wealth in the auditorium, the two most prominent advertisers in the program were Paschal's and Citizen's Trust. A final page rehearsed the history of fighters unsuccessfully attempting to make returns after long layoffs—but Ali was different. He was "the superman of heavyweights. Maybe, because he has constantly kept in condition despite his rise in weight, and the fact that he is only 28, he can remedy the ravages of time." Perhaps most telling of all, the back cover of the program included a photo of the city skyline with Atlanta Stadium in the foreground. Atlanta was a major-league city; sports had made it so, and sports would do so again.[92]

Table 2. Tale of the Tape

Muhammad Ali (Cassius Clay)		Jerry Quarry
28	AGE	25
215	WEIGHT	196
6 FEET 3 INCHES	HEIGHT	6 FEET ½ INCH
82 INCHES	REACH	76½ INCHES
42 INCHES	CHEST (NORMAL)	43 INCHES
44½ INCHES	CHEST (EXPANDED)	45½ INCHES
16¼ INCHES	BICEP	16½ INCHES
13½ INCHES	FOREARM	15 INCHES
34 INCHES	WAIST	33 INCHES
25 INCHES	THIGH	25 INCHES

Muhammad Ali (Cassius Clay)		Jerry Quarry
17 INCHES	CALF	16½ INCHES
17 INCHES	NECK	18¼ INCHES
1½ INCHES	WRIST	7¼ INCHES
12 INCHES	FIST	13 INCHES
9½ INCHES	ANKLE	12 INCHES

In the opening contest of the night, Muhammad Ali's brother Rahman, one year younger than his more famous sibling, knocked out his opponent, Hurricane Grant, in the third round. In the second preliminary bout, Quarry's sparring partner, Eddie "Bossman" Jones, knocked down Texan Willis Earls three times in the seventh round, stopping the fight. The third prelim also ended in a three-knockdown technical knockout when Herman "Bunky" Akins of Los Angeles felled Charleston's Jimmy Brown three times in the fourth round.[93]

After the preliminary bouts Leroy Johnson entered the ring, again receiving an ovation. He presented the promised $50,000 check, or at least a ceremonial version of it, to Sam Massell, who said into the microphone that the night's event was a "demonstration in democracy." One Black fan shouted back, "Right on, baby. That cat's gonna show whitey!" Finally, just before 10:30, Curtis Mayfield entered the ring and sang the national anthem. He was followed by ring announcer Johnny Addie, who introduced celebrities at ringside. Johnson was celebrated as the facilitator of the event. Then Bill Cosby and Sidney Poitier entered the ring, shadowboxing in opposite corners to entertain the crowd and kill time before the closed-circuit broadcast was scheduled to start. At ringside was Tom Harmon, broadcaster and former Heisman Trophy–winning halfback from the University of Michigan, joined for color commentary on the closed-circuit broadcast by Cosby.[94]

Cosby seemed like an odd choice, but the comedian was an aficionado of the sport. In 1967 he joined fellow Hollywood stars Ryan O'Neal and Robert Goulet, along with more experienced boxing people like Eddie Futch and Dell Jackson, to form January Fighters, Inc., a boxing management company. The group began by signing welterweight Hedgemon

Lewis, and in the months before the Ali-Quarry fight, January Fighters had signed Walter E. Moore, Jr., the 1969 Golden Gloves national heavyweight champion. Cosby was a famous name, and he was funny, but he also had a substantive relationship with the sport.[95]

Ali, meanwhile, was preparing, despite arriving at his small dressing room, along with two busloads of friends and acquaintances, still in his street clothes, an hour before the bout. When he finally dressed, Ali didn't like the foul-proof belt that Bundini Brown had brought for him. Conscious of his weight and his appearance, Ali preferred a small metal cup that didn't add bulk and make him look, in his assessment, fat. When Brown looked for the red belt that he and Dundee insisted on, he found that it was missing. Ali had taken it out of the suitcase; it was found under his bed the next morning. So Dundee improvised by raiding Rahaman's gear and using the black foul-proof belt of Muhammad's brother. Ali wasn't thrilled, but he continued shadowboxing as his team prepared.[96]

But there were other problems. Boxing publicists Murray and Bob Goodman were in Atlanta to fix some of the mistakes first-time promoters might make. "The people in charge knew nothing whatever," said Bob. "They forgot to order the gloves for the main eventers." So the Goodmans ordered some, then sent a taxi to the airport to pick them up. "We sweated it out," he remembered. "The cab didn't show until 10 minutes before the fight was scheduled to go on. That's why there was a delay in starting the fight on closed circuit."[97]

Ferdie Pacheco, worried about bursitis in Ali's hands and pain during the fight, gave Ali numbing shots in each of his hands before the gloves went on. He numbed them first with ethyl chloride, then shot a combination of cortisone and Xylacene into each hand. "The shots didn't violate any rules that I know of, although we didn't brag about them," Pacheco said. "The shots gave Ali comfort and the security of knowing he could punch without pain."[98]

With roughly forty minutes to go, Ali went to the restroom, passing Quarry's dressing room along the way. He opened the door. "You best be in good shape," he told Quarry, sitting in front of him, "because if you whup me, you've whupped the greatest fighter in the whole wide world." He closed the door before Quarry had a chance to reply. When he returned to his team, he lay on a table and received a rubdown. Then a member of Quarry's camp, Willie Ketchum, arrived to monitor the taping of Ali's late-arriving gloves. "You all in trouble tonight," Ali told him. "Your man's in for a new experience. He's up against the fastest heavyweight alive, quick and trim."

"You won't be when Jerry finishes," said Ketchum. "I know he's going to hit you."

"How's he going to do that? Angelo, how can he get away from the jab? How will he ever see it?" Dundee just shrugged and began taping Ali's hands.

Ketchum, however, wasn't done. "And if Jerry moves in on you, throwing the big ones? Ho, ho."

"He's goin' to get hit right in the banana," said Ali. "He never seen a right like that."

"If you beat Quarry tonight," Ketchum responded, "you are the greatest heavyweight who ever lived." To that Ali could never disagree. But Ketchum added, "And if that happens I'll come in here and kiss you."

"Oh, my, no," said Ali, changing the subject. "Hey, we will give you guys $500,000, *cash*, if you let me put a horseshoe in my gloves."

When the tape job was complete and Ketchum had approved, Ali stood up and moved in close. "Look into my eyes," he said. "I'm the real heavyweight. I am the fastest heavyweight that ever lived."

Ketchum chomped on his gum, unflinching. "I won some money on you once," he told Ali. "I bet $50 at 7 to 1 that you'd whip Sonny Liston." The two parted amicably.[99]

Ali told his team that he was thinking about all the television sets being turned on around the world, all the traffic jams around closed-circuit venues. An intern asked him for a poem, and the fighter responded, "Quarry sorry." He talked about Allah, about the gifts that Allah had given him. As he continued to pump himself up, a trainer smeared petroleum jelly on his shoulders and torso. "The Temptations are out there," he told himself. "The Supremes are out there. Sidney Poitier's out there." He combed his hair and reluctantly put on the foul protector when Dundee brought it to him. Then he decided that he didn't like his trunks. "Where are my brother's trunks?" he asked. Someone opened Rahaman's bag and brought them to him. He put those on instead. "This is better."[100]

Jesse Jackson joined the group in the dressing room and led everyone in prayer. He told them that he was glad that Ali's return to boxing had come in the hometown of Martin Luther King, Jr. "He would have loved it this way." Six years earlier, before Ali's first fight with Liston, Malcolm X had been the minister talking to Ali before he walked to the ring, describing that bout as a battle between "the Cross and the Crescent." Now it was a Christian prayer and the invocation of King, leader of a movement that Malcolm and Ali had often disagreed with. In a corner, George Plimpton sat taking notes and watching the preparations.[101]

Just before it was time to go, Sidney Poitier entered the room. "Sidney's here!" shouted Ali. "I'm really ready to rumble!" The two hugged and joked together before Poitier headed out to his seat. Before they left Ali asked about the ring; he asked about closed-circuit cameras. Then came the knock on the door. "It's time." He looked at himself once more in the mirror, then stepped out into the hallway.[102]

Quarry appeared to the crowd at 10:35, wearing a kelly green robe. There was scattered respectful applause for the challenger. But after he was in the ring, Ali appeared "wearing the kind of terry-cloth robe that can be bought at nickle [*sic*] and dime stores." The crowd, roughly 90 percent Black, erupted. There were some boos in the audience but there were far more cheers as Ali walked to the ring. "We didn't have a clearly defined aisle to the ring," Pacheco remembered. "We were going through a crowd where anyone could touch you or pull out a snub-nosed revolver and shoot you. That walk into the ring was one of the worst experiences of my life. We were just hoping no one could get through to us."[103] But the crowd: "It was like a scene from Lester Maddox's strangest nightmare," Jonathan Eig explained, "like watching Paul Robeson play Rhett in *Gone with the Wind*."[104] When Ali got to the ring Bundini Brown pointed to a small group of white fans in the crowd, describing them as "white buttons on a black silk shirt." He whispered to Ali, "Jack Johnson's ghost is watching you," then throughout the fight shouted, "Ghost in the house! Jack Johnson's here!" to encourage his fighter.[105]

Addie reintroduced the celebrities, including Johnson. He introduced Quarry, who received a polite ovation. His introduction of Ali, however, was drowned out in the roar of the crowd. "Ali is not introduced as a champion," José Torres remembered. "But everyone there knows he is the real champion." When the two came to the middle of the ring at referee Tony Perez's signal, Ali told his opponent, "You are in trouble, man. I'm going to get rid of you, fast." A stoic Quarry responded, "Shut up and fight."[106]

Ali came into the fight sixteen pounds heavier than Quarry and immediately used his weight advantage with left jabs in the first round. He threw sixty-one punches and landed twenty-five. Quarry responded with rights that failed to land. It was clear that Ali's corner felt that he was far too aggressive in that first round, wearing himself out in three minutes. Dundee explained that after a close first round, "it appeared Quarry was setting him up for the sucker left so I told him to change directions, first move one way and then another." The plan was to "snake-hit Quarry, move around." Dundee encouraged him before round two to "stay at a distance" and use his reach advantage.[107]

And in round two he did, opening with two quick jabs and throwing forty-nine punches, landing twenty. He was also able to back away from Quarry's right hooks, making for a generally uneventful round until Quarry landed a significant body shot before the bell. Ali had thrown more than double the punches of Quarry, and had landed them at an even greater rate, but Quarry's late second-round surge allowed him to claim more power punches in the second round than Ali. Though the two had appeared at least relatively even for the first two rounds, Ali won them with his left hand and Quarry landed only six effective punches. Round three seemed more of the same, with Ali "bordering on exhaustion," until Quarry pinned Ali on the ropes and attempted a flurry of blows that mostly missed their target. Ali parried with shots of his own, and when they were finally separated, blood appeared for the first time over Quarry's eye. Quarry narrowly missed with a right hand and Ali countered with an overhand right that further opened the cut above the eye, which eventually required fifteen stitches. That immediately became Ali's target as he directed right hands to the eye, opening the wound more and sending blood gushing down Quarry's cheek. "It was so brutal," said Andrew Young, who was sitting in the fourth row with his wife, "that blood spattered on my wife's dress."[108]

Table 3. Statistics[1]

	Ali	Quarry
PUNCHES LANDED	57	17
PERCENTAGE OF TOTAL	38%	25%
JABS	38	4

PERCENTAGE OF TOTAL	38%	18%
POWER PUNCHES	19	13
PERCENTAGE OF TOTAL	40%	28%

1. Groves, "Muhammad Ali—Jerry Quarry I."

Though his corner was able to stanch the bleeding, Quarry's second, Teddy Bentham, made the decision to keep his fighter back, not letting him answer the bell for the fourth round, giving Ali a victory by technical knockout. Quarry attempted to shove Bentham out of the way and move to the middle for the fourth round, but referee Tony Perez stopped him and convinced him to listen to his cornerman. "No, no, no," he screamed, but after a brief conclave with Perez, he walked, dejected, back to his corner. Perez later remembered, "I'd never seen a cut like that before. You could see the bone." They didn't consult any of the four doctors present because the chaos at ringside would never have allowed them to reach the ring.[109]

"I didn't want it stopped," Quarry said after the fight, "but [Bentham] did the right thing." To that point, Quarry had been following his game plan, keeping it close in the first five rounds before becoming more aggressive later in the bout. The cut above his eye, however, stopped that strategy short. Jack Quarry, the fighter's father and manager, also agreed with the call, even though he thought his son's strategy had worked well to that point. "It was a bad cut, a real bad cut, the worst I've seen." The punch that did it was "not a particularly hard punch but one coming down on him. But that's life in the big city," he said. "You can't fight that." Throughout his comments, the elder Quarry referred to his son's opponent only as Clay, as he had in the week leading up to the fight. He would give Ali credit for the win, but he would never call him by his name.[110]

Despite the Quarry family insisting that their plan was working until the stoppage, the judges' scorecards unanimously gave every round to Ali. Ali claimed that the only Quarry punch that really hurt him was the body shot late in the second round. Ali, in the words of Norman Mailer, "beat Quarry in the flurry of a missed hundred punches, ho! how his timing was off! beat him with a calculated whip, snake-lick whip, to the corrugated sponge of dead flesh over Quarry's Irish eyes."[111]

Kassel, in the ring after the fight, claimed that he was there when Dundee was cutting off Ali's gloves. "Inside the left-hand cuff, in the soft cotton part, it was written in a ballpoint pen, 'TKO, 3rd Round.' So help me God. That glove was taped on, so nobody could have slipped in there and written that." It was true. Dundee had written his prediction in the glove before putting it on his fighter.[112]

With the kind of gash Quarry had sustained over his eye, some questioned whether the cut was the result of a headbutt. But Quarry denied that after the fight. "It wasn't a butt," he said. "And I don't want anybody saying it was. It was a right hand." Quarry's sister Dianna later claimed that the cut was actually created by Bentham, who cut Quarry's eye, at the fighter's request, before the third round to reduce swelling. A punch by Ali right on the cut opened it. If not for that, she wondered, "who knows what would have happened" if Quarry had won. "A white, good-looking heavyweight champion who had just defeated Muhammad Ali—that would have opened up the door to everything."[113]

Despite the early loss, Quarry emerged confident and cocky in defeat. "The crowd was 90 percent black and all for Ali, but that didn't motivate me or intimidate me either," remembered Quarry. "When I got in the ring, it was just another fight, even though the opponent was Ali. I wasn't fighting against a symbol. I was fighting a fighter, who had two arms and two legs just like me."[114] Quarry had gone "out there thinking he [Ali] was going to be the greatest. Heck, he's a good fighter, but he ain't the greatest. He couldn't whip my four-year-old son," Quarry said. "I wasn't beaten by a better fighter, I was beaten by a miracle."[115] It was a unique turn for an Ali fight, with the former champion humble in victory and his defeated foe crowing about his superiority.

Ali, for his part, was satisfied with the win but disappointed in the fight. "Frankly, I don't like the idea of the fight ending on a cut," he told reporters. Quarry "was tough and tricky." He "has a hard style to get away from. I couldn't get in and out the way I had planned." Ali was sure that Quarry could have gone at least ten rounds if not for the cut, "and that would have been better for me," he said. "The longer the better."[116]

Of course, reporters' focus almost immediately turned to Frazier after the final bell had sounded in Atlanta. Ali projected confidence, even without the ten rounds he had hoped for. Quarry was "a harder man to fight than Frazier. He was clever and he moved well and brought that left hook in well. Frankly, he gave me some pause to think. Frazier, on the other hand, comes right at you. He's a straightaway fighter and much easier to go against." Dundee was even more dismissive. "Frazier said he wasn't interested in this fight and wasn't even going to watch it on TV. Well, we're not interested in Frazier."[117]

After the questions had run their course, the press conference after the fight closed with Coretta Scott King, who had championed Ali's return to boxing since the SCLC International Freedom Games earlier in the year, presenting an award to Ali in memory of her husband, for the fighter's contribution "to the dignity of man." She told him at the event, "You are not only our champion in the boxing area, but you're also our champion of justice and peace and human dignity."[118]

More than 100 million viewers around the world, the largest boxing audience in history to that point, watched the Ali-Quarry fight. In New York, 17,800 fans packed into Madison Square Garden to watch. The Los Angeles Forum sold out. Journalist Robert Lipsyte argued that the bout "reestablished Ali's credibility with the closed-circuit television network," which had become the most important driver of revenue in the sport over the course of the 1960s. The fight was, for Scott Freeman, all to the glory of the city. "It marked the moment that Atlanta ascended to the undisputed black political capital of America."[119]

But not everyone was pleased. Nat Fleischer's *Ring Magazine*, already on record as opposed to the Mansfield ruling, described the Atlanta fight as "a hoax" and a "mess." The bout was "devoid of excitement, and utterly lacking in information concerning Cassius' present condition for a fight lasting more than nine minutes." The magazine, which almost always referred to Ali as Clay, explained that it normally presented action photographs of important fights, but in the Quarry contest, "the most eligible camera shots showed Muhammad Ali laughing his way to his bank." The statement was in fact surrounded by action photographs of the important fight, but consistency was less important than finding reasons to criticize the former champion.[120]

"The fight didn't figure to be one of boxing's great moments, and it wasn't," wrote Jesse Outlar. "The story of this fight was important simply because it was held."[121] But for Black Americans, at least those represented by the Black press, the win was indeed a great moment. "The cat is back," the *Chicago Defender*'s Norman Unger celebrated. "Muhammad

Ali proved to the world that he is still just as good as 'Cassius Clay' ever was."[122] According to the *Los Angeles Sentinel*, "the critics have been silenced." Ali had made his comeback, "but most important, he showed the same class that was his trademark more than 40 months ago." He had "risked everything," demonstrating "the strength of his convictions" and that he "was not afraid to stand up for them." So the victory against Quarry was partly his, and partly for those who supported him all those months. "His followers have the pride of knowing that their faith in Cassius Clay has paid off. He has been persecuted on every side and there were times when a lesser man would have thrown in the towel. But he remained strong and the prize for his perseverance is gradually becoming obvious."[123]

Chicago Defender columnist Louis Martin was even more circumspect. He celebrated Ali's victory, noting "that the bout took place in Governor Maddox's bailiwick where fistic encounters between blacks and whites are rarely governed by any rules or held in the presence of impartial judges or referees. The Governor must have gulped when the future of the new White Hope went up in smoke." And he was right. The fight was surely one of, if not the first instance of a Black man in Georgia publicly whipping a white man without violent retributive consequences. In that sense it had to be a devastating blow for Maddox and his acolytes, a symbolic changing of the Southern guard. But the guard itself—white supremacy—could accept symbolic victories as long as it stayed in a position of power. "We live in a society which has historically sought to intimidate and inhibit the citizen with a black skin," Martin wrote. But "the single most important development in the so-called black revolution in the past decade has been the growth of pride and a new sense of dignity." Ali was the embodiment of that new pride and dignity. For many in the younger generation, Martin assumed, much of their talk was just that: sound and fury without much action behind it. But Ali put his money where his mouth was. He fought to get back into the ring, then went into it and dominated. Ali wasn't simply a boxer, then; he was an example to those now manning the rhetorical barricades of the "black revolution."[124]

"Muhammad Ali upset the Establishment 'Joes,' the flag-wavers and all of the antis over the world," wrote Dick Edwards of the *New York Amsterdam News*, having watched the fight on closed-circuit broadcast in Harlem, "but he was the greatest before a good crowd at the 369th Armory." The "Joes" comment wasn't an accident. Edwards used Ali's success as a rebuke of Joe Frazier. "At least Ali didn't fake patriotism, like one heavyweight champion allegedly did. And, he didn't have a photo taken of himself playing at being a longshoreman—with patent leather shoes on—as this same ex-champion did. How about that Joe? Did that get to you at all—too?"[125]

The *Pittsburgh Courier*'s Jess Peters noted that despite the rhetoric of Maddox, the American Legion, and the VFW, "there was no real boycott of the fight." That said, a group of veterans in Scranton, Pennsylvania, did conduct a boycott of the closed-circuit broadcast. "Wild," wrote Peters, "a brother can get more consideration in Georgia and human decency than he can in a Pennsylvania community."[126] For the Baltimore *Afro-American*, "Muhammad Ali is back, thank you. He looks as flashy and effective as ever." Surely his next victory would come in the Supreme Court after "another example of the white majority using its weight to put a black man in his place by one means or another." But the champ would win that one, too. "Ali will have back his crown. He will be more popular than ever before."[127]

Still, the response to Ali's victory wasn't a total coronation. In the week after the fight, Missouri representative Richard Ichord, chair of the committee formerly known as the House Un-American Activities Committee, released a list of "Radical Campus Speakers." His committee requested reports on campus speakers from 179 universities. From the ninety-five replies the representatives received, they compiled a list of names of sixty-five "radicals" who, they argued, may have used honoraria to fund left-wing organizing. At the top of the list was Muhammad Ali. While his regular campus tours had come to an end, Ali's move back into the national spotlight also returned him to the attention of white conservatives who sought to remind America that he was a threat, a member of a "Black hate group."[128]

There were also more pragmatic frustrations. In Ali's hometown of Louisville, fans who paid either $5 or $7.50 to watch the fight on screens at the city's Freedom Hall were unable to see the first two rounds because of technical difficulties. When the fight finally appeared on-screen, the third round was about to begin. Fans began chanting for their money back. Some threw liquor bottles and beer cans. Eventually twenty policemen arrived to quiet the crowd. One of the promoter's assistants was injured in the scrum, and one of the patrons was arrested for "inciting to riot." The promoter, William King, would ultimately face a lawsuit over the failure.[129]

Back in Atlanta, as Julian Bond remembered, Black residents felt as though they had won, as well. None of them had punched Jerry Quarry, but "people said, 'We got the Ali fight. Nobody else can have an Ali fight. We're the only people in the country that can have an Ali fight.'" And "we're the only people in the country that can attract a crowd like this."[130] The overwhelming feeling was that they—the crowd and Black Atlanta more broadly—had gotten Ali back in the ring, a much more difficult task than cutting Quarry's eye. And they were right. Crowds often claim a role in helping their combatants to victory, but this one had an actual argument to make. Black Atlanta had resurrected Ali. In a city that provided its Black population a series of losses, often hidden under the veneer of racial moderation, this time they had won.

As fans were leaving Municipal Auditorium and streaming out into the street, invitations were handed out by Black bystanders outside of the arena, directing them to a private house for a party. But the invitations went only to Black fans. "They were," remembered Bert Sugar, "purposely passing over the white people." Others claimed to have received phone calls inviting them to the party, and mailed invitations had also gone out weeks before. When the fight was over, some two hundred fans, most of them from out of town, attended a post-match party at the home of Gordon "Chicken Man" Williams at 2819 Handy Drive in northwest Atlanta. But the party ended early when masked gunmen arrived and stole cash, jewelry, and clothing, a haul valued at more than a million dollars.[131]

The party and its robbery demonstrated a different kind of hierarchy in Black Atlanta. There was the mass of the Black working class, there were the activists, and there were the business and civic leaders who served as conduits to white power structures. But there was also a different class of Black influencers—the criminal underworld. That group constituted another power elite, one that didn't negotiate with white businessmen and politicians. Wesley Merrit, for example, one of the leaders in the Atlanta loan sharking and gambling game, owned a pool hall and used much of his profit to develop the community and help individuals in need. He and those like him were often seen as a more reliable source of Black leadership than the politicians who necessarily made compromises with leading whites as part of their jobs. Hustlers were pillars of the community, people who gamed a system hostile to Black interests.[132]

It was the hustlers, the high-rolling criminals, who would be holding and attending the Handy Drive party. Chicken Man had been told to organize the gathering. He was a military veteran who had become a bootlegger and numbers runner; eventually he became a drug dealer. Williams had earned the name Chicken Man by offering to buy pretty girls chicken sandwiches at Paschal's restaurant. He was part of the criminal underground in Atlanta, but he was also connected around the country. He often ran drugs from Miami, the home of Dundee's gym, bringing them back to Atlanta and transporting them to other urban hubs. Chicken Man saw the party as an opportunity to make money and to demonstrate his competence among the country's leading Black criminal element. He would play host to a massive collection of illicit Black wealth, coming from all over the country, drawn by Ali's return to the ring. It was a perfect opportunity for him—but it was also a perfect opportunity for someone to make the biggest score of his life.[133]

Invitations to the party had been printed in Harlem and shared with those streaming to Atlanta for the fight. People from New York came down and built craps tables, roulette wheels, card tables, and other amenities for the party, fitting out Chicken Man's house to make the event the best it could be. The party started days prior to the contest, running virtually twenty-four hours a day, with pimps, drug dealers, and racketeers using the house as a home base for fun and excitement in the lead-up to Ali's return. But the party would be busiest after the boxing match.[134]

Richard Wheeler, the mastermind of the robbery, staged one Cadillac on the street behind the house and another on the street in front of it, several blocks away, the two groups communicating with walkie-talkies about people going in and out of the party. Two or three people from each Cadillac then got out and went to the house, one of the groups wearing masks. When two unmasked robbers, Fast Eddie Parker and McKinley Rogers, both from Brunswick, knocked on the door, a man named William Knox answered. He greeted them fondly because the robbers had been at the party the last two nights, but soon they pulled their guns and announced the robbery. Wheeler, however, was not with them. He had been in Atlanta in preparation for the heist, but had then boarded a plane, returned to New York, and was watching the fight at Madison Square Garden to give himself an alibi.[135]

The robbers forced the partygoers downstairs to the house's basement at gunpoint, made them strip down to their underwear, then robbed them of all of their possessions. One of the robbers used a broom to sweep the valuables into a pile on the floor. Meanwhile they kept the party lights on and the music loud, hoping to ensure that new arrivals would assume the party was still going so that they could rob them, as well.[136]

Not every victim was a part of the criminal underworld, of course. Many were just people hoping to party after the fight. Andrew West, a New York City detective, was robbed of a diamond ring, a watch, and almost $500 in cash, along with his police badge. "I don't know why I went to that party," said another New Yorker. "Someone gave me an invitation to 'Come to the Party,' and I went like a fool." She lost $200 and her wedding ring. "They cleaned everyone like a farmer cleaning chicken for dinner," remembered another victim. "We all had to undress, dumped our valuables on the floor." The robbers took everything. "We went downstairs in the nude."[137] Among those robbed was Muhammad Ali's father, who had worn a double-breasted white suit to the fight. Family friend Gene Kilroy remembered going to the Hyatt with Ali after his victory to enjoy the win with fans. But later that night he got a telephone call from Cassius Clay, Sr. "I had to bring him some clothes because they went in and took all their clothes. People were standing there naked with sheets around them."[138]

When the heist began, Chicken Man was not at home. He had been at the fight, then went to the Hyatt Regency, where he met Frank Molton, a former Atlanta numbers runner who had moved to New York to become a leading drug dealer, one of the most important men in the world of Black organized crime. He was known as the Black Godfather and was the one who originally orchestrated the party. Molton traveled with bodyguards; when he got to the party, the robbers attacked his bodyguards and took their guns. Then he and Chicken Man were stripped and robbed like everyone else.[139]

When one large crowd of revelers arrived, however, someone in their party saw a gun and screamed; someone else went next door and called the police. At that point the robbers left, desperate, taking with them two women as hostages. After they got away, they let the women go, allowing them to make their way back to the house on Handy Drive.[140]

Chief of Police Herbert Jenkins appointed J. D. Hudson, who had served as the leader of Ali's security detail, to be lead investigator on the case, assuming a Black officer would be better able to get information from the hustlers. They trusted Hudson. That was important, as most victims chose not to press charges, fearing negative publicity for themselves and consequences for their generally illicit lifestyle. Hudson knew Chicken Man didn't have anything to do with the robbery. But most others, including many of the hustlers who had been robbed, assumed Chicken Man had staged it. Williams and his family received death threats and other intimidations. To try to solve his dilemma, Chicken Man gave a television interview proclaiming his innocence; he traveled to New York to meet with the leaders of Black organized crime, aided by the good word of Molton. Williams even arrived at police headquarters with a lawyer, claiming that he and his girlfriend had also been robbed. It surprised the police, some of whom assumed that Williams had orchestrated the plot to pay off underworld debts and had subsequently been killed by gangsters.[141]

Meanwhile there were the actual robbers: Bookie Brown, James Henry Hall, Charles Lee, Houston Hammons, Baby Ray Humphrey, Emerson Dorsey, and Lillian Dabney (the only woman involved in the heist). Hudson was able to capture Houston Hammons after tracing a shotgun found at the scene to the twenty-seven-year-old. When he wouldn't talk, Hudson threatened to tell the press he was part of the robbery, then to release him to be killed by the gangsters. So Hammons talked. He described where the group purchased supplies and how they were instructed to do so. He named his coconspirators. He told Hudson everything.[142]

Despite his capture, Hammons was one of the lucky ones. One of Molton's bodyguards, who had been waiting on the road behind Chicken Man's house on the night of the robbery, captured Bookie Brown and Lillian Dabney and killed them. Their bodies were found days later. The next person to turn up dead was Emerson Dorsey. He and his girlfriend, Rachel Worthy, had been tortured in Dorsey's home in Decatur to get information about the robbery, then he had been shot in the head. Worthy was found with several knives stuck in her body. Then Charles Lee and Baby Ray Humphrey were killed—shot near Atlanta Stadium. Humphrey had $35,000 in cash on him and hundreds of thousands of dollars in heroin, and his killers didn't take any of it. This wasn't about money; it was about revenge.[143]

McKinley Rogers, James Henry Hall, Fast Eddie Parker, and others escaped to Brunswick, where some of the robbers were originally from. They stayed at a Holiday Inn, spent a lot of money, stayed in their rooms, and wouldn't let cleaning crews or anyone else come in. It was suspicious, but they left before Hudson and his team could get to Brunswick. They went to New York, the home of so many gangsters who had been robbed on the night of the Ali-Quarry fight. It came as little surprise that at least four of them were killed in the city. Finally, Richard Wheeler himself was executed.[144]

Four years after the Ali-Quarry bout, Poitier and Cosby made *Uptown Saturday Night*, a film that featured a robbery similar to the one following the fight that both attended. Cosby had been the color commentator for the Ali-Quarry fight, and Poitier had been prominent in the front row. They clearly knew the story of the robbery. In the movie, directed by Poitier, an after-hours house party at which revelers are playing craps, drinking, and dancing comes to a halt when masked gunmen enter the basement casino. They rob everyone of money, wallets, and jewelry. The robbers force the guests to strip to their underwear, collecting their clothes in a pile. Poitier and Cosby are victims of the robbery and spend the rest of the film mired in the shady underworld of criminals and hustlers with names like Sharp Eye Washington, Geechie Dan Beauford, and Silky Slim, trying to retrieve a wallet that holds a winning lottery ticket. They even seek help from their congressman, a Leroy Johnson–esque politician played by Roscoe Lee Browne, who is involved in shady dealings and shifts allegiances with the political winds. In one of the film's best comic bits, the congressman learns from his secretary that those asking to see him are constituents from his Black district rather than white political players, so he dons a dashiki and turns around a prominent photo of Richard Nixon, displaying instead a portrait of

Malcolm X before letting them into his office. Poitier claimed that any similarities between the events of the movie and the events in Atlanta were "serendipitous," but you certainly couldn't tell that to anyone in Atlanta. Those who had been at Chicken Man's house that night, and even those who just read the newspapers, would have noticed the obvious parody of the events four years earlier. "The movie didn't do justice to what actually happened," said Andrew Young, but he did know that it was based on what actually happened.[145]

Ali, of course, attended his own afterparty at the Hyatt Regency, where celebrity entertainers like Poitier and Cosby joined wealthy influencers and businesspeople to drink and dance alongside political leaders like Leroy Johnson, Whitney Young, Coretta Scott King, and Roy Wilkins. Demonstrating the NOI's renewed interest in its cash cow, Herbert Muhammad was also conspicuously present at the gathering, which continued into the morning even though Ali had long since retired to bed.[146]

The next day Ali traveled back to Philadelphia, spending time with his newborn daughters, now out of danger. The one exception to his seclusion with his family came days after the fight when he appeared on *The Tonight Show* with Johnny Carson, ensuring that even those who didn't follow boxing knew that the former champion was back and fighting again. That, too, like so many other things in Ali's life, had been negotiated. He had been scheduled to appear before his fight with Quarry, but Johnson and other Atlanta officials feared an unscripted national television appearance might spark local antagonism and hurt chances of the fight taking place. So Ali told Carson that he would appear after his trip to Atlanta.[147]

"Were you worried a little bit fighting down in Atlanta?" Carson asked. "Things were a little hot down there for a while. How'd they treat you down there?"

"Oh, it was beautiful," Ali said. "I figured it might be a little rough. You hear a lot of things about the South, this and that." But he had met the press every day, and they hadn't asked questions that might have caused problems with keeping the fight as scheduled. "Everything was to help the fight. Running in the mornings on the back roads, red clay and the dirt, all the farmers and the people would ride by. They would holler, 'How you doing, champ? Good luck!' and not one word of violence or racism. Nothing that you might think if you've never been down to the South. Not one boo at the fight. Not one. I was really amazed at the outcome of the whole thing." That was not exactly an accurate account, but it helped Atlanta's image. He did bring up Maddox's day of mourning, bomb threats at the arena, and other forms of pressure on him. But he was complimentary of the city; he was cheered by the audience; he was back.[148]

7. AFTER OCTOBER

1970–1996

The day after the fight, attention turned to the possibility of a match between Ali and Frazier. Despite the early assurances of Leroy Johnson, the assumption of virtually everyone was that the bout would take place in Madison Square Garden, the venue's promoter Harry Markson publicly stumping for a February 1971 date. Even before the Quarry fight, Jesse Outlar was certain that the success of the evening would not lead to an Ali-Frazier bout in Atlanta. "Sorry about that, Sen. Johnson, but I think you'll then have to visit New York to see Ali and Frazier," he wrote. "Once Atlanta opened the door, New York stuck its official foot in, and chances are boxing is making a one-night stand here." So it was best for no one to get their hopes up. "Sen. Leroy Johnson, Jesse Hill and Harry Pett had a monopoly on Clay's services a mere six weeks ago, but it isn't likely they'll be able to sign him for an encore."[1]

Frazier still had a November bout to contend with, and the proposed three-month window for Ali led to speculation about another warm-up fight for the former champ, possibly with Oscar Bonavena. Miami and Houston were seen as possible destinations for the potential bout, though Atlanta wanted that one, too. Meanwhile, there was still the pending decision of the U.S. Supreme Court, which was slated to rule on Ali's 1967 conviction for avoiding the draft. If its opinion went against the boxer, it was at least possible "that Ali must spend the next five years in Atlanta in the Federal Penitentiary."[2]

Quarry, for his part, left Atlanta embittered by the fight's outcome. "If you came to hear me say Ali's a great fighter," he told reporters in a press conference the day after the contest, "you wasted a trip." He admitted that the cut over his eye was the deepest he'd ever experienced, but "it was circumstances that beat me, not a better fighter. Ali knew if he hadn't cut me that there was no way he could stop me. And I knew I would have killed him if it had lasted just a little longer." Frazier was a far superior fighter, he thought, and would easily defeat Ali when the bout eventually happened. When asked about his own future and the possibility of retirement, the twenty-five-year-old said that he healed quickly. "But I'll go home, have myself a turkey dinner on Thanksgiving and then think about the future."[3] The fight itself was lucrative for Quarry. He made the largest purse of his career, over $300,000, and after paying his trainers and sparring partners, he netted $95,000.[4]

Constitution political columnist Reg Murphy wrote about the "sociology" of the contest, one "that probably is an event unparalleled in Negro social history." It was, for the white Southerner, "unparalleled because it should have destroyed, once and forever, the stereotype of black Americans as shuffling, nodding failures. It should have made clear to the world that there are thousands on thousands of black Americans who have found success in the biggest possible way." He described the long black limousines, the "mad mod hats," the sequins on men's jackets, and even a "silver mink bow tie." There was a throng of celebrities, "Negroes who have made their mark on the nation." After the fight, "one of the biggest social events in black American history," the crowd filed out into Courtland Street, returning to their limousines. "Some would go off to glittering parties for the night, and others would go to a private residence to be robbed at the point of a shotgun." Murphy was certain that "black Atlantans had just brought a special social dimension to the sport that had dragged their heroes of the past out of the ghettoes into the limelight."[5] Murphy's was a well-intentioned but problematic compliment to the seeming majesty of the evening, a kind of boilerplate white reification of the trope of the talented tenth. "See," he seemed to be saying, "they aren't all ghetto failures." Still, it was a summary of the evening intended to be complimentary in the principal white newspaper in the city, one that had not always been on the right side of history. The paper did its best, problematic as that best may have been, to credit the Black population for doing credit to Atlanta.

While the white Atlanta press thrilled to global accounts of Ali's stunning return, it also looked with a jaundiced eye to "leftist political comments" related to the bout. It quoted the Soviet news agency TASS as seeing the win as "a blow to racists and reactionary forces that had unlawfully deprived him [Ali] of the title of world champion." Austria's *Die Presse* saw the victory as "a rehabilitation, a settlement of accounts with hypocrisy and political business." Ali "became the shooting alley figure of white racial fanatics," and his fight against Quarry finally gave him a chance to shoot back. White Atlanta clearly resented such framings. The racial story for them was the fancy Negroes coming "out of the ghettoes into the limelight," the death of their own artificially generated stereotype of "black Americans as shuffling, nodding failures."[6]

Only adding to such racist commentary, former champion Gene Tunney, seventy-three years old at the time of the fight, claimed that Ali should have been disqualified. He hadn't actually watched the contest, but he was confident that no one blow could cause fifteen stitches. "You can never be cut like that by a glove," he claimed. "It's too round and soft. He got bumped by a head, Clay's head." Luckily, argued the *Los Angeles Sentinel*'s Brad Pye, "this is 1970, and it isn't necessarily so that a person has to be correct because he is old and has the right paint job."[7]

The Municipal Auditorium gate for the night was $206,450, the largest in the sixty-one-year history of the building. As the city of Atlanta was scheduled to receive 10 percent of gross revenue, it received a check for $20,645. Madison Square Garden's closed-circuit broadcast reaped $201,000, and more than fourteen thousand fans watched at the Los Angeles Forum.[8] Sports Action's Michael Malitz estimated the gross income from the roughly two hundred American locations at more than $3 million and that a minimum of $250,000 would come from overseas, making the total take for the fight more than $3.5 million. With 42.5 percent of gross revenues, Ali ultimately made roughly $1 million for the fight, Quarry roughly $400,000. Johnson walked away with roughly $175,000. He came through with his promised payment, as well. In early November the Atlanta board of aldermen accepted $50,000 from Johnson and other promoters to be used "for rewards for information leading to the arrest and conviction of drug pushers." Jesse Hill noted that the $50,000 payoff also made a substantial impact on the way cities approached prize fights. Promoters in Philadelphia, for example, tried to convince the city to greenlight the Ali-Frazier contest there by offering the mayor $150,000 to fight drug abuse.[9]

Big money was back in boxing, and whether or not Atlanta was going to be part of it going forward, everyone knew that Ali drove revenue, and they waited for his next move. At some point before the Ali-Quarry fight, Bonavena held a press conference in his hometown of Buenos Aires, announcing that he had signed to meet the winner of the Ali-Quarry contest.[10] That wasn't true, but it demonstrated that Bonavena had been in contact with Ali's team about another potential fight before the former champ finally took on Frazier. On October 29, three days after his Atlanta bout, Ali announced that he would, in fact, fight Bonavena in December. The location had yet to be determined, but waiting until February for Frazier was too long a layoff. Bonavena, for his part, felt confident. "Ali is a mere myth," he told reporters. "He has defects like any other fighter." He had defeated Quarry. Quarry, however, "fought like a coward, but I will not act with the cowardice he showed."[11]

It was ultimately decided that Ali's fight with Bonavena would take place in Madison Square Garden on December 7, demonstrating to many that New York's prowess had robbed Atlanta of ever having Ali return to fight in Georgia again.[12] But Leroy Johnson was not giving up. "Nothing has been signed as far as a [Frazier] fight or a site are concerned." He claimed, with at least some credibility, "We feel we have better than a 50–50 chance to get an Ali-Frazier championship fight in Atlanta." Johnson had pulled off one coup for the city; why couldn't he pull off another? As part of his House of Sports promotion, Johnson and Jesse Hill traveled across the country in early November, attempting to book future boxing matches in Atlanta. House of Sports was also promoting the local closed-circuit broadcast of the fight between Frazier and Bob Foster from Detroit, which had as its principal undercard match a bout between top heavyweight contenders Boone Kirkman and George Foreman, who would later play such a large part in Ali's career.[13]

But getting another Ali fight in Atlanta was Johnson's main priority. "We put Ali back in the ring in Atlanta," he said. "We did what 72 other cities tried to do and couldn't do, for one thing. And we in Atlanta are now looked upon as the good guys in boxing—the ones in the white hats." He contrasted the city's image with that of its New York rival. "We have no connection with any of the past bad images of boxing—gang control, syndicate or anything like that." The fact that Ali enjoyed his time in Atlanta, and that a Black man with such public infamy was able to fight "without anything of a bad nature happening, proved that Atlanta has a relationship between black and white to be envied by other cities. It has had effects in a lot of areas outside of sports." That rosy racial picture of Atlanta was true for only a small portion of the city's Black residents, but Johnson was correct in his assessment of the fight's influence on the city. He acknowledged that Municipal Auditorium and its five thousand seats didn't compare to the Garden, but he explained that closed-circuit television is what really drove revenue. Besides, "a live fight in Madison Square Garden blacks out a television market of eight million people. I believe we can show as much total revenue from a live championship fight in Atlanta." One of the original sticking points for such a fight had been Yank Durham's doubt that Johnson would be able to get Ali into the ring, but Johnson had proven him wrong. "I've discussed possibilities with him in recent weeks," said Johnson of Durham. "He's a straight talking man. We have been able to communicate with him."[14]

Meanwhile, the election season that had occupied so many other people in Georgia came and went. Andrew Young was unsuccessful in challenging incumbent Fletcher Thompson for his congressional seat, and Jimmy Carter, who won a race-baiting primary in which he claimed that he didn't need a single Black vote, had been proven correct, defeating Republican former television news anchor Hal Suit to succeed Maddox as governor. Maddox then won his own race to become lieutenant governor. Eleven Black men won seats in the state legislature, including Johnson, who ran unopposed, but the election was one of white reactionary politics in which furor in predominantly white rural areas over the Ali fight surely played a role.[15]

Toward the end of the early November election cycle in Atlanta, Ali reconnected with his friend Walt Bellamy when the Hawks traveled to Philadelphia for a game against the 76ers. During halftime, Ali attempted a half-court shot to earn a $1,000 donation to the Young Great Society. Though he missed the shot, 76ers owner Irv Kosloff still made a donation to the YGS in Ali's name. That month Ali was named boxer of the month by the World Boxing Council, which named him the number one contender for Frazier's title, replacing Quarry, who was dropped from the rankings.[16]

On November 4 *a.k.a. Cassius Clay* officially opened in theaters, profiling Ali's career and the controversies surrounding him.[17] In Atlanta the film premiered at Loew's Grand on Peachtree, where Ali and his entourage had seen a special screening before the Quarry fight. "See the punches that won the championship," the theater's advertisement read, "and the ideals that lost it!"[18]

Ali missed the Atlanta premiere, but he returned to the city to watch the Frazier-Foster and Kirkland-Foreman fights. The closed-circuit broadcast at Municipal Auditorium was promoted by Johnson's House of Sports, and Johnson explained that Ali would watch from the auditorium "because of his great affection for this city." He arrived in Atlanta the day before the contest and seemed to have recovered much of the boisterous posturing that he had suppressed in preparing for his Quarry fight. At the airport upon his arrival, Ali told reporters that he was confident that Frazier would defeat Foster, but "against me, it'll be no contest. He'll be a joke," he said. "My reflection could beat the guy!" Frazier was "nothing but a machine." He "has no skills. He has no sense. He's just like a robot." Ali's humility seemed to have left with Jerry Quarry.[19]

More importantly for Johnson and the hopes of Atlanta, Ali explained that he had been asked to stay in Miami Beach, where he was training for Bonavena, but "I wanted to witness the fight with my many friends and fans in Atlanta, though. You folks—especially brothers Johnson and Hill—have been real good to me. And I enjoy being with you." So he was "gonna be right out there—among the people—watching tomorrow night. I want to shake a lot of hands . . . and thank a lot of people."[20]

On fight night Ali arrived at Municipal Auditorium early. He joked with the crowd and gladhanded, getting popcorn and sitting with the rest of those who had paid to see the fights. Both Foreman and Frazier won easily in second-round technical knockouts, but Ali's presence at the auditorium ensured that the crowd did not leave disappointed at the brevity of the event. When Frazier was being interviewed in the ring after his victory, Ali stood and yelled at the screen. "I'm on your trail," he told the image of Frazier. "You ain't whipped anybody yet. Anybody can whip a stringbean." Ali shadowboxed and continued yelling, promising to whip Frazier, to the delight of everyone present. It was the kind of bravado the fighter had denied Atlanta in the run-up to the Quarry fight, and he had returned to give the city one more show.[21]

But if Ali saw the closed-circuit viewing as a fitting end to his time in Atlanta, he wasn't giving the information away. When asked if he would be willing to fight Frazier in the city, he said, "You can put me on the book for that." Either way, Ali's presence in Atlanta mattered. Because of the quick knockouts, Frazier's closed-circuit broadcast was roundly considered a failure across the country—except in Atlanta, because Ali made it a show.[22]

The next time the former champ would appear at Municipal Auditorium, he would be the one on-screen when Johnson's House of Sports presented the closed-circuit broadcast of Ali's fight with Bonavena in early December. In promoting the bout, Johnson urged people to attend not only to see the action but to "help the city's chance of landing the Ali-Joe Frazier heavyweight title bout." He argued that a poor showing at the venue "could be used against us in our efforts." Besides, "we broke the ice," he said, referencing the opportunity the city gave to Ali, "and we deserve it more than anyone else."[23]

But not everyone was excited about the prospect of another fight in the city. Positive press reports about the attention Ali's presence brought to Atlanta hid an undercurrent of anger among many conservative whites about the opportunity that the city gave a Black activist. On December 4 Johnson's wife received a threatening phone call telling her that her husband "would be sorry" if the Ali-Frazier fight came to Atlanta. Two days later, around 1:00 a.m., less than forty-eight hours before the closed-circuit broadcast of Ali-Bonavena, three shots were fired into Johnson's northwest Atlanta home. Johnson and his wife were asleep upstairs when the shots crashed through a first-floor window. While no one saw the shooter, neighbors said that it sounded like an automatic weapon. A taxi driver who had ridden down Johnson's street between midnight and 12:30 a.m. had noticed a white station wagon backed into the driveway of his home. Tires screeched after the shots as a car, perhaps the white station wagon, sped away. Johnson was certain that the gunshots were "redneck" attempts to keep the senator from bringing Frazier and Ali to the city, but he would not be scared away, even though "my wife is extremely upset." Police had no suspects, though they claimed to be on the lookout for a white station wagon, and the bullets in the house were too smashed to allow for ballistics tests.[24]

"I know of no country other than the United States whereby one can refuse to serve his country and be allowed to make a fortune while laughing in its face," read one anonymous letter to the *Constitution* opposing another Atlanta Ali fight. "I have a retarded child just turned 18 whom under the draft laws of this country I had to register and then prove by medical evidence that he is retarded in order not to be drafted. This I believe is more legitimate than Muhammad Ali's religion." It was an odd comparison, as both religion and medical conditions had always been valid reasons for not participating in American military service. But the writer, a disabled veteran associated with the VFW, saw no problem with it. "No wonder the draft is a joke to so many of draft age."[25]

In December the Fulton County senate delegation, of which Johnson had been the chair, voted for Horace Ward, the only other Black senator in the county and the state, to replace Johnson in 1971 as head of the eight-man roster of senators from the county. There was no specific evidence that Johnson's advocacy for Ali played a role in the change of leadership, but the majority-white delegation made the change nonetheless.[26] Less than a week later Lester Maddox, still governor but acting in his new role as lieutenant governor–elect, stripped Johnson of the chairmanship of the senate's Scientific Research Committee, the only committee chair held by Georgia's first Black senator since Reconstruction. Maddox claimed that the "committee has not been active. I want to get it moving." Most, however, including Johnson, understood what was really going on. "The only reason I don't have a committee chairmanship is because of discrimination on the part of the governor," he said. "If you use longevity as a yardstick, if you use ability, if you use political acuteness, if you use educational attainment, if you use any yardstick you want except color, I deserve a chairmanship." Maddox kept Ward as chairman of the County and Urban Affairs Committee's Urban Development Subcommittee, but there was no leadership role for Johnson. The difference between Johnson and Ward, of course, was that one had shown up the governor in bringing the Ali-Quarry fight to Atlanta.[27]

Maddox also capitalized on Georgia's newfound national attention by appearing on *The Dick Cavett Show*. It was inevitably controversial. Cavett asked Maddox about race, and Maddox touted his record of Black appointments, but when Jim Brown, who was also on the program, asked Maddox what white bigots who had supported him thought about his moderate racial record, the conversation devolved, as Maddox railed against calling his supporters bigots and eventually stormed off the set. Maddox's supporters saw the show as an ambush. Cavett was "a rable [*sic*] rouser in the ethnic corner," one correspondent told the governor. He assured Maddox of white Georgia's support. "We need more people like you and fewer James Brown's, Truman Capote's and Muhammad Ali's in this country."[28]

But most wanted more James Browns, and whether they supported him or not, everyone seemed to want more Muhammad Alis. The Ali fight with Bonavena took place just prior to the Maddox appearance with Dick Cavett. Bonavena gave Ali what he wanted: a long fight that went into the fifteenth round before Ali won on a technical knockout after putting the Argentine down three times. Bonavena stunned Ali in the ninth and almost won, but Ali hugged his opponent, recovered, and eventually triumphed six rounds later. Still, it left many wondering whether the Ali who fought Bonavena could have beaten Frazier. More importantly for Atlanta, the crowd that watched the fight in person—more than nineteen thousand fans—paid a gate of $615,401, a total that left Madison Square Garden authorities reasonably confident they could draw Ali's next match.[29] The large crowd was filled with even more celebrities. Jesse Jackson and other Black leaders were joined by members of the New York Yankees, Woody Allen, Dustin Hoffman, and others. Black vendors sold portraits of Ali and of activist Angela Davis, charged at the time with a California courthouse murder. Everything coming from the Garden that night seemed to be saying to Atlanta's Municipal Auditorium: we are not the same. But Johnson was there, too, watching his friend and representing Atlanta in the hopes that Ali's next bout would be back in the South.[30] So was Joe Frazier, who had easily defeated Bob Foster, worrying that Ali would not defeat Bonavena and thus ruin the possibility of their lucrative contest. After Ali knocked out Bonavena, Frazier said, "Now he's mine." Durham told him to go into the ring and shake Ali's hand. "I got nothin' to say to that clown," an angry Frazier told him.[31]

After Ali's Bonavena victory, New York seemed like the most likely destination for his next fight, but Houston also had reason to assume that it could attract Ali-Frazier. Officials from the Astrodome noted that their venue sat sixty-five thousand people, far more than the twenty-two thousand of Madison Square Garden, to say nothing of the paltry five thousand of Atlanta's Municipal Auditorium. The Garden, one Astrodome official explained, would have to average a $60 ticket price to gross $1.5 million at the gate, while the Astrodome could gross $2 million with only a $30 average ticket, allowing more people to afford to see the bout live. "We think a fight of this magnitude should be seen by everyone who really wants to see it." It was a good argument, and in making their pitch to representatives of the two fighters, Astrodome officials brought with them Thomas Smith, commissioner of the Texas Bureau of Labor Statistics, under whose jurisdiction boxing and wrestling events were regulated, indicating that licensing Ali in Texas would not be a problem. In fact, the day after the Houston conclave with Ali's representatives, Smith granted the fighter a license. In 1969 Ali had filed a lawsuit against Smith to force a reinstatement, and at the end of 1970 Smith agreed to reinstate the boxer if Ali dropped the lawsuit. Ali did, and with his license, Houston became a prime contender for the championship bout.[32]

Still, there were those in Texas, as in Georgia, who adamantly hoped that Ali would not fight in Houston, the city where the fighter had refused military induction. The American Legion petitioned Texas governor Preston Smith to use his authority to stop any fight at the Astrodome. "This would be an insult to the 1.3 million ex-service-men of Texas and to those now on active duty," said a department commander for the Legion.[33]

It was the kind of opposition that had characterized a segment of white Georgia when Ali arrived, and it was a problem for officials who could easily avoid such headaches by staging the bout in New York. After Christmas word began to leak that the Frazier-Ali fight would be scheduled for March 8 in Madison Square Garden. At that point Atlantans saw the writing on the wall. The reaction of some in white Atlanta, the thinly veiled racism, the gunshots into Johnson's home, and the political retribution against him all took their toll, leaving Georgia on the outside looking in when it came to the championship fight. The *New York Daily News* broke the story that the Garden would handle the fight promotion in conjunction with Chartwell, a Los Angeles personal management corporation that also owned the NBA's Phoenix Suns. Ali, it seemed, preferred Houston, but the Garden was the safer choice.[34]

On December 30 Frazier and Ali signed a contract for guarantees of $2.5 million each for a March 8 title fight in Madison Square Garden. A Chartwell representative predicted that the worldwide gross could be between $20 and $30 million. "We think this is the single most important event in the history of sports in the area of one-night events," he said.

When Ali heard the predicted total at the press luncheon to announce the deal, he stood and pointed to Frazier. "Five million dollars [combined for the fighters]. Frazier, we've been taken!" The crowd laughed. They were excited. This was what everyone had been waiting for. Fifteen rounds in the Garden between two champions who had never lost their titles. The money promised to be huge; the fight promised to be one of the most important in history. Big-time boxing was back in New York, as Atlanta faded quietly into the distance.[35]

The Nation of Islam also reemerged into the spotlight, once again embracing Ali and the millions of dollars he would earn for the fight. The suspension, Dave Kindred has argued, "never really began and never was officially ended." Ali never gave up his name, and when his return to the ring began producing sizable revenue, the Nation was back in his corner. Fitting the change, Ali used the "Uncle Tom" rhetoric against Frazier that he had used against Liston, against Patterson, and against Terrell. He was no longer facing a Great White Hope, so he effectively turned his Black opponent into a white hope. "The only people rooting for Joe Frazier are white people in suits, Alabama sheriffs, and members of the Ku Klux Klan," Ali said. "I'm fighting for the little man in the ghetto."[36] *Time* magazine interpreted the fight publicity as "Frazier the good citizen v. Ali the draft dodger, Frazier the white man's champ v. Ali the great black hope, Frazier the quiet loner v. Ali the irrepressible loudmouth, Frazier the simple Bible-reading Baptist v. Ali the slogan-spouting Black Muslim." And that was as Ali wanted it, despite the fact that Frazier had been good to Ali, loaning him money and publicly supporting his conscientious objector status. "There were moments when Joe was so hurt," remembered Dave Wolf. "Joe is not, and never was, an Uncle Tom, whatever that means, but Ali branded him with that label." Ali "was going around saying Joe was a tool of the white man," even though "the significant people around Joe were a lot blacker than the significant people around Ali." Ultimately, "what he did was turn Joe into a black white hope. He isolated Joe from the black community. He constantly equated Joe with the white power structure, and said things like, 'Any black person who's for Joe Frazier is a traitor.' He did it on purpose; he did it far beyond what was necessary to sell tickets. It was cruel."[37]

In the run-up to the Ali-Frazier fight, both the Congress of Racial Equality and Southern Christian Leadership Conference protested the contest and its closed-circuit promotion, claiming they would continue until Black groups were allowed to purchase television rights. Though an agreement with promoters granted CORE licensing rights to show the fight in several cities, allowing the group to raise money for civil rights causes across the country, SCLC's efforts were more troubled. The organization argued that Black fans were being priced out of the closed-circuit market and Black fighters were being exploited by white promoters. The SCLC joined the Consumer Education Protective Association to lead a series of pickets in Philadelphia. When Yank Durham heard about the group's actions, he announced that the SCLC could "drop dead." Before signing the deal for the bout, "our doors were open to everyone, black or white, as long as the color of their money was green." The concern from rights groups and the lack of Black representation in promotional leadership was a glaring regression from the mean created by Leroy Johnson in Atlanta. In the wake of Ali-Frazier, Black activists and journalists maintained frustration with what they saw as economic exploitation of Black fighters and a lack of Black leadership in boxing. That frustration, that lack of a Johnson figure in Ali's next major fight after his time in Atlanta, ultimately led to the rise of the first major Black boxing promoter, Don King. As Gregory Kaliss explains, Ali-Frazier "revealed the serious, on-going limitations for athletics to provide financial empowerment to the black community." Ali and Frazier each made a small fortune, but without figures like Johnson involved, "the promotional rights went to two white men who had the pre-existing capital necessary to swing the deal their way."[38]

Ali and Frazier attempted to stanch such charges. In a joint statement, the two camps claimed, "There has been more significant Black involvement in the Joe Frazier–Muhammad Ali heavyweight championship fight than in any other major sporting or entertainment event in the history of this country." They noted that both fighters, both managers, and over two hundred employees of the teams were Black. There were several Black promoters involved in staging the bout. Financial donations from the gate were being made to a variety of Black charities. All of that was true, but coming on the heels of the parade of Black excellence in Atlanta and the protests of groups like the SCLC and CORE, the statement rang hollow to many.[39]

Back in Atlanta, headquarters of the SCLC, Johnson was reaping the benefits of his boxing coup. He wore tailored suits and a diamond ring. His fancy cars were fancier, his expensive cigars more expensive. He built a swimming pool in his backyard. That kind of bravado led many to accuse him of being on the take, mistaking his business acumen for a willingness to shift political positions based on bribes. But that was all untrue, said Julian Bond. "Even when he trades votes in the legislature, I've never known him to trade away his integrity." Bond attributed much of that talk to the assumption among Southern whites that Black men couldn't work hard and accumulate money through legal means.[40]

But Johnson had made his money legally. He had made a small fortune on lecture tours early in his career and had invested that income in businesses like a taxi company, a bakery, a fast-food restaurant, service stations, and convenience stores. Then he had his law practice, which brought him roughly $50,000 per year. He had even represented James Brown during his 1969 divorce from his first wife. No payday, however, matched his payday with Ali.[41]

But politics was where his heart was. He took it upon himself to turn out Fulton County's Black vote for the candidate that he believed was the best choice, and Fulton County's Black population constituted almost a quarter of the state's four hundred thousand Black voters. Before the November elections his team made telephone calls to all ninety-two thousand Black voters in the county; they sent mailings that contained a reference card listing all the candidates endorsed by Johnson. On election day Johnson employed sixty drivers to take as many as ten thousand voters to and from the polls. There had been accusations, however, recurring from previous election cycles, that those seeking rides who were planning to vote for a candidate not on Johnson's preferred list were dropped at the wrong voting precinct to keep them from being able to vote.[42]

Johnson could only really control what happened in Atlanta, however, and his efforts wouldn't be enough in the gubernatorial election of 1970. Jimmy Carter took the oath of office as governor in January 1971, and despite the race-baiting of his campaign, he announced in his inaugural address that "the time for racial discrimination is over." When he came into office, Carter consulted with Johnson, who advocated for

Black appointments to state government agencies. Carter responded by appointing them.[43]

Carter's administration proved a pleasant surprise, but the time for discrimination was not over. Less than two weeks after Carter's inauguration, state senators Hugh Gillis and Edward Zipperer offered a bill to create a state athletic commission. Gillis was a rural Democrat from Montgomery County; Zipperer was a Savannah native, head of the Chatham County Farm Bureau. Johnson called it the "Muhammad Ali Bill." The *Atlanta Inquirer* called it "clearly racist." Though the paper didn't deny the utility of an athletic commission, the Gillis and Zipperer bill was motivated solely by Ali's fight in Atlanta. Proof, the *Inquirer* argued, was that auto racing was omitted from the legislation. In March 1969 the possibility of an athletic commission had been debated after a drag-racing accident at Yellow River, forty miles outside of Atlanta, killed eleven spectators. An oversight bill, however, never appeared. "But three months after Muhammad Ali climbs into a ring and kills no one, but fills city coffers, the solons see a need for a commission." The *Inquirer* encouraged the new governor to end "such racist folly," to "send that bill back with a note attached, 'Remember Yellow River.'"[44]

In response to white conservatives in the state legislature, Atlanta's 100 Percent Wrong Club publicly honored House of Sports that month for bringing the Ali-Quarry fight to the city. The 100 Percent Wrong Club had been created in 1934 by sportswriters Ric Roberts and Lucius Jones of the *Atlanta Daily World* to pick college football winners and recognize outstanding athletes. In January 1971 the club recognized Johnson, Hill, and Pett. Johnson, the club explained, "used his experience as a legal expert and his influence as a Senator to take care of the legal barriers that faced the fight." Jesse Hill "used his business experience as Actuary of Atlanta Life, plus the many contacts that he had gained from his legal battles. He also helped to draw up the plan of presentation to the camp of Ali" to convince him that a fight was possible. Pett's business acumen served to "complement the talents of Johnson and Hill." Together, they were able to create a "history-making event," despite the desperate frustration of rural white Georgians and their representatives.[45]

Meanwhile, Massell was still mayor, and in October 1971 he demonstrated that much of his work in facilitating the Ali-Quarry fight was less about racial reckoning and more about economic growth. In a speech at the Butler Street YMCA he warned about too much Black influence in Atlanta politics. The creation of a predominantly Black city would be "a terribly confined and costly ambition." He told his audience to "think white," urging them not to let "the vast majority of blacks be sold out for the little prestige of a few demagogues." It was not a popular address to a group that had largely been responsible for putting him in office—a "with friends like these, who needs enemies" moment. That the mayor would come speak at the Butler Street YMCA was progress, to be sure, but his admonition that his audience "think white" was a demonstration that the city's racial woes had not magically disappeared after a third-round TKO the previous year.[46]

In late 1971 the city's alternative newspaper, *The Great Speckled Bird*, published a series of exposés on slum housing in Atlanta, and the resulting pressure on the city forced the release of a list compiled by the Building Department's housing code enforcement division of low-income slum housing and its ownership. The *Bird*, in turn, published the list, showing that Leroy Johnson owned two slum rental properties; alderman and Johnson ally Q. V. Williamson owned five. Citizens Trust Bank owned seven. In the wake of the report it seemed to many that the Black power structure in the city was not only disconnected from the mass of working-class Black citizens but was actively exploiting them. White slumlords were seemingly everywhere, but they were not alone. It was, for many, a Kafkaesque experience to know that the man fighting for racial equity, for a King holiday, for Ali in Atlanta, also owned and operated slum housing. The disconnect between Black power brokers and their working-class counterparts was only further widened at the news.[47]

Ali was blissfully unaware of those frictions. He had moved on to fights in New York and Washington. To the disappointment of many who saw themselves reflected in Ali's glory, the former champion would lose a split decision to Joe Frazier in Madison Square Garden. But he would finally win his appeal to the Supreme Court on June 28, 1971. John Marshall Harlan, among the unanimous votes to rule in Ali's favor, was the grandson of the original Supreme Court Justice John Marshall Harlan, who had been friends with the white Cassius Marcellus Clay in Kentucky. And he was originally part of a 5–3 majority ready to affirm Ali's conviction. His law clerks, however, changed his mind, using the case of a Jehovah's Witness during the Korean War. Anthony Sicurella had claimed conscientious objector status because his faith allowed him to fight only "in the interests of defending Kingdom interests, our preaching work, our meetings, our fellow brethren and sisters, and our property against attack." The court ruled in Sicurella's favor in the 1950s and now, the clerks argued, the court should rule in favor of Ali, noting that Ali's willingness to fight only in a war "declared by Allah himself" was even more limited than that of the Witnesses. Harlan's changed vote led Potter Stewart to seek a compromise position on the issue with the four remaining justices who had voted to affirm Ali's conviction. He argued to his colleagues that even if they couldn't get past the fighter's willingness to participate in some theoretical Muslim war, that didn't necessarily matter because the draft appeal board never mentioned that as a reason. The board considered the sincerity of the claim and the religious status of Black Muslims, which the government now conceded were no longer in question. The other justices agreed to go along, and the court issued its ruling unanimously.[48]

The decision established that any registrant for conscientious objector status had to demonstrate that they were opposed to war in any form, that their opposition was sincere, and that it was based "on religious, moral, or ethical beliefs." The government conceded that the Justice Department's original conclusion that Ali wasn't sincere and that his faith didn't count as religious belief were wrong. But it maintained its initial contention that Ali wasn't opposed to "war in any form"—that his opposition to war was selective. The Supreme Court ruled, essentially, that even if that contention could be proven, there were other reasons for reversal. Neither the Louisville selective service draft board nor the Kentucky Appeal Board gave a specific reason for rejecting Ali's claim, so it was impossible for the court to determine which of the three basic contentions caused his classification. So even conceding the possibility that Ali wasn't opposed to war in any form, there was a two-thirds chance that Kentucky ruled on insufficient grounds, and therefore its decision had to be invalidated.[49]

Ali, now free of his legal burden and ready to again put himself in contention for the heavyweight crown, would fight Quarry again in June 1972 in Las Vegas for the NABF heavyweight title. Quarry had aged significantly in the two previous years. He was heavier, slower. Ali again won by technical knockout, this time in the seventh round. The undercard featured Quarry's brother Mike taking on Bob Foster for the world light heavyweight title. The Quarrys would lose both fights that night.[50]

It was, for Jerry Quarry, his chance at redemption, but it went similarly awry. Ali even had equipment problems in the dressing room prior to the fight, just as he had in Atlanta. While the undercard matches were progressing, the team realized that they had forgotten Ali's ring gear. He had no trunks, no shoes, no robe, no anything. Bundini Brown was dispatched back to the hotel several blocks away. Meanwhile, the celebrities in Ali's dressing room for the second Quarry fight were decidedly different. Howard Cossell was a constant presence. NFL receiver Otis Taylor entered, as did Joe Louis, now out of the hospital and working as a promoter in Las Vegas. Ali verbally sparred with Cossell, as befit their relationship, but he spoke meaningfully with Louis. The discussion was ultimately interrupted by Joe DiMaggio, then referee Mike Kaplan.[51]

After Foster knocked out Mike Quarry in the final fight of the undercard, it was finally time for the rematch. In the first round Jerry Quarry brought the crowd to its feet when he hugged Ali and lifted him off the ground, almost like a football tackle. It took Ali by surprise, but it would in retrospect be Quarry's most notable highlight. Throughout the first six rounds Ali pummeled his opponent unmercifully, and when the beating continued in the seventh, the referee finally stopped the contest. Ali was no longer working his way back into boxing shape; he was a complete fighter, and he completely took Quarry apart.[52]

As his career developed after his days with Quarry, Jack Johnson's legacy and *a.k.a. Cassius Clay* remained vital parts of Ali's life. "Ain't he [Johnson] sump'n?" Ali asked a reporter from *Ebony* in the months after his second Quarry fight. "That's me. Jack Johnson's a bad n—— who didn't take no stuff. I'm just as bad." He would often screen *a.k.a. Cassius Clay* for reporters and his entourage. His time with Quarry had ended, but it wasn't just his ability to box again that remained from his time in Atlanta.[53]

Quarry, meanwhile, soldiered on. He defeated Randy Neumann, top-ranked contender Ron Lyle, and Earnie Shavers, earning himself another chance to fight Joe Frazier. Again the fight was halted, this time in the fifth round, again because of Quarry's bleeding. This time he had cuts over both eyes. Blood was coming from his nose and mouth. He was twenty-nine years old. His last major opportunity had passed him by—almost. The following year, in 1975, just after his thirtieth birthday, Quarry fought Ken Norton, who had defeated Muhammad Ali in March 1973. Again the blood, again a fifth-round stoppage. After the fight a disappointed Quarry announced his retirement.[54]

But he wouldn't yet actually retire. Quarry made brief comebacks in the seventies, eighties, and nineties. He amassed a record of 53-9-4 with thirty-three knockouts, earning more than $2 million in purses. He fought for the heavyweight title twice and shared the ring with the biggest names in the sport.[55]

By the late 1970s, however, Quarry was drinking heavily. He had divorced, then married, then divorced, then married, then divorced. Ali's time at Atlanta's Municipal Auditorium had, for him, initiated an upward trajectory and a return to the limelight, but for Quarry it had begun a downward spiral. His son Jerry Lynn called the 1980s "the hard years." Quarry would "come home drunk, then go into his room and cry. He didn't know what he was going to do with his life." In 1983 Quarry participated in a study conducted by *Sports Illustrated* about brain damage among boxers. Neurologists scanned Quarry's brain, concluding that he had "problems with certain cognitive functions—short-term memory and perceptual motor ability." He was still able to function, but it was clear that boxing had taken its toll.[56]

Though Quarry had earned millions in his fight career, his alimony, child support payments, and addictions drained whatever he was able to save over the years. He had to make money somehow, so he tried his hand at being a fight analyst. He became a roadie for Three Dog Night. He tried acting, singing. Nothing worked, and nothing filled the void left by his absence from the ring. In 1992 he tried one more fight. He wasn't licensed anymore, he wasn't in shape, and he wasn't particularly qualified. So he fought in Colorado, a state without a boxing commission, where he lost a six-round decision for a $1,000 payday. He was forty-seven years old, and after that last bout he started to demonstrate substantial mental decline.[57]

Later in his life Quarry would change the stance he took immediately after his first fight with Ali and begin claiming that the cut that stopped the bout had been caused by a headbutt. By that time the signs of dementia were prevalent. He began to be confused, to not understand where he was. His sister Dianna took him to a neuropsychologist, who determined that Quarry had "suffered significant cerebral atrophy and neurological impairment" from the beatings he had taken to the head over his years in the ring. In October 1995 Quarry was inducted into the World Boxing Hall of Fame, but he was already suffering from severe pugilistica dementia, chronic brain damage, brought on by the head trauma from his fights. He had short-term memory loss and difficulty with directions and simple tasks. He couldn't sustain his equilibrium or maintain consistent depth perception, making it impossible to drive. Quarry lived with his older brother Jimmy, who was responsible for his care, in a small townhouse in San Jacinto, California. Though the former fighter received a monthly Social Security check, he had no other source of income. Quarry spent his days sitting with a home nurse, watching videos of his old fights, surrounded by photos of his career.[58]

Jimmy, a bank officer, created the Jerry Quarry Foundation to raise money for retired boxers suffering dementia and other forms of brain damage related to their days in the ring. Jimmy was frustrated that his brother had made so many people so much money over the years, yet was left with nothing but severe mental decline.[59] By the end of the decade Jerry began hallucinating. He walked out of the house and wandered the streets, forcing his family to call the police to help find him and bring him home. Ultimately he contracted pneumonia, suffered complications from it, and died in 1999. He was fifty-three years old.[60]

Two days after the Ali-Quarry fight in Atlanta, the Internal Revenue Service opened an investigation into Leroy Johnson, who claimed that the effort was an act of retribution for facilitating Ali's return to the ring. Still, protest or no, the probe continued, and in 1974 Johnson was charged with income tax evasion. That year, with the cloud of scandal looming over him, he lost his state senate seat. He lost it to Horace Tate, whom he had refused to support in the 1969 mayoral race in favor of Sam Massell. It was a measure of satisfaction for Tate, spurned five years prior, and a devastating blow for Johnson. After his defeat the government dropped the tax evasion charges but convicted him on a lesser charge of filing a false affidavit. Johnson maintained his innocence, framing the conviction as a face-saving effort by the government after phony tax evasion charges had sabotaged his reelection. Carl Sanders, Benjamin Mays, and Martin Luther King, Sr., all spoke at the trial in his defense, but he received a sixty-day sentence and a year of probation nonetheless. His political career was over. Thus it was that the pinnacle of Johnson's political triumph also proved to be his downfall. That the tax charges were dropped, and that they were dropped immediately following his electoral defeat, seems to justify many of Johnson's claims about the retributive nature of the IRS investigation. There is no way to be sure. But if it was a punishment for staging the Ali fight, it worked. Johnson continued his businesses after 1974, but the political influence he wielded for more than a decade was gone.[61]

For Ali, meanwhile, 1974 was a turning point in the other direction. On October 30 he upset the undefeated heavyweight champion, George Foreman, in Kinshasa, Zaire, to reclaim the heavyweight title. Foreman was in many ways the antithesis of Ali. He had also won the Olympic gold medal, in his case in 1968. While Smith and Carlos were using the Mexico City games as a stage for protest, Foreman waved the American flag and refused to participate in racial demonstrations. Six years later, Ali was a 4–1 underdog in what became known as "the Rumble in the Jungle," and his eighth-round knockout of the champion was one of the most-watched events in global history. Johnson watched just like everyone else, days away from electoral defeat and the end of his political career. The champion was champion once again.[62]

In March 1973, while he was still under criminal investigation, Johnson decided that he, too, wanted a championship of sorts. He announced that he was finally running for mayor. His announcement came, however, after originally pledging his support for the other Black candidate in the race, Maynard Jackson. Maurice Hobson has concluded that the rivalry between the two marked the final split in the original political divergence of the Atlanta Negro Voters League, with Jackson standing in for his grandfather, John Wesley Dobbs, and Johnson standing in for his mentor, Austin Walden.[63] Though Johnson was the choice of the established Black elite, and even won the endorsement of the *Atlanta Constitution*, Jackson ultimately had the support of the people. Johnson's role in the Ali promotion actually aided in that support, since many Black residents saw him as "too much a hustler" after the Quarry fight. In the campaign, Jesse Hill, Johnson's longtime ally, originally supported his friend, but ultimately gave his support to Jackson after seeing poll results that demonstrated his greater viability. Hill even served as Jackson's campaign manager. It seemed like a real rift in the governing coalition of Black Atlanta, but after Johnson's loss he, too, endorsed Jackson, and the wounds caused by the bitterness of the race were at least superficially healed. Jackson would ultimately win the election, becoming in October 1973 the first Black mayor of Atlanta.[64]

Ali, in the years after the Quarry fight, became close to Jackson. In January 1975 the champion actually returned to Atlanta to fight the mayor in a one-round charity bout, with Julian Bond serving as referee. The brief match was a benefit for the creation of the city's Martin Luther King Center, a project Ali would continue to donate to in the 1980s. More than ten thousand people came to the Southeastern Fairgrounds to see the overweight Jackson prance around the ring in paisley shorts and an Atlanta Falcons T-shirt. Jackson met the heavyweight champion with a poem of his own.

> They tell me the champ is Muhammad Ali,
> But that's just because he never fought me . . .
> Liston is strong and Foreman was tough,
> But when you mess with the Big M the going is rough!

Late in the round Ali fell dramatically to the canvas, giving the mayor a symbolic victory.[65]

Johnson's fall from grace came as Jackson's profile rose. But his wasn't the only one. The year of the 1973 mayoral election, Jesse Hill, who had been so instrumental in so many of the city's civil rights efforts and a vital part of House of Sports, took over as president and chief executive officer of Atlanta Life Insurance, the largest Black company in the nation.[66] In the wake of Ali's time in Atlanta, everyone seemed to benefit except for Johnson and Quarry.

In September 1978 Ali would again fight in the Deep South, defeating Leon Spinks in the Superdome in front of more than sixty-three thousand fans. While both Spinks and Ali were Black, four years later, in November 1982, Larry Holmes would take on white fighter Randall "Tex" Cobb in the Houston Astrodome. Holmes battered Cobb for fifteen rounds, a beating so brutal and bloody that Howard Cosell was prompted to describe the fight as "an advertisement for the abolition of boxing." Gone were the racial connotations of the mauling. It was the 1980s; far more concern was directed toward head trauma and the long-term effects of a fight career. The race of those doing the fighting was at least somewhat beside the point, even in the South.[67]

Before them, though, had been Muhammad Ali and Jerry Quarry. *Ring Magazine*'s Bernard Fernandez has argued that Ali's fights with Frazier, Liston, Foreman, and Ken Norton are rightfully celebrated as "the principal building blocks Ali assembled on his path to boxing immortality," but he argues that "the first clash with Quarry deserves to be on that list," even though historians seldom place it in that category.[68] "Nobody realized it at the time, but it was one of the most political fights of the golden era of boxing," concluded Quarry's sister Dianna. "After that fight is when the big money came into boxing."[69] For historian Johnny Smith, the Ali-Quarry fight "marked a turning point in boxing history. Leroy Johnson and his business partners had not only resurrected the career of Muhammad Ali, but they had also staged a match that breathed new life into a sport that critics pronounced dead."[70]

For all the fight did for Ali and for boxing, it was also a boon to a city that had presented itself as a racial oasis in a sea of turmoil but was anything but in the tumultuous years of the late 1960s. "The progressive city of Atlanta offered a case study in tolerance and sanity," concluded *Newsweek*'s Pete Axthelm, though Black residents knew that the city's progressive bona fides were largely shibboleths. "Many Northerners may have clucked smugly when the site [for Ali-Quarry] was announced, assuming the fight belonged in some more 'liberal' city," but "Atlanta's citizens treated Ali and the many black visitors with respect and cordiality. The two newspapers, which probably could have whipped up local emotions and killed the fight if they had desired, offered only fair and enthusiastic commentary." There were Maddox and his outbursts, to be sure, but even those led nowhere. And for its trouble, Atlanta got "a glittering black fashion show among the spectators, a brilliant display of black power in the ring, and also a step, however small, toward righting an injustice."[71]

The focus of much of that celebratory rhetoric was Johnson himself. As the Baltimore *Afro-American* reported, "men like State Senator Leroy Johnson of Georgia and the City of Atlanta, deserve great credit for helping get the United States to back away from this disgraceful episode in its history before Ali grew too old to make it possible for a happy ending."[72] The Black press understood that race relations in Atlanta were not all they seemed to be, but "Muhammad Ali got his chance to flatten Jerry Quarry and make a handsome buck," wrote the *Chicago Defender*'s Charlie Cherokee, "because of the skill and finesse of a black Georgia politician who knew how to handle Governor Lester Maddox and all the white wheels of Georgia."[73]

And there seemed to be real payoffs for the flexing of Black political muscle in Atlanta. The year after the Ali-Quarry fight, in 1971, for example, Emory University's Delores Aldridge began directing the first Black Studies program in the South.[74] "The fight showed the emergence of African-American political power and influence in Atlanta," said Jesse Hill. "It indicated this was a city that had progressive associations among its black and white leadership." For Andrew Young, "the fight meant recognition of Atlanta as the capital of the civil rights movement in that we were having an impact, not only on the South, but on the nation."[75]

Then there were the city's civic and business interests. "The fight was a feather in Atlanta's cap," concluded Johnson, "and a feather in the South's cap—for having this person, who was a Muslim and who had been kicked out of the ring by the liberal state of New York, to come back in a state with, at the time, a questionable admiration for blacks."[76] *Atlanta Magazine*'s David Davis argued that the fight helped make the city a sports destination, ultimately "paving the way" for major events like Super Bowls, Final Fours, and the Olympics. "Perhaps more importantly, the fight cemented the city's growing reputation as a 'black Mecca,'" he wrote. "Nothing better defines the emergence of modern-day Atlanta than the night Muhammad Ali defeated Jerry Quarry."[77]

Ali's relationship with Atlanta didn't end in the 1970s. He returned to the city in 1981 for a benefit. He was no longer heavyweight champion, but he was still Muhammad Ali. At the time of his arrival, the city was gripped by a series of child murders in Atlanta's Black neighborhoods. Ali phoned his friend Maynard Jackson and pledged $400,000 to the cause, endearing him further to Black residents.[78]

Almost two decades after Ali's return to the ring, in September 1990, the ascension of Atlanta reached its peak when the city won its bid to host the 1996 Summer Olympics. As preparations were being made for the games, questions about who would light the Olympic cauldron animated the city, the state, and the country. The secret, however, was closely guarded. Perhaps it would be Jimmy Carter. Or the current president.

Or one of the country's many past Olympic champions. Roughly ten thousand people handled the torch in the eighty-four days prior to the start of the games. It came into the stadium at the hands of Al Oerter, who won discus gold in four consecutive Olympics in the 1950s and 1960s. He passed it to a boxer, Atlanta's Evander Holyfield, who carried it around the track before handing it to swimmer Janet Evans, who ran it up a ramp to the cauldron. But when the spotlight landed on the man who would actually light the flame, the crowd in the stadium and in front of televisions all over the world audibly gasped. "At first it was complete surprise," remembered Scott Freeman. But it was "followed by the same collective thought: This time, they got it right. And then, then came the tears."[79]

That was, probably, correct. Muhammad Ali was the most important American athlete of the twentieth century, a man who embodied the best that sports was supposed to be. "He was once the most dynamic figure in sports, a gregarious man, now trapped inside that mask created by Parkinson's syndrome," said Bob Costas over the scene. "The response he evokes is part affection, part excitement, but especially respect."[80] But for me, watching from my small apartment in Arkansas, it was confusing. What did Ali have to do with Atlanta? He was from Louisville, but Louisville wasn't really the South. So what did he have to do with representing the first Southern Olympics? Of course, there were so many reasons. He was the athletic embodiment of the fight to change the South, a symbol of the power of sports to influence the personal and collective morality of those who cared about them. But, as it turned out, he had been an embodiment of those broader changes in Georgia, too. Muhammad Ali mattered to the country and the world. But he also mattered to Atlanta.

Joe Frazier was not among those touched by the moment. "I hope he falls in the flame," he said upon seeing Ali light the Olympic cauldron.[81] He was not alone. Hosea Williams, the former sparring partner of Leroy Johnson, stood outside the stadium with a small group of protesters attempting to use the event to draw attention to the Georgia flag, which still boldly incorporated the Confederate battle flag as it flew over Olympic Stadium, just as it still flew over the venue where the former champ performed for an adoring crowd twenty-six years earlier.[82]

The Georgia state flag would finally change in 2001, after growing calls to remove the battle flag iconography. A brief and unpopular replacement was used for two years and was changed again in 2003. The new flag still used Confederate iconography, but did so in a more subtle way. The government based its new choice on the First National Flag of the Confederacy, less well-known and thus less despised as a racist symbol. But it was still a version of a Confederate flag. Atlanta had consistently presented itself as a city too busy to hate, but the rest of Georgia was far less busy and was rarely shy about proclaiming white supremacy as a value added to Southern identity.[83]

Ali had been suggested to the Atlanta Olympic Committee by Dick Ebersol, president of NBC Sports. Originally the committee was dismissive of the suggestion, citing the former champion's Parkinson's disease and his divisive political legacy.[84] Ali, too, had originally rejected the idea, not wanting to be seen publicly in the reduced state brought on by his Parkinson's. Even after Ali was convinced, Ebersol had to persuade the Atlanta Committee for the Olympic Games, led by Billy Payne. "As a nineteen-year-old freshman at the University of Georgia who considered himself a patriot," Payne said, "I had considered Ali a draft-dodger." Payne had argued for Hank Aaron as a representative of the city, or Evander Holyfield, an Atlanta fighter who had participated in the Olympics as an amateur and won a bronze medal. But Ebersol was persuasive, making a sustained case for Ali that never included the fighter's pivotal role in Atlanta. Payne reluctantly agreed.[85]

His appearance was surely inspirational, but Amy Bass has argued that it served to "erase the battles he fought so long ago in the face of vitriolic discrimination, because society, in all of its white liberal tolerance, rests easy that it now 'gets it.'"[86] Mike Marqusee has noted that Ali served "as the principal public role model for conscientious objectors and draft resisters." He became something more than a boxer, a symbol who "gave courage to thousands of young men, many of them isolated from the organized movement. He made dissent visible, audible and attractive."[87] And none of that symbolism was visible on the Atlanta platform at the 1996 Olympics. The Ali on public display in Atlanta in 1996 was a hero to everyone, whereas a quarter-century earlier the Ali on public display in Atlanta had been a hero only to a certain segment of a dispossessed population, one that saw in his victory a chance for victory themselves.

Because Ali no longer had his 1960 Olympic gold medal, the apocryphal story claiming that he flung it into the Ohio River after experiencing segregation, the International Olympic Committee presented him with a new one during halftime of the gold-medal basketball game between the United States and Yugoslavia. Costas explained in commentary both the story often told and the reality that the medal was simply lost during Ali's long career. "It makes a good symbolic story. It could have happened. It actually did not," said Costas. "And now that situation will be rectified."[88]

So much of Ali's career was and is enmeshed in both apocrypha and symbol. His image served as an empty vessel for so many different actors to fill with their own political interests that the meaning of his life had become, by the 1996 Olympics, inevitably malleable. But on a cool October night in 1970, less than two miles away from where the opening Olympic ceremonies would be held, his symbolism was perhaps most acute. That night he was a draft dodger. He was a Black radical. A Black Muslim. He was the target of white racial bigotry. He was a fighter finally able to practice his craft in what was ostensibly a free country. He was a hero to Black residents of a city who had endured so much discrimination under the thin veneer of the city's progressive identity. When his fight was stopped after the third round that cool October night, Ali finally had a measure of redemption. But the winners that night were boxing and Black Atlanta.

NOTES

PROLOGUE

1. Elliot J. Gorn, "John L. Sullivan: 'The Champion of All Champions,'" *Virginia Quarterly Review* 62 (Autumn 1986): 626–632; Adam J. Pollack, *John L. Sullivan: The Career of the First Gloved Heavyweight Champion* (McFarland, 2015), 211–219; Michael T. Isenberg, *John L. Sullivan and His America* (University of Illinois Press, 1994), 321–322; Armond Fields, *James J. Corbett: A Biography of the Heavyweight Boxing Champion and Popular Theater Headliner* (McFarland, 2017), 51–66.
2. Gorn, "John L. Sullivan," 629–630; Steven Laffoley, *Shadowboxing: The Rise and Fall of George Dixon* (Pottersfield, 2012), 112–122; Dan Streible, "A History of the Boxing Film, 1894–1915: Social Control and Social Reform in the Progressive Era," *Film History* 3, no. 3 (1989): 242; Louis Moore, "Fine Specimens of Manhood: The Black Boxer's Body and the Avenue to Equality, Racial Advancement, and Manhood in the Nineteenth Century," *MELUS* 35 (Winter 2010): 76–79.
3. *Chicago Tribune* and *New Orleans Times-Democrat* quoted in Dale Somers, *The Rise of Sports in New Orleans, 1850–1900* (Louisiana State University Press, 1972), 180–183; Laffoley, *Shadowboxing*, 122–124; Randy Roberts, *Papa Jack: Jack Johnson and the Era of White Hopes* (Free Press, 1983), 18.
4. Roberts, *Papa Jack*, 17.
5. Lerone Bennett, Jr., "Georgia's Negro Senator," *Ebony*, March 1963, 25–34. Quote from 34.
6. *Baker v. Carr*, 369 US 186 (1962); David Davis, "Knockout: Muhammad Ali, Atlanta, and the Fight Nobody Wanted," *Atlanta*, October 2005, 120; *Atlanta Constitution [AC]*, 13 January 1969, 9A; Bennett, "Georgia's Negro Senator," 32.
7. Alex Poinsett, "A Look At Cassius Clay: Biggest Mouth in Boxing," *Ebony*, March 1963, 35, 36–38.

8. David Remnick, *King of the World: Muhammad Ali and the Rise of an American Hero* (Random House, 1998), 101–107; Dick Schaap, "The Happiest Heavyweight," *Saturday Evening Post*, 25 March 1961, 101; Dave Kindred, *Sound and Fury: Two Powerful Lives, One Fateful Friendship* (Free Press, 2006), 34–35.
9. Andres F. Quintana, "Muhammad Ali: The Greatest in Court," *Marquette Sports Law Review* 18, no. 1 (2007): 180–181; Jon David Rutter, "White Hopes: Heavyweight Boxing and the Repercussions of Race" (PhD diss., University of Texas at Austin, 2001), 195; Jack Olsen, "A Case of Conscience," *Sports Illustrated*, 11 April 1966, 101.
10. Randy Roberts and Johnny Smith, *Blood Brothers: The Fatal Friendship Between Muhammad Ali and Malcolm X* (Basic, 2016), 14–16; David K. Wiggins, "Victory for Allah: Muhammad Ali, the Nation of Islam, and American Society," in *Muhammad Ali: The People's Champ*, ed. Elliott J. Gorn (University of Illinois Press, 1995), 90.
11. "Cassius Marcellus Clay, Jr.," 25–531360, 13 June 1966, File No. 25–330971, Muhammad Ali, FOIA, Federal Bureau of Investigation; Wiggins, "Victory for Allah," 98; Rutter, "White Hopes," 196.
12. AC, 20 August 1969, 1C, 2C, 22 August 1969, 5C; "Muhammad Ali Chronology," received from M.A. Project, Inc., vol. 2, Permanent Collection, Muhammad Ali Center, Louisville, Kentucky; Howard Bingham and Max Wallace, *Muhammad Ali's Greatest Fight: Cassius Clay vs. The United States of America* (M. Evans, 2000), 209–210; *Muhammad Speaks*, 11 April 1969, 2, 3; *Atlanta Voice [AV]*, 13 April 1969, 9.
13. David Andrew Harmon, "Beneath the Image: The Civil Rights Movement and Race Relations in Atlanta, Georgia, 1946–1981" (PhD diss., Emory University, 1993), 90; Clifford M. Kuhn, Harlon E. Joye, and Bernard West, *Living Atlanta: An Oral History of the City, 1914–1948* (University of Georgia Press, 2005), 39; Elizabeth Tandy Shermer, *Sunbelt Capitalism: Phoenix and the Transformation of American Politics* (University of Pennsylvania Press, 2013), 36.
14. August Meier and David Lewis, "History of the Negro Upper Class in Atlanta, Georgia, 1890–1958," *Journal of Negro Education* 28 (Spring 1959): 131–132; Virginia H. Hein, "The Image of 'A City Too Busy Too Hate': Atlanta in the 1960's," *Phylon* 33 (Fall 1972): 215; Tomiko Brown-Nagin, "Class Actions: The Impact of Black and Middle-Class Conservatism on Civil Rights Lawyering in a New South Political Economy, Atlanta, 1946–1979" (PhD diss., Duke University, 2002), 70–73.
15. Peter K. Eisinger, *The Politics of Displacement: Racial and Ethnic Transition in Three American Cities* (Academic Press, 1980), 58; Bruce J. Schulman,

From Cotton Belt to Sunbelt: Federal Policy, Economic Development, and the Transformation of the South, 1938–1980 (Oxford University Press, 1991), 208; Alton Hornsby, Jr., "A City That Was Too Busy to Hate: Atlanta Businessmen and Desegregation," in *Southern Businessmen and Desegregation*, eds. Elizabeth Jacoway and David R. Colburn (Louisiana State University Press, 1982), 121; *New York Times [NYT]*, 16 November 1964, 49, 5 May 1974, D21.

16. Brown-Nagin, "Class Actions," 13; Alton Hornsby, Jr., "Black Public Education in Atlanta, Georgia, 1954–1973: From Segregation to Segregation," *Journal of Negro History* 76 (Winter-Autumn 1991): 30; Adam Fairclough, *To Redeem the Soul of America: The Southern Christian Leadership Conference and Martin Luther King, Jr.* (University of Georgia Press, 1987), 175.
17. Charles Rutheiser, *Imagineering Atlanta: The Politics of Place in the City of Dreams* (Verso, 1996), 153–154; Clarence N. Stone, *Regime Politics: Governing Atlanta, 1946–1988* (University of Kansas Press, 1989), 70; Winston A. Grady-Willis, "A Changing Tide: Black Politics and Activism in Atlanta, Georgia, 1960–1977" (PhD diss., Emory University, 1998), 176; Julian Bond, *A Time to Speak, a Time to Act: The Movement in Politics* (Simon & Schuster, 1972), 78.
18. Bob Short, *Everything Is Pickrick: The Life of Lester Maddox* (Mercer University Press, 1999), 69–81; "Oral history interview with Governor Lester Maddox, 1986 April 17," uwg_phc_maddox2, Georgia Political Papers and Oral History Program, Special Collections, Ingram Library, University of West Georgia, Carrollton GA; Bruce Galphin, *The Riddle of Lester Maddox* (Camelot Publishing, 1968), 2–3.
19. Frederick Allen, *Atlanta Rising: The Invention of an International City, 1946–1996* (Longstreet, 1996), 144–145; Furman Bisher, *Miracle in Atlanta: The Atlanta Braves Story* (World Publishing, 1966); Clayton Trutor, *Loserville: How Professional Sports Remade Atlanta—And How Atlanta Remade Professional Sports* (University of Nebraska Press, 2022), 67, 79–89, 108–115; Glen Gendzel, "Competitive Boosterism: How Milwaukee Lost the Braves," *Business History Review* 69 (Winter 1995): 530–566; Furman Bisher, *Atlanta Falcons: Violence and Victory* (Prentice Hall, 1973).
20. Alton Hornsby, Jr., "The Negro in Atlanta Politics," *Atlanta Historical Bulletin* 21 (Spring 1977): 20; Grady-Willis, "A Changing Tide," 179–184; *Atlanta Journal [AJ]*, 7 September 1966, 2; Daniel S. Lucks, *Selma to Saigon: The Civil Rights Movement and the Vietnam War* (University Press of Kentucky, 2014), 114–119; Frank J. Lower, "Julian Bond: A Case Study in a Legislator's Freedom of Speech," *Free Speech Yearbook* 13, no. 1 (1974): 35–44; "Legislative Exclusion: Julian Bond and Adam Clayton Powell," *University of Chicago Law Review* 35 (Autumn 1967): 151–172.

21. Thomas Aiello, *Dixieball: Race and Professional Basketball in the Deep South, 1947–1979* (University of Tennessee Press, 2019), 59–86; Thomas Aiello, *White Ice: Race and the Making of Atlanta Hockey* (University of Tennessee Press, 2019), 53–68.
22. Bingham and Wallace, *Muhammad Ali's Greatest Fight*, 230; Davis, "Knockout," 120; Jonathan Eig, *Ali: A Life* (Houghton Mifflin Harcourt, 2017), 288–289; AC, 13 August 1970, 1D, 6D; *Atlanta Daily World [ADW]*, 28 April 1970, 5.
23. Thomas Hauser, *Muhammad Ali: His Life and Times* (Simon & Schuster, 1991), 209; AC, 14 August 1970, 1D; *NYT*, 14 August 1970, 39.
24. AC, 10 September 1970, 1D, 7D; Hauser, *Muhammad Ali*, 210; *NYT*, 10 September 1970, 67; Rutter, "White Hopes," 209; David Davis, "The 13th Round: How Boxing Made and Destroyed Jerry Quarry," *L.A. Weekly*, 17–23 March 1995, 23, 26.
25. Muhammad Ali with Richard Durham, *The Greatest: My Own Story* (Random House, 1975), 268; Davis, "Knockout," *Atlanta*, October 2005, 119; Angelo Dundee with Bert Randolph Sugar, *My View from the Corner: A Life in Boxing* (McGraw Hill, 2008), 137.
26. Mark Kram, "Smashing Return of the Old Ali," *Sports Illustrated*, 2 November 1970, 18; Jack Richardson, "Ali on Peachtree," *Harper's Magazine*, January 1971, 49; Budd Schulberg, *Loser and Still Champion: Muhammad Ali* (Doubleday, 1972), 69.
27. AC, 9 January 1969, 45, 30 April 1969, 16, 12 July 1969, 16A, 21 August 1969, 11D, 6 February 1970, 23A, 29 October 1970, 3D; John Matthew Smith, "The Resurrection: Atlanta, Racial Politics, and the Return of Muhammad Ali," *Southern Cultures* 21 (Summer 2015): 24.
28. Alton Hornsby, Jr., *Black Power in Dixie: A Political History of African Americans in Atlanta* (University Press of Florida, 2009), 136–138; Harmon, "Beneath the Image," 537, 543; Eisinger, *The Politics of Displacement*, 67; Gary M. Pomerantz, *Where Peachtree Meets Sweet Auburn: The Saga of Two Families and the Making of Atlanta* (Lisa Drew/Scribner, 1996), 403–405.
29. Othello Harris, "Muhammad Ali and the Revolt of the Black Athlete," in *Muhammad Ali: The People's Champ*, ed. Elliott J. Gorn (University of Illinois Press, 1995), 66.
30. Gary Wills, "Muhammad Ali," in *The Muhammad Ali Reader*, ed. Gerald Early (HarperCollins, 1998), 163.

1. RISE OF LEROY JOHNSON

1. Brown-Nagin, "Class Actions," 7.

2. Meier and Lewis, "History of the Negro Upper Class," 128–131.
3. Alexa Benson Henderson, *Atlanta Life Insurance Company: Guardian of Black Economic Dignity* (University of Alabama Press, 1990), xi, xiii, 3; Meier and Lewis, "History of the Negro Upper Class," 131–132.
4. Meier and Lewis, "History of the Negro Upper Class," 133–135.
5. Hein, "The Image," 215; Anne Rivers Siddons, "The Seeds of Sanity," *Atlanta*, July 1967, 55–56; James C. Cobb, *The Selling of the South: The Southern Crusade for Industrial Development, 1936–1980* (Louisiana State University Press, 1982), 122.
6. Hornsby, "A City," 123; *Chapman v. King*, 154 F.2d 460 (1946); Brown-Nagin, "Class Actions," 9; Charles S. Rooks, *The Atlanta Elections of 1969* (Voter Education Project, 1970), 1; Jack Walker, "Negro Voting in Atlanta: 1953–1961," *Phylon* 24 (4th Qtr. 1964): 380–382; Stone, *Regime Politics*, 18–21, 27–35; Allen, *Atlanta Rising*, 25–28, 69.
7. Brown-Nagin, "Class Actions," 10; Matthew D. Lassiter, *The Silent Majority: Suburban Politics in the Sunbelt South* (Princeton University Press, 2006), 48; William Seth LaShier, "'To Secure Improvements in Their Material and Social Conditions': Atlanta's Civil Rights Movement, Middle-Class Reformers, and Workplace Protests, 1960–1977" (PhD diss., George Washington University, 2020), 19.
8. Harmon, "Beneath the Image," 90; Eisinger, *The Politics of Displacement*, 58; Brown-Nagin, "Class Actions," 70–73; Henderson, *Atlanta Life Insurance Company*, 71–72; Kuhn, Joye, and West, *Living Atlanta*, 39; Shermer, *Sunbelt Capitalism*, 36.
9. Ronald H. Bayor, "Roads to Racial Segregation: Atlanta in the Twentieth Century," *Journal of Urban History* 15 (November 1988): 4–5, 7–8, 14–15; Joan Browning, "The Atlanta Wall," *Southern Patriot* (January 1963): 1, 4, MS/124, Department of Archives and Special Collections, Valdosta State University, Valdosta GA; Kevin M. Kruse, *White Flight: Atlanta and the Making of Modern Conservatism* (Princeton University Press, 2005), 3–5; Lassiter, *The Silent Majority*, 50.
10. LaShier, "To Secure Improvements," 16; Lassiter, *The Silent Majority*, 47; Eisinger, *The Politics of Displacement*, 58; Schulman, *Cotton Belt to Sunbelt*, 208; Smith, "The Resurrection," 12; Hornsby, "A City," 121; *NYT*, 16 November 1964, 49, 5 May 1974, D21.
11. Helen Fuller, "Southerners and the Schools: Atlanta Is Different," *New Republic* (repr., 1959): 14–17, box 1, folder 18, Civil Rights Papers, MS-134, Department of Archives and Special Collections, Valdosta State University, Valdosta GA; Hornsby, "A City," 129–131; Ronald L. Bayor, *Race and the Shaping of Twentieth-Century Atlanta* (University of North Carolina Press,

1996), 223–224; Lassiter, *The Silent Majority*, 60–61; Hornsby, "Black Public Education," 21–22, 25; Cobb, *The Selling of the South*, 127.

12. Cobb, *The Selling of the South*, 129.
13. Hornsby, "Black Public Education," 21; Brown-Nagin, "Class Actions," 11; NYT, 31 August 1961, A10; "The 'Deep South'–Land with a Future: Atlanta," *US News & World Report*, 6 November 1961, 68; George McMillan, "Atlanta's Peaceful Blow for Justice: With the Police on an Integration Job," *Life*, 16 September 1961, 35–36; Grace Walker, "How Women Won the Quiet Battle of Atlanta," *Good Housekeeping*, May 1961, 76; "Glad to See You," *Newsweek*, 11 September 1961, 93; Kyle Haselden, "Too Busy to Hate," *Christian Century*, 27 March 1963, 392; William S. Ellis, "Atlanta, Pacesetter City of the South," *National Geographic* 135 (February 1969): 249.
14. Hornsby, "A City," 120; Brown-Nagin, "Class Actions," 12; Bayor, *Race and the Shaping of Twentieth-Century Atlanta*, 225–227; Rutheiser, *Imagineering Atlanta*, 52, 62; Phyl Garland, "Atlanta: Black Mecca of the South," *Ebony*, August 1971, 152–157. Johnson quoted in Hein, "The Image," 210.
15. Bond, *A Time to Speak*, 75.
16. Brown-Nagin, "Class Actions," 13; and Hornsby, "Black Public Education," 30. King quoted in Fairclough, *To Redeem the Soul of America*, 175.
17. *Heart of Atlanta Motel v. United States*, 379 U.S. 241 (1964); *Calhoun v. Latimer*, 377 U.S. 263 (1964); Brown-Nagin, "Class Actions," 14–15; David Andrew Harmon, *Beneath the Image of the Civil Rights Movement and Race Relations: Atlanta, Georgia. 1946–1981* (Garland, 1996), 163–165; Short, *Everything Is Pickrick*, 59.
18. *Armour v. Nix*, 446 U.S. 930 (1980); and Brown-Nagin, "Class Actions," 15–16.
19. Brown-Nagin, "Class Actions," 16–17, 20; LaShier, "To Secure Improvements," 21–22; Adolph Reed, Jr., *Stirrings in the Jug: Black Politics in the Post-Segregation Era* (University of Minnesota Press, 1999), 167. Bond quote from Peter Ross Range, "Making It in Atlanta: Capital of Black-Is-Bountiful," *New York Times Magazine*, 7 April 1974, 268.
20. Brown-Nagin, "Class Actions," 24, 26–27.
21. Grady-Willis, "A Changing Tide," 175; James Baldwin, "Nobody Knows My Name: A Letter from the South," in *James Baldwin, Collected Essays*, ed. Toni Morrison (Literary Classics, 1998), 199; Eisinger, *The Politics of Displacement*, 56–60.
22. Grady-Willis, "A Changing Tide," 177; "Dr. King Views Atlanta Slum Areas," *SCLC Newsletter* 3 (January-February 1966), 3.
23. Rutheiser, *Imagineering Atlanta*, 153–154; Stone, *Regime Politics*, 70; Grady-Willis, "A Changing Tide," 176.

24. Rutheiser, *Imagineering Atlanta*, 155; *Report of the National Advisory Commission on Civil Disorders* (USGPO, 1968), 28; Hornsby, "The Negro in Atlanta Politics," 20; Grady-Willis, "A Changing Tide," 179–184; *AJ*, 7 September 1966, 2.
25. *AJ*, 8 September 1966, 1; Grady-Willis, "A Changing Tide," 188–189.
26. Brown-Nagin, "Class Actions," 38–41, 151–153, quote from 41.
27. Harmon, *Beneath the Image*, 134; Henderson, *Atlanta Life Insurance Company*, 181–182; Bayor, *Race and the Shaping of Twentieth-Century Atlanta*, 32; Harmon, "Beneath the Image," 274.
28. Henderson, *Atlanta Life Insurance Company*, 165, 180–181; "Muhammad Ali versus Jerry Quarry Souvenir Program," 26 October 1970, Greatest of All Time Collection, Muhammad Ali Center, Louisville ky [hereinafter cited as "Souvenir Program"].
29. Kruse, *White Flight*, 185; Brown-Nagin, "Class Actions," 139.
30. Grady-Willis, "A Changing Tide," 63.
31. Kruse, *White Flight*, 182–183, 203.
32. Grady-Willis, "A Changing Tide," 111.
33. Brown-Nagin, "Class Actions," 161–162; Ivan Allen, *Mayor: Notes on the Sixties* (Simon & Schuster, 1971), 101–116.
34. Harmon, "Beneath the Image," 465–466; Rooks, *Atlanta Elections*, 2; Walker, "Negro Voting in Atlanta," 385.
35. Kruse, *White Flight*, 12.
36. Kruse, *White Flight*, 15; Eisinger, *The Politics of Displacement*, 65.
37. Kruse, *White Flight*, 234; Eisinger, *The Politics of Displacement*, 59.
38. Stephen Lesher, "Leroy Johnson Outslicks Mister Charlie," *New York Times Magazine*, 8 November 1970, 35.
39. Lesher, "Leroy Johnson," 35; "Souvenir Program"; Pomerantz, *Where Peachtree Meets Sweet Auburn*, 385; Bennett, "Georgia's Negro Senator," 26–27; Maurice J. Hobson, *The Legend of the Black Mecca: Politics and Class in the Making of Modern Atlanta* (University of North Carolina Press, 2017), 56–57.
40. Lesher, "Leroy Johnson," 36; Bennett, "Georgia's Negro Senator," 28; "Interview with Leroy Johnson, February 27, 2007," RBRL220ROGP-016, Reflections on Georgia Politics Oral History Collection, Richard B. Russell Library for Political Research and Studies, University of Georgia, Athens GA.
41. *Chapman v. King*, 154 F.2d 460 (1946); Brown-Nagin, "Class Actions," 51–52; Bayor, *Race and the Shaping of Twentieth-Century Atlanta*, 23–24; Allen, *Atlanta Rising*, 35.
42. *Baker v. Carr*, 369 U.S. 186 (1962).

43. *Truman v. Duckworth*, 68 F. Supp. 744 (N.D. Ga. 1946); *Cook v. Fortson*, 68 F. Supp. 624 (N.D. Ga. 1946); Cobb, *The Selling of the South*, 159.
44. Lassiter, *The Silent Majority*, 54; Lesher, "Leroy Johnson," 36; Bennett, "Georgia's Negro Senator," 28, 30; Walker, "Negro Voting in Atlanta," 385; Allen, *Atlanta Rising*, 121; Harmon, "Beneath the Image," 403; Grady-Willis, "A Changing Tide," 101–102; Tim S. R. Boyd, *Georgia Democrats, the Civil Rights Movement, and the Shaping of the New South* (University Press of Florida, 2012), 145.
45. Bennett, "Georgia's Negro Senator," 32, 34; Donald L. Grant, *The Way It Was in the South: The Black Experience in Georgia* (Birch Lane, 1993), 421.
46. Soon after the Commerce Club incident, the club would reluctantly desegregate. Allen, *Atlanta Rising*, 124; Hornsby, *Black Power in Dixie*, 125–126; Schulberg, *Loser and Still Champion*, 62.
47. Bennett, "Georgia's Negro Senator," 32; Lesher, "Leroy Johnson," 36.
48. Lesher, "Leroy Johnson," 36; Grant, *The Way It Was*, 438; Bayor, *Race and the Shaping of Twentieth-Century Atlanta*, 39; "Souvenir Program"; Boyd, *Georgia Democrats*, 137, 146; Bennett, "Georgia's Negro Senator," 25–26, 32.
49. Sanders quoted in Davis, "Knockout," 120. This book will use citations from Muhammad Ali's FBI file, but it does not use the FBI's surveillance on Johnson, as records relevant to a FOIA request were destroyed under the supervision of the National Archives and Records Administration. US Department of Justice, FOIPA Request No. 1621846-000, 18 March 2024.
50. Paul Stephen Hudson and Lora Pond Mirza, "Controversial Comeback in Atlanta: The 1970 Return of Muhammad Ali in 'The City Too Busy to Hate,'" *Georgia Historical Quarterly* 95 (Spring 2011): 42.
51. "December 29–30: State Legislators Seminar," box 41, folder 7, Voter Education Project Organizational Records, 0000-0000-0000-0076, Robert W. Woodruff Library of the Atlanta University Center, Inc., Atlanta GA; Evan Faulkenbury, *Poll Power: The Voter Education Project and the Movement for the Ballot in the American South* (University of North Carolina Press, 2019), 90–91, 105; Howard Romaine, "Black Politics," *The Great Speckled Bird*, 23 December 1968, 3.
52. Lesher, "Leroy Johnson," 36–37; Grady-Willis, "A Changing Tide," 157; Lucks, *Selma to Saigon*, 114–119; Lower, "Julian Bond," 35–44; "Legislative Exclusion," 151–172; L.H.B., Jr. and A.S.C., "The Julian Bond Case," *Virginia Law Review* 52 (November 1966): 1309–1335; *Bond v. Floyd*, 385 U.S. 116 (1966); Harmon, *Beneath the Image*, 199; Harmon, "Beneath the Image," 407, 458.
53. Short, *Everything Is Pickrick*, 69–81; and "Oral history interview with Governor Lester Maddox, 1986 April 17," uwg_phc_maddox2, Georgia Political

Papers and Oral History Program, Special Collections, Ingram Library, University of West Georgia, Carrollton GA.

54. Donnie Summerlin, "'We Represented the Best of Georgia in Chicago': The Georgia Loyalist Delegate Challenge at the 1968 Democratic National Convention," *Georgia Historical Quarterly* 103, no. 3 (2019): 213; Short, *Everything Is Pickrick*, 95–99; *Fortson v. Morris*, 385 U.S. 231 (1966); Lesher, "Leroy Johnson," 38.
55. Short, *Everything Is Pickrick*, 56–58, 63; Lester Maddox, *Speaking Out: The Autobiography of Lester Garfield Maddox* (Doubleday, 1975), 54, 57, 62, 65; Galphin, *Riddle of Lester Maddox*, 2–3.
56. Galphin, *The Riddle of Lester Maddox*, 2–3; Maddox, *Speaking Out*, 101; Short, *Everything Is Pickrick*, 108, 123–124; *Atlanta Inquirer [AI]*, 13 December 1969, 1; Allen, *Atlanta Rising*, 155; "Interview with Leroy Johnson."
57. Norman Mailer, *Miami and the Siege of Chicago: An Informal History of the Republican and Democratic Conventions of 1968* (Donald I. Fine, 1968), 131; Maddox, *Speaking Out*, 127, 129; "Oral history interview with Governor Lester Maddox"; Galphin, *Riddle of Lester Maddox*, 208–210.
58. Lesher, "Leroy Johnson," 37; Joseph Foote, ed., *The Presidential Nominating Conventions, 1968* (Congressional Quarterly Service, 1968), 108–109.
59. Foote, *The Presidential Nominating Conventions*, 117–118, 128, 277–278, quote from 128; Democratic National Convention, *Report of the Proceedings of the 35th Quadrennial Convention of the Democratic National Committee, August 26–30, 1968* (Democratic National Committee, 1968), 154, 179–180, 433, quote from 154; Summerlin, "We Represented the Best," 230–232.
60. Summerlin, "We Represented the Best," 236–240; Mailer, *Miami and the Siege of Chicago*, 160.
61. Foote, *Presidential Nominating Conventions*, 155, 159; Summerlin, "We Represented the Best," 240, 244–245; Mailer, *Miami and the Siege of Chicago*, 207; Neary, *Julian Bond*, 206, 212–215.
62. Lesher, "Leroy Johnson," 37.
63. Walker, "Negro Voting in Atlanta," 387.
64. Lesher, "Leroy Johnson," 39–40.
65. Eliza Paschall, "Black Male Chauvinists," *The Great Speckled Bird*, 24 February 1969, 7.
66. Allen, *Atlanta Rising*, 144–145; Bisher, *Miracle in Atlanta*; Trutor, *Loserville*, 67, 114; Gendzel, "Competitive Boosterism," 530–566. Portions of the following narrative of the development of professional team sports in Atlanta come from two of my previous works, *Dixieball* and *White Ice*.
67. Bisher, *Atlanta Falcons*; Trutor, *Loserville*, 79–89, 108–116.

68. Kathryn Jay, *More Than Just a Game: Sports in American Life Since 1945* (Columbia University Press, 2004), 79–81, 82.
69. Kruse, *White Flight*, 6–10, quote from p. 8; Benjamin D. Lisle, *Modern Coliseum: Stadiums and American Culture* (University of Pennsylvania Press, 2017), 4–6; ADW, 10 May 1968, 7.
70. *Report of the National Advisory Commission on Civil Disorders*, 28–30; Hobson, *Legend of the Black Mecca*, 47; Stone, *Regime Politics*, 70; Hein, "The Image," 215–216; Harmon, *Beneath the Image*, 212; Grady-Willis, "A Changing Tide," 194–196; Winston Grady-Willis, *Challenging US Apartheid: Atlanta and Black Struggles for Human Rights, 1960–1977* (Duke University Press, 2006), 129–130.
71. Harmon, "Beneath the Image," 437.
72. Grady-Willis, "A Changing Tide," 198–199.
73. Grady-Willis, "A Changing Tide," 200–201, 203; Hornsby, "The Negro in Atlanta Politics," 20–21; Lassiter, *The Silent Majority*, 49; *Detroit News*, 1 August 1967, 10D.
74. *Report of the National Advisory Commission on Civil Disorders*, 29.
75. Hobson, *Legend of the Black Mecca*, 51–53, 63; Tomiko Brown-Nagin, *Courage to Dissent: Atlanta and the Long History of the Civil Rights Movement* (Oxford University Press, 2011), 3; Brown-Nagin, "Class Actions," 64.
76. Nasrolah Rashid Farokhi, "The Influences of Nongovernmental, Business, and Interest Group Organizations on Urban Politics and Policy Making: A Case Study of the Leadership Role and Influence of the Atlanta Chamber of Commerce, 1960–1978" (PhD diss., Atlanta University, 1979), 8.

2. FALL OF MUHAMMAD ALI

1. Gerald Early, "The Mortality of Kings: Ali versus Frazier," in *Rivals: Legendary Matchups That Made Sports History*, ed. David K. Wiggins and R. Pierre Rodgers (University of Arkansas Press, 2010), 53–55; Schaap, "The Happiest Heavyweight," 101; Mikal Gilmore, "The Greatest of All Time, 1942–2016," *Rolling Stone*, 1 July 2016, 28.
2. Thomas R. Hietala, "Muhammad Ali and the Age of Bare-Knuckle Politics," in *Muhammad Ali: The People's Champ*, ed. Elliott J. Gorn (University of Illinois Press, 1995), 119.
3. Early, "The Mortality of Kings," 53–55; Remnick, *King of the World*, 101–107.
4. Kindred, *Sound and Fury*, 34–35; Early, "The Mortality of Kings," 53–55; Remnick, *King of the World*, 101–107; Schaap, "The Happiest Heavyweight," 101; Gilmore, "The Greatest of All Time," 28; Fiaz Rafiq, *Muhammad Ali: The Life of a Legend* (Arena Sport, 2020), 29.
5. Kindred, *Sound and Fury*, 36–37.

6. Roberts and Smith, *Blood Brothers*, 3–4; AC, 22 October 1970, 1D.
7. Schaap, "The Happiest Heavyweight," 36, 100–102.
8. Rutter, "White Hopes," 177, 179; Howard M. Tuckner, "Man, It's Great to be Great," *New York Times Magazine*, 9 December 1962, 47–50.
9. Roberts and Smith, *Blood Brothers*, 14–16; Jack Olsen, *Black Is Best: The Riddle of Cassius Clay* (n.p., 2014); Shawn Lamar Williams, "'The People's Champion': Folk Heroism and the Oral Artistry of Muhammad Ali" (PhD diss., Clark Atlanta University, 2000), 18; Kindred, *Sound and Fury*, 42.
10. Pete Axthelm, "The Return of an Exiled Champ," *Newsweek*, 9 November 1970, 59; Wiggins, "Victory for Allah," 90; Roberts and Smith, *Blood Brothers*, 12, 33, 55–56.
11. Roberts and Smith, *Blood Brothers*, 63.
12. Claude Andrew Clegg, III, *An Original Man: The Life and Times of Elijah Muhammad* (St. Martin's, 1997), 11–15, 21–22, 60, 90–92; Herbert Berg, *Elijah Muhammad and Islam* (New York University Press, 2009), 31–52.
13. Wiggins, "Victory for Allah," 91; Rutter, "White Hopes," 181, 182–183; George Plimpton, "Miami Notebook: Cassius Clay and Malcolm X," *The Muhammad Ali Reader*, ed. Gerald Early (HarperCollins, 1998), 32.
14. Roberts and Smith, *Blood Brothers*, xvi, 171; Plimpton, "Miami Notebook," 30–31.
15. Phillip J. Hutchinson, "From Bad Buck to White Hope: Journalism and Sonny Liston, 1958–1965," *Journal of Sports Media* 10 (Spring 2015): 119–137; Early, "The Mortality of Kings," 56; Rutter, "White Hopes," 181, 184.
16. Olsen, "A Case of Conscience," 104.
17. Jack Newfield, "The Meaning of Muhammad," *The Nation*, 4 February 2002, 26; Rutter, "White Hopes," 183–184; Early, "The Mortality of Kings," 57–58; Wiggins, "Victory for Allah," 97; Roberts and Smith, *Blood Brothers*, 143, 162.
18. Roberts and Smith, *Blood Brothers*, 155, 184–185.
19. Roberts and Smith, *Blood Brothers*, 200, 205.
20. NYT, 27 February 1964, 34, 28 February 1964, 34; Rutter, "White Hopes," 186–187.
21. ADW, 22 February 1964, 5.
22. *New York Amsterdam News [AN]*, 7 March 1964, 1, 2, 51; Roberts and Smith, *Blood Brothers*, 214.
23. Roberts and Smith, *Blood Brothers*, 218; Williams, "'The People's Champion,'" 36–37; Rutter, "White Hopes," 188; Taylor Branch, *Pillar of Fire: America in the King Years, 1963–1965* (Simon & Schuster, 1998), 251.
24. Kindred, *Sound and Fury*, 74.
25. Wiggins, "Victory for Allah," 95; Roberts and Smith, *Blood Brothers*, 245.

26. Quintana, "Muhammad Ali," 179.
27. Roberts and Smith, *Blood Brothers*, 216.
28. "Clay's 2d Army Test Is Reported a Failure," *NYT*, 18 March 1964, Draft Issue folder, Muhammad Ali Center, Louisville ky; Roberts and Smith, *Blood Brothers*, 235.
29. Rutter, "White Hopes," 189–190.
30. Rutter, "White Hopes," 191.
31. George Plimpton, *Shadow Box: An Amateur in the Ring* (Little, Brown, 2016), 105, 109–111; Kindred, *Sound and Fury*, 89–90.
32. Kindred, *Sound and Fury*, 92; Plimpton, *Shadow Box*, 113–116.
33. Kindred, *Sound and Fury*, 96.
34. Grant A. Farred, "What's My Name? Organic and Vernacular Intellectuals" (Phd diss., Princeton University, 1997), 176–177; Williams, "The People's Champion," 34.
35. Rutter, "White Hopes," 192–193; Hauser, *Muhammad Ali*, 139.
36. Michael Ezra, "Muhammad Ali's Main Bout: African American Economic Power and the World Heavyweight Title," in *The Economic Civil Rights Movement: African Americans and the Struggle for Economic Power*, ed. Michael Ezra (Routledge, 2013), 104–124; Gregory Kaliss, "Ali-Frazier 1: Black Gladiators, White Promoters, and the Economics of Big-Time Boxing," *International Journal of the History of Sport* 34, no. 11 (2017): 1006; "Nation of Islam, Internal Security—Nation of Islam," 11 January 1966, File No. 25-330971, Muhammad Ali, FOIA, Federal Bureau of Investigation [FBI].
37. SAC, Chicago (100–35635) to Director, FBI (25–330971), 17 January 1966, file no. 25–330971, Muhammad Ali, FOIA, FBI.
38. Roberts and Smith, *Blood Brothers*, 305; SAC, Miami (105–544) to Director, FBI (25–330971), 13 January 1966, and SAC, Miami (105–544) to Director, FBI (25–330971), 4 April 1966, file no. 25–330971, Muhammad Ali, FOIA, FBI; Olsen, *Black Is Best*.
39. SAC, Chicago (100–35635) to Director, FBI (25–330971), 28 February 1966, file no. 25–330971, Muhammad Ali, FOIA, FBI.
40. SAC, Miami (105–5262) to Director, FBI (25–330971), 10 March 1966, file no. 25–330971, Muhammad Ali, FOIA, FBI.
41. Olsen, "A Case of Conscience," 90.
42. Olsen, "A Case of Conscience," 90–92.
43. Kindred, *Sound and Fury*, 100.
44. Olsen, "A Case of Conscience," 95.
45. Olsen, "A Case of Conscience," 101.
46. Roberts and Smith, *Blood Brothers*, 220–221.
47. Olsen, "A Case of Conscience," 102.

48. "Cassius Clay Rejected by Army," Draft Issue folder, Muhammad Ali Center, Louisville, Kentucky; *Chicago Defender [CD]*, 26 September 1970, 35; Remnick, *King of the World*, 285; Quintana, "Muhammad Ali," 180–181; Rutter, "White Hopes," 195; Kindred, *Sound and Fury*, 110.
49. Newfield, "The Meaning of Muhammad," 29; Mike Marqusee, *Redemption Song: Muhammad Ali and the Spirit of the Sixties*, 2nd ed. (Verso, 2005), 178–179.
50. "Cassius Marcellus Clay, Jr.," 25–531360, 13 June 1966, file no. 25–330971, Muhammad Ali, FOIA, FBI; Leigh Montville, *Sting Like a Bee: Muhammad Ali vs. the United States of America, 1966–1971* (Doubleday, 2017), 11–21.
51. Rutter, "White Hopes," 196–199; Momodu Christopher Taylor, "An Examination of the Life and Times of Muhammad Ali: Boxing, Politics, Cultural Identity, and Transformational Leadership" (PhD diss., North Carolina A&T State University, 2016), 146–147; Daniel Bennett Coy, "Imagining Dissent: Muhammad Ali, Daily Newspapers, and the State, 1966–1971" (Master's thesis, University of Tennessee, Knoxville, 2004), 55; Remnick, *King of the World*, 289; Howard Cosell, *Cosell* (Pocket Books, 1974), 205–206; Dave Zirin, *A People's History of Sports in the United States: 250 Years of Politics, Protest, People and Play* (New Press, 2008), 146.
52. C. D. Brennan to Mr. Sullivan, 15 February 1967 and 14 February 1967, file no. 25–330971, Muhammad Ali, FOIA, FBI.
53. "Report of Hearing Conducted by the Department of Justice Pursuant to Section 6(1) of the Universal Military Training and Service Act, in re: Cassius Marcellus Clay, Jr.," 7 September 1966, box 1, folder 15, "Clippings on Muhammad Ali, 1977, 1971," box 1, folder 16, Lawrence S. Grauman Papers, 1902–1971, Hanna Holborn Gray Special Collections Research Center, University of Chicago Library, Chicago IL; "Indictment of Cassius Clay on May 8, 1967, by Federal Grand Jury, Houston, Texas," LS 100–4558, file no. 25–330971, Muhammad Ali, FOIA, FBI; Montville, *Sting Like a Bee*, 79–101.
54. T. Oscar Smith to Chairman, Appeal Board, Western District of Kentucky Selective Service System, 25 November 1966, box 1, folder 15, Lawrence S. Grauman Papers, 1902–1971, Hanna Holborn Gray Special Collections Research Center, University of Chicago Library, Chicago IL; Quintana, "Muhammad Ali," 181–183; Wiggins, "Victory for Allah," 98; Kindred, *Sound and Fury*, 102; Rutter, "White Hopes," 196; Brandon E. Allen, "Black Athletic Activism and How It Shapes Africana Cultural Memory" (Master's thesis, Clark Atlanta University, 2022), 55.
55. After Ali defeated George Foreman and regained the heavyweight title in Zaire in 1974, he told Dave Kindred that he would have left the NOI years earlier, "but you saw what they did to Malcolm X." He couldn't leave the

organization, he said. "They'd shoot me, too." Kindred, *Sound and Fury*, 204; Leonard Shecter, "The Passion of Muhammad Ali," *Esquire*, April 1968, 158; *NYT*, 29 April 1967, 1; Roberts and Smith, *Blood Brothers*, 306.

56. Kindred, *Sound and Fury*, 109; and Remnick, *King of the World*, 285–291.

57. "Indictment of Cassius Clay on May 8, 1967, by Federal Grand Jury, Houston, Texas," LS 100–4558, file no. 25-330971, Muhammad Ali, FOIA, FBI; Hayden C. Covington, "Petition for a Writ of Certiorari to the United States Court of Appeals for the Sixth Circuit," Supreme Court of the United States, October Term, 1966; Covington, "Notice of Petition for an Order Staying Orders of District Court and for an Injunction Pending Appeal," Supreme Court of the United States, October Term, 1966; Covington, "Motion for Leave to File Petition and Petition for Writ of Mandamus and Supporting Brief," Supreme Court of the United States, October Term, 1966; Covington and Ernest Woodward, II, "Petition for Rehearing," Supreme Court of the United States, October Term, 1966; *Ali v. Breathitt*, 268 F. Supp. 63, 65 (W.D. Ky. 1967), stay denied, sub nom., *Ali v. Gordon*, 386 U.S. 1002 (1967); *Muhammad Ali, etc., et al. v. Edward T. Breathitt, Jr., Governor, etc., et al.*—Civil Action No. 5621, United States District Court for the Western District of Kentucky, Appendix, United States Court of Appeals for the Sixth Circuit, Lynn Covington-Elfers Collection, Muhammad Ali Center, Louisville KY; *Ali v. Connally*, 266 F. Supp. 345, 347 (S.D. Tex. 1967); Shecter, "The Passion of Muhammad Ali," 158; *NYT*, 29 April 1967, 1, 12, 10 September 1970, 67; Rutter, "White Hopes," 200–201.

58. Rutter, "White Hopes," 200–201; Taylor, "An Examination," 150–151.

59. *NYT*, 29 April 1967, 12; "Indictment of Cassius Clay on May 8, 1967, by Federal Grand Jury, Houston, Texas," LS 100–4558, file no. 25-330971, Muhammad Ali, FOIA, FBI; Quintana, "Muhammad Ali," 184–186; Rutter, "White Hopes," 201–202; Allen, "Black Athletic Activism," 53–54.

60. Plimpton, *Shadow Box*, 130; Quintana, "Muhammad Ali," 185.

61. Quintana, "Muhammad Ali," 185; Harry Edwards, *The Revolt of the Black Athlete* (Free Press, 1969), 31; Kindred, *Sound and Fury*, 113.

62. "The Dissenting Champion," *National Review*, 16 May 1967, 504–506; Taylor, "An Examination," 154.

63. Richardson, "Ali on Peachtree," 47.

64. Roberts and Smith, *Blood Brothers*, 226.

65. Schulberg, *Loser and Still Champion*, 61; Smith, "The Resurrection," 19, 24; Taylor, "An Examination," 173.

66. Marqusee, *Redemption Song*, 179–180, 221.

67. Zirin, *A People's History of Sports*, 144.

68. Marqusee, *Redemption Song*, 222–223; "Dr. Martin Luther King, Jr. speaking at a press conference held at Ebenezer Baptist Church, Atlanta, Georgia, June 25, 1967," wsbn51565, WSB-TV Newsfilm Reel #1387, wsbn_1387, "Dr. Martin Luther King, Jr. criticizing the Vietnam War and praising Muhammad Ali for being a conscientious objector, April 30, 1967," wsbn51358, WSB-TV Newsfilm Reel #1381, wsbn_1381, WSB-TV Newsfilm Collection, Walter J. Brown Media Archives and Peabody Awards Collection, University of Georgia, Athens GA.
69. Early, "The Mortality of Kings," 53; Kindred, *Sound and Fury*, 131.
70. Tex Maule, "The Once and Future King?," *Sports Illustrated*, 10 July 1967, 18–21; "Souvenir Program."
71. *Chicago Tribune*, 21 June 1967, 1, 2; NYT, 20 June 1967, 1; "Special Investigative Division Report," 5 June 1967, file no. 25-330971, Muhammad Ali, FOIA, FBI; Rutter, "White Hopes," 203; Taylor, "An Examination," 157.
72. *Clay v. United States* (Clay I), 397 F.2d 901, 905 (5th Cir. 1968); *United States v. Clay* (Clay II), 430 F.2d 165, 166 (5th Cir. 1970); J.H. Gale to Mr. DeLoach, 21 May 1969, and SAC Houston (25-17618) to Director, FBI (25-531360), 4 June 1969, file no. 25-330971, Muhammad Ali, FOIA, FBI; Kindred, *Sound and Fury*, 127; Quintana, "Muhammad Ali," 187–188.
73. *Ali v. Div. of State Athletic Comm'n of N.Y.*, 308 F. Supp. 11, 14 (S.D.N.Y. 1969); Quintana, "Muhammad Ali," 188–189.
74. Gilmore, "The Greatest of All Time," 35; Gerald Early, "Tales of the Wonderboy," in *The Muhammad Ali Reader*, ed. Gerald Early (Ecco, 1998), xix; Hauser, *Muhammad Ali*, 209; Shecter, "The Passion of Muhammad Ali," 129.
75. Kindred, *Sound and Fury*, 123–124.
76. Shecter, "The Passion of Muhammad Ali," 158; Cleveland (100-26690) to Director, Houton, Chicago and Louisville, 4 June 1967, file no. 25-330971, Muhammad Ali, FOIA, FBI; Taylor, "An Examination," 156.
77. Williams, "'The People's Champion,'" 19; Zirin, *A People's History of Sports*, 155.
78. Amy Bass, *Not the Triumph but the Struggle: The 1968 Olympics and the Making of the Black Athlete* (University of Minnesota Press, 2002), 135; Harry Edwards, *The Struggle That Must Be* (Macmillan, 1980), 174–175; Edwards, *The Revolt of the Black Athlete*, 58–59.
79. Bass, *Not the Triumph but the Struggle*, 33–35.
80. Edwards, *The Revolt*, 74, 89–90; Roberts and Smith, *Blood Brothers*, xviii, 112; Jeffrey T. Sammons, "Rebel with a Cause: Muhammad Ali as Sixties Protest Symbol," *Muhammad Ali: The People's Champ*, ed. Elliott J. Gorn (University of Illinois Press, 1995), 159; Othello Harris, "Muhammad Ali," 66.

81. Bass, *Not the Triumph*, 138.
82. Harris, "Muhammad Ali," 64.
83. Edwards, *The Revolt*, 142–166; Sammons, "Rebel with a Cause," 162.
84. Bass, *Not the Triumph*, 193–194.
85. Pete Axthelm, "The Angry Black Athlete," *Newsweek*, 15 July 1968, 56; Bass, *Not the Triumph*, 211.
86. NYT, 14 August 1967, 22; Taylor, "An Examination," 171; Shecter, "The Passion of Muhammad Ali," 128.
87. Joe Frazier with Phil Berger, *Smokin' Joe: The Autobiography* (Macmillan, 1996), 67; Early, "The Mortality of Kings," 61–62; Mark Kram, *Ghosts of Manila: The Fateful Blood Feud Between Muhammad Ali and Joe Frazier* (HarperCollins, 2001), 24–25.

3. GROWING PAINS

1. James Earl Jones with Penelope Niven, *James Earl Jones: Voices and Silences* (Charles Scribner's Sons, 1993), 197–198; Roberts, *Papa Jack*, 228; "Jack Johnson Goes to Hollywood," *The Ring* 49 (October 1970): 13; Kindred, *Sound and Fury*, 219; Rutter, "White Hopes," 206–207; AV, 12 January 1969, 5; NYT, 4 October 1968, 40.
2. Roberts, *Papa Jack*, 11; Al-Tony Gilmore, *Bad Nigger! The National Impact of Jack Johnson* (Kennikat, 1975), 5.
3. William H. Wiggins, Jr., "Jack Johnson as Bad Nigger: The Folklore of His Life," *Black Scholar* 2 (January 1971): 4–19; Gilmore, *Bad Nigger!*, 12, 16, 18, 21, 149–150.
4. Mark Kram, "He Moves Like Silk, Hits Like a Ton," *Sports Illustrated*, 26 October 1970, 16.
5. Bond, *A Time to Speak, A Time to Act*, 74.
6. AC, 14 January 1969, 10A, 21 January 1969, 7A.
7. ADW, 16 January 1970, 3; AC, 16 January 1969, 1A, 11A, 22 January 1969, 6A, 24 January 1969, 11A, 27 March 1969, 14A; "Leroy Johnson on MLK Day in Georgia 1969," WALB-TV Newsfilm Collection [1968–1969], walb_0787, WALB-TV Newsfilm Collection, Walter J. Brown Media Archives and Peabody Awards Collection, University of Georgia, Athens GA.
8. Eliza Paschall, "Urban Observatory," *The Great Speckled Bird*, 13 January 1969, 6.
9. AC, 29 January 1969, 12A, 30 January 1969, 8A.
10. AC, 10 March 1969, 40A, 20 March 1969, 14A, 20 April 1969, 27A.
11. Harmon, "Beneath the Image," 465, 467–468; Allen, *Mayor*, 220–222.
12. Quotes from Hobson, *The Legend of the Black Mecca*, 57. Hobson even characterizes Johnson's politics as "white business in blackface."

13. AC, 23 April 1969, 5A; AI, 3 May 1969, 1, 12; Eliza Paschall, "Paschall On . . . ," *The Great Speckled Bird*, 5 May 1969, 12; Harmon, "Beneath the Image," 468–469; Hobson, *The Legend of the Black Mecca*, 53–54; Stone, *Regime Politics*, 78; Hornsby, "The Negro in Atlanta Politics," 23–24; Allen, *Atlanta Rising*, 164.
14. "A Statement by Senator Leroy Johnson," 27 August 1969, box 88, folder 18, James P. Brawley Collection, Atlanta University Center Robert W. Woodruff Library Archives Research Center, Atlanta GA; AC, 30 April 1969, 3A, 2 May 1969, 31A, 23 May 1969, 6A, 20 June 1969, 4A, 25 August 1969, 1A, 8A, 28 August 1969, 1A; AI, 13 September 1969, 1; Stone, *Regime Politics*, 78–79; Bayor, *Race and the Shaping of Twentieth-Century Atlanta*, 42–43.
15. Donald Grant went so far as to say, "In part, Jackson had Leroy Johnson's shrewd machinations to thank for his rise." AC, 3 October 1969, 1A; AI, 15 March 1969, 1, 21 June 1969, 1, 13 September 1969, 1, 12; Lesher, "Leroy Johnson Outslicks Mister Charlie," 40–41; Grant, *The Way It Was*, 438; Hornsby, *Black Power in Dixie*, 126; Harmon, *Beneath the Image*, 231–234. Franklin quote from Pomerantz, *Where Peachtree Meets Sweet Auburn*, 386.
16. AI, 3 May 1969, 1, 4 October 1969, 2; AV, 12 January 1969, 1, 14 August 1969, 12.
17. The two were both alumni of North Carolina College in Durham; they would remain relative allies, though their different strategies often created tension. Pomerantz, *Where Peachtree Meets Sweet Auburn*, 385.
18. Hobson, *The Legend of the Black Mecca*, 54–55; AV, 5 October 1969, 1, 3, 4, 26; Rooks, *The Atlanta Elections*, 6; Bond, *A Time to Speak*, 79–80.
19. AI, 11 October 1969, 1, 18 October 1969, 1, 20 October 1969, 1, 25 October 1969, 1, 2; AV, 12 October 1969, 1, 26 October 1969, 1, 2; Farokhi, "The Influences," 4, 123–124; Rooks, *The Atlanta Elections*, 2–3, 17, 19, 34–35, 41, 60, 68; Pomerantz, *Where Peachtree Meets Sweet Auburn*, 389–392; Fred Powledge, "Profiles—A New Politics in Atlanta," *New Yorker*, 31 December 1973, 34; Hein, "The Image," 220–221.
20. Harmon, *Beneath the Image*, 19–20; Hornsby, *Black Power in Dixie*, xvii.
21. Maude, "Politics: Hurrah for the Red, Black, and Blue!" *The Great Speckled Bird*, 12 May 1969, 12.
22. Smith, "The Resurrection," 10.
23. AC, 30 March 1969, 18B, 11 July 1969, 69.
24. *Macon Telegraph*, 21 August 1969, 12.
25. AC, 9 January 1969, 45, 30 April 1969, 16, 12 July 1969, 16A, 21 August 1969, 11D, 6 February 1970, 23A.
26. AI, 26 April 1969, 1, 14; AV, 27 April 1969, 3; Grady-Willis, "A Changing Tide," 217–218.

27. Grady-Willis, "A Changing Tide," 217–218; *AI*, 26 April 1969, 1, 14.
28. *AI*, 3 May 1969, 2.
29. *AV*, 27 April 1969, 4, 5.
30. *AV*, 6 July 1969, 4; Grady-Willis, "A Changing Tide," 221.
31. *AC*, 19 August 1969, 1A, 9A; *Macon Telegraph*, 20 August 1969, 17.
32. Bingham and Wallace, *Muhammad Ali's Greatest Fight*, 209–210; *Muhammad Speaks*, 11 April 1969, 2, 3; *AV*, 13 April 1969, 9; Kindred, *Sound and Fury*, 133; Taylor, "An Examination," 158–159.
33. Bingham and Wallace, *Muhammad Ali's Greatest Fight*, 209–210.
34. Shecter, "The Passion of Muhammad Ali," 130.
35. Clegg, *Life and Times*, 248.
36. Bingham and Wallace, *Muhammad Ali's Greatest Fight*, 211.
37. Schulberg, *Loser and Still Champion*, 58–59; Kindred, *Sound and Fury*, 48.
38. Eig, *Ali*, 288; Bingham and Wallace, *Muhammad Ali's Greatest Fight*, 212; "Muhammad Ali and the Negro Movement," 12 December 1968, Program 130, 80040.130, Firing Line Broadcast Records, Hoover Institution Library and Archives, Stanford University, Palo Alto CA.
39. *AC*, 20 August 1969, 1C, 2C, 22 August 1969, 5C; *Macon Telegraph*, 26 August 1969, 6, 28 August 1969, 1, 2; "Muhammad Ali Chronology," received from M.A. Project, Inc., volume II, permanent collection, Muhammad Ali Center, Louisville KY. Howard Bingham and Max Wallace have claimed that Lester Maddox was behind the Macon rejection, but that is not the case. Bingham and Wallace, *Muhammad Ali's Greatest Fight*, 226.
40. Bingham and Wallace, *Muhammad Ali's Greatest Fight*, 230.
41. Shecter, "The Passion of Muhammad Ali," 130; Bingham and Wallace, *Muhammad Ali's Greatest Fight*, 217, 218; "Muhammad Ali Chronology"; Kindred, *Sound and Fury*, 122, 130; "Chauncey Eskridge Dies; Legal Counsel To MLK, Ali," *Jet*, 8 February 1988, 14; Smith, "The Resurrection," 9; Taylor, "An Examination," 158.
42. Pete Hamill, "The Disintegration of a Folk Hero," in *The Muhammad Ali Reader*, ed. Gerald Early (HarperCollins, 1998), 123.
43. Kram, *Ghosts of Manila*, 26; Hauser, *Muhammad Ali*, 185–186; Montville, *Sting Like a Bee*, 185–200.
44. "Champburger Corporation Prospectus," 23 December 1968, permanent collection, Muhammad Ali Center, Louisville KY; Bingham and Wallace, *Muhammad Ali's Greatest Fight*, 220–221.
45. "Muhammad Ali Chronology"; *AV*, 14 June 1969, 1, 2.
46. *AC*, 6 April 1969, 3A.
47. See in particular Montville, *Sting Like a Bee*; Bingham and Wallace, *Muhammad Ali's Greatest Fight*.

48. AC, 1 June 1969, 24A.
49. AC, 8 June 1969, 2A.
50. Hauser, *Muhammad Ali*, 211; Davis, "The 13th Round," 23, 26.
51. AC, 17 October 1970, 2C; NYT, 5 January 1999, A15; Davis, "The 13th Round," 23, 26.
52. Davis, "The 13th Round," 26.
53. Norman Mailer, "Ego," in *The Muhammad Ali Reader*, ed. Gerald Early (HarperCollins, 1998), 103.
54. Davis, "The 13th Round," 26. In 1964 Quarry married Mary Kathleen O'Casey; they met while working in a pizza parlor. At the time of his fight with Ali, they had two children, Jerry and Keri. "Souvenir Program."
55. Angelo Dundee with Mike Winters, *I Only Talk Winning* (Contemporary Books, 1985), 209–211; NYT, 5 January 1999, A15. It was also because Quarry was legitimately good. He had lost to Ellis, but he defeated Floyd Patterson, Buster Mathis, and Thad Spencer. He had solid showings, if losses, against Ellis, Frazier, and Chuvalo. One could only become a Great White Hope by giving white fans a reason to hope. Bernard Fernandez, "50 Years Ago, Muhammad Ali Launched a Comeback Unlike Any Other vs. Jerry Quarry," *Ring Magazine*, 26 October 2020, https://www.ringtv.com/612011-50-years-ago-muhammad-ali-launched-a-comeback-unlike-any-other-vs-jerry-quarry/.
56. AC, 5 June 1969, 55.
57. Early, "The Mortality of Kings," 51.
58. *AI*, 14 June 1969, 11.
59. AV, 14 June 1969, 3, 15.
60. NYT, 5 January 1999, A15; Davis, "The 13th Round," 26.
61. AV, 22 June 1969, 15.
62. "Bob Foster," BoxRec, https://boxrec.com/en/proboxer/9000.
63. "Community Relations Commission," 16 February 1967, box 7, folder 19, document 14, Ivan Allen Jr. Mayoral Records, Ivan Allen College of Liberal Arts, Georgia Institute of Technology, Atlanta GA, https://ivanallen.iac.gatech.edu/mayoral-records/traditional/items/show/3159.
64. Irwin Shaw, "Muhammad Ali and the Little People," *Esquire*, November 1969, 125–129, 100, 102, 104, 106.
65. AC, 14 October 1969, 2C.
66. Bingham and Wallace, *Muhammad Ali's Greatest Fight*, 213; Kindred, *Sound and Fury*, 132.
67. AC, 12 December 1969, 3D, 13 December 1968, 2C.
68. AC, 19 December 1969, 3D.

69. Bingham and Wallace, *Muhammad Ali's Greatest Fight*, 213–214; *Miami Herald*, 12 January 1970, 5D.
70. AC, 2 February 1970, 1C, 4C; Rutter, "White Hopes," 206; Bingham and Wallace, *Muhammad Ali's Greatest Fight*, 217.
71. AC, 2 February 1970, 1C, 4C; *Michigan Chronicle [MC]*, 18 July 1970, A1; *Philadelphia Tribune [PT]*, 24 October 1970, 21; "Muhammad Ali Chronology"; Bingham and Wallace, *Muhammad Ali's Greatest Fight*, 217.
72. *Los Angeles Sentinel [LAS]*, 9 July 1970, B1.
73. Bingham and Wallace, *Muhammad Ali's Greatest Fight*, 217–218; Jeffrey T. Sammons, *Beyond the Ring: The Role of Boxing in American Society* (University of Illinois Press, 1990), 209.
74. Martin Kane, "Welcome Back, Ali!" *Sports Illustrated*, 14 September 1970, 23.
75. *AI*, 28 June 1969, 4; AC, 26 June 1969, 27A.
76. AV, 14 June 1969, 4, 6 July 1969, 1, 3.
77. AC, 17 July 1969, 14A.
78. *AJ*, 11 September 1969, 4C, 18 September 1969, 1A, 12A, 20 September 1969, 5A, 5 October 1969, 16A; AC, 19 September 1969, 1C; *AI*, 20 September 1969, 1, 16, 27 September 1969, 1; AV, 21 September 1969, 1, 2.
79. *AJ*, 11 September 1969, 4C, 18 September 1969, 1A, 12A, 20 September 1969, 5A, 5 October 1969, 16A; AC, 19 September 1969, 1C; AV, 12 January 1969, 2; Kimberly Marissa James, "Challenges to Control? Atlanta's Maynard Jackson and the Politics of Police Reform" (PhD diss., University of Michigan, 2002), 126–127, 141–142, 158.
80. AC, 14 October 1969, 10A; Hobson, *The Legend of the Black Mecca*, 68.
81. AC, 20 October 1969, 4A; Grant, *The Way It Was*, 438; Hobson, *The Legend of the Black Mecca*, 53–55, 57.
82. AV, 16 March 1969, 4.
83. "Johnson, Jordan Map Races," 10 March 1969, Voter Education Project Organizational Records, Atlanta University Center Robert W. Woodruff Library Archives Research Center, Atlanta GA; Hobson, *The Legend of the Black Mecca*, 55–56; Hudson and Mirza, "Controversial Comeback in Atlanta," 42; Allen, *Atlanta Rising*, 164; Pomerantz, *Where Peachtree Meets Sweet Auburn*, 384; James, "Challenges to Control?," 48.
84. AC, 21 October 1969, 1A, 8A; Hudson and Mirza, "Controversial Comeback in Atlanta," 43.
85. Minutes, Board of Aldermen, City of Atlanta, book 12, 5 January 1970, 602, 603, 605, City of Atlanta Records, Atlanta History Center, Atlanta GA; AV, 12 January 1969, 14; AC, 22 October 1969, 1A, 11A.
86. AC, 27 October 1969, 7C.

87. *AV*, 8 February 1970, 3, 8.
88. *AC*, 6 November 1969, 14A, 8 November 1969, 10A, 13 November 1969, 1B, 14 November 1969, 23A; *AV*, 2 November 1969, 1, 2; Grady-Willis, "A Changing Tide," 209–210.
89. *AV*, 9 November 1969, 1, 8, 16 November 1969, 1, 3, 23 November 1969, 1, 2, 30 November 1969, 3, 7 December 1969, 3, 18 January 1970, 3; Brown-Nagin, "Class Actions," 173, 178–179, 187, 191.
90. *AC*, 27 November 1969, 4A, 30 November 1969, 16C, 13 December 1969, 5A, 29 January 1970, 8B, 4 February 1970, 10A, June 30 1970, 6A, 2 July 1970, 7B; *AV*, 8 February 1970, 2.
91. Harmon, "Beneath the Image," 493–494; Harmon, *Beneath the Image*, 244; Bayor, *Race and the Shaping of Twentieth-Century Atlanta*, 88; James, "Challenges to Control?," 44–45.
92. *AV*, 23 November 1969, 1, 2; *AC*, 18 November 1969, 6A; *AI*, 1 March 1969, 1, 9.
93. *AC*, 30 November 1969, 1C.
94. *AC*, 29 January 1970, 1A, 8A, 30 January 1970, 9A.
95. Lesher, "Leroy Johnson," 43.
96. Minutes, Board of Aldermen, City of Atlanta, book 12, 19 January 1970, 605, 627, 653–654, City of Atlanta Records, Atlanta History Center, Atlanta GA; *ADW*, 12 February 1970, 1; *AC*, 8 February 1970, 1A, 12 February 1970, 8A, 15 February 1970, 26A, 17 February 1970, 6A, 20 February 1970, 14A, 22 February 1970, 22A.
97. Bingham and Wallace, *Muhammad Ali's Greatest Fight*, 219; "Muhammad Ali Chronology"; Montville, *Sting Like a Bee*, 238–252; Rutter, "White Hopes," 206.

4. POLITICS OF RACE

1. *AI*, 10 January 1970, 1.
2. *AC*, 10 January 1970, 1A, 9A, 11A, 24 January 1970, 10A.
3. *AC*, 10 January 1970, 1A, 9A, 11A.
4. *ADW*, 15 January 1970, 4.
5. *ADW*, 20 January 1970, 6.
6. Odum-Hinmon, "The Cautious Crusader," 7–8; Gloria Blackwell, "Black-Controlled Media in Atlanta, 1960–1970: The Burden of the Message and the Struggle for Survival" (PhD diss., Emory University, 1973), v, 1.
7. *NYT*, 30 August 1970, 32.
8. *AI*, 17 January 1970, 1, 12, 24 January 1970, 2.
9. *AC*, 22 February 1970, 9A.
10. *AI*, 28 February 1970, 1, 3.

11. *AI*, 28 February 1970, 1, 6, 7 March 1970, 13; "Azira Hill," *Jet*, 20 December 1999, 20; Aiello, *White Ice*, 55–56; Lois Benjamin, *Three Black Generations at the Crossroads: Community, Culture, and Consciousness* (Rowman & Littlefield, 2007), 108–110.
12. *AI*, 28 February 1970, 1, 6, 7 March 1970, 13; "Vernon Beale," BoxRec, https://boxrec.com/ru/box-pro/91468.
13. *CD*, 3 March 1970, 26; *MC*, 21 March 1970, A5.
14. Allen, "Black Athletic Activism," 59; Roberts and Smith, *Blood Brothers*, 168–169; Rob Sneddon, *The Phantom Punch: The Story Behind Boxing's Most Controversial Bout* (Down East Books, 2016), 216.
15. Hauser, *Muhammad Ali*, 208; Bingham and Wallace, *Muhammad Ali's Greatest Fight*, 223; "Muhammad Ali Chronology"; Eig, *Ali*, 288.
16. Kindred, *Sound and Fury*, 132.
17. Davis, "Knockout," 119; *MC*, 7 March 1970, A3; *PT*, 2 May 1970, 12; *LAS*, 7 May 1970, B1.
18. *ADW*, 27 March 1970, 7.
19. *ADW*, 27 March 1970, 7.
20. Jones with Niven, *James Earl Jones*, 202, 210–211; Ali with Durham, *The Greatest*, 320; Roberts, *Papa Jack*, 228; *ADW*, 27 March 1970, 7, 2 April 1970, 6, 15 November 1970, 6.
21. *ADW*, 20 September 1970, 6; Kram, "He Moves Like Silk," 16; *CD*, 19 September 1970, 17.
22. *Norfolk Journal and Guide*, 7 March 1970, 13; *Afro-American [AA]*, 4 July 1970, 9; Dundee, *I Only Talk Winning*, 217; Earl Lewis, *In Their Own Interests: Race, Class, and Power in Twentieth-Century Norfolk, Virginia* (University of California Press, 1991), 26.
23. *Pittsburgh Courier [PC]*, 7 March 1970, 10, 14 March 1970, 12; Eldridge Cleaver, *Soul On Ice* (Dell, 1992), 117; Roberts and Smith, *Blood Brothers*, xvii.
24. For more, see Sammons, *Beyond the Ring*, 1, 30–47; David Scott, "Boxing: From Male Vocation to Neurotic Masculinity," *Sport in History* 37, no. 4 (2017): 469–482; David Scott, "The Boxing Gym as Masculine Space," *Sports in History* 40, no. 3 (2020): 356–369; John Hoberman, *Darwin's Athletes: How Sport Has Damaged Black America and Preserved the Myth of Race* (Mariner Books, 1997), 52–60.
25. *AA*, 21 March 1970, 8; *MC*, 21 March 1970, A2; *Norfolk Journal and Guide*, 28 March 1970, 12.
26. Hobson, *The Legend of the Black Mecca*, 58–59; Grady-Willis, "A Changing Tide," 255–256; *AV*, 22 March 1970, 1, 29 March 1970, 1, 19 April 1970, 1; *AI*, 21 March 1970, 1, 6; LaShier, "To Secure Improvements," 334, 335, 340, 342; Joseph A. McCartin, "'Fire the Hell Out of Them': Sanitation Workers'

Struggles and the Normalization of the Striker Replacement Strategy in the 1970s," *Labor: Studies in Working Class History of the Americas* 2 (Fall 2005): 69–70.

27. ADW, 27 March 1970, 1, 10 April 1970, 1, 12 April 1970, 1, 14 April 1970, 6; AC, 26 March 1970, 1A, 31 March 1970, 1A, 7 April 1970, 1A, 8 April 1970, 1A, 14A; AJ, 22 March 1970, 1A; AI, 28 March 1970, 1, 18 April 1970, 1, 3; Bob Goodman, "Strike Escalates," *The Great Speckled Bird*, 20 April 1970, 5; Harmon, *Beneath the Image of the Civil Rights Movement and Race Relations*, 241; Hornsby, *Black Power in Dixie*, 130–133; Grady-Willis, "A Changing Tide," 256–257; LaShier, "To Secure Improvements," 335, 347, 351.
28. Gene Guerrero, Jr., "Strike: Slim Victory," *The Great Speckled Bird*, 4 May 1970, 5; AI, 18 April 1970, 1; LaShier, "To Secure Improvements," 26–27, 154, 336; CD, 30 April 1970, 8.
29. AI, 11 April 1970, 1, 11 April 1970, 2; and LaShier, "To Secure Improvements," 360, 363.
30. LaShier, "To Secure Improvements," 339.
31. ADW, 6 April 1970, 4, 12 April 1970, 1, 14 April 1970, 6; AV, 5 April 1970, 1, 12 April 1970, 1, 19 April 1970, 1, 11, 26 April 1970, 1, 26 April 1970, 1, 11, 3 May 1970, 1, 2; AI, 4 April 1970, 1, 11 April 1970, 1, 10; AC, 9 April 1970, 1A, 10 April 1970, 4A, 11 April 1970, 1A, 5A, 13 April 1970, 14A, 17 April 1970, 1A, 20A, 23 April 1970, 1A, 4A, 19A, 27 April 1970, 4A, 5C; McCartin, "Fire the Hell Out of Them," 69–70; LaShier, "To Secure Improvements," 14; Grady-Willis, "A Changing Tide," 257; Harmon, "Beneath the Image," 487; Hobson, *The Legend of the Black Mecca*, 59.
32. AV, 26 April 1970, 1; PC, 2 May 1970, 1; Grady-Willis, "A Changing Tide," 258–259; LaShier, "To Secure Improvements," 370, 372.
33. AC, 14 May 1970, 1B, 26 May 1970, 6A; ADW, 17 May 1970, 1. Hill quoted in Davis, "Knockout," 120.
34. Hornsby, *Black Power in Dixie*, 138.
35. Stephen Tuck, "A City Too Dignified to Hate: Civic Pride, Civil Rights, and Savannah in Comparative Perspective," *Georgia Historical Quarterly* 79 (Fall 1995): 539–559; Matthew F. Delmont, *Half American: The Epic Story of African Americans Fighting World War II at Home and Abroad* (Viking, 2022), 288–289; Clare Russell, "Upheaval in Savannah: The Protest Cycle of a 'Short' Civil Rights Movement," *Journal of Contemporary History* 47 (October 2012): 773–792; Robert A. Pratt, *Selma's Bloody Sunday: Protest, Voting Rights, and the Struggle for Racial Equality* (Johns Hopkins University Press, 2017), 58–64, 67, 87–89; Hornsby, *Black Power in Dixie*, 139; Branch, *Pillar of Fire*, 124. See also Rolundus R. Rice, *Hosea Williams: A Lifetime of Defiance and Protest* (University of South Carolina Press, 2022).

36. AC, 2 August 1970, 14A.
37. ADW, 1 March 1970, 4.
38. AC, 11 August 1970, 3A.
39. ADW, 24 March 1970, 1.
40. AC, 16 January 1969, 7A; AJ, 6 May 1968, 1A; Robert Coram and Remer Tyson, "The Loser Who Won," *Atlanta Magazine*, November 1970, 43.
41. Muhammad Ali, "I'm Sorry, but I'm Through Fighting Now," *Esquire*, May 1970, 120–122; CD, 14 April 1970, 26; MC, 25 April 1970, A4; Bingham and Wallace, *Muhammad Ali's Greatest Fight*, 221.
42. Ali, "I'm Sorry," 122, 226–227.
43. MC, 16 May 1970, A3; CD, 26 September 1970, 35; "Messenger, Ex-Champ Mum on Ali's Reinstatement," *Jet*, 14 May 1970, 49.
44. Muhammad Ali, "The Black Scholar Interviews Muhammad Ali," in *The Muhammad Ali Reader*, ed. Gerald Early (HarperCollins, 1998), 87.
45. Roberts and Smith, *Blood Brothers*, 307.
46. AA, 25 April 1970, 7.
47. PC, 16 May 1970, 1.
48. PT, 16 May 1970, 1; *Norfolk Journal and Guide*, 23 May 1970, 1, 2.
49. John M. Shaw, *The Cambodian Campaign: The 1970 Offensive and America's Vietnam War* (University Press of Kansas, 2005); Wilfred P. Deac, *Road to the Killing Fields: The Cambodian War of 1970–1975* (Texas A&M University Press, 1997); Howard Means, *67 Shots: Kent State and the End of American Innocence* (Da Capo, 2016); Nancy K. Bristow, *Steeped in the Blood of Racism: Black Power, Law and Order, and the 1970 Shootings at Jackson State College* (Oxford University Press, 2020).
50. PT, 13 June 1970, 26.
51. William F. Russell, "Success is a Journey," *Sports Illustrated*, 8 June 1970, 82; AA, 13 June 1970, 8.
52. LAS, 14 May 1970, B2; CD, 13 June 1970, 35; AA, 20 June 1970, 4; Eig, *Ali*, 288; Hauser, *Muhammad Ali*, 208; Bingham and Wallace, *Muhammad Ali's Greatest Fight*, 225–226.
53. CD, 13 June 1970, 36.
54. AA, 27 June 1970, 1, 9; Dan Daniel, "The Real Story: Clay Fight Cash Lures Grabbers Galore but Vets Put Kibosh on Cassius," *The Ring*, October 1970, 6; Bingham and Wallace, *Muhammad Ali's Greatest Fight*, 226.
55. AA, 20 June 1970, 4.
56. LAS, 25 June 1970, B1.
57. *Mulloy v. United States*, 398 US 410 (1970). The ruling also overturned the conviction of Elliot Ashton Welsh, similarly sentenced after refusing to

say that he believed in a supreme being. *Welsh v. United States*, 398 US 333 (1970); AA, 27 June 1970, 1.

58. AA, 27 June 1970, 1, 9; *Norfolk Journal and Guide*, 4 July 1970, 12.
59. AA, 27 June 1970, 4; MC, 27 June 1970, A1.
60. *Michigan Catholic* editorial reprinted in MC, 11 July 1970, A4.
61. PT, 27 June 1970, 1; Matthew Countryman, *Up South: Civil Rights and Black Power in Philadelphia* (University of Pennsylvania Press, 2006), 120–129, 134–138, 164–178.
62. CD, 1 July 1970, 28; MC, 18 July 1970, A4.
63. LAS, 2 July 1970, B1, 24 August 1970, B1; Daniel, "The Real Story," 6.
64. Daniel, "The Real Story," 56.
65. John M. Smith, "The Riot of May 1970: A Humanistic Perspective," *Richmond County History* 7 (Summer 1975): 109; C. W. Herndon, "Summary of Investigation of the Augusta Riot," 30 November 1970, Georgia Bureau of Investigation, case no. 27–3001, p. 10–12, Lester Maddox Papers, box 1, folder 3, ahc.MSS135, Atlanta History Center, Atlanta GA [hereinafter cited as Herndon, "Summary"]; William Winn with D. L. Inman, "Augusta, Georgia," in *Augusta, Georgia and Jackson State University: Southern Episodes in a National Tragedy* (Southern Regional Council 1970), 35.
66. Herndon, "Summary," 42; Winn with Inman, "Augusta, Georgia," 17, 19–20, 27–30.
67. Herndon, "Summary," 25; Alexander J. Azarian and Eden Fesshazion, "The State Flag of Georgia: The 1956 Change In Its Historical Context," Senate Research Office (August 2000), Atlanta GA.
68. Winn with Inman, "Augusta, Georgia," 15, 45; Herndon, "Summary," 37, 40; Southern Regional Council, *Augusta, Georgia and Jackson State University: Southern Episodes in a National Tragedy* (Southern Regional Council, 1970), 10.
69. Winn with Inman, "Augusta, Georgia," 37–39.
70. AI, 4 July 1970, 1.
71. Lester G. Maddox, "Epitaph of World's Greatest Free Republic," Office of Georgia Governor, 1970, Lester Maddox Papers, box 2, folder 11, ahc.MSS135, Atlanta History Center, Atlanta GA.
72. AV, 5 July 1970, 2.

5. POLITICS OF BOXING

1. AA, 4 July 1970, 1; MC, 4 July 1970, 8, A6, 22 August 1970, 16; LAS, 16 July 1970, A1, A12, 23 July 1970, B1; Daniel, "The Real Story," 6.
2. AA, 4 July 1970, 8; *Norfolk Journal and Guide*, 4 July 1970, 12.

3. MC, 4 July 1970, 8; LAS, 16 July 1970, B1.
4. MC, 1 August 1970, D1.
5. PT, 7 July 1970, 16; AA, 11 July 1970, 8; *Norfolk Journal and Guide*, 18 July 1970, B21.
6. LAS, 25 June 1970, B1; Davis, "The 13th Round," 26.
7. Remnick, *King of the World*, 292.
8. Ali, "The Black Scholar," 83, 85.
9. Bingham and Wallace, *Muhammad Ali's Greatest Fight*, 224; Ali with Durham, *The Greatest*, 268; Davis, "Knockout," 119.
10. Dundee with Sugar, *My View from the Corner*, 137.
11. AC, 8 July 1970, 4C, 9 July 1970, 1D; LAS, 9 July 1970, B1, 16 July 1970, B1; PT, 11 July 1970, 18; Ali with Durham, *The Greatest*, 269; Dan Daniel, "Kiss of Death Lurks in World Heavy Ratings," *The Ring*, October 1970, 8; Bingham and Wallace, *Muhammad Ali's Greatest Fight*, 225.
12. MC, 15 August 1970, 1, 4, 22 August 1970, A1; AA, 29 August 1970, 8.
13. *Detroit Free Press*, 12 July 1970, 52; Bingham and Wallace, *Muhammad Ali's Greatest Fight*, 224.
14. AI, 8 August 1970, 1, 16.
15. AI, 8 August 1970, 1, 16, 22 August 1970, 1, 3; AV, 23 August 1970, 1, 6, 23 September 1970, 1.
16. ADW, 7 August 1970, 2, 20 August 1970, 5.
17. "Souvenir Program"; Lesher, "Leroy Johnson," 42; Smith, "The Resurrection," 13.
18. "Interview with Leroy Johnson, February 27, 2007," RBRL220ROGP-016, Reflections on Georgia Politics Oral History Collection, Richard B. Russell Library for Political Research and Studies, University of Georgia, Athens GA; Lesher, "Leroy Johnson," 42; Smith, "The Resurrection," 13; "Souvenir Program"; Hudson and Mirza, "Controversial Comeback in Atlanta," 42; Eig, *Ali*, 288. Johnson quoted in Davis, "Knockout," 120.
19. Kassel and Johnson quoted in Davis, "Knockout," 120, 121; *Fight Night*, episode 4, "If You Build It They Will Come," produced by Jeff Keating, aired 16 November 2020, on iHeart, https://www.iheart.com/podcast/1119-fight-night-72737532/episode/if-you-build-it-they-will-73897405/; "Souvenir Program"; Lesher, "Leroy Johnson," 42; Eig, *Ali*, 288.
20. Lesher, "Leroy Johnson," 41.
21. Davis, "Knockout," 120; Eig, *Ali*, 288–289; Scott Freeman, "Carrying the Torch," *Atlanta*, May 2001, 113.
22. AC, 13 August 1970, 1D, 6D; ADW, 28 April 1970, 5.
23. Scot M. Beekman, *Ringside: A History of Professional Wrestling in America* (Praeger, 2006), 110–122; David Shoemaker, *The Squared Circle: Life,*

Death, and Professional Wrestling (Penguin, 2014), 44; Tim Hornbaker, *National Wrestling Alliance: The Untold Story of the Monopoly that Strangled Professional Wrestling* (ECW, 2007), 294–295.

24. "Interview with Leroy Johnson, February 27, 2007."
25. Davis, "Knockout," 121; Hudson and Mirza, "Controversial Comeback in Atlanta," 42; Eig, *Ali*, 289.
26. Hudson and Mirza, "Controversial Comeback in Atlanta," 44; *AC*, 15 May 1970, 12B, 2 September, 1970, 14A; *NYT*, 5 September 1970, 27; "Interview with Leroy Johnson, February 27, 2007."
27. *AC*, 26 October 1970, 3C; Hauser, *Muhammad Ali*, 210.
28. Hauser, *Muhammad Ali*, 209; *AC*, 14 August 1970, 1D; *NYT*, 14 August 1970, 39.
29. Early, "The Mortality of Kings," 62.
30. *AC*, 14 August 1970, 1D, 4D; Bingham and Wallace, *Muhammad Ali's Greatest Fight*, 227.
31. *AC*, 14 August 1970, 1D, 4D; *AI*, 29 August 1970, 1, 5 September 1970, 1; *AV*, 6 September 1970, 10; Smith, "The Resurrection," 15.
32. Ali with Durham, *The Greatest*, 268–270.
33. Ali with Durham, *The Greatest*, 270–271.
34. James Vaughn Paschal and Mae Armster Kendall, *Paschal: Living the Dream* (iUniverse, 2006), 103–104; Ali with Durham, *The Greatest*, 272–275.
35. Lesher, "Leroy Johnson," 42.
36. Michael Ezra, *Muhammad Ali: The Making of an Icon* (Temple University Press, 2009), 149; *AC*, 15 August 1970, 4A.
37. *ADW*, 16 August 1970, 1.
38. "Man on the Street Comments on the Idea of Atlanta Hosting the Boxing Championship, August 14, 1970," wsbn60449, WSB-TV Newsfilm Reel #1664, wsbn_1664, WSB-TV Newsfilm Collection, Walter J. Brown Media Archives and Peabody Awards Collection, University of Georgia, Athens GA.
39. *AC*, 16 August 1970, 2C; *AI*, 3 October 1970, 2; "Interview with Leroy Johnson, February 27, 2007"; Bingham and Wallace, *Muhammad Ali's Greatest Fight*, 227.
40. *AC*, 16 August 1970, 2C.
41. *AC*, 18 August 1970, 1C, 4C.
42. *AC*, 19 August 1970, 1C.
43. *NYT*, 26 August 1970, 51; *AC*, 20 August 1970, 1C, 3C; Early, "The Mortality of Kings," 52–53.
44. *AC*, 20 August 1970, 1C, 3C.
45. *AC*, 20 August 1970, 6A, 21 August 1970, 14A, 27 August 1970, 9A.

46. *AC*, 30 August 1970, 1A, 9A.
47. *NYT*, 30 August 1970, 32; Grant, *The Way It Was*, 436–437.
48. *AC*, 11 June 1970, 17A; Randy Sanders, "The Sad Duty of Politics: Jimmy Carter and the Issue of Race in His 1970 Gubernatorial Campaign," *Georgia Historical Quarterly* 76 (Fall 1992): 627–628; Kenneth E. Morris, *Jimmy Carter: American Moralist* (University of Georgia Press, 1996), 187.
49. *PT*, 25 August 1970, 1; *CD*, 29 August 1970, 26; *LAS*, 3 September 1970, A1; *AC*, 23 August 1970, 8A.
50. *ADW*, 1 September 1970, 5; *NYT*, 2 September 1970, 44; Eig, *Ali*, 288; Rafiq, *Muhammad Ali*, 177–178; Davis, "Knockout," 121.
51. *AC*, 29 August 1970, 4C; *ADW*, 1 September 1970, 5; *NYT*, 2 September 1970, 44; *CD*, 29 August 1970, 25; Kane, "Welcome Back, Ali!" 20.
52. *AC*, 2 September 1970, 1C, 4C.
53. *AC*, 2 September 1970, 1C, 4C; *PC*, 31 October 1970, 8.
54. *ADW*, 3 September 1970, 6.
55. *AA*, 5 September 1970, 10; *PT*, 8 September 1970, 17; *MC*, 12 September 1970, A6.
56. *CD*, 9 September 1970, 5.
57. Kane, "Welcome Back, Ali!" 20.
58. *ADW*, 6 September 1970, 1; *AI*, 12 September 1970, 13; *AC*, 3 September 1970, 1D; *Norfolk Journal and Guide*, 19 September 1970, 12, 13; Ali with Durham, *The Greatest*, 279–280.
59. Kane, "Welcome Back, Ali!" 20.
60. *AC*, 3 September 1970, 1D, 7D; *AA*, 12 September 1970, 9; *LAS*, 10 September 1970, B4; Davis, "Knockout," 121.
61. Davis, "Knockout," 121.
62. Kane, "Welcome Back, Ali!" 23; Eig, *Ali*, 289.
63. *AC*, 3 September 1970, 7D.
64. *AA*, 12 September 1970, 4, 8, 9.
65. Hornsby, "Black Public Education," 35.
66. Kane, "Welcome Back, Ali!" 23.
67. *AI*, 19 September 1970, 12; *ADW*, 15 September 1970, 5.
68. *PT*, 12 September 1970, 18.
69. *AC*, 3 September 1970, 7D.
70. *AC*, 5 September 1970, 2C; Davis, "Knockout," 121.
71. Ali had fought white fighters in Europe since 1962, including German Karl Mildenberger in 1966 and Englishman Henry Cooper twice—once in 1963 before Clay's conversion and again as Ali in 1966. *AC*, 10 September 1970, 1D, 7D; Eig, *Ali*, 290, 294; Hauser, *Muhammad Ali*, 210; *NYT*, 10 September 1970, 67; Rutter, "White Hopes," 209; Richardson, "Ali on Peachtree," 49.

72. AC, 10 September 1970, 1D, 7D, 11 September 1970, 1D; Les Krantz, *Ali in Action: The Man, the Moves, the Mouth* (Lyons, 2008), 67; Bingham and Wallace, *Muhammad Ali's Greatest Fight*, 227; Eig, *Ali*, 290, 294; Hauser, *Muhammad Ali*, 210; NYT, 10 September 1970, 67; LAS, 10 September 1970, B1, 17 September 1970, B2; CD, 12 September 1970, 30, 19 September 1970, 29; *Cleveland Call and Post*, 19 September 1970, 11B, 26 September 1970, 11B; AA, 19 September 1970, 8. Kassel quote from Davis, "Knockout," 149.
73. NYT, 10 September 1970, 67.
74. AC, 2 July 1910, 8, 3 July 1910, A3; Augustus Clark Wood, "The Sixth Finger: Jack Johnson, Muhammad Ali, and the Unconscious Race Hero in Hero" (Master's thesis, Clark Atlanta University, 2012), 132, 133.
75. Gilmore, *Bad Nigger!*, 3–4; Roberts, *Papa Jack*, 68, 91, 104, 105.
76. Roberts, *Papa Jack*, 108–110; AC, 5 July 1910, 1, 2, 3, 6 July 1910, 1.
77. Kram, "He Moves Like Silk," 19; Eig, *Ali*, 291–292; Hietala, "Muhammad Ali," 146; Kindred, *Sound and Fury*, 42.
78. Kram, "He Moves Like Silk," 19; Ali with Durham, *The Greatest*, 286–288.
79. NYT, 12 September 1970, 34.
80. Bingham and Wallace, *Muhammad Ali's Greatest Fight*, 227–228.
81. Axthelm, "The Return," 62.
82. Axthelm, "The Return," 62.
83. AC, 13 September 1970, 6A.
84. ADW, 20 September 1970, 4; and Boyd, *Georgia Democrats*, 165.
85. AC, 15 September 1970, 1C.
86. CD, 26 September 1970, 35; MC, 24 October 1970, A4.
87. AN, 17 October 1970, 38, 24 October 1970, 44.
88. LAS, 17 September 1970, B1, 24 September 1970, B1; AN, 19 September 1970, 16, 39; AA, 26 September 1970, 4; AC, 15 September 1970, 1C; "Muhammad Ali Chronology"; "The Ring Believes . . ." *The Ring*, January 1971, 6–7; Quintana, "Muhammad Ali," 189–190; Cosell, *Cosell*, 222; Hauser, *Muhammad Ali*, 214; Eig, *Ali*, 290; Bingham and Wallace, *Muhammad Ali's Greatest Fight*, 231.
89. Nat Fleischer, "Nat Fleischer Speaks Out," *The Ring*, January 1971, 5; L. Vettor, "The Clay Case, Again," *The Ring*, January 1971, 34.
90. AN, 19 September 1970, 16, 39; AA, 26 September 1970, 4.
91. LAS, 24 September 1970, B1.
92. AC, 15 September 1970, 1C.
93. ADW, 15 September 1970, 5.
94. AJ, 28 October 1983, 1C; Kindred, *Sound and Fury*, 135.
95. Minutes, Board of Aldermen, City of Atlanta, book 13, 21 September 1970, p. 73, City of Atlanta Records, Atlanta History Center, Atlanta GA.

96. AC, 20 September 1970, 11F; CD, 19 September 1970, 17; "Jack Johnson Goes to Hollywood," *The Ring*, October 1970, 13, 45.
97. AC, 20 September 1970, 11H, 2 October 1970, 1D.
98. AC, 20 September 1970, 11H; Davis, "Knockout," 121, 149; Eig, *Ali*, 288.
99. AC, 23 September 1970, 5C, 11 October 1970, 4H.
100. ADW, 18 October 1970, 10; AC, 25 September 1970, 2D, 29 September 1970, 2C; CD, 29 September 1970, 25; *Norfolk Journal and Guide*, 17 October 1970, 13.
101. ADW, 15 September 1970, 3.
102. AC, 24 September 1970, 6D.
103. CD, 3 October 1970, 30; AC, 26 September 1970, 1A, 4A.
104. ADW, 2 October 1970, 5; CD, 3 October 1970, 30; AC, 26 September 1970, 1A, 4A; NYT, 30 September 1970, 52.
105. Lesher, "Leroy Johnson," 39.
106. LAS, 1 October 1970, B1; *Norfolk Journal and Guide*, 17 October 1970, 12.
107. MC, 3 October 1970, B16.
108. AC, 1 October 1970, 4A.

6. RETURN OF THE KING

1. Kram, "He Moves Like Silk," 16, 18.
2. Kram, "He Moves Like Silk," 18.
3. Bingham and Wallace, *Muhammad Ali's Greatest Fight*, 228; Hietala, "Muhammad Ali," 146.
4. Ali with Durham, *The Greatest*, 290–292.
5. Ali with Durham, *The Greatest*, 294–299.
6. AC, 11 October 1970, 4H; CD, 14 October 1970, 30, 15 October 1970, 42.
7. AC, 16 October 1970, 3D; Torres, *Sting Like a Bee*, 22–23.
8. Davis, "Knockout," 149.
9. AN, 17 October 1970, 39; George Plimpton, "Watching the Man in the Mirror," *Sports Illustrated*, 23 November 1970, 87; Kindred, *Sound and Fury*, 90; Roberts and Smith, *Blood Brothers*, 97, 278; CD, 17 October 1970, 36.
10. LAS, 15 October 1970, B1; AC, 17 October 1970, 2C; Ali with Durham, *The Greatest*, 312–313.
11. Ali with Durham, *The Greatest*, 303–304; Bingham and Wallace, *Muhammad Ali's Greatest Fight*, 228; Smith, "The Resurrection," 22; Davis, "Knockout," 149. George Plimpton described the cook as Johnson's cousin, not his sister. Plimpton, "Watching the Man in the Mirror," 82.
12. Ali with Durham, *The Greatest*, 314–317; *Fight Night*, episode 1, "The Case of a Lifetime," produced by Jeff Keating, aired 26 October 2020, on iHeart, https://www.iheart.com/podcast/1119-fight-night-72737532/episode/the-case-of-a-lifetime-72956476/.

13. Davis, "Knockout," 149, 151.
14. "Cassius M. Clay, Sr., 1970, at Atlanta," Permanent Collection, Muhammad Ali Center, Louisville KY.
15. *AC*, 17 October 1970, 7T; *LAS*, 15 October 1970, B3A; *AN*, 17 October 1970, 21, 31 October 1970, 44; *PT*, 31 October 1970, 20; *CD*, 14 November 1970, 16.
16. *a.k.a. Cassius Clay*, dir. Jim Jacobs, Metro Goldwyn Mayer, 1970.
17. *AC*, 18 October 1970, 12H.
18. *CD*, 26 October 1970, 13, 24; *PT*, 20 October 1970, 19.
19. *LAS*, 22 October 1970, B2, B6.
20. *PT*, 24 October 1970, 19, 20.
21. *AC*, 18 October 1970, 12H.
22. *AN*, 24 October 1970, 5, 42; *CD*, 21 October 1970, 32; *LAS*, 8 October 1970, B4, 15 October 1970, B4, 22 October 1970, B6.
23. *CD*, 20 October 1970, 26; *AV*, 9 August 1970, 11; *PT*, 24 October 1970, 19; Roberts and Smith, *Blood Brothers*, 52.
24. *CD*, 20 October, 1970, 24; *AC*, 19 October 1970, 4C.
25. Enrico Beltramini, "S.C.L.C. Operation Breadbasket, from Economic Civil Rights to Black Economic Power," *Fire!!!* 2, no. 2 (2013): 6–7; LaShier, "To Secure Improvements," 22, 36.
26. *AC*, 20 October 1970, 1C, 6C, 22 October 1970, 1D.
27. *PT*, 27 October 1970, 2.
28. Kindred, *Sound and Fury*, 135; *AC*, 21 October 1970, 1C, 6C, 22 October 1970, 1D.
29. *CD*, 21 October 1970, 32, 24 October 1970, 29; *AC*, 21 October 1970, 1C, 6C; *MC*, 24 October 1970, A1; *AA*, 31 October 1970, 8.
30. *AC*, 21 October 1970, 1C.
31. *AC*, 21 October 1970, 3C.
32. *AC*, 22 October 1970, 1D, 8D; Schulberg, *Loser and Still Champion*, 65–66.
33. *AC*, 22 October 1970, 1D.
34. *AC*, 22 October 1970, 1D, 4D.
35. *NYT*, 24 October 1970, 45.
36. *ADW*, 25 October 1970, 10.
37. Daniel Lucks, "African American Soldiers and the Vietnam War: No More Vietnams," *The Sixties* 10, no. 2 (2017): 196–220; Wesley Abney, *Random Destiny: How the Vietnam War Draft Lottery Shaped a Generation* (Vernon, 2019), 57–58.
38. *AC*, 22 October 1970, 3D; *AI*, 24 October 1970, 1.
39. *AC*, 23 October 1970, 1D; *ADW*, 30 October 1970, 8; Fernandez, "50 Years Ago"; Krantz, *Ali in Action*, 68.
40. *AC*, 23 October 1970, 1D.

41. CD, 26 October 1970, 24; AC, 24 October 1970, 2C.
42. AC, 23 October 1970, 1D.
43. Ali with Durham, *The Greatest*, 308–310.
44. AC, 23 October 1970, 1D, 5D, 8D.
45. AC, 24 October 1970, 2C.
46. AC, 23 October 1970, 1D, 11D.
47. AC, 23 October 1970, 1D, 11D.
48. Schulberg, *Loser and Still Champion*, 78.
49. Smith, "The Resurrection," 19.
50. AC, 24 October 1970, 1C, 25 October 1970, 1H.
51. AC, 25 October 1970, 1H, 3H.
52. AC, 24 October 1970, 1C, 3C; AA, 31 October 1970, 8; Roberts and Smith, *Blood Brothers*, 41; Rafiq, *Muhammad Ali*, 178–179; Newfield, "The Meaning of Muhammad," 26.
53. PT, 24 October 1970, 21.
54. AC, 26 October 1970, 3C; CD, 28 October 1970, 32.
55. AC, 25 October 1970, 3H, 26 October 1970, 3C.
56. AC, 25 October 1970, 3H.
57. Davis, "Knockout," 151.
58. Richardson, "Ali on Peachtree," 46; Schulberg, *Loser and Still Champion*, 67.
59. Torres, *Sting Like a Bee*, 17–20.
60. AC, 26 October 1970, 1C.
61. AC, 26 October 1970, 1C, 3C; *Chicago Tribune*, 24 October 1970, B3; Smith, "The Resurrection," 7.
62. "Ali And Unidentified White Boxer Weigh In Before Boxing Match, October 26, 1970," wsbn61202, WSB-TV Newsfilm Reel #1685, wsbn_1685, WSB-TV Newsfilm Collection, Walter J. Brown Media Archives and Peabody Awards Collection, University of Georgia, Athens GA; Ali with Durham, *The Greatest*, 304–307; AC, 26 October 1970, 3C; Richardson, "Ali on Peachtree," 49.
63. "Ali And Unidentified White Boxer Weight In Before Boxing Match, October 26, 1970"; Richardson, "Ali on Peachtree," 49; Ali with Durham, *The Greatest*, 304–307; Lee Groves, "Muhammad Ali-Jerry Quarry I: Half a Century on from the Return of the Champion," *Ring Magazine*, 26 October 2020, https://www.ringtv.com/612026-muhammad-ali-jerry-quarry-i-half-a-century-on-from-the-return-of-the-champion/.
64. Quarry, meanwhile, was staying at the Matador Inn, a local motel. NYT, 23 October 1970, 57; Davis, "Knockout," 149.
65. Kindred, *Sound and Fury*, 136; Schulberg, *Loser and Still Champion*, 73; Robert Lipsyte, "'I Don't Have to Be What You Want Me to Be,' Says

Muhammad Ali," in *The Muhammad Ali Reader*, ed. Gerald Early (HarperCollins, 1998), 96.

66. Andrew J. Hale, "How Voice Operates in Popular Culture through the Performance Persona of Muhammad Ali" (Master's thesis, San Jose State University, 1994), 28; Art Evans, "Joe Louis as a Key Functionary: White Reactions toward a Black Champion," *Journal of Black Studies* 16 (September 1985): 100.
67. Dundee with Sugar, *My View from the Corner*, 65.
68. AC, 29 October 1970, 1D; Plimpton, "Watching the Man in the Mirror," 82–83; Plimpton, *Shadow Box: An Amateur in the Ring* (Little, Brown, 2016), 148–152; Hale, "How Voice Operates," 26–27; Schulberg, *Loser and Still Champion*, 72; Hietala, "Muhammad Ali," 147; Davis, "Knockout," 149.
69. Plimpton, "Watching the Man in the Mirror," 87–88.
70. Kram, "Smashing Return," 18.
71. Schulberg, *Loser and Still Champion*, 74–75.
72. Plimpton, "Watching the Man in the Mirror," 88; Torres, *Sting Like a Bee*, 23.
73. Schulberg, *Loser and Still Champion*, 81–83.
74. Kassel's claim seems plausible, but no record of any formal injunction exists. The only case law on record for the Federal District Court for the Northern District of Georgia on the day of the fight dealt with a Socialist Workers Party lawsuit against the state's attorney general. Davis, "Knockout," 152; *Georgia Socialist Workers Party v. Fortson*, 315 F. Supp. 1035.
75. Torres, *Sting Like a Bee*, 26; Schulberg, *Loser and Still Champion*, 81–83.
76. *LAS*, 22 October 1970, B2; *MC*, 24 October 1970, A2; *AN*, 24 October 1970, 42; *CD*, 24 October 1970, 30.
77. AC, 26 October 1970, 1A, 3C.
78. *LAS*, 22 October 1970, B1, 29 October 1970, B1, B2, B4, 5 November 1970, B4; *AN*, 31 October 1970, 1, 38; *PT*, 31 October 1970, 20.
79. Richardson, "Ali on Peachtree," 49; Schulberg, *Loser and Still Champion*, 69. Sugar quoted in Davis, "Knockout," 118.
80. Eig, *Ali*, 292–293; Kindred, *Sound and Fury*, 135; Davis, "Knockout," 150.
81. Richardson, "Ali on Peachtree," 48; Rutter, "White Hopes," 210.
82. AC, 27 October 1970, 4C.
83. *Fight Night*, episode 3, "Chicken Man," produced by Jeff Keating, aired 9 November 2020, on iHeart, https://www.iheart.com/podcast/1119-fight-night-72737532/episode/chicken-man-73479112/; Davis, "Knockout," 150; Kindred, *Sound and Fury*, 134; Richardson, "Ali on Peachtree," 48.
84. Richardson, "Ali on Peachtree," 49; Rutter, "White Hopes," 209–210.
85. Richardson, "Ali on Peachtree," 53.

86. AC, 27 October 1970, 4C, 28 October 1970, 4A; LAS, 29 October 1970, B4; PT, 31 October 1970, 20, 21; Torres, *Sting Like a Bee*, 26.
87. Lesher, "Leroy Johnson," 34; Bingham and Wallace, *Muhammad Ali's Greatest Fight*, 228.
88. Roberts and Smith, *Blood Brothers*, 277.
89. ADW, 29 October 1970, 8.
90. Ali with Durham, *The Greatest*, 332; Montville, *Sting Like a Bee*, 268–275.
91. "Souvenir Program."
92. "Souvenir Program."
93. AC, 27 October 1970, 3C.
94. Davis, "Knockout," 151; Torres, *Sting Like a Bee*, 27; Smith, "The Resurrection," 23–24.
95. Roy Raskin, "Cosby Group Inks Golden Gloves Heavy Champ Moore," *The Ring*, October 1970, 32.
96. Plimpton, "Watching the Man in the Mirror," 88–91.
97. Fernandez, "50 Years Ago."
98. Davis, "Knockout," 151; Hauser, *Muhammad Ali*, 213.
99. Plimpton, "Watching the Man in the Mirror," 95–96.
100. Plimpton, "Watching the Man in the Mirror," 96, 101.
101. Davis, "Knockout," 151; Hietala, "Muhammad Ali," 146; Eig, *Ali*, 292–294; Hauser, *Muhammad Ali*, 213.
102. Plimpton, "Watching the Man in the Mirror," 102.
103. AC, 27 October 1970, 3C; Bingham and Wallace, *Muhammad Ali's Greatest Fight*, 229; Davis, "Knockout," 151.
104. Eig, *Ali*, 292.
105. Hauser, *Muhammad Ali*, 212; Ali with Durham, *The Greatest*, 324; Plimpton, *Shadow Box*, 161; Kindred, *Sound and Fury*, 136; Wood, "The Sixth Finger," 187.
106. Torres, *Sting Like a Bee*, 28.
107. AC, 27 October 1970, 6C; *Cleveland Call and Post*, 31 October 1970, 2A; PC, 31 October 1970, 8; "Return of the Ringmaster," *Time*, 9 November 1970, 35.
108. ADW, 29 October 1970, 8; AC, 27 October 1970, 3C; AI, 31 October 1970, 14; Torres, *Sting Like a Bee*, 29–35; Eig, *Ali*, 295; CD, 27 October 1970, 24; *Cleveland Call and Post*, 31 October 1970, 2A; PC, 31 October 1970, 8; "Return of the Ringmaster," 35; Cosell, *Cosell*, 224–226; Groves, "Muhammad Ali-Jerry Quarry I." Young quote from Davis, "Knockout," 152.
109. AC, 27 October 1970, 1A, 3C; Hauser, *Muhammad Ali*, 212.
110. ADW, 29 October 1970, 8; AC, 27 October 1970, 1C, 3C, 4C; LAS, 29 October 1970, B1, B3; CD, 27 October 1970, 24; *Norfolk Journal and Guide*, 7 November 1970, 13; "Return of the Ringmaster," 35.

111. AC, 27 October 1970, 1C, 3C, 4C; Norman Mailer, "Ego," in *The Muhammad Ali Reader*, ed. Gerald Early (HarperCollins, 1998), 111.
112. Davis, "Knockout," 152; Kram, "Smashing Return of the Old Ali," 18; Eig, *Ali*, 295.
113. Hauser, *Muhammad Ali*, 212; Davis, "Knockout," 152.
114. Hauser, *Muhammad Ali*, 211.
115. CD, 28 October 1970, 32.
116. AC, 27 October 1970, 1C, 6C; CD, 27 October 1970, 24.
117. AC, 27 October 1970, 6C; MC, 31 October 1970, A1.
118. AC, 27 October 1970, 6C; Wiggins, "Victory for Allah," 105–106; Panos J. Voulgaris, "Muhammad Ali: An Unusual Leader in the Advancement of Black America" (Master's thesis, Harvard University, 2016), 74.
119. *Chicago Tribune*, 24 October 1970, B3; Ezra, *Muhammad Ali*, 150; Smith, "The Resurrection," 7, 24; Lipsyte, "I Don't Have to," 97; Freeman, "Carrying the Torch," 113.
120. Nat Loubet, "Now It's Frazier vs. Clay," *The Ring*, January 1971, 8–9.
121. AC, 27 October 1970, 4C.
122. CD, 27 October 1970, 24.
123. LAS, 29 October 1970, A6.
124. CD, 31 October 1970, 3; MC, 7 November 1970, 8; PC, 7 November 1970, 11.
125. AN, 31 October 1970, 42.
126. PC, 31 October 1970, 16.
127. AA, 7 November 1970, 4.
128. "Muhammad Ali Chronology."
129. "Muhammad Ali Chronology"; NYT, 28 October 1970, 79.
130. Julian Bond, "We Got Ali," Loose Leaf: Southern Cultures Unbound, Center for the Study of the American South, University of North Carolina, https://vimeo.com/127075065.
131. AC, 1 November 1970, 1E; Plimpton, *Shadow Box*, 162; Eig, *Ali*, 295.
132. *Fight Night*, episode 2, "A Hustler's Life," produced by Jeff Keating, aired 2 November 2020, on iHeart, https://www.iheart.com/podcast/1119-fight-night-72737532/episode/a-hustlers-life-73240767/.
133. *Fight Night*, episode 2, "A Hustler's Life"; *Fight Night*, episode 3, "Chicken Man," produced by Jeff Keating, aired 9 November 2020, on iHeart, https://www.iheart.com/podcast/1119-fight-night-72737532/episode/chicken-man-73479112/.
134. *Fight Night*, episode 4, "If You Build It They Will Come," produced by Jeff Keating, aired 16 November 2020, on iHeart, https://www.iheart.com/podcast/1119-fight-night-72737532/episode/if-you-build-it-they-will-73897405/.

135. Plimpton, *Shadow Box*, 168, 171; *Fight Night*, episode 5, "Fight Night," produced by Jeff Keating, aired 23 November 2020, on iHeart, https://www.iheart.com/podcast/1119-fight-night-72737532/episode/fight-night-74280495/.
136. ADW, 29 October 1970, 1; AN, 31 October 1970, 1; *Fight Night*, episode 6, "Everyone That Showed Up Got Held Up," produced by Jeff Keating, aired 30 November 2020, on iHeart, https://www.iheart.com/podcast/1119-fight-night-72737532/episode/everyone-that-showed-up-got-held-74538347/.
137. ADW, 29 October 1970, 1; AN, 31 October 1970, 1; PT, 31 October 1970, 36.
138. Eig, *Ali*, 293; Davis, "Knockout," 152.
139. Plimpton, *Shadow Box*, 167; *Fight Night*, episode 6, "Everyone That Showed Up Got Held Up"; *Fight Night*, episode 2, "A Hustler's Life."
140. Plimpton, *Shadow Box*, 163; *Fight Night*, episode 7, "Where The F*ck Are My Keys?!," produced by Jeff Keating, aired 7 December 2020, on iHeart, https://www.iheart.com/podcast/1119-fight-night-72737532/episode/where-the-fck-are-my-keys-74824978/.
141. *Fight Night*, episode 7, "Where The F*ck Are My Keys?!"; *Fight Night*, episode 8, "Into the Lion's Den," produced by Jeff Keating, aired 14 December 2020, on iHeart, https://www.iheart.com/podcast/1119-fight-night-72737532/episode/into-the-lions-den-75119208/; CD, 31 October 1970, 2; PT, 31 October 1970, 36; AN, 7 November 1970, 40.
142. AN, 7 November 1970, 1, 40; Plimpton, *Shadow Box*, 165; *Fight Night*, episode 6, "Everyone That Showed Up Got Held Up"; *Fight Night*, episode 8, "Into the Lion's Den."
143. Eig, *Ali*, 296; *Fight Night*, episode 8, "Into the Lion's Den"; *Fight Night*, episode 9, "From Atlanta to the Grave," produced by Jeff Keating, aired 21 December 2020, on iHeart, https://www.iheart.com/podcast/1119-fight-night-72737532/episode/from-atlanta-to-the-grave-75410367/.
144. Plimpton, *Shadow Box*, 165, 172; *Fight Night*, episode 9, "From Atlanta to the Grave"; *Fight Night*, episode 10, "Aftermath," produced by Jeff Keating, aired 28 December 2020, on iHeart, https://www.iheart.com/podcast/1119-fight-night-72737532/episode/aftermath-75622455/.
145. *Uptown Saturday Night*, dir. Sidney Poitier (First Artists/Warner Brothers, 1974), film; Davis, "Knockout," 152–154.
146. Schulberg, *Loser and Still Champion*, 80–81.
147. "Muhammad Ali Chronology"; Ali with Durham, *The Greatest*, 286, 332–333.
148. "Muhammad Ali on *The Tonight Show* October 1970," YouTube, https://www.youtube.com/watch?v=sfNouojnqhe, accessed 24 April 2024.

7. AFTER OCTOBER

1. AC, 26 October 1970, 3C, 28 October 1970, 1C.
2. AC, 28 October 1970, 1C, 5C; "Return of the Ringmaster," 35.
3. AC, 28 October 1970, 5C; CD, 4 November 1970, 34.
4. Hauser, *Muhammad Ali*, 211.
5. AC, 28 October 1970, 4A.
6. AC, 29 October 1970, 1D, 6D.
7. LAS, 5 November 1970, B3.
8. AC, 29 October 1970, 3D; Smith, "The Resurrection," 24.
9. AC, 29 October 1970, 3D, 3 November 1970, 3A, 10 November 1970, 4C, 15 November 1970, 15H; CD, 10 November 1970, 24; Minutes, Board of Aldermen, City of Atlanta, book 13, 2 November 1970, p. 120, City of Atlanta Records, Atlanta History Center, Atlanta GA; PT, 31 October 1970, 21; Fernandez, "50 Years Ago"; Smith, "The Resurrection," 24.
10. AC, 27 October 1970, 4C.
11. AC, 30 October 1970, 1D; AS, 31 October 1970, 42; PT, 3 November 1970, 17; CD, 5 November 1970, 37.
12. AC, 15 November 1970, 12H.
13. AC, 15 November 1970, 15H.
14. AC, 15 November 1970, 15H.
15. ADW, 5 November 1970, 1.
16. PT, 10 November 1970, 15; CD, 14 November 1970, 30.
17. PT, 31 October 1970, 20, 3 November 1970, 18; CD, 4 November 1970, 15; AN, 7 November 1970, 42.
18. AI, 7 November 1970, 14; AV, 8 November 1970, 4.
19. AI, 14 November 1970, 1, 14; AC, 16 November 1970, 5C, 18 November 1970, 4C; MC, 7 November 1970, A4.
20. AC, 18 November 1970, 4C.
21. AC, 19 November 1970, 1D, 3D.
22. AC, 19 November 1970, 1D, 3D, 20 November 1970, 1D.
23. AC, 3 December 1970, 1D.
24. ADW, 8 December 1970, 1; AC, 7 November 1970, 1A.
25. AC, 14 December 1970, 4A.
26. AC, 18 December 1970, 3C.
27. AC, 23 December 1970, 1A, 18A.
28. *The Dick Cavett Show*, "Lester Maddox Storms Off the Show," 18 December 1970, https://www.youtube.com/watch?v=7-8wnl5bspg, accessed 24 April 2024; "Dorothy Heckert to Lester Maddox, 19 December 1970," and

"Edward Miller to Lester Maddox, 19 December 1970," Lester Maddox Papers, box 1, folder 10, ahc.MSS135, Atlanta History Center, Atlanta GA.

29. AC, 9 December 1970, 1D; AI, 19 December 1970, 12; Torres, *Sting Like a Bee*, 53–58; Krantz, *Ali in Action*, 67; Montville, *Sting Like a Bee*, 275–280; Kindred, *Sound and Fury*, 137.
30. During the fight, at a closed-circuit venue in Philadelphia, a Black man was killed by an off-duty policeman after pulling a knife in an argument with another customer. Ali visited the funeral home to pay his respects to the man who was killed. NYT, 8 December 1970, 64; Kindred, *Sound and Fury*, 138–139.
31. Kram, *Ghosts of Manila*, 104.
32. AC, 10 December 1970, 1D, 11 December 1970, 1D, 3D; Krantz, *Ali in Action*, 69.
33. AC, 19 December 1970, 3C.
34. AC, 28 December 1970, 4C.
35. Early, "The Mortality of Kings," 63; AC, 30 December 1970, 2C, 31 December 1970, 3C.
36. Kindred, *Sound and Fury*, 154, 165.
37. "Bull v. Butterfly: A Clash of Champions," *Time*, 8 March 1971, 63; Lacy J. Banks, "The Biggest Fight in History," *Ebony*, March 1971, 135; Rutter, "White Hopes," 215; Hauser, *Muhammad Ali*, 219–220.
38. NYT, 19 January 1971, 43; PT, 16 February 1971, 1, 3, 20 February 1971, 22, 2 March 1971, 14; *Washington Times*, 4 April 1971, 161; Art Fisher and Neal Marshall, *Garden of Innocents* (E. P. Dutton, 1972), 16; Schulberg, *Loser and Still Champion*, 105; Robert E. Johnson, "World's Biggest Event Brings Mixed Reactions," *Jet*, 25 March 1971, 12; Kaliss, "Ali-Frazier 1," 1007–1008, 1013–1014.
39. AI, 27 February 1971, 10.
40. Lesher, "Leroy Johnson," 40.
41. Lesher, "Leroy Johnson," 40; Grant, *The Way It Was*, 438.
42. Lesher, "Leroy Johnson," 43–44.
43. AC, 13 January 1971, 1; Boyd, *Georgia Democrats*, 8, 202–203, 217.
44. AI, 24 January 1971, 2.
45. AI, 30 January 1971, 15. See also "Clippings, 1970–1971," box 9, folder 126, series VI, 100% Wrong Club Records, aarl011-007, Auburn Avenue Research Library on African-American Culture and History, Atlanta GA.
46. Pomerantz, *Where Peachtree Meets Sweet Auburn*, 395.
47. Mike Raffauf, "Lords of Squalor," *The Great Speckled Bird*, 27 December 1971, 5.

48. *Clay v. United States* (Clay III), 403 U.S. 698 (1971); *United States v. Clay* (Clay IV), 446 F.2d 1406 (5th Cir. 1971); *Sicurella v. United States*, 348 U.S. 385; *In the Matter of: Cassius Marcellus Clay, Jr. a/k/a Muhammad Ali, Petitioner vs. United States of America, Respondent, Supreme Court of the United States* [transcript] (Alderson Reporting Company, 1971); Montville, *Sting Like a Bee*, 310–313; Kindred, *Sound and Fury*, 172–174.
49. Quintana, "Muhammad Ali," 180, 194; Early, "The Mortality of Kings," 61; Newfield, "The Meaning of Muhammad," 29. See also *United States v. Reese*, 331 F. Supp. 1088 (1971).
50. Davis, "The 13th Round," 27; "Jerry Quarry versus Muhammad Ali Fight Poster," 27 June 1972, Permanent Collection, Muhammad Ali Center, Louisville KY; Davis, "Knockout," 154.
51. Ali with Durham, *The Greatest*, 324–328.
52. Ibid., 328–329.
53. Hans J. Massaquoi, "The Private World of Muhammad Ali," *Ebony*, September 1972, 148.
54. Davis, "The 13th Round," 27.
55. *NYT*, 5 January 1999, A15.
56. Davis, "The 13th Round," 27, 28.
57. Davis, "The 13th Round," 27–28.
58. Davis, "The 13th Round," 21, 23, 26–27, 28.
59. Davis, "The 13th Round," 21.
60. *NYT*, 5 January 1999, A15; Davis, "Knockout," 154.
61. Grant, *The Way It Was*, 438.
62. Harris, "Muhammad Ali," 65. For more, see Lewis A. Erenberg, *The Rumble in the Jungle: Muhammad Ali and George Foreman on the Global Stage* (University of Chicago Press, 2019).
63. "Campaign Flier, Leroy Johnson circa 1973," Maynard Jackson Mayoral Administrative Records, Atlanta University Center Robert W. Woodruff Library Archives Research Center, Atlanta GA; Hobson, *The Legend of the Black Mecca*, 65–66; Reed, *Stirrings in the Jug*, 167; Pomerantz, *Where Peachtree Meets Sweet Auburn*, 403; Farokhi, "The Influences," 128.
64. Hornsby, *Black Power in Dixie*, 136–138; Harmon, "Beneath the Image," 537, 543; Eisinger, *The Politics of Displacement*, 67; Pomerantz, *Where Peachtree Meets Sweet Auburn*, 403–405; Allen, *Atlanta Rising*, 177; James, "Challenges to Control?," 53.
65. Pomerantz, *Where Peachtree Meets Sweet Auburn*, 443; "Muhammad Ali Challenges Atlanta Mayor Maynard Jackson To Boxing Match, January 22, 1975," wsbn39359, WSB-TV Newsfilm Reel #245, wsbn_0245, WSB-

TV Newsfilm Collection, Walter J. Brown Media Archives and Peabody Awards Collection, University of Georgia, Athens ga.

66. Henderson, *Atlanta Life Insurance Company*, 198–199.
67. Kindred, *Sound and Fury*, 229, 249.
68. Fernandez, "50 Years Ago."
69. Davis, "Knockout," 154.
70. Smith, "The Resurrection," 24.
71. Axthelm, "The Return of an Exiled Champ," 67.
72. *AA*, 7 November 1970, 4.
73. *CD*, 11 November 1970, 5.
74. Grady-Willis, "A Changing Tide," 6.
75. Davis, "Knockout," 154.
76. Davis, "Knockout," 154.
77. Davis, "Knockout," 118.
78. Pomerantz, *Where Peachtree Meets Sweet Auburn*, 483.
79. Freeman, "Carrying the Torch," 114; Ezra, *Muhammad Ali*, 175; Rafiq, *Muhammad Ali*, 73, 216, 304.
80. Ezra, *Muhammad Ali*, 175–176.
81. Kram, *Ghosts of Manila*, 30.
82. Marqusee, *Redemption Song*, 2.
83. J. Michael Martinez, "The Georgia Confederate Flag Dispute," *Georgia Historical Quarterly* 92 (Summer 2008): 200–228.
84. Wood, "The Sixth Finger," 286.
85. Kindred, *Sound and Fury*, 308.
86. Bass, *Not the Triumph*, 348.
87. Marqusee, *Redemption Song*, 234.
88. Marqusee, *Redemption Song*, 2; Ezra, *Muhammad Ali*, 176–177.

BIBLIOGRAPHY

ARCHIVES AND MANUSCRIPT MATERIALS

100% Wrong Club Records, aarl011–007, Auburn Avenue Research Library on African-American Culture and History, Atlanta GA.

Carl E. Sanders Papers, Richard B. Russell Library for Political Research and Studies, University of Georgia Libraries, Athens GA.

City of Atlanta Records, Atlanta History Center, Atlanta GA.

Civil Rights Papers, MS-134, Department of Archives and Special Collections, Valdosta State University, Valdosta GA.

Democratic National Convention Records, Special Collections, Chicago Public Library, Chicago IL.

Draft Issue folder, Muhammad Ali Center, Louisville KY.

Firing Line Broadcast Records, Hoover Institution Library and Archives, Stanford University, Palo Alto CA.

Georgia Political Papers and Oral History Program, Special Collections, Ingram Library, University of West Georgia, Carrollton GA.

Greatest of All Time Collection, Muhammad Ali Center, Louisville KY.

Ivan Allen Jr. Mayoral Records, Ivan Allen College of Liberal Arts, Georgia Institute of Technology, Atlanta GA.

James P. Brawley Collection, Atlanta University Center Robert W. Woodruff Library Archives Research Center, Atlanta GA.

Jimmy Carter Papers-Pre-Presidential, 1962–1976, accession no. 80–1, Jimmy Carter Library, Atlanta GA.

Lawrence S. Grauman Papers, 1902–1971, Hanna Holborn Gray Special Collections Research Center, University of Chicago Library, Chicago IL.

Lester Maddox Papers, ahc.MSS135, Atlanta History Center, Atlanta GA.

Lynn Covington-Elfers Collection, Muhammad Ali Center, Louisville KY.

Maynard Jackson Mayoral Administrative Records, Atlanta University Center Robert W. Woodruff Library Archives Research Center, Atlanta GA.

Muhammad Ali, File No. 25-330971, Federal Bureau of Investigation, Washington DC.

Permanent Collection, Muhammad Ali Center, Louisville KY.

Reflections on Georgia Politics Oral History Collection, Richard B. Russell Library for Political Research and Studies, University of Georgia, Athens GA.

Thomas Gresham Collection of Lester Maddox Speech/Press Files, RBRL/022/TGLM, Richard B. Russell Library for Political Research and Studies, University of Georgia, Athens GA.

Voter Education Project Organizational Records, 0000-0000-0000-0076, Robert W. Woodruff Library of the Atlanta University Center, Inc., Atlanta GA.

WALB-TV Newsfilm Collection, Walter J. Brown Media Archives and Peabody Awards Collection, University of Georgia, Athens GA.

WSB-TV Newsfilm Collection, Walter J. Brown Media Archives and Peabody Awards Collection, University of Georgia, Athens GA.

PUBLISHED WORKS

Abney, Wesley. *Random Destiny: How the Vietnam War Draft Lottery Shaped a Generation*. Vernon, 2019.

Aiello, Thomas. *Dixieball: Race and Professional Basketball in the Deep South, 1947–1979*. University of Tennessee Press, 2019.

Aiello, Thomas. *White Ice: Race and the Making of Atlanta Hockey*. University of Tennessee Press, 2024.

a.k.a. Cassius Clay, dir. Jim Jacobs. Metro Goldwyn Mayer, 1970.

Ali, Muhammad. "The Black Scholar Interviews Muhammad Ali." In *The Muhammad Ali Reader*, edited by Gerald Early, 83–89. HarperCollins, 1998.

Ali, Muhammad, with Richard Durham. *The Greatest: My Own Story*. Random House, 1975.

Ali, Muhammad. "I'm Sorry, but I'm Through Fighting Now." *Esquire*, May 1970, 120–127.

Allen, Brandon E. "Black Athletic Activism and How It Shapes Africana Cultural Memory." Master's thesis, Clark Atlanta University, 2022.

Allen, Frederick. *Atlanta Rising: The Invention of an International City, 1946–1996*. Longstreet, 1996.

Allen, Ivan. *Mayor: Notes on the Sixties*. Simon & Schuster, 1971.

Axthelm, Pete. "The Angry Black Athlete." *Newsweek*, 15 July 1968, 56–60.

Axthelm, Pete. "The Return of an Exiled Champ." *Newsweek*, 9 November 1970, 56–67.

Azarian, Alexander J., and Eden Fesshazion. "The State Flag of Georgia: The 1956 Change in Its Historical Context." Senate Research Office (August 2000), Atlanta GA.

"Azira Hill." *Jet*, 20 December 1999, 20.

Baldwin, James. "Nobody Knows My Name: A Letter from the South." In *James Baldwin, Collected Essays*, edited by Toni Morrison, 199. Literary Classics, 1998.

Banks, Lacy J. "The Biggest Fight in History." *Ebony*, March 1971, 134–142.

Bass, Amy. *Not the Triumph but the Struggle: The 1968 Olympics and the Making of the Black Athlete*. University of Minnesota Press, 2002.

Bayor, Ronald H. *Race and the Shaping of Twentieth-Century Atlanta*. University of North Carolina Press, 1996.

Bayor, Ronald H. "Roads to Racial Segregation: Atlanta in the Twentieth Century." *Journal of Urban History* 15 (November 1988): 3–21.

Beekman, Scot M. *Ringside: A History of Professional Wrestling in America*. Praeger, 2006.

Beltramini, Enrico. "S.C.L.C. Operation Breadbasket, from Economic Civil Rights to Black Economic Power." *Fire!!!* 2, no. 2 (2013): 5–47.

Benjamin, Lois. *Three Black Generations at the Crossroads: Community, Culture, and Consciousness*. Rowman & Littlefield, 2007.

Bennett, Jr., Lerone. "Georgia's Negro Senator." *Ebony*, March 1963, 25–34.

Berg, Herbert. *Elijah Muhammad and Islam*. New York University Press, 2009.

Bingham, Howard, and Max Wallace. *Muhammad Ali's Greatest Fight: Cassius Clay vs. The United States of America*. M. Evans, 2000.

Bisher, Furman. *Atlanta Falcons: Violence and Victory*. Prentice Hall, 1973.

Bisher, Furman. *Miracle in Atlanta: The Atlanta Braves Story*. World Publishing, 1966.

Blackwell, Gloria. "Black-Controlled Media in Atlanta, 1960–1970: The Burden of the Message and the Struggle for Survival." PhD dissertation, Emory University, 1973.

"Bob Foster." BoxRec, https://boxrec.com/en/proboxer/9000.

Bond, Julian. *A Time to Speak, a Time to Act: The Movement in Politics*. Simon & Schuster, 1972.

Bond, Julian. "We Got Ali." Loose Leaf: Southern Cultures Unbound, Center for the Study of the American South, University of North Carolina, https://vimeo.com/127075065.

Boyd, Tim S. R. *Georgia Democrats, the Civil Rights Movement, and the Shaping of the New South*. University Press of Florida, 2012.

Branch, Taylor. *Pillar of Fire: America in the King Years, 1963–1965*. Simon & Schuster, 1998.

Brill, Steven. "Jimmy Carter's Pathetic Lies." *Harper's*, March 1976, 79.

Bristow, Nancy K. *Steeped in the Blood of Racism: Black Power, Law and Order, and the 1970 Shootings at Jackson State College*. Oxford University Press, 2020.

Brown-Nagin, Tomiko. "Class Actions: The Impact of Black and Middle-Class Conservatism on Civil Rights Lawyering in a New South Political Economy, Atlanta, 1946–1979." PhD diss., Duke University, 2002.

Brown-Nagin, Tomiko. *Courage to Dissent: Atlanta and the Long History of the Civil Rights Movement*. Oxford University Press, 2011.

Browning, Joan. "The Atlanta Wall." *Southern Patriot*, January 1963, 1, 4. MS/124, Department of Archives and Special Collections, Valdosta State University, Valdosta GA.

"Bull v. Butterfly: A Clash of Champions." *Time*, 8 March 1971, 63.

"Chauncey Eskridge Dies; Legal Counsel To MLK, Ali." *Jet*, 8 February 1988, 14.

Cleaver, Eldridge. *Soul on Ice*. Dell, 1992.

Clegg, III, Claude Andrew. *An Original Man: The Life and Times of Elijah Muhammad*. St. Martin's, 1997.

Cobb, James C. *The Selling of the South: The Southern Crusade for Industrial Development, 1936–1980*. Louisiana State University Press, 1982.

Cook, James F. *Carl Sanders: Spokesman of the New South*. Mercer University Press, 1993.

Coram, Robert, and Remer Tyson. "The Loser Who Won." *Atlanta*, November 1970, 43.

Cosell, Howard. *Cosell*. Pocket Books, 1974.

Countryman, Matthew. *Up South: Civil Rights and Black Power in Philadelphia*. University of Pennsylvania Press, 2006.

Coy, Daniel Bennett. "Imagining Dissent: Muhammad Ali, Daily Newspapers, and the State, 1966–1971." Master's thesis, University of Tennessee, Knoxville, 2004.

Daniel, Dan. "Kiss of Death Lurks in World Heavy Ratings." *The Ring*, October 1970, 8–9, 45.

Daniel, Dan. "The Real Story: Clay Fight Cash Lures Grabbers Galore but Vets Put Kibosh on Cassius." *The Ring*, October 1970, 6–7, 56.

Davis, David. "The 13th Round: How Boxing Made and Destroyed Jerry Quarry." *L.A. Weekly*, 17–23 March 1995, 21–30.

Davis, David. "Knockout: Muhammad Ali, Atlanta, and the Fight Nobody Wanted," *Atlanta*, October 2005, 116–121, 149–154.

Deac, Wilfred P. *Road to the Killing Fields: The Cambodian War of 1970–1975*. Texas A&M University Press, 1997.

""The 'Deep South'–Land With A Future: Atlanta." *US News & World Report*, 6 November 1961, 68.

Delmont, Matthew F. *Half American: The Epic Story of African Americans Fighting World War II at Home and Abroad*. Viking, 2022.

Denberg, Jeffrey, Roland Lazenby, and Tom Stinson. *From Sweet Lou to 'Nique*. Longstreet, 1992.

The Dick Cavett Show. "Lester Maddox Storms Off the Show," 18 December 1970, https://www.youtube.com/watch?v=7-8wnl5bspg. Accessed 24 April 2024.

"The Dissenting Champion." *National Review*, 16 May 1967, 504–506.

"Dr. King Views Atlanta Slum Areas." *SCLC Newsletter*, January-February 1966, 3.

Dundee, Angelo, with Bert Randolph Sugar. *My View from the Corner: A Life in Boxing*. McGraw Hill, 2008.

Dundee, Angelo, with Mike Winters. *I Only Talk Winning*. Contemporary Books, 1985.

Early, Gerald. "The Mortality of Kings: Ali versus Frazier." In *Rivals: Legendary Matchups That Made Sports History*, edited by David K. Wiggins and R. Pierre Rodgers, 49–67. University of Arkansas Press, 2010.

Early, Gerald. "Tales of the Wonderboy." In *The Muhammad Ali Reader*, edited by Gerald Early, vii—xx. Ecco, 1998.

Edwards, Harry. "The Olympic Project for Human Rights: An Assessment Ten Years Later." *Black Scholar* (March-April 1979): 2–8.

Edwards, Harry. *The Revolt of the Black Athlete*. Free Press, 1969.

Edwards, Harry. *The Struggle That Must Be*. Macmillan, 1980.

Egerton, John. *Speak Now Against the Day: The Generation Before the Civil Rights Movement in the South*. University of North Carolina Press, 1995.

Eig, Jonathan. *Ali: A Life*. Houghton Mifflin Harcourt, 2017.

Eisinger, Peter K. *The Politics of Displacement: Racial and Ethnic Transition in Three American Cities*. Academic, 1980.

Ellis, William S. "Atlanta, Pacesetter City of the South." *National Geographic* 135 (February 1969): 246–281.

Erenberg, Lewis A. *The Rumble in the Jungle: Muhammad Ali and George Foreman on the Global Stage*. University of Chicago Press, 2019.

Evans, Art. "Joe Louis as a Key Functionary: White Reactions Toward a Black Champion." *Journal of Black Studies* 16 (September 1985): 95–111.

Ezra, Michael. *Muhammad Ali: The Making of an Icon*. Temple University Press, 2009.

Ezra, Michael. "Muhammad Ali's Main Bout: African American Economic Power and the World Heavyweight Title." In *The Economic Civil Rights*

Movement: African Americans and the Struggle for Economic Power, edited by Michael Ezra, 104–124. Routledge, 2013.

Fairclough, Adam. *To Redeem the Soul of America: The Southern Christian Leadership Conference and Martin Luther King, Jr.* University of Georgia Press, 1987.

Farokhi, Nasrolah Rashid. "The Influences of Nongovernmental, Business, and Interest Group Organizations on Urban Politics and Policy Making: A Case Study of the Leadership Role and Influence of the Atlanta Chamber of Commerce, 1960–1978." PhD diss., Atlanta University, 1979.

Farred, Grant A. "What's My Name? Organic and Vernacular Intellectuals." Phd diss., Princeton University, 1997.

Faulkenbury, Evan. *Poll Power: The Voter Education Project and the Movement for the Ballot in the American South*. University of North Carolina Press, 2019.

Fernandez, Bernard. "50 Years Ago, Muhammad Ali Launched a Comeback Unlike Any Other vs. Jerry Quarry." *Ring Magazine*, 26 October 2020, https://www.ringtv.com/612011-50-years-ago-muhammad-ali-launched-a-comeback-unlike-any-other-vs-jerry-quarry/.

Fields, Armond. *James J. Corbett: A Biography of the Heavyweight Boxing Champion and Popular Theater Headliner*. McFarland, 2017.

Fisher, Art, and Neal Marshall. *Garden of Innocents*. E. P. Dutton, 1972.

Fleischer, Nat. "Nat Fleischer Speaks Out." *The Ring*, January 1971, 5.

Fogelson, Robert M. *The Great Rent Wars: New York, 1917–1929*. Yale University Press, 2013.

Frazier, Joe, with Phil Berger. *Smokin' Joe: The Autobiography*. Macmillan, 1996.

Freeman, Scott. "Carrying the Torch." *Atlanta*, May 2001, 112–114.

Fuller, Helen. "Southerners and the Schools: Atlanta Is Different." *New Republic* (Repr., 1959): 14–17.

Galphin, Bruce. "MARTA Tries a Wider Track." *Atlanta Magazine*, October 1971, 46–49, 66–70.

Galphin, Bruce. *The Riddle of Lester Maddox*. Camelot, 1968.

Garland, Phyl. "Atlanta: Black Mecca of the South." *Ebony*, August 1971, 152–157.

Gendzel, Glen. "Competitive Boosterism: How Milwaukee Lost the Braves." *Business History Review* 69 (Winter 1995): 530–566.

Gilmore, Al-Tony. *Bad Nigger! The National Impact of Jack Johnson*. Kennikat, 1975.

Gilmore, Mikal. "The Greatest of All Time, 1942–2016." *Rolling Stone*, 1 July 2016, 28–41.

"Glad to See You." *Newsweek*, 11 September 1961, 93.

Glad, Betty. *Jimmy Carter: In Search of the Great White House*. Norton, 1980.

Gorn, Elliot J. "John L. Sullivan: 'The Champion of All Champions.'" *Virginia Quarterly Review* 62 (Autumn 1986): 614–633.

Grady-Willis, Winston. *Challenging US Apartheid: Atlanta and Black Struggles for Human Rights, 1960–1977*. Duke University Press, 2006.

Grady-Willis, Winston A. "A Changing Tide: Black Politics and Activism in Atlanta, Georgia, 1960–1977." PhD diss., Emory University, 1998.

Grant, Donald L. *The Way It Was in the South: The Black Experience in Georgia*. Birch Lane, 1993.

Groves, Lee. "Muhammad Ali-Jerry Quarry I: Half a Century On from the Return of the Champion." *Ring Magazine*, 26 October 2020, https://www.ringtv.com/612026-muhammad-ali-jerry-quarry-i-half-a-century-on-from-the-return-of-the-champion/.

Halberstam, David. *The Breaks of the Game*. Knopf, 1981.

Hale, Andrew J. "How Voice Operates in Popular Culture through the Performance Persona of Muhammad Ali." Master's thesis, San Jose State University, 1994.

Hamill, Pete. "The Disintegration of a Folk Hero." In *The Muhammad Ali Reader*, edited by Gerald Early, 122–124. HarperCollins, 1998.

Harmon, David Andrew. "Beneath the Image: The Civil Rights Movement and Race Relations in Atlanta, Georgia, 1946–1981." PhD diss., Emory University, 1993.

Harmon, David Andrew. *Beneath the Image of the Civil Rights Movement and Race Relations: Atlanta, Georgia. 1946–1981*. Garland, 1996.

Harris, Othello. "Muhammad Ali and the Revolt of the Black Athlete." In *Muhammad Ali: The People's Champ*, edited by Elliott J. Gorn, 54–69. University of Illinois Press, 1995.

Haselden, Kyle. "Too Busy to Hate." *Christian Century*, 27 March 1963, 392.

Hauser, Thomas. *Muhammad Ali: His Life and Times*. Simon & Schuster, 1991.

Hein, Virginia H. "The Image of 'A City Too Busy Too Hate': Atlanta in the 1960's." *Phylon* 33 (Fall 1972): 205–221.

Henderson, Alexa Benson. *Atlanta Life Insurance Company: Guardian of Black Economic Dignity*. University of Alabama Press, 1990.

Hietala, Thomas R. "Muhammad Ali and the Age of Bare-Knuckle Politics." In *Muhammad Ali: The People's Champ*, edited by Elliott J. Gorn, 117–153. University of Illinois Press, 1995.

Hoberman, John. *Darwin's Athletes: How Sport Has Damaged Black America and Preserved the Myth of Race*. Mariner Books, 1997.

Hobson, Maurice J. *The Legend of the Black Mecca: Politics and Class in the Making of Modern Atlanta*. University of North Carolina Press, 2017.

Hornbaker, Tim. *National Wrestling Alliance: The Untold Story of the Monopoly that Strangled Professional Wrestling*. ECW, 2007.

Hornsby, Jr., Alton. *Black Power in Dixie: A Political History of African Americans in Atlanta*. University Press of Florida, 2009.

Hornsby, Jr., Alton. "Black Public Education in Atlanta, Georgia, 1954–1973: From Segregation to Segregation." *Journal of Negro History* 76 (Winter—Autumn 1991): 21–47.

Hornsby, Jr., Alton. "A City That Was Too Busy to Hate: Atlanta Businessmen and Desegregation." In *Southern Businessmen and Desegregation*, edited by Elizabeth Jacoway and David R. Colburn, 120–136. Louisiana State University Press, 1982.

Hornsby, Jr., Alton. "The Negro in Atlanta Politics." *Atlanta Historical Bulletin* 21 (Spring 1977): 7–33.

Hudson, Paul Stephen, and Lora Pond Mirza. "Controversial Comeback in Atlanta: The 1970 Return of Muhammad Ali in 'The City Too Busy to Hate.'" *Georgia Historical Quarterly* 95 (Spring 2011): 42–55.

Hutchinson, Phillip J. "From Bad Buck to White Hope: Journalism and Sonny Liston, 1958–1965." *Journal of Sports Media* 10 (Spring 2015): 119–137.

In the Matter of: Cassius Marcellus Clay, Jr. a/k/a Muhammad Ali, Petitioner vs. United States of America, Respondent, Supreme Court of the United States [transcript]. Alderson Reporting Company, 1971.

Isenberg, Michael T. *John L. Sullivan and His America*. University of Illinois Press, 1994.

"Jack Johnson Goes to Hollywood." *The Ring*, October 1970, 13, 45.

James, Kimberly Marissa. "Challenges to Control? Atlanta's Maynard Jackson and the Politics of Police Reform." PhD diss., University of Michigan, 2002.

Jay, Kathryn. *More Than Just a Game: Sports In American Life Since 1945*. Columbia University Press, 2004.

Johnson, Robert E. "World's Biggest Event Brings Mixed Reactions." *Jet*, 25 March 1971, 12–17.

Jones, James Earl, with Penelope Niven. *James Earl Jones: Voices and Silences*. Charles Scribner's Sons, 1993.

Kallina, Edmund Frank. *Claude Kirk and the Politics of Confrontation*. University Press of Florida, 1993.

Kaliss, Gregory. "Ali-Frazier 1: Black Gladiators, White Promoters, and the Economics of Big-Time Boxing." *International Journal of the History of Sport* 34, no. 11 (2017): 1003–1019.

Kane, Martin. "Welcome Back, Ali!" *Sports Illustrated*, September 14, 1970, 20, 23.

Kindred, Dave. *Sound and Fury: Two Powerful Lives, One Fateful Friendship*. Free Press, 2006.

Kram, Mark. *Ghosts of Manila: The Fateful Blood Feud between Muhammad Ali and Joe Frazier*. HarperCollins, 2001.

Kram, Mark. "He Moves Like Silk, Hits Like a Ton." *Sports Illustrated*, 26 October 1970, 16–19.

Kram, Mark. "Smashing Return of the Old Ali." *Sports Illustrated*, 2 November 1970, 18–19.

Krantz, Les. *Ali in Action: The Man, the Moves, the Mouth*. Lyons, 2008.

Kruse, Kevin M. *White Flight: Atlanta and the Making of Modern Conservatism*. Princeton University Press, 2005.

Kuhn, Clifford M., Harlon E. Joye, and Bernard West. *Living Atlanta: An Oral History of the City, 1914–1948*. University of Georgia Press, 2005.

L.H.B., Jr., and A.S.C. "The Julian Bond Case." *Virginia Law Review* 52 (November 1966): 1309–1335.

Laffoley, Steven. *Shadowboxing: The Rise and Fall of George Dixon*. Pottersfield, 2012.

Lassiter, Matthew D. *The Silent Majority: Suburban Politics in the Sunbelt South*. Princeton University Press, 2006.

LaShier, William Seth. "'To Secure Improvements in Their Material and Social Conditions': Atlanta's Civil Rights Movement, Middle-Class Reformers, and Workplace Protests, 1960–1977." PhD diss., George Washington University, 2020.

"Legislative Exclusion: Julian Bond and Adam Clayton Powell." *University of Chicago Law Review* 35 (Autumn 1967): 151–172.

Lesher, Stephen. "Leroy Johnson Outslicks Mister Charlie." *New York Times Magazine*, 8 November 1970, 34–50.

Lewis, Earl. *In Their Own Interests: Race, Class, and Power in Twentieth-Century Norfolk, Virginia*. University of California Press, 1991.

Lipsyte, Robert. "'I Don't Have to Be What You Want Me to Be,' Says Muhammad Ali." In *The Muhammad Ali Reader*, edited by Gerald Early, 90–100. HarperCollins, 1998.

Lisle, Benjamin D. *Modern Coliseum: Stadiums and American Culture*. University of Pennsylvania Press, 2017.

Loubet, Nat. "Now It's Frazier vs. Clay." *The Ring*, January 1971, 8–11.

Lower, Frank J. "Julian Bond: A Case Study in a Legislator's Freedom of Speech." *Free Speech Yearbook* 13, no. 1 (1974): 35–44.

Lucks, Daniel. "African American Soldiers and the Vietnam War: No More Vietnams." *The Sixties* 10, no. 2 (2017): 196–220.

Lucks, Daniel S. *Selma to Saigon: The Civil Rights Movement and the Vietnam War*. University Press of Kentucky, 2014.

Maddox, Lester. "Maddox for President Press Conference." In *Addresses of Lester Garfield Maddox, 1967–1971*, edited by Frank Daniel, 197–200. Ben W. Fortson, Jr., 1971.

Maddox, Lester. *Speaking Out: The Autobiography of Lester Garfield Maddox*. Doubleday, 1975.

Mailer, Norman. "Ego." In *The Muhammad Ali Reader*, edited by Gerald Early, 101–121. HarperCollins, 1998.

Mailer, Norman. *Miami and the Siege of Chicago: An Informal History of the Republican and Democratic Conventions of 1968*. Donald I. Fine, 1968.

Marqusee, Mike. *Redemption Song: Muhammad Ali and the Spirit of the Sixties*, 2nd ed. Verso, 2005.

Martinez, J. Michael. "The Georgia Confederate Flag Dispute." *Georgia Historical Quarterly* 92 (Summer 2008): 200–228.

Massaquoi, Hans J. "The Private World of Muhammad Ali." *Ebony*, September 1972, 145–152.

Maule, Tex. "The Once and Future King?" *Sports Illustrated*, 10 July 1967, 18–21.

McCartin, Joseph A. "'Fire the Hell Out of Them': Sanitation Workers' Struggles and the Normalization of the Striker Replacement Strategy in the 1970s." *Labor: Studies in Working Class History of the Americas* 2 (Fall 2005): 67–92.

McCurdy, Charles W. *The Anti-Rent Era in New York Law and Politics, 1839–1865*. University of North Carolina Press, 2003.

McMillan, George. "Atlanta's Peaceful Blow for Justice: With the Police on an Integration Job." *Life*, 16 September 1961, 35–36.

Means, Howard. *67 Shots: Kent State and the End of American Innocence*. Da Capo, 2016.

Meier, August, and David Lewis. "History of the Negro Upper Class in Atlanta, Georgia, 1890–1958," *Journal of Negro Education* 28 (Spring 1959): 128–139.

"Messenger, Ex-Champ Mum on Ali's Reinstatement." *Jet*, 14 May 1970, 49.

Montville, Leigh. *Sting Like a Bee: Muhammad Ali vs. the United States of America, 1966–1971*. Doubleday, 2017.

Moore, Louis. "Fine Specimens of Manhood: The Black Boxer's Body and the Avenue to Equality, Racial Advancement, and Manhood in the Nineteenth Century." *MELUS* 35 (Winter 2010): 59–84.

Morris, Kenneth E. *Jimmy Carter: American Moralist*. University of Georgia Press, 1996.

"Muhammad Ali on *The Tonight Show* October 1970." YouTube, https://www.youtube.com/watch?v=sfNouojnqhe. Accessed 24 April 2024.

Neary, John. *Julian Bond: Black Rebel*. William Morrow, 1971.

Newfield, Jack. "The Meaning of Muhammad." *The Nation*, 4 February 2002, 25–30.

Odum-Hinmon, Maria E. "The Cautious Crusader: How the *Atlanta Daily World* Covered the Struggle for African American Rights from 1945 to 1985." PhD diss., University of Maryland, 2005.

Olsen, Jack. *The Black Athlete: A Shameful Story*. Time-Life Books, 1968.

Olsen, Jack. *Black Is Best: The Riddle of Cassius Clay*. Jack Olsen, 2014.

Olsen, Jack. "A Case of Conscience." *Sports Illustrated*, 11 April 1966, 89–104.

Paschal, James Vaughn, and Mae Armster Kendall. *Paschal: Living the Dream*. iUniverse, 2006.

"Plight of Girl Jailed in Ga. for Cursing." *Jet*, 27 February 1969, 14–19.

Plimpton, George. "Miami Notebook: Cassius Clay and Malcolm X." In *The Muhammad Ali Reader*, edited by Gerald Early, 27–40. HarperCollins, 1998.

Plimpton, George. *Shadow Box: An Amateur in the Ring*. Little, Brown, 2016.

Plimpton, George. "Watching the Man in the Mirror." *Sports Illustrated*, 23 November 1970, 80–83, 87–96, 101–102.

Poinsett, Alex. "A Look At Cassius Clay: Biggest Mouth in Boxing." *Ebony*, March 1963, 35–42.

Poitier, Sidney, dir. *Uptown Saturday Night*. First Artists/Warner Brothers, 1974. Film.

Pollack, Adam J. *John L. Sullivan: The Career of the First Gloved Heavyweight Champion*. McFarland, 2015.

Pomerantz, Gary M. *Where Peachtree Meets Sweet Auburn: The Saga of Two Families and the Making of Atlanta*. Lisa Drew/Scribner, 1996.

Powledge, Fred. "Profiles—A New Politics in Atlanta." *New Yorker*, 31 December 1973, 28–40.

Pratt, Robert A. *Selma's Bloody Sunday: Protest, Voting Rights, and the Struggle for Racial Equality*. Johns Hopkins University Press, 2017.

Quintana, Andres F. "Muhammad Ali: The Greatest in Court." *Marquette Sports Law Review* 18, no. 1 (2007): 171–204.

Rafiq, Fiaz. *Muhammad Ali: The Life of a Legend*. Arena Sport, 2020.

Range, Peter Ross. "Making It in Atlanta: Capital of Black-Is-Bountiful." *New York Times Magazine*, 7 April 1974, 268–275.

Raskin, Roy. "Cosby Group Inks Golden Gloves Heavy Champ Moore." *The Ring*, October 1970, 32.

Reed, Jr., Adolph. *Stirrings in the Jug: Black Politics in the Post-Segregation Era*. University of Minnesota Press, 1999.

Remnick, David. *King of the World: Muhammad Ali and the Rise of an American Hero*. Random House, 1998.

Report of the National Advisory Commission on Civil Disorders. USGPO, 1968.
"Return of the Ringmaster." *Time*, 9 November 1970, 35.
Rice, Rolundus R. *Hosea Williams: A Lifetime of Defiance and Protest.* University of South Carolina Press, 2022.
Richardson, Jack. "Ali on Peachtree." *Harper's Magazine*, January 1971, 46–53.
"The Ring Believes . . ." *The Ring*, January 1971, 6–7.
Roberts, Randy. *Papa Jack: Jack Johnson and the Era of White Hopes.* Free Press, 1983.
Roberts, Randy, and Johnny Smith. *Blood Brothers: The Fatal Friendship between Muhammad Ali and Malcolm X.* Basic, 2016.
Rooks, Charles S. *The Atlanta Elections of 1969.* Voter Education Project, 1970.
Russell, Clare. "Upheaval in Savannah: The Protest Cycle of a 'Short' Civil Rights Movement." *Journal of Contemporary History* 47 (October 2012): 773–792.
Russell, William F. "Success is a Journey." *Sports Illustrated*, 8 June 1970, 80–93.
Rutheiser, Charles. *Imagineering Atlanta: The Politics of Place in the City of Dreams.* Verso, 1996.
Rutter, Jon David. "White Hopes: Heavyweight Boxing and the Repercussions of Race." PhD diss., University of Texas at Austin, 2001.
Sammons, Jeffrey T. *Beyond the Ring: The Role of Boxing in American Society.* University of Illinois Press, 1990.
Sammons, Jeffrey T. "Rebel with a Cause: Muhammad Ali as Sixties Protest Symbol." In *Muhammad Ali: The People's Champ*, edited by Elliott J. Gorn, 154–180. University of Illinois Press, 1995.
Sanders, Randy. "The Sad Duty of Politics: Jimmy Carter and the Issue of Race in His 1970 Gubernatorial Campaign." *Georgia Historical Quarterly* 76 (Fall 1992): 612–638.
Schaap, Dick. "The Happiest Heavyweight." *Saturday Evening Post*, 25 March 1961, 101.
Schulberg, Budd. *Loser and Still Champion: Muhammad Ali.* Doubleday, 1972.
Schulman, Bruce J. *From Cotton Belt to Sunbelt: Federal Policy, Economic Development, and the Transformation of the South, 1938–1980.* Oxford University Press, 1991.
Scott, David. "Boxing: From Male Vocation to Neurotic Masculinity." *Sport in History* 37, no. 4 (2017): 469–482.
Scott, David. "The Boxing Gym as Masculine Space." *Sports in History* 40, no. 3 (2020): 356–369.
Shaw, Irwin. "Muhammad Ali and the Little People." *Esquire*, November 1969, 100, 102, 104, 106, 125–129.
Shaw, John M. *The Cambodian Campaign: The 1970 Offensive and America's Vietnam War.* University Press of Kansas, 2005.

Shecter, Leonard. "The Passion of Muhammad Ali." *Esquire*, April 1968, 129–131, 140, 148–160.

Shermer, Elizabeth Tandy. *Sunbelt Capitalism: Phoenix and the Transformation of American Politics*. University of Pennsylvania Press, 2013.

Shoemaker, David. *The Squared Circle: Life, Death, and Professional Wrestling*. Penguin, 2014.

Short, Bob. *Everything Is Pickrick: The Life of Lester Maddox*. Mercer University Press, 1999.

Siddons, Anne Rivers. "The Seeds of Sanity." *Atlanta*, July 1967, 55–56.

Silver, Murray. *Daddy King and Me: Memories of the Forgotten Father of the Civil Rights Movement*. Continental Shelf, 2009.

Silver, Murray. *When Elvis Meets the Dalai Lama*. Bonaventure, 2003.

Smith, John M. "The Riot of May 1970: A Humanistic Perspective." *Richmond County History* 7 (Summer 1975): 103–115.

Smith, John Matthew. "The Resurrection: Atlanta, Racial Politics, and the Return of Muhammad Ali." *Southern Cultures* 21 (Summer 2015): 5–26.

Sneddon, Rob. *The Phantom Punch: The Story behind Boxing's Most Controversial Bout*. Down East, 2016.

Somers, Dale. *The Rise of Sports in New Orleans, 1850–1900*. Louisiana State University Press, 1972.

Southern Regional Council. *Augusta, Georgia and Jackson State University: Southern Episodes in a National Tragedy*. Southern Regional Council, 1970.

Stone, Clarence N. *Regime Politics: Governing Atlanta, 1946–1988*. University of Kansas Press, 1989.

Streible, Dan. "A History of the Boxing Film, 1894–1915: Social Control and Social Reform in the Progressive Era." *Film History* 3, no. 3 (1989): 235–257.

Summerlin, Donnie. "'We Represented the Best of Georgia in Chicago': The Georgia Loyalist Delegate Challenge at the 1968 Democratic National Convention." *Georgia Historical Quarterly* 103, no. 3 (2019): 211–253.

Taylor, Momodu Christopher. "An Examination of the Life and Times of Muhammad Ali: Boxing, Politics, Cultural Identity, and Transformational Leadership." PhD diss., North Carolina A&T State University, 2016.

Torres, José. *Sting Like a Bee: The Muhammad Ali Story*. Abelard-Schuman, 1971.

Trutor, Clayton. *Loserville: How Professional Sports Remade Atlanta—and How Atlanta Remade Professional Sports*. University of Nebraska Press, 2022.

Tuck, Stephen. "A City Too Dignified to Hate: Civic Pride, Civil Rights, and Savannah in Comparative Perspective." *Georgia Historical Quarterly* 79 (Fall 1995): 539–559.

Tuckner, Howard M. "Man, It's Great to be Great." *New York Times Magazine*, 9 December 1962, 47–50.

"Vernon Beale." BoxRec, https://boxrec.com/ru/box-pro/91468.

Vettor, L. "The Clay Case, Again." *The Ring*, January 1971, 34.

Voulgaris, Panos J. "Muhammad Ali: An Unusual Leader in the Advancement of Black America." Master's thesis, Harvard University, 2016.

Walker, Grace. "How Women Won the Quiet Battle of Atlanta." *Good Housekeeping*, May 1961, 76.

Walker, Jack. "Negro Voting in Atlanta: 1953–1961." *Phylon* 24 (4th Qtr. 1964): 379–387.

Wiggins, David K. "Victory for Allah: Muhammad Ali, the Nation of Islam, and American Society." In *Muhammad Ali: The People's Champ*, edited by Elliott J. Gorn, 88–116. University of Illinois Press, 1995.

Wiggins, Jr., William H. "Jack Johnson as Bad Nigger: The Folklore of His Life." *Black Scholar* 2 (January 1971): 4–19.

Williams, Shawn Lamar. "'The People's Champion': Folk Heroism and the Oral Artistry of Muhammad Ali." PhD diss., Clark Atlanta University, 2000.

Wills, Gary. "Muhammad Ali." In *The Muhammad Ali Reader*, edited by Gerald Early, 160–164. HarperCollins, 1998.

Winn, William, with D. L. Inman. "Augusta, Georgia." In *Augusta, Georgia and Jackson State University: Southern Episodes in a National Tragedy*, 12–56. Southern Regional Council, 1970.

Wood, Augustus Clark. "The Sixth Finger: Jack Johnson, Muhammad Ali, and the Unconscious Race Hero in Hero." Master's thesis, Clark Atlanta University, 2012.

Zirin, Dave. *A People's History of Sports in the United States: 250 Years of Politics, Protest, People and Play*. New Press, 2008.

ACKNOWLEDGMENTS

No book like this one could exist without archivists, and many helped in the creation of *Return of the King*. Most vital were the great people at the Atlanta History Center, the Atlanta University Center Robert W. Woodruff Library Archives Research Center, and, perhaps most vitally, the Muhammad Ali Center in Louisville, Kentucky. The Center's Amelia McGrath was inordinately helpful; this book would not have its current form without her assistance and that of the Center. I am also indebted, as always, to Pickle Clark, who makes everything possible.

INDEX